Lecture Notes in Computer Science 925

Edited by G. Goos, J. Ha

Advisory Board: W. Brau

Springer

Berlin
Heidelberg
New York
Barcelona
Budapest
Hong Kong
London
Milan
Paris
Tokyo

Johan Jeuring Erik Meijer (Eds.)

Advanced
Functional Programming

First International Spring School
on Advanced Functional Programming Techniques
Båstad, Sweden, May 24–30, 1995
Tutorial Text

 Springer

Series Editors

Gerhard Goos
Universität Karlsruhe
Vincenz-Priessnitz-Straße 3, D-76128 Karlsruhe, Germany

Juris Hartmanis
Department of Computer Science, Cornell University
4130 Upson Hall, Ithaca, NY 14853, USA

Jan van Leeuwen
Department of Computer Science, Utrecht University
Padualaan 14, 3584 CH Utrecht, The Netherlands

Volume Editors

Johan Jeuring
Department of Computing Science, Chalmers University
of Technology and University of Göteborg
S-412 96 Göteborg, Sweden

Erik Meijer
Department of Computer Science, Utrecht University
P.O. Box 80.089, NL-3508 TB Utrecht, The Netherlands

CR Subject Classification (1991): D.1.1, D.3.2, D.2.2, D.2.10

ISBN 3-540-59451-5 Springer-Verlag Berlin Heidelberg New York

CIP data applied for

© Springer-Verlag Berlin Heidelberg 1995
Printed in Germany

Typesetting: Camera-ready by author
SPIN: 10485985   06/3142-543210 - Printed on acid-free paper

Preface

This volume contains the lecture notes used at the *First International Spring School on advanced Functional Programming Techniques*, held May 24 – 31, 1995 in Båstad, Sweden. The school was organized by the department of Computing Science of Chalmers University of Technology and University of Göteborg.

Functional programming languages offer a number of benefits to programmers. Using functional languages often results in fast development times, and shorter code that is easier to adjust, reason about and reuse. The last few years have seen new developments in functional programming techniques. Concepts such as monads, type classes, and several new special purpose libraries of higher-order functions are new and powerful methods for structuring programs.

These notes focus on how-to-write-functional-programs. The notes aim to bring computer scientists up-to-date with the latest advanced functional programming techniques. It is assumed that the reader has some basic knowledge of functional programming, i.e., on the level of Bird and Wadler's "Introduction to functional programming". Most of the notes contain exercises that enable the reader to familiarize him/herself thoroughly with the material and the techniques.

These notes cover a wide range of topics within functional programming. The topics covered include:

- Programming user interfaces with fudgets;

- Using monads for programming with for example exceptions and state;

- Using type classes and constructor classes in functional programming;

- Using folds and monadic folds in a programs for type checking and in the calculation of a version of the G-machine and;

Acknowledgements
We are very happy that a team of top level researchers in the field of functional programming agreed to present their most recent work both in these lecture notes and at the Spring School itself. The Computing Science department of Chalmers University of Technology and University of Göteborg provided financial and secretarial support.

Johan Jeuring
Erik Meijer
Göteborg, March 1995

Contents

Functional Parsers

Jeroen Fokker

Dept. of Computer Science, Utrecht University
P.O.Box 80.089, 3508 TB Utrecht, The Netherlands
e-mail jeroen@cs.ruu.nl

Abstract. In an informal way the 'list of successes' method for writing parsers using a lazy functional language (Gofer) is described. The library of higher-order functions (known as 'parser combinators') that is developed is used for writing parsers for nested parentheses and operator expressions with an arbitrary number of priorities. The method is applied on itself to write a parser for grammars, that yields a parser for the language of the grammar. In the text exercises are provided, the solutions of which are given at the end of the article.

1 Introduction

This article is an informal introduction to writing parsers in a lazy functional language using 'parser combinators'. Most of the techniques have been described by Burge [2], Wadler [5] and Hutton [3]. Recently, the use of so-called *monads* has become quite popular in connection with parser combinators [6, 7]. We will not use them in this article, however, to show that no magic is involved in using parser combinators. You are nevertheless encouraged to study monads at some time, because they form a useful generalization of the techniques described here.

In this article we stick to standard functional language constructs like higher-order functions, lists, and algebraic types. All programs are written in Gofer [4]. List comprehensions are used in a few places, but they are not essential, and could be easily rephrased using the `map`, `filter` and `concat` functions [1]. Type classes are only used for overloading the equality and arithmetic operators.

We will start by motivating the definition of the type of parser functions. Using that type, we will be capable to build parsers for the language of ambiguous grammars. Next, we will introduce some elementary parsers that can be used for parsing the terminal symbols of a language.

In section 4 the first parser combinators are introduced, which can be used for sequentially and alternatively combining parsers. In section 5 some functions are defined, which make it possible to calculate a value during parsing. You may use these functions for what traditionally is called 'defining semantic functions': some useful meaning can be associated to syntactic structures. As an example, in section 6 we construct a parser for strings of matching parentheses, where different semantic values are calculated: a tree describing the structure, and an integer indicating the nesting depth.

In sections 7 and 8 we introduce some new parser combinators. Not only these will make life easier later, but also their definitions are nice examples of using parser combinators. A real application is given in section 9, where a parser for arithmetical expressions is developed. Next, the expression parser is generalized to expressions with an arbitrary number of precedence levels. This is done without coding the priorities of operators as integers, and we will avoid using indices and ellipses.

In the last section parser combinators are used to parse the string representation of a grammar. As a semantic value, a parser is derived for the language of the grammar, which in turn can be applied to an input string. Thus we will essentially have a parser generator.

2 The type 'Parser'

The *parsing problem* is: given a string, construct a tree that describes the structure of the string. In a functional language we can define a datatype `Tree`. A parser could be implemented by function of the following type:

```
type Parser  =  String -> Tree
```

For parsing substructures, a parser could call other parsers, or itself recursively. These calls need not only communicate their result, but also which part of the input string is left unprocessed. As this cannot be done using a global variable, the unprocessed input string has to be part of the result of the parser. The two results can be grouped in a tuple. A better definition for the type `Parser` is thus:

```
type Parser  =  String -> ( String, Tree )
```

The type `String` is defined in the standard prelude as a list of characters. The type `Tree`, however, is not yet defined. The type of tree that is returned depends on the application. Therefore it is better to make the parser type into a polymorphic type, by parameterizing it with the type of the parse tree. Thus we abstract from the type of the parse tree at hand, substituting the type variable a for it:

```
type Parser a  =  String -> ( String , a )
```

For example, a parser that returns a structure of type `Oak` now has type `Parser Oak`. For parse trees that represent an 'expression' we could define a type `Expr`, making it possible to develop parsers returning an expression: `Parser Expr`. Another instance of a parser is a parse function that recognizes a string of digits, and yields the number represented by it as a parse 'tree'. In this case the function is of type `Parser Int`.

Until now, we have been assuming that every string can be parsed in exactly one way. In general, this need not be the case: it may be that a single string can be parsed in various ways, or that there is no possible way of parsing a string. As another refinement of the type definition, instead of returning one parse tree (and its associated rest string), we let a parser return a *list* of trees. Each element of the result consists of a tree, paired with the rest string that was left unprocessed whil parsing it. The type definition of `Parser` therefore had better be:

```
type Parser a  =  String -> [ (String,a) ]
```

If there is just one parsing, the result of the parse function will be a singleton list. If no parsing is possible, the result will be an empty list. In the case of an ambiguous grammar, alternative parsings make up the elements of the result.

This method is called the *list of successes* method, described by Wadler [5]. It can be used in situations where in other languages you would use backtracking techniques. In the Bird and Wadler textbook it is used to solve combinatorial problems like the eight queens problem [1]. If only one solution is required rather than all possible solutions, you can take the **head** of the list of successes. Thanks to lazy evaluation, not all elements of the list are determined if only the first value is needed, so there will be no loss of efficiency. Lazy evaluation provides a backtracking approach to finding the first solution.

Parsers with the type described so far operate on strings, that is lists of characters. There is however no reason for not allowing parsing strings of elements other than characters. You may imagine a situation in which a preprocessor prepares a list of tokens, which is subsequently parsed. To cater for this situation, as a final refinement of the parser type we again abstract from a type: that of the elements of the input string. Calling it a, and the result type b, the type of parsers is defined by:

```
type Parser a b  =  [a] -> [([a],b)]
```

or if you prefer meaningful identifiers over conciseness:

```
type Parser symbol result  =  [symbol] -> [([symbol],result)]
```

We will use this type definition in the rest of this article.

3 Elementary parsers

We will start quite simply, defining a parse function that just recognizes the symbol 'a'. The type of the input string symbols is Char in this case, and as a parse 'tree' we also simply use a Char:

```
symbola  ::  Parser Char Char
symbola []                   =  []
symbola (x:xs) | x=='a'      =  [ (xs, 'a') ]
               | otherwise   =  []
```

The list of successes method immediately pays off, because now we can return an empty list if no parsing is possible (because the input is empty, or does not start with an 'a').

In the same fashion, we can write parsers that recognize other symbols. As always, rather than defining a lot of closely related functions, it is better to abstract from the symbol to be recognized by making it an extra parameter of the function. Also, the function can operate on strings other than characters, so that it can be used in other applications than character oriented ones. The only prerequisite is that the symbols to be parsed can be tested for equality. In Gofer, this is indicated by the Eq predicate in the type of the function:

```
symbol  ::  Eq s  => s -> Parser s s
symbol a []                  =  []
symbol a (x:xs) | a==x       =  [ (xs,x) ]
                | otherwise  =  []
```

As usual, there are a number of ways to define the same function. If you like list comprehensions, you might prefer the following definition:

```
symbol a []     = []
symbol a (x:xs) = [ (xs,a) | a==x ]
```

In Gofer, a list comprehension with no generators but only a condition is defined to be empty or singleton, depending on the condition.

The function `symbol` is a function that, given a symbol, yields a parser for that symbol. A parser in turn is a function, too. This is why two parameters appear in the definition of `symbol`.

We will now define some elementary parsers that can do the work traditionally taken care of by lexical analyzers. For example, a useful parser is one that recognizes a fixed string of symbols, such as 'begin' or 'end'. We will call this function `token`.

```
token k xs | k==take n xs = [ (drop n xs, k) ]
           | otherwise    = []
                     where  n = length k
```

As in the case of the `symbol` function we have parameterized this function with the string to be recognized, effectively making it into a family of functions. Of course, this function is not confined to strings of characters. However, we do need an equality test on the input string type; the type of `token` is:

```
token  ::  Eq [s]  =>  [s] -> Parser s [s]
```

The function `token` is a generalization of the `symbol` function, in that it recognizes more than one character.

Another generalization of `symbol` is a function which may, depending on the input, return different parse results. The function `satisfy` is an example of this. Where the `symbol` function tests for equality to a given symbol, in `satisfy` an arbitrary predicate can be specified. Again, `satisfy` effectively is a family of parser functions. It is defined here using the list comprehension notation:

```
satisfy ::  (s->Bool) -> Parser s s
satisfy p []     = []
satisfy p (x:xs) = [ (xs,x) | p x ]
```

Exercise 1. Since `satisfy` is a generalization of `symbol`, the function `symbol` could have been defined as an instance of `satisfy`. How can this be done?

In books on grammar theory an empty string is often called 'epsilon'. In this tradition, we will define a function `epsilon` that 'parses' the empty string. It does not consume any input, and thus always returns an empty parse tree and unmodified input. A zero-tuple can be used as a result value: () is the only value of the type ().

```
epsilon    ::  Parser s ()
epsilon xs  = [ ( xs, () ) ]
```

A variation is the function `succeed`, that neither consumes input, but does always return a given, fixed value (or 'parse tree', if you could call the result of processing zero symbols a parse tree...)

```
succeed        ::  r -> Parser s r
succeed v xs  =  [ (xs,v) ]
```

Of course, epsilon can be defined using succeed:

```
epsilon  ::  Parser s ()
epsilon  =  succeed ()
```

Dual to the function succeed is the function fail, that fails to recognize any symbol on the input string. It always returns an empty list of successes:

```
fail     ::  Parser s r
fail xs  =  []
```

We will need this trivial parser as a neutral element for foldr later. Note the difference with epsilon, which *does* have one element in its list of successes (albeit an empty one).

4 Parser combinators

Using the elementary parsers from the previous section, parsers can be constructed for terminal symbols from a grammar. More interesting are parsers for *non*terminal symbols. Of course, you could write these by hand, but it is more convenient to *construct* them by partially parameterizing higher-order functions.

Important operations on parsers are sequential and alternative composition. We will develop two functions for this, which for notational convenience are defined as operators: <*> for sequential composition, and <|> for alternative composition. Priorities of these operators are defined so as to minimize parentheses in practical situations:

```
infixr 6 <*>
infixr 4 <|>
```

Both operators have two parsers as parameter, and yield a parser as result. By again combining the result with other parsers, you may construct even more involved parsers.

In the definitions below, the functions operate on parsers p1 and p2. Apart from the parameters p1 and p2, the function operates on a string, which can be thought of as the string that is parsed by the parser that is the result of combining p1 and p2.

To start, we will write the operator <*>. For sequential composition, first p1 must be applied to the input. After that, p2 is applied to the rest string part of the result. Because p1 yields a *list* of solutions, we use a list comprehension in which p2 is applied to all rest strings in the list:

```
(<*>)           ::  Parser s a -> Parser s b -> Parser s (a,b)
(p1 <*> p2) xs  =  [ (xs2, (v1,v2))
                   | (xs1, v1)  <-  p1 xs
                   , (xs2, v2)  <-  p2 xs1
                   ]
```

The result of the function is a list of all possible tuples (v1,v2) with rest string xs2, where v1 is the parse tree computed by p1, and where rest string xs1 is used to let p2 compute v2 and xs2.

Apart from 'sequential composition' we need a parser combinator for representing 'choice'. For this, we have the parser combinator operator <|>:

```
(<|>)              ::  Parser s a -> Parser s a -> Parser s a
(p1 <|> p2) xs  =  p1 xs ++ p2 xs
```

Thanks to the list of successes method, both p1 and p2 yield lists of possible parsings. To obtain all possible successes of choice between p1 and p2, we only need to concatenate these two lists.

Exercise 2. When defining the priority of the <|> operator, using the infixr keyword we also specified that the operator associates to the right. Why is this a better choice than association to the left?

The result of parser combinators is again a parser, which can be combined with other parsers. The resulting parse trees are intricate tuples which reflect the way in which the parsers were combined. Thus, the term 'parse tree' is really appropriate. For example, the parser p where

```
p  =  symbol 'a' <*> symbol 'b' <*> symbol 'c'
```

is of type Parser Char (Char,(Char,Char)).

Although the tuples clearly describe the structure of the parse tree, it is a problem that we cannot combine parsers in an arbitrary way. For example, it is impossible to alternatively compose the parser p above with symbol 'a', because the latter is of type Parser Char Char, and only parsers of the same type can be composed alternatively. Even worse, it is not possible to recursively combine a parser with itself, as this would result in infinitely nested tuple types. What we need is a way to alter the structure of the parse tree that a given parser returns.

5 Parser transformers

Apart from the operators <*> and <|>, that combine parsers, we can define some functions that modify or *transform* existing parsers. We will develop three of them: sp lets a given parser neglect initial spaces, just transforms a parser into one that insists on empty rest string, and <@ applies a given function to the resulting parse trees.

The first parser transformer is sp. It drops spaces from the input, and then applies a given parser:

```
sp  ::  Parser Char a -> Parser Char a
sp p  =  p . dropWhile (==' ')
```

or if you prefer functional definitions:

```
sp  =  ( . dropWhile (==' '))
```

The second parser transformer is just. Given a parser p it yields a parser that does the same as p, but also guarantees that the rest string is empty. It does so by filtering the list of successes for null rest strings. Because the rest string is the first component of the list, the function can be defined as:

```
just       :: Parser s a -> Parser s a
just p     = filter (null.fst) . p
```

Exercise 3. Define the function just using a list comprehension instead of the filter function.

The most important parser transformer is the one that transforms a parser into a parser which modifies its result value. We will define it as an operator <@, that applies a given function to the result parse trees of a given parser. We have chosen the symbol so that you might pronounce it as 'apply'; the arrow points away from the function. Given a parser p and a function f, the operator <@ returns a parser that does the same as p, but in addition applies f to the resulting parse tree. It is most easily defined using a list comprehension:

```
infixr 5 <@
(<@)          :: Parser s a -> (a->b) -> Parser s b
(p <@ f) xs   = [ (ys, f v)
                | (ys,    v) <- p xs
                ]
```

Using this operator, we can transform the parser that recognizes a digit character into one that delivers the result as an integer:

```
digit         :: Parser Char Int
digit         = satisfy isDigit <@ f
           where f c = ord c - ord '0'
```

In practice, the <@ operator is used to build a certain value during parsing (in the case of parsing a computer program this value may be the generated code, or a list of all variables with their types, etc.). Put more generally: using <@ we can add *semantic functions* to parsers.

While testing your self-made parsers, you can use just for discarding the parses which leave a non-empty rest string. But you might become bored of seeing the empty list as rest string in the results. Also, more often than not you may be interested in just *some* parsing rather than *all* possibilities.

As we have reserved the word 'parser' for a function that returns *all* parsings, accompanied with their rest string. Let's therefore define a new type for a function that parses a text, guarantees empty rest string, picks the first solution, and delivers the parse tree only (discarding the rest string, because it is known to be empty at this stage). The functional program for converting a parser in such a 'deterministic parser' is more concise and readable than the description above:

```
type DetPars symbol result = [symbol] -> result
some    :: Parser s a -> DetPars s a
some p  = snd . head . just p
```

Use the **some** function with care: this function assumes that there is at least one solution, so it fails when the resulting DetPars is applied to a text which contains a syntax error.

6 Matching parentheses

Using the parser combinators and transformers developed thus far, we can construct a parser that recognizes matching pairs of parentheses. A first attempt, that is not type correct however, is:

```
parens  ::  Parser Char ???
parens  =  (   symbol '('
            <*> parens
            <*> symbol ')'
            <*> parens
            )
            <|> epsilon
```

This definition is inspired strongly by the well known grammar for nested parentheses. The type of the parse tree, however, is a problem. If this type would be a, then the type of the composition of the four subtrees in the first alternative would be (Char,(a,(Char,a))), which is not the same or unifiable. Also, the second alternative (epsilon) must yield a parse tree of the same type. Therefore we need to define a type for the parse tree first, and use the operator <@ in both alternatives to construct a tree of the correct type. The type of the parse tree can be for example:

```
data Tree  =  Nil
           |  Bin (Tree,Tree)
```

Now we can add 'semantic functions' to the parser:

```
parens  ::  Parser Char Tree
parens  =  (   symbol '('
            <*> parens
            <*> symbol ')'
            <*> parens
            )              <@  ( \(_,(x,(_,y))) -> Bin(x,y) )
            <|> epsilon <@  const Nil
```

The rather obscure text \(_,(x,(_,y))) is a lambda pattern describing a function with as first parameter a tuple containing the four parts of the first alternative, of which only the second and fourth matter.

Exercise 4. Why don't we use a four-tuple in the lambda pattern instead of a tuple with as second element a tuple with as second element a tuple?

Exercise 5. Why is the function const, which is defined by const x y = x in the prelude, needed? Can you write the second alternative more concisely without using const and <@?

In the lambda pattern, underscores are used as placeholders for the parse trees of symbol '(' and symbol ')', which are not needed in the result. In order to not having to use these complicated tuples, it might be easier to discard the parse trees for symbols in an earlier stage. For this, we introduce two auxiliary parser combinators, which will prove useful in more situations. These operators behave the same as <*>, except that they discard the result of one of their two parser arguments:

```
(<*)     ::  Parser s a -> Parser s b -> Parser s a
p <* q   =   p <*> q <@ fst

(*>)     ::  Parser s a -> Parser s b -> Parser s b
p *> q   =   p <*> q <@ snd
```

We can use these new parser combinators for improving the readability of the parser parens:

```
open     =  symbol '('
close    =  symbol ')'

parens   ::  Parser Char Tree
parens   =  (open *> parens <* close) <*> parens  <@  Bin
            <|> succeed Nil
```

By judiciously choosing the priorities of the operators involved:

```
infixr 6  <*> , <*  , *>
infixl 5  <@
infixr 4  <|>
```

we minimize on the number of parentheses needed.

Exercise 6. The parentheses around open*>parens<*close in the first alternative, are required in spite of our clever priorities. What would happen if we left them out?

By varying the function used after <@ (the 'semantic function'), we can yield other things than parse trees. As an example we write a parser that calculates the nesting depth of nested parentheses:

```
nesting  ::  Parser Char Int
nesting  =  (open *> nesting <* close) <*> nesting <@  f
            <|> succeed 0
         where  f (x,y) = (1+x) `max` y
```

If more variations are of interest, it may be worthwhile to make the semantic function and the value to yield in the 'empty' case into two additional parameters. The higher order function foldparens parses nested parentheses, using the given function and constant respectively, after parsing one of the two alternatives:

```
foldparens  ::  ((a,a)->a) -> a -> Parser Char a
foldparens f e  =  p
            where  p = (open *> p <* close) <*> p <@  f
                       <|> succeed e
```

Exercise 7. The function `foldparens` is a generalization of `parens` and `nesting`. Write the latter two as an instantiation of the former.

A session in which `nesting` is used may look like this:

```
? just nesting "()(())()"
[(2,[])]
? just nesting "())"
[]
```

Indeed `nesting` only recognizes correctly formed nested parentheses, and calculates the nesting depth on the fly.

Exercise 8. What would happen if we omit the `just` transformer in these examples?

7 More parser combinators

Although in principle you can build parsers for any context-free language using the combinators `<*>` and `<|>`, in practice it is easier to have some more parser combinators available. In traditional grammar formalisms, too, additional symbols are used to describe for example optional or repeated constructions. Consider for example the BNF formalism, in which originally only sequential and alternative composition could be used (denoted by juxtaposition and vertical bars, respectively), but which was later extended to also allow for repetition, denoted by asterisks.

It is very easy to make new parser combinators for extensions like that. As a first example we consider repetition. Given a parser for a construction, `many` makes a parser for zero or more occurrences of that construction:

```
many   :: Parser s a  -> Parser s [a]
many p =  p <*> many p  <@ list
          <|> succeed []
```

The auxiliary function `list` is defined as the uncurried version of the list constructor:

```
list (x,xs) = x:xs
```

The recursive definition of the parser follows the recursive structure of lists. Perhaps even nicer is the version in which the `epsilon` parser is used instead of `succeed`:

```
many   :: Parser s a  -> Parser s [a]
many p =  p <*> many p   <@ (\(x,xs)->x:xs)
          <|> epsilon     <@ (\_      ->[] )
```

Exercise 9. But to obtain symmetry, we could also try and avoid the `<@` operator in both alternatives. Earlier we defined the operator `<*` as an abbreviation of applying `<@ fst` to the result of `<*>`. In the function `many`, also the result of `<*>` is postprocessed. Define an utility function `<:*>` for this case, and use it to simplify the definition of `many` even more.

The order in which the alternatives are given only influences the order in which solutions are placed in the list of successes.

Exercise 10. Consider application of the parser many (symbol 'a') to the string "aaa". In what order do the four possible parsings appear in the list of successes?

An example in which the many combinator can be used is parsing of a natural number:

```
natural  ::  Parser Char Int
natural  =  many digit  <@  foldl f 0
       where  f a b = a*10 + b
```

Defined in this way, the natural parser also accepts empty input as a number. If this is not desired, we'd better use the many1 parser combinator, which accepts one or more occurrences of a construction.

Exercise 11. Define the many1 parser combinator.

Another combinator that you may know from other formalisms is the option combinator. The constructed parser generates a list with zero or one element, depending on whether the construction was recognized or not.

```
option  ::  Parser s a -> Parser s [a]
option p  =      p        <@  (\x->[x])
            <|> epsilon  <@  (\x->[] )
```

For æsthetic reasons we used epsilon in this definition; another way to write the second alternative is succeed [].

The combinators many, many1 and option are classical in compiler constructions, but there is no need to leave it at that. For example, in many languages constructions are frequently enclosed between two meaningless symbols, most often some sort of parentheses. For this we design a parser combinator pack. Given a parser for an opening token, a body, and a closing token, it constructs a parser for the enclosed body:

```
pack  ::  Parser s a -> Parser s b -> Parser s c -> Parser s b
pack s1 p s2  =  s1 *> p <* s2
```

Special cases of this combinator are:

```
parenthesized p =  pack (symbol '(')    p  (symbol ')')
bracketed p     =  pack (symbol '[')    p  (symbol ']')
compound p      =  pack (token "begin") p  (token "end")
```

Another frequently occurring construction is repetition of a certain construction, where the elements are separated by some symbol. You may think of lists of parameters (expressions separated by commas), or compound statements (statements separated by semicolons). For the parse trees, the separators are of no importance. The function listOf below generates a parser for a (possibly empty) list, given a parser for the items and a parser for the separators:

```
listOf       ::  Parser s a -> Parser s b -> Parser s [a]
listOf p s   =  p <:*> many (s *> p)  <|>  succeed []
```

Useful instatiations are:

```
commaList, semicList  ::  Parser Char a -> Parser Char [a]
commaList p = listOf p (symbol ',')
semicList p = listOf p (symbol ';')
```

Exercise 12. As another variation on the theme 'repetition', define a parser sequence combinator that transforms a *list of parsers* for some type into a *parser yielding a list* of elements of that type. Also define a combinator choice that iterates the operator <|>.

Exercise 13. As an application of sequence, define the function token that was discussed in section 3.

A somewhat more complicated variant of the function listOf is the case where the separators carry a meaning themselves. For example, an arithmetical expressions, where the operators that separate the subexpressions have to be part of the parse tree. For this case we will develop the functions chainr and chainl. These functions expect that the parser for the separators yields a function (!); that function is used by chain to combine parse trees for the items. In the case of chainr the operator is applied right-to-left, in the case of chainl it is applied left-to-right. The basic structure of chainl is the same as that of listOf. But where the function listOf discards the separators using the operator *>, we will keep it in the result now using <*>. Furthermore, postprocessing is more difficult now than just applying list.

```
chainl     ::  Parser s a -> Parser s (a->a->a) -> Parser s a
chainl p s =  p <*> many (s <*> p)  <@  f
```

The function f should operate on an element and a list of tuples, each containing an operator and an element. For example, $f(e_0, [(\oplus_1, e_1), (\oplus_2, e_2), (\oplus_3, e_3)])$ should return $((e_o \oplus_1 e_1) \oplus_2 e_2) \oplus_3 e_3$. You may recognize a version of foldl in this (albeit an uncurried one), where a tuple $(\oplus, y)$ from the list and intermediate result x are combined applying $x \oplus y$. If we define

```
ap2 (op,y) x = x 'op' y
```

or even

```
ap2 (op,y) = ('op' y)
```

then we may define

```
chainl     :: Parser s a -> Parser s (a->a->a) -> Parser s a
chainl p s = p <*> many (s <*> p)
                  <@  uncurry (foldl (flip ap2))
```

Dual to this function is chainr, which applies the operators associating to the right.

Exercise 14. Try to define chainr. The definition is beautifully symmetric to chainl, but you only experience the beauty when you discover it yourself...

8 Analyzing options

The `option` function constructs a parser which yields a list of elements: an empty list if the optional construct was not recognized, and a singleton list if it was present. Postprocessing functions may therefore safely assume that the list consists of zero or one element, and will in practice do a case analysis. You will therefore often need constructions like:

```
option p  <@  f
      where  f [] = a
             f [x] = b x
```

As this necessitates a new function name for every optional symbol in our grammar, we had better provide a higher order function for this situation. We will define a special version `<?@` of the `<@` operator, which provides a semantics for both the case that the optional construct was present and that it was not. The right argument of `<?@` consists of two parts: a constant to be used in absence, and a function to be used in presence of the optional construct. The new transformer is defined by:

```
p <?@ (no,yes)  =  p <@ f
             where  f [] = no
                    f [x] = yes x
```

For a practical use of this, let's extend the parser for natural numbers to floating point numbers:

```
natural  ::  Parser Char Int
natural  =  many digit  <@  foldl f 0
      where  f n d = n*10 + d
```

The fractional part of a floating point number is parsed by:

```
fract  ::  Parser Char Float
fract  =  many digit  <@  foldr f 0.0
      where  f d x = (x + fromInteger d)/10.0
```

But the fractional part is optional in a floating point number.

```
fixed  ::  Parser Char Float
fixed  =  (integer <@ fromInteger)
          <*>
          (option (symbol '.' *> fract) <?@ (0.0,id))
          <@  uncurry (+)
```

The decimal point is for separation only, and therefore immediately discarded by the operator `*>`. The decimal point and the fractional part together are optional. In their absence, the number `0.0` should be used, in there presence, the identity function should be applied to the fractional part. Finally, integer and fractional part are added.

Exercise 15. Define a parser for a (possibly negative) integer number, which consists of an optional minus sign followed by a natural number.

Exercise 16. Let the parser for floating point numbers recognize an optional exponent.

In the solution of exercise 15 you will find a nice construct, in which the first construct parsed yields a function which is subsequently applied to the second construct parsed. We can use that for yet another refinement of the `chainr` function. It was defined in the previous section using the `many` function. The parser yields a list of tuples (operator,element), which immediately afterwards is destroyed by `foldr`. Why bothering building the list, then, anyway? We can apply the function that is folded with directly during parsing, without first building a list. For this, we need to substitute the body of `many` in the definition of `chainr`. We can further abbreviate the phrase p <|> epsilon by option p. By directly applying the function that was previously used during `foldr` we obtain:

```
chainr' p s  =  q
    where  q =  p <*> (option (s <*> q) <?@ (id,ap2) )
                <@ flip ap
```

Exercise 17. You want to try `chainl` yourself?

By the use of the `option` and `many` functions, a large amount of backtracking possibilities are introduced. This is not always advantageous. For example, if we define a parser for identifiers by

```
identifier  =  many1 (satisfy isAlpha)
```

a single word may also be parsed as two identifiers. Caused by the order of the alternatives in the definition of `many`, the 'greedy' parsing, which accumulates as many letters as possible in the identifier is tried first, but if parsing fails elsewhere in the sentence, also less greedy parsings of the identifier are tried – in vain.

In situations where from the way the grammar is built we can predict that it is hopeless to try non-greedy successes of `many`. We can define a parser transformer `first`, that transforms a parser into a parser that only yields the first possibility. It does so by taking the first element of the list of successes.

```
first :: Parser a b -> Parser a b
first p xs | null r    =  []
           | otherwise =  [head r]
                where r = p xs
```

Using this function, we can create a special 'take all or nothing' version of `many`:

```
greedy   =  first . many
greedy1  =  first . many1
```

If we compose the `first` function with the `option` parser combinator:

```
compulsion  =  first . option
```

we get a parser which must accept a construction if it is present, but which does not fail if it is not present.

9 Arithmetical expressions

In this section we will use the parser combinators in a concrete application. We will develop a parser for arithmetical expressions, of which parse trees are of type `Expr`:

```
data Expr  =  Con Int
           |  Var String
           |  Fun String [Expr]
           |  Expr :+: Expr
           |  Expr :-: Expr
           |  Expr :*: Expr
           |  Expr :/: Expr
```

In order to account for the priorities of the operators, we will use a grammar with non-terminals 'expression', 'term' and 'factor': an expression is composed of terms separated by + or −; a term is composed of factors separated by * or /, and a factor is a constant, variable, function call, or expression between parentheses.

This grammar is represented in the functions below:

```
fact  ::  Parser Char Expr
fact  =       integer <@ Con
          <|> identifier
              <*> ( option (parenthesized (commaList expr))
                   <?@ (Var,flip Fun))
              <@  ap'
          <|> parenthesized expr
```

The first alternative is a constant, which is fed into the 'semantic function' `Var`. The second alternative is a variable or function call, depending on the presence of a parameterlist. In absence of the latter, the function `Var` is applied, in presence the function `Fun`. For the third alternative there is no semantic function, because the meaning of an expression between parentheses is the same as that of the expression without parentheses.

For the definition of a term as a list of factors separated by multiplicative operators we will use the function `chainr`:

```
term  ::  Parser Char Expr
term  =  chainr fact
             (    symbol '*' <@ const (:*:)
              <|> symbol '/' <@ const (:/:)
             )
```

Recall that `chainr` repeatedly recognizes its first parameter (`fact`), separated by its second parameter (an * or /). The parse trees for the individual factors are joined by the constructor functions mentioned after `<@`.

The function `expr` is analogous to `term`, only with additive operators instead of multiplicative operators, and with `terms` instead of `factors`:

```
expr  ::  Parser Char Expr
```

```
expr   =  chainr term
                 (    symbol '+' <@ const (:+:)
                <|> symbol '-' <@ const (:-:)
                )
```

From this example the strength of the method becomes clear. There is no need for a separate formalism for grammars; the production rules of the grammar are joined using higher-order functions. Also, there is no need for a separate parser generator (like 'yacc'); the functions can be viewed both as description of the grammar and as an executable parser.

10 Generalized expressions

Arithmetical expressions in which operators have more than two levels of priority can be parsed by writing more auxiliary functions between term and expr. The function chainr is used in each definition, with as first parameter the function of one priority level lower.

If there are nine levels of priority, we obtain nine copies of almost the same text. This would not be as it should be. Functions that resemble each other are an indication that we should write a generalized function, where the differences are described using extra parameters. Therefore, let's inspect the differences in the definitions of term and expr again. These are:

- The operators and associated tree constructors that are used in the second parameter of chainr
- The parser that is used as first parameter of chainr

The generalized function will take these two differences as extra parameters: the first in the form of a list of pairs, the second in the form of a parse function:

```
type Op a  =  (Char, a->a->a)
gen         ::  [Op a] -> Parser Char a -> Parser Char a
gen ops p  =  chainr p (choice (map f ops))
        where  f (s,c) = symbol s <@ const c
```

If furthermore we define as shorthand:

```
multis  =  [ ('*',(:*:)), ('/',(:/:)) ]
addis   =  [ ('+',(:+:)), ('-',(:-:)) ]
```

then expr and term can be defined as partial parametrizations of gen:

```
expr  =  gen addis  term
term  =  gen multis fact
```

By expanding the definition of term in that of expr we obtain:

```
expr  =  addis 'gen' (multis 'gen' fact)
```

which an experienced functional programmer immediately recognizes as an application of foldr:

```
expr = foldr gen fact [addis, multis]
```

From this definition a generalization to more levels of priority is simply a matter of extending the list of operator-lists.

The very compact formulation of the parser for expressions with an arbitrary number of priority levels was possible because the parser combinators could be used in conjunction with the existing mechanisms for generalization and partial parametrization in the functional language.

Contrary to conventional approaches, the levels of priority need not be coded explicitly with integers. The only thing that matters is the relative position of an operator in the list of 'list with operators of the same priority'. Also, the insertion of new priority levels is very easy.

11 Self application

Although in the preceding sections it is shown that a separate formalism for grammars is not needed, users might want to stick to, for example, BNF-notation for writing grammars. Therefore in this section we will write a function that transforms a BNF-grammar into a parser. The BNF-grammar is given a a string, and is analyzed itself of course by a parser. This parser is a parser that as parse 'tree' yields a parser! Thus, the title of this section is justified.

This section is structured as follows. First we write some functions that are needed to manipulate an *environment*. Next, we describe how a grammar can be parsed. Then we will define a data structure in which parse trees for an arbitrary grammar can be represented. Finally we will show how the parser for grammars can yield a parser for the language described by the grammar.

Environments An environment is a list of pairs, in which a finite mapping can be represented. The function assoc can be used to associate a value to its image under the mapping.

```
type Env a b   =   [(a,b)]
assoc :: Eq s  =>  Env s d -> s -> d
assoc ((u,v):ws) x | x==u      = v
                   | otherwise = assoc ws x
```

We also define a function mapenv that applies a function to all images in an environment.

```
mapenv :: (a->b) -> Env s a -> Env s b
mapenv f [] = []
mapenv f ((x,v):ws) = (x,f v) : mapenv f ws
```

Grammars In a grammar, terminal symbols and nonterminal symbols are used. Both are represented by a string. We provide a datatype with two cases for the two kinds of symbols:

```
data Symbol = Term String
            | Nont String
```

The right hand side of a production rule consists of a number of alternatives, each of which is a list of symbols:

```
type Alt   =   [Symbol]
type Rhs   =   [Alt]
```

Finally, a grammar is an association between a (nonterminal) symbol an the right hand side of the production rule for it:

```
type Gram   =   Env Symbol Rhs
```

Grammars can easily be denoted using the BNF-notation. For this notation we will write a parser, that as a parse tree yields a value of type Gram. The parser for BNF-grammars in parameterized with a parser for nonterminals and a parser for terminals, so that we can adopt different conventions for representing them later. We use the elementary parsers sptoken and spsymbol rather than token and symbol to allow for extra spaces in the grammar representation.

```
bnf :: Parser Char String -> Parser Char String
        -> Parser Char Gram
bnf nontp termp = many rule
    where rule = (     nont
                 <*>  sptoken "::="  *> rhs <*  spsymbol '.'
                 )
          rhs  =  listOf alt (spsymbol '|')
          alt  =  many (term <|> nont)
          term =  sp termp  <@  Term
          nont =  sp nontp  <@  Nont
```

A BNF-grammar consists of 'many' rules, each consisting of a nonterminal separated by a ::=-symbol from the rhs and followed by a full stop. The rhs is a list of alternatives, separated by |-symbols, where each alternative consists of 'many' symbols, terminal or nonterminal. Terminals and nonterminals are recognized by the parsers provided as parameter to the bnf function.

An example of a grammar representation that can be parsed with this parser is the grammar for block structured statements:

```
blockgram = "BLOCK ::= begin BLOCK end BLOCK  |  ."
```

Here we used the convention to denote nonterminals by upper case and terminals by lower case characters. In a call of the bnf functions we should specify these conventions. For example:

```
test = some (bnf nont term) blockgram
    where nont = greedy1 (satisfy isUpper)
          term = greedy1 (satisfy isLower)
```

The output of this test is the following environment:

```
[ (Nont "BLOCK",[  [ Term "begin"
                   , Nont "BLOCK"
```

```
                         , Term "end"
                         , Nont "BLOCK"
                         ]
                    ,   []
                    ]

         )
    ]
```

Parse trees We can no longer use a data structure that is specially designed for one
particular grammar, like the Expr type in section 9. Instead, we define a generic data
structure, that describes parse trees for sentences from an arbitrary grammar. We
simply call them Tree; they are instances of multibranching trees or 'rose trees':

```
data Tree  =  Node Symbol [Tree]
```

Parsers instead of grammars Using the bfn function, we can easily generate values
of the Gram type. But what we really need in practice is a parser for the language
that is described by a BNF grammar. So let's define a function

```
parsGram :: Gram -> Symbol -> Parser Symbol Tree
```

that given a grammar and a start symbol generates a parser for the language described by the grammar. Having defined it, we can let is postprocess the output of
the bnf function.

The function parsGram uses some auxiliary functions, which generate a parser
for a symbol, an alternative, and the rhs of a rule, respectively:

```
parsGram :: Gram -> Symbol -> Parser Symbol Tree
parsGram gram start = parsSym start
   where
      parsSym :: Symbol -> Parser Symbol Tree
      parsSym s@(Term t)  =  symbol s <@ const []    <@ Node s
      parsSym s@(Nont n)  =  parsRhs (assoc gram s) <@ Node s
      parsAlt ::  Alt -> Parser Symbol [Tree]
      parsAlt  =  sequence . map parsSym
      parsRhs ::  Rhs -> Parser Symbol [Tree]
      parsRhs  =  choice . map parsAlt
```

The parsSym function distinguishes cases for terminal and nonterminal functions.
For terminal symbols a parser is generated that just recognizes that symbol, and
subsequently a Node for the parse tree is build.

Exercise 18. What is the <@ const [] transformation used for?

For nonterminal symbols, the corresponding rule is looked up in the grammar, which
is an environment after all. Then the function parsRhs is used to construct a parser
for a rhs. The function parsRhs generates parsers for each alternative, and makes
a choice from them. Finally, the function parseAlt generates parsers for the individual symbols in the alternative, and combines them using the sequence function.

A parser generator In theoretical textbooks a context-free grammar is usually described as a four-tuple (N, T, R, S) consisting of a set of nonterminals, a set of terminals, a set of rules and a start symbol. Let's do so, representing a set of symbols by a parser:

```
type SymbolSet = Parser Char String
type CFG = (SymbolSet, SymbolSet, String, Symbol)
```

Now we will define a function that takes such a four-tuple and returns a parser for its language. Would it be too immodest to call this a 'parser generator'?

```
parsgen ::  CFG -> Parser Symbol Tree
parsgen (nontp,termp,bnfstring,start)
          = some (bnf nontp termp <@ parsGram) bnfstring start
```

The sets of nonterminals and terminals are represented by parsers for them. The grammar is a string in BNF notation. The resulting parser accepts a list of (terminal) Symbols and yields a parse Tree.

Lexical scanners The parser that is generated accepts Symbols instead of Chars. If we want to apply it to a character string, this string first has to be 'tokenized' by a lexical scanner.

For this, we will make a library function twopass, which takes two parsers: one that converts characters into tokens, and one that converts tokens into trees. The function does not need any properties of 'character', 'token' and 'tree', and thus has a polymorphic type:

```
twopass ::  Parser a b -> Parser b c -> Parser a c
twopass lex synt xs = [ (rest,tree)
                      | (rest,tokens) <- many lex xs
                      , (_,tree)      <- just synt tokens
                      ]
```

Using this function, we can finally parse a string from the language that was described by a BNF grammar:

```
blockgram =  "BLOCK ::= begin BLOCK end BLOCK |   ."
block4tup =  (upperId, lowerId, blockgram, Nont "BLOCK")
upperId   =  greedy1 (satisfy isUpper)
lowerId   =  greedy1 (satisfy isLower)
final     =  twopass (sp lowerId <@ Term) (parsgen block4tup)
input     =  "begin end begin begin end end"
```

This can really be used in a session:

```
? some final input
Node (Nont "BLOCK") [Node (Term "begin") [], Node (Nont
"BLOCK") [], Node (Term "end") [], Node (Nont "BLOCK")
[Node (Term "begin") [], Node (Nont "BLOCK") [Node (Term
"begin") [], Node (Nont "BLOCK") [], Node (Term "end")
```

```
[], Node (Nont "BLOCK") []], Node (Term "end") [], Node
(Nont "BLOCK") []]]
(1061 reductions, 2722 cells)
```

Exercise 19. We used uppercase and lowercase identifiers to distinguish between non-terminals an terminals. If the namespaces of nonterminals and terminals overlap, we have to adopt other mechanisms to distinguish them, for example angle brackets around nonterminals and quotes around terminals. How can this be done?

Exercise 20. Make a parser for your favourite language.

Acknowledgement

I would like to thank Doaitse Swierstra and Erik Meijer for their comments on a draft of this paper and stimulating ideas.

References

1. R. Bird and P. Wadler, *Introduction to Functional Programming.* Prentice Hall, 1988.
2. W.H. Burge, 'Parsing'. In *Recursive Programming Techniques*, Addison-Wesley, 1975.
3. Graham Hutton, 'Higher-order functions for parsing'. *J. Functional Programming* 2:323–343.
4. Mark Jones, *Gofer 2.30 release notes.*
   http://www.cs.nott.ac.uk:80/Department/Staff/mpj/.
5. P. Wadler, 'How to replace failure by a list of successes: a method for exception handling, backtracking, and pattern matching in lazy functional languages'. In *Functional Programming Languages and Computer Architecture*, (J.P.Jouannaud, ed.), Springer, 1985 (LNCS 201), pp. 113–128.
6. Philip Wadler, 'Monads for functional programming'. In *Program design calculi, proc. of the Marktoberdorf Summer School*, (M. Broy, ed.) Springer, 1992.
7. Philip Wadler, 'Monads for functional programming'. In J. Jeuring and E. Meijer, editors. *Lecture notes on Advanced Functional Programming Techniques*, LNCS, Springer-Verlag, 1995.

Solutions to exercises

1. A symbol equal to *a* satisfies equality to *a*:

   ```
   symbol a  =  satisfy  (==a)
   ```

2. As <|> is a lifted version of ++, it is more efficiently evaluated right associative.
3. The function just can be written as a list comprehension:

   ```
   just p xs  =  [ ([],v)
                 | (ys,v) <- p xs
                 , null ys
                 ]
   ```

4. The operator `<*>` associates to the right, so `a <*> b <*> c <*> d` really means `a <*> (b <*> (c <*> d))`, which explains the structure of the result.

5. The parser epsilon yields the empty tuple () as parse tree. The function `const Nil` is applied to this result, thus effectively discarding the empty tuple and substituting `Nil` for it. Instead of `epsilon <@ const Nil` we can also write `succeed Nil`.

6. Without parentheses, we obtain `open *> (parens <* (close<*>parens))`, and we would only keep the result of the first recursive use of the `parens` parser.

7. The functions `parens` and `nesting` can be written as partial parametrizations of `foldparens`, by supplying the functions to be used for the first and second alternative:

```
parens  = foldparens Bin        Nil
nesting = foldparens (max.(1+)) 0
```

8. Without the `just` transformer, also partial parses are reported in the successes list

```
? nesting "()(())()"
[([],2), ("()",2), ("(())()",1), ("()(())()",0)]
? nesting "())"
[(")",1), ("())",0)]
```

9. The empty alternative is presented last, because the `<|>` combinator uses list concatenation for concatenating lists of successes. This also holds for the recursive calls; thus the 'greedy' parsing of all three a's is presented first, then two a's with singleton rest string, then one a, and finally the empty result with untouched rest string.

10. We define `<:*>` as an abbreviation of postprocessing `<*>` with the `list` function:

```
p <:*> q = p <*> q <@ list
```

Then we can define

```
many p =  p <:*> many p  <|>  succeed []
```

11. The `many1` combinator can be defined using the `many` combinator:

```
many1  :: Parser s a -> Parser s [a]
many1 p = p <*> many p <@ list
```

12.
```
sequence   :: [Parser s a] -> Parser s [a]
sequence   = foldr (<:*>) (succeed [])
choice     :: [Parser s a] -> Parser s a
choice     = foldr (<|>) fail
```

13.
```
token :: Eq [s] => [s] -> Parser s [s]
token = sequence . map symbol
```

14. This was chainl:

```
chainl :: Parser s a -> Parser s (a->a->a) -> Parser s a
chainl p s = p <*> many (s <*> p)
                <@ uncurry (foldl (flip ap2))
```

To obtain `chainr`, change `foldl` into `foldr`, swap `flip` and `fold`, change `ap2` into `ap1` and reorder the distribution of `many` over the `<*>` operators:

```
chainr :: Parser s a -> Parser s (a->a->a) -> Parser s a
chainr p s = many (p <*> s) <*> p
                  <@ uncurry (flip (foldr ap1))
```

The auxiliary functions used are:

```
ap2 (op,y)   = ('op' y)
ap1 (x,op)   = (x 'op')
```

15. Easiest is to do the case analysis explicitly:

```
integer  ::  Parser Char Int
integer   =  option (symbol '-') <*> natural <@ f
        where f ([],n) =  n
              f (_ ,n) =  -n
```

But nicest is to use the `<?@` operator, yielding the identity or negation function in absence or presence of the minus sign, which is finally applied to the natural number:

```
integer ::  Parser Char Int
integer =  (option (symbol '-')  <?@  (id,const negate))
             <*> natural
             <@ ap
        where ap (f,x) = f x
```

16. A floating point number is a fixed point number with an optional exponent part:

```
float  ::  Parser Char Float
float   =  fixed
           <*>
           (option (symbol 'E' *> integer) <?@ (0,id) )
           <@ f
       where f (m,e)  =  m * power e
             power e | e<0       = 1.0 / power (-e)
                     | otherwise = fromInteger(10^e)
```

17. This would be nice:

```
chainl' p s  =  q
       where  q = (option (q <*> s) <?@ (id,ap1) )
                  <*> p <@ ap
```

Alas, this function will not terminate...

18. The symbol s that is parsed is discarded, and an empty list is substituted for it. Then the function `Node s` is applied to this empty list, resulting in `Node s []`, which is a terminal node in the parse tree.

Monads for functional programming

Philip Wadler, University of Glasgow*

Department of Computing Science, University of Glasgow, G12 8QQ, Scotland
(wadler@dcs.glasgow.ac.uk)

Abstract. The use of monads to structure functional programs is described. Monads provide a convenient framework for simulating effects found in other languages, such as global state, exception handling, output, or non-determinism. Three case studies are looked at in detail: how monads ease the modification of a simple evaluator; how monads act as the basis of a datatype of arrays subject to in-place update; and how monads can be used to build parsers.

1   Introduction

Shall I be pure or impure?

The functional programming community divides into two camps. *Pure* languages, such as Miranda[2] and Haskell, are lambda calculus pure and simple. *Impure* languages, such as Scheme and Standard ML, augment lambda calculus with a number of possible *effects*, such as assignment, exceptions, or continuations. Pure languages are easier to reason about and may benefit from lazy evaluation, while impure languages offer efficiency benefits and sometimes make possible a more compact mode of expression.

Recent advances in theoretical computing science, notably in the areas of type theory and category theory, have suggested new approaches that may integrate the benefits of the pure and impure schools. These notes describe one, the use of *monads* to integrate impure effects into pure functional languages.

The concept of a monad, which arises from category theory, has been applied by Moggi to structure the denotational semantics of programming languages [13, 14]. The same technique can be applied to structure functional programs [21, 23].

The applications of monads will be illustrated with three case studies. Section 2 introduces monads by showing how they can be used to structure a simple evaluator so that it is easy to modify. Section 3 describes the laws satisfied by monads. Section 4 shows how monads provide a new solution to the old problem of providing updatable state in pure functional languages. Section 5 applies monads to the problem of building recursive descent parsers; this is of interest in its own right, and because it provides a paradigm for sequencing and alternation, two of the central concepts of computing.

It is doubtful that the structuring methods presented here would have been discovered without the insight afforded by category theory. But once discovered

---

* A previous version of this note appeared in: M. Broy, editor, *Program Design Calculi*, Proceedings of the Marktoberdorf Summer School, 30 July–8 August 1992.

[2] Miranda is a trademark of Research Software Limited.

they are easily expressed without any reference to things categorical. No knowledge of category theory is required to read these notes.

The examples will be given in Haskell, but no knowledge of that is required either. What is required is a passing familiarity with the basics of pure and impure functional programming; for general background see [3, 12]. The languages refered to are Haskell [4], Miranda [20], Standard ML [11], and Scheme [17].

2 Evaluating monads

Pure functional languages have this advantage: all flow of data is made explicit. And this disadvantage: sometimes it is painfully explicit.

A program in a pure functional language is written as a set of equations. Explicit data flow ensures that the value of an expression depends only on its free variables. Hence substitution of equals for equals is always valid, making such programs especially easy to reason about. Explicit data flow also ensures that the order of computation is irrelevant, making such programs susceptible to lazy evaluation.

It is with regard to modularity that explicit data flow becomes both a blessing and a curse. On the one hand, it is the ultimate in modularity. All data in and all data out are rendered manifest and accessible, providing a maximum of flexibility. On the other hand, it is the nadir of modularity. The essence of an algorithm can become buried under the plumbing required to carry data from its point of creation to its point of use.

Say I write an evaluator in a pure functional language.

- To add error handling to it, I need to modify each recursive call to check for and handle errors appropriately. Had I used an impure language with exceptions, no such restructuring would be needed.
- To add a count of operations performed to it, I need to modify each recursive call to pass around such counts appropriately. Had I used an impure language with a global variable that could be incremented, no such restructuring would be needed.
- To add an execution trace to it, I need to modify each recursive call to pass around such traces appropriately. Had I used an impure language that performed output as a side effect, no such restructuring would be needed.

Or I could use a *monad*.

These notes show how to use monads to structure an evaluator so that the changes mentioned above are simple to make. In each case, all that is required is to redefine the monad and to make a few local changes.

This programming style regains some of the flexibility provided by various features of impure languages. It also may apply when there is no corresponding impure feature. It does not eliminate the tension between the flexibility afforded by explicit data and the brevity afforded by implicit plumbing; but it does ameliorate it to some extent.

The technique applies not just to evaluators, but to a wide range of functional programs. For a number of years, Glasgow has been involved in constructing a compiler for the functional language Haskell. The compiler is itself written in Haskell, and uses the structuring technique described here. Though this paper describes the use of monads in a program tens of lines long, we have experience of using them in a program three orders of magnitude larger.

We begin with the basic evaluator for simple terms, then consider variations that mimic exceptions, state, and output. We analyse these for commonalities, and abstract from these the concept of a monad. We then show how each of the variations fits into the monadic framework.

2.1 Variation zero: The basic evaluator

The evaluator acts on terms, which for purposes of illustration have been taken to be excessively simple.

$$\textbf{data } Term = Con \, Int \mid Div \, Term \, Term$$

A term is either a constant $Con \, a$, where a is an integer, or a quotient, $Div \, t \, u$, where t and u are terms.

The basic evaluator is simplicity itself.

$$
\begin{aligned}
&eval && :: Term \rightarrow Int \\
&eval \, (Con \, a) &&= a \\
&eval \, (Div \, t \, u) &&= eval \, t \div eval \, u
\end{aligned}
$$

The function $eval$ takes a term to an integer. If the term is a constant, the constant is returned. If the term is a quotient, its subterms are evaluated and the quotient computed. We use '$\div$' to denote integer division.

The following will provide running examples.

$$
\begin{aligned}
&answer, error &&:: Term \\
&answer &&= (Div \, (Div \, (Con \, 1972) \, (Con \, 2)) \, (Con \, 23)) \\
&error &&= (Div \, (Con \, 1) \, (Con \, 0))
\end{aligned}
$$

Computing $eval \, answer$ yields the value of $((1972 \div 2) \div 23)$, which is 42. The basic evaluator does not incorporate error handling, so the result of $eval \, error$ is undefined.

2.2 Variation one: Exceptions

Say it is desired to add error checking, so that the second example above returns a sensible error message. In an impure language, this is easily achieved with the use of exceptions.

In a pure language, exception handling may be mimicked by introducing a type to represent computations that may raise an exception.

$$
\begin{aligned}
&\textbf{data } M \, a && = Raise \, Exception \mid Return \, a \\
&\textbf{type } Exception = String
\end{aligned}
$$

A value of type $M \, a$ either has the form $Raise \, e$, where e is an exception, or $Return \, a$, where a is a value of type a. By convention, a will be used both as a type variable, as in $M \, a$, and as a variable ranging over values of that type, as in $Return \, a$.

(A word on the difference between 'data' and 'type' declarations. A 'data' declaration introduces a new data type, in this case M, and new constructors for values of that type, in this case *Raise* and *Return*. A 'type' declaration introduces a new name for an existing type, in this case *Exception* becomes another name for *String*.)

It is straightforward, but tedious, to adapt the evaluator to this representation.

$$
\begin{aligned}
&eval && :: Term \rightarrow M\,Int \\
&eval\,(Con\,a) &&= Return\,a \\
&eval\,(Div\,t\,u) &&= \textbf{case }\ eval\,t\ \textbf{ of} \\
&&&\quad Raise\,e \rightarrow Raise\,e \\
&&&\quad Return\,a \rightarrow \\
&&&\qquad \textbf{case }\ eval\,u\ \textbf{ of} \\
&&&\qquad\quad Raise\,e \rightarrow Raise\,e \\
&&&\qquad\quad Return\,b \rightarrow \\
&&&\qquad\qquad \textbf{if }\ b = 0 \\
&&&\qquad\qquad\quad \textbf{then }\ Raise\ \text{``divide by zero''} \\
&&&\qquad\qquad\quad \textbf{else }\ \ Return\,(a \div b)
\end{aligned}
$$

At each call of the evaluator, the form of the result must be checked: if an exception was raised it is re-raised, and if a value was returned it is processed. Applying the new evaluator to *answer* yields (*Return* 42), while applying it to *error* yields (*Raise "divide by zero"*).

2.3 Variation two: State

Forgetting errors for the moment, say it is desired to count the number of divisions performed during evaluation. In an impure language, this is easily achieved by the use of state. Set a given variable to zero initially, and increment it by one each time a division occurs.

In a pure language, state may be mimicked by introducing a type to represent computations that act on state.

$$
\begin{aligned}
&\textbf{type }\ M\,a &&= State \rightarrow (a, State) \\
&\textbf{type }\ State &&= Int
\end{aligned}
$$

Now a value of type $M\,a$ is a function that accepts the initial state, and returns the computed value paired with the final state.

Again, it is straightforward but tedious to adapt the evaluator to this representation.

$$
\begin{aligned}
&eval && :: Term \rightarrow M\,Int \\
&eval\,(Con\,a)\,x &&= (a, x) \\
&eval\,(Div\,t\,u)\,x &&= \textbf{let }\ (a, y) = eval\,t\,x\ \textbf{ in} \\
&&&\quad\ \ \textbf{let }\ (b, z) = eval\,u\,y\ \textbf{ in} \\
&&&\quad\ \ (a \div b, z + 1)
\end{aligned}
$$

At each call of the evaluator, the old state must be passed in, and the new state extracted from the result and passed on appropriately. Computing *eval answer* 0 yields (42, 2), so with initial state 0 the answer is 42 and the final state is 2, indicating that two divisions were performed.

2.4 Variation three: Output

Finally, say it is desired to display a trace of execution. In an impure language, this is easily done by inserting output commands at appropriate points.

In a pure language, output may be mimicked by introducing a type to represent computations that generate output.

$$\textbf{type } M\, a \quad = (Output, a)$$
$$\textbf{type } Output = String$$

Now a value of type $M\, a$ consists of the output generated paired with the value computed.

Yet again, it is straightforward but tedious to adapt the evaluator to this representation.

$$
\begin{aligned}
&eval &&:: Term \to M\, Int \\
&eval\,(Con\, a) &&= (line\,(Con\, a)\, a, a) \\
&eval\,(Div\, t\, u) &&= \textbf{let } (x, a) = eval\, t \textbf{ in} \\
& && \quad \textbf{let } (y, b) = eval\, u \textbf{ in} \\
& && \quad (x +\!\!+ y +\!\!+ line\,(Div\, t\, u)\,(a \div b), a \div b) \\[4pt]
&line &&:: Term \to Int \to Output \\
&line\, t\, a &&= \text{"}eval\,(" +\!\!+ showterm\, t +\!\!+ ")\text{"} \Leftarrow \text{"} +\!\!+ showint\, a +\!\!+ \text{"}\hookleftarrow\text{"}
\end{aligned}
$$

At each call of the evaluator, the outputs must be collected and assembled to form the output of the enclosing call. The function $line$ generates one line of the output. Here $showterm$ and $showint$ convert terms and integers to strings, $+\!\!+$ concatenates strings, and "$\hookleftarrow$" represents the string consisting of a newline.

Computing $eval\, answer$ returns the pair $(x, 42)$, where x is the string

$$
\begin{aligned}
&eval\,(Con\, 1972) \Leftarrow 1972 \\
&eval\,(Con\, 2) \Leftarrow 2 \\
&eval\,(Div\,(Con\, 1972)\,(Con\, 2)) \Leftarrow 986 \\
&eval\,(Con\, 23) \Leftarrow 23 \\
&eval\,(Div\,(Div\,(Con\, 1972)\,(Con\, 2))\,(Con\, 23))) \Leftarrow 42
\end{aligned}
$$

which represents a trace of the computation.

From the discussion so far, it may appear that programs in impure languages are easier to modify than those in pure languages. But sometimes the reverse is true. Say that it was desired to modify the previous program to display the execution trace in the reverse order:

$$
\begin{aligned}
&eval\,(Div\,(Div\,(Con\, 1972)\,(Con\, 2))\,(Con\, 23))) \Leftarrow 42 \\
&eval\,(Con\, 23) \Leftarrow 23 \\
&eval\,(Div\,(Con\, 1972)\,(Con\, 2)) \Leftarrow 986 \\
&eval\,(Con\, 2) \Leftarrow 2 \\
&eval\,(Con\, 1972) \Leftarrow 1972
\end{aligned}
$$

This is simplicity itself to achieve with the pure program: just replace the term

$$x +\!\!+ y +\!\!+ line\,(Div\, t\, u)\,(a \div b)$$

with the term

$$line\,(Div\,t\,u)\,(a \div b) + \!\!\!+ y + \!\!\!+ x.$$

It is not so easy to modify the impure program to achieve this effect. The problem is that output occurs as a side-effect of computation, but one now desires to display the result of computing a term *before* displaying the output generated by that computation. This can be achieved in a variety of ways, but all require substantial modification to the impure program.

2.5 A monadic evaluator

Each of the variations on the interpreter has a similar structure, which may be abstracted to yield the notion of a *monad*.

In each variation, we introduced a type of computations. Respectively, M represented computations that could raise exceptions, act on state, and generate output. By now the reader will have guessed that M stands for *monad*.

The original evaluator has the type $Term \to Int$, while in each variation its type took the form $Term \to M\,Int$. In general, a function of type $a \to b$ is replaced by a function of type $a \to M\,b$. This can be read as a function that accepts an argument of type a and returns a result of type b, with a possible additional effect captured by M. This effect may be to act on state, generate output, raise an exception, or what have you.

What sort of operations are required on the type M? Examination of the examples reveals two. First, we need a way to turn a value into the computation that returns that value and does nothing else.

$$unit :: a \to M\,a$$

Second, we need a way to apply a function of type $a \to M\,b$ to a computation of type $M\,a$. It is convenient to write these in an order where the argument comes before the function.

$$(\star) :: M\,a \to (a \to M\,b) \to M\,b$$

A *monad* is a triple $(M, unit, \star)$ consisting of a type constructor M and two operations of the given polymorphic types. These operations must satisfy three laws given in Section 3.

We will often write expressions in the form

$$m \star \lambda a.\,n$$

where m and n are expressions, and a is a variable. The form $\lambda a.\,n$ is a lambda expression, with the scope of the bound variable a being the expression n. The above can be read as follows: perform computation m, bind a to the resulting value, and then perform computation n. Types provide a useful guide. From the type of $(\star)$, we can see that expression m has type $M\,a$, variable a has type a, expression n has type $M\,b$, lambda expression $\lambda a.\,n$ has type $a \to M\,b$, and the whole expression has type $M\,b$.

The above is analogous to the expression

$$\textbf{let}\ \ a = m\ \ \textbf{in}\ \ n.$$

In an impure language, this has the same reading: perform computation m, bind a to the resulting value, then perform computation n and return its value. Here the types say nothing to distinguish values from computations: expression m has type a, variable a has type a, expression n has type b, and the whole expression has type b. The analogy with 'let' explains the choice of the order of arguments to $\star$. It is convenient for argument m to appear before the function $\lambda a. n$, since computation m is performed before computation n.

The evaluator is easily rewritten in terms of these abstractions.

$$
\begin{aligned}
&eval && :: Term \to M\,Int \\
&eval\,(Con\,a) &&= unit\,a \\
&eval\,(Div\,t\,u) &&= eval\,t \star \lambda a.\,eval\,u \star \lambda b.\,unit\,(a \div b)
\end{aligned}
$$

A word on precedence: lambda abstraction binds least tightly and application binds most tightly, so the last equation is equivalent to the following.

$$
eval\,(Div\,t\,u) = ((eval\,t) \star (\lambda a.\,((eval\,u) \star (\lambda b.\,(unit\,(a \div b))))))
$$

The type $Term \to M\,Int$ indicates that the evaluator takes a term and performs a computation yielding an integer. To compute $(Con\,a)$, just return a. To compute $(Div\,t\,u)$, first compute t, bind a to the result, then compute u, bind b to the result, and then return $a \div b$.

The new evaluator is a little more complex than the original basic evaluator, but it is much more flexible. Each of the variations given above may be achieved by simply changing the definitions of M, $unit$, and $\star$, and by making one or two local modifications. It is no longer necessary to re-write the entire evaluator to achieve these simple changes.

2.6 Variation zero, revisited: The basic evaluator

In the simplest monad, a computation is no different from a value.

$$
\begin{aligned}
&\textbf{type}\ \ M\,a = a \\
\\
&unit && :: a \to I\,a \\
&unit\,a && = a \\
\\
&(\star) && :: M\,a \to (a \to M\,b) \to M\,b \\
&a \star k && = k\,a
\end{aligned}
$$

This is called the *identity* monad: M is the identity function on types, $unit$ is the identity function, and $\star$ is just application.

Taking M, $unit$, and $\star$ as above in the monadic evaluator of Section 2.5 and simplifying yields the basic evaluator of Section 2.1

2.7 Variation one, revisited: Exceptions

In the exception monad, a computation may either raise an exception or return a value.

$$
\begin{aligned}
&\textbf{data } M\,a && = Raise\,Exception \mid Return\,a \\
&\textbf{type } Exception && = String
\end{aligned}
$$

$$
\begin{aligned}
&unit && :: a \to M\,a \\
&unit\,a && = Return\,a
\end{aligned}
$$

$$
\begin{aligned}
&(\star) && :: M\,a \to (a \to M\,b) \to M\,b \\
&m \star k && = \textbf{case } m \textbf{ of} \\
& && \quad Raise\,e \to Raise\,e \\
& && \quad Return\,a \to k\,a
\end{aligned}
$$

$$
\begin{aligned}
&raise && :: Exception \to M\,a \\
&raise\,e && = Raise\,e
\end{aligned}
$$

The call $unit\,a$ simply returns the value a. The call $m \star k$ examines the result of the computation m: if it is an exception it is re-raised, otherwise the function k is applied to the value returned. Just as $\star$ in the identity monad is function application, $\star$ in the exception monad may be considered as a form of *strict* function application. Finally, the call $raise\,e$ raises the exception e.

To add error handling to the monadic evaluator, take the monad as above. Then just replace $unit\,(a \div b)$ by

$$
\begin{aligned}
&\textbf{if } b = 0 \\
&\textbf{then } raise \text{ ``divide by zero''} \\
&\textbf{else } unit\,(a \div b)
\end{aligned}
$$

This is commensurate with change required in an impure language.

As one might expect, this evaluator is equivalent to the evaluator with exceptions of Section 2.2. In particular, unfolding the definitions of $unit$ and $\star$ in this section and simplifying yields the evaluator of that section.

2.8 Variation two, revisited: State

In the state monad, a computation accepts an initial state and returns a value paired with the final state.

$$
\begin{aligned}
&\textbf{type } M\,a && = State \to (a, State) \\
&\textbf{type } State && = Int
\end{aligned}
$$

$$
\begin{aligned}
&unit && :: a \to M\,a \\
&unit\,a && = \lambda x.\,(a, x)
\end{aligned}
$$

$$
\begin{aligned}
&(\star) && :: M\,a \to (a \to M\,b) \to M\,b \\
&m \star k && = \lambda x.\,\textbf{let } (a, y) = m\,x \textbf{ in} \\
& && \quad\quad \textbf{let } (b, z) = k\,a\,y \textbf{ in} \\
& && \quad\quad (b, z)
\end{aligned}
$$

$$
\begin{aligned}
&tick && :: M\,() \\
&tick && = \lambda x.\,((), x + 1)
\end{aligned}
$$

The call *unit a* returns the computation that accept initial state x and returns value a and final state x; that is, it returns a and leaves the state unchanged. The call $m \star k$ performs computation m in the initial state x, yielding value a and intermediate state y; then performs computation $k\,a$ in state y, yielding value b and final state z. The call *tick* increments the state, and returns the empty value (), whose type is also written ().

In an impure language, an operation like *tick* would be represented by a function of type () → (). The spurious argument () is required to delay the effect until the function is applied, and since the output type is () one may guess that the function's purpose lies in a side effect. In contrast, here *tick* has type M (): no spurious argument is needed, and the appearance of M explicitly indicates what sort of effect may occur.

To add execution counts to the monadic evaluator, take the monad as above. Then just replace $unit\,(a \div b)$ by

$$tick \star \lambda().\,unit\,(a \div b)$$

(Here $\lambda\_.\,e$ is equivalent to $\lambda x.e$ where $x :: ()$ is some fresh variable that does not appear in e; it indicates that the value bound by the lambda expression must be ().) Again, this is commensurate with change required in an impure language. Simplifying yields the evaluator with state of Section 2.3.

2.9 Variation three, revisited: Output

In the output monad, a computation consists of the output generated paired with the value returned.

```
type  M a     = (Output, a)
type  Output  = String

unit          :: a → M a
unit a        = ( " ", a)

(*)           :: M a → (a → M b) → M b
m * k         = let  (x, a) = m  in
                let  (y, b) = k a  in
                (x ++ y, b)

out           :: Output → M ()
out x         = (x, ())
```

The call *unit a* returns no output paired with a. The call $m \star k$ extracts output x and value a from computation m, then extracts output y and value b from computation $k\,a$, and returns the output formed by concatenating x and y paired with the value b. The call *out x* returns the computation with output x and empty value ().

To add execution traces to the monadic evaluator, take the monad as above. Then in the clause for *Con a* replace *unit a* by

$$out\,(line\,(Con\,a)\,a) \star \lambda().\,unit\,a$$

and in the clause for $Div\,t\,u$ replace $unit\,(a \div b)$ by

$$out\,(line\,(Div\,t\,u)\,(a \div b)) \star \lambda(). \, unit\,(a \div b)$$

Yet again, this is commensurate with change required in an impure language. Simplifying yields the evaluator with output of Section 2.4.

To get the output in the reverse order, all that is required is to change the definition of $\star$, replacing $x \mathbin{+\!\!+} y$ by $y \mathbin{+\!\!+} x$. This is commensurate with the change required in the pure program, and rather simpler than the change required in an impure program.

You might think that one difference between the pure and impure versions is that the impure version displays output as it computes, while the pure version will display nothing until the entire computation completes. In fact, if the pure language is lazy then output will be displayed in an incremental fashion as the computation occurs. Furthermore, this will also happen if the order of output is reversed, which is much more difficult to arrange in an impure language. Indeed, the easiest way to arrange it may be to simulate lazy evaluation.

3 Monad laws

The operations of a monad satisfy three laws.

- *Left unit.* Compute the value a, bind b to the result, and compute n. The result is the same as n with value a substituted for variable b.

$$unit\,a \star \lambda b. \, n = n[a/b].$$

- *Right unit.* Compute m, bind the result to a, and return a. The result is the same as m.

$$m \star \lambda a. \, unit\,a = m.$$

- *Associative.* Compute m, bind the result to a, compute n, bind the result to b, compute o. The order of parentheses in such a computation is irrelevant.

$$m \star (\lambda a. \, n \star \lambda b. \, o) = (m \star \lambda a. \, n) \star \lambda b. \, o.$$

The scope of the variable a includes o on the left but excludes o on the right, so this law is valid only when a does not appear free in o.

A binary operation with left and right unit that is associative is called a *monoid*. A monad differs from a monoid in that the right operand involves a binding operation.

To demonstrate the utility of these laws, we prove that addition is associative. Consider a variant of the evaluator based on addition rather than division.

```
data Term    = Con Int | Add Term Term
eval         :: Term → M Int
eval (Con a) = unit a
eval (Add t u) = eval t ⋆ λa. eval u ⋆ λb. unit (a ÷ b)
```

We show that evaluation of

$$Add\,t\,(Add\,u\,v) \quad \text{and} \quad Add\,(Add\,t\,u)\,v,$$

both compute the same result. Simplify the left term:

$$eval\,(Add\,t\,(Add\,u\,v))$$
$$= \{ \text{ def'n } eval \}$$
$$eval\,t \star \lambda a.\,eval\,(Add\,u\,v) \star \lambda x.\,unit\,(a+x)$$
$$= \{ \text{ def'n } eval \}$$
$$eval\,t \star \lambda a.\,(eval\,u \star \lambda b.\,eval\,v \star \lambda c.\,unit\,(b+c)) \star \lambda x.\,unit\,(a+x)$$
$$= \{ \text{ associative } \}$$
$$eval\,t \star \lambda a.\,eval\,u \star \lambda b.\,eval\,v \star \lambda c.\,unit\,(b+c) \star \lambda x.\,unit\,(a+x)$$
$$= \{ \text{ left unit } \}$$
$$eval\,t \star \lambda a.\,eval\,u \star \lambda b.\,eval\,v \star \lambda c.\,unit\,(a+(b+c))$$

Simplify the right term similarly:

$$eval\,(Add\,(Add\,t\,u)\,v)$$
$$= \{ \text{ as before } \}$$
$$eval\,t \star \lambda a.\,eval\,u \star \lambda b.\,eval\,v \star \lambda c.\,unit\,((a+b)+c)$$

The result follows by the associativity of addition. This proof is trivial; without the monad laws, it would be impossible.

The proof works in any monad: exception, state, output. This assumes that the code is as above: if it is modified then the proof also must be modified. Section 2.3 modified the program by adding calls to *tick*. In this case, associativity still holds, as can be demonstrated using the law

$$tick \star \lambda().\,m = m \star \lambda().\,tick$$

which holds so long at *tick* is the only action on state within m. Section 2.4 modified the program by adding calls to *line*. In this case, the addition is no longer associative, in the sense that changing parentheses will change the trace, though the computations will still yield the same value.

As another example, note that for each monad we can define the following operations.

$$map \quad :: (a \to b) \to (M\,a \to M\,b)$$
$$map\,f\,m = m \star \lambda a.\,unit\,(f\,a)$$

$$join \quad :: M\,(M\,a) \to M\,a$$
$$join\,z \quad = z \star \lambda m.\,m$$

The *map* operation simply applies a function to the result yielded by a computation. To compute $map\,f\,m$, first compute m, bind a to the result, and then return $f\,a$. The *join* operation is trickier. Let z be a computation that *itself* yields a computation. To compute $join\,z$, first compute z, binds m to the result, and then behaves as computation m. Thus, *join* flattens a mind-boggling double layer of computation into a run-of-the-mill single layer of computation. As we will see in Section 5.1, lists form a monad, and for this monad *map* applies a function to each element of a list, and *join* concatenates a list of lists.

Using id for the identity function ($id\, x = x$), and ($\cdot$) for function composition ($(f \cdot g)\, x = f\,(g\, x)$), one can then formulate a number of laws.

$$
\begin{aligned}
map\, id &= id \\
map\,(f \cdot g) &= map\, f \cdot map\, g \\
map\, f \cdot unit &= unit \cdot f \\
map\, f \cdot join &= join \cdot map\,(map\, f) \\
join \cdot unit &= id \\
join \cdot map\, unit &= id \\
join \cdot map\, join &= join \cdot join \\
m \star k &= join\,(map\, k\, m)
\end{aligned}
$$

The proof of each is a simple consequence of the definitions of map and $join$ and the three monad laws.

Often, monads are defined not in terms of $unit$ and $\star$, but rather in terms of $unit$, $join$, and map [10, 13]. The three monad laws are replaced by the first seven of the eight laws above. If one defines $\star$ by the eighth law, then the three monad laws follow. Hence the two definitions are equivalent.

4   State

Arrays play a central role in computing because they closely match current architectures. Programs are littered with array lookups such as $x[i]$ and array updates such as $x[i] := v$. These operations are popular because array lookup is implemented by a single indexed fetch instruction, and array update by a single indexed store.

It is easy to add arrays to a functional language, and easy to provide efficient array lookup. How to provide efficient array update, on the other hand, is a question with a long history. Monads provide a new answer to this old question.

Another question with a long history is whether it is *desirable* to base programs on array update. Since so much effort has gone into developing algorithms and architectures based on arrays, we will sidestep this debate and simply assume the answer is yes.

There is an important difference between the way monads are used in the previous section and the way monads are used here. The previous section showed monads help to use existing language features more effectively; this section shows how monads can help define new language features. No change to the programming language is required, but the implementation must provide a new abstract data type, perhaps as part of the standard prelude.

Here monads are used to manipulate state internal to the program, but the same techniques can be use to manipulate extenal state: to perform input/output, or to communicate with other programming languages. The Glasgow implementation of Haskell uses a design based on monads to provide input/output and interlanguage working with the imperative programming language C [15]. This design has been adopted for version 1.3 of the Haskell standard.

4.1 Arrays

Let *Arr* be the type of arrays taking indexes of type *Ix* and yielding values of type *Val*. The key operations on this type are

$$newarray :: Val \rightarrow Arr,$$
$$index \quad :: Ix \rightarrow Arr \rightarrow Val,$$
$$update \quad :: Ix \rightarrow Val \rightarrow Arr \rightarrow Arr.$$

The call *newarray v* returns an array with all entries set to v; the call *index i x* returns the value at index i in array x; and the call *update i v x* returns an array where index i has value v and the remainder is identical to x. The behaviour of these operations is specified by the laws

$$index\,i\,(newarray\,v) = v,$$
$$index\,i\,(update\,i\,v\,x) = v,$$
$$index\,i\,(update\,j\,v\,x) = index\,i\,x, \text{ if } i \neq j.$$

In practice, these operations would be more complex; one needs a way to specify the index bounds, for instance. But the above suffices to explicate the main points.

The efficient way to implement the update operation is to overwrite the specified entry of the array, but in a pure functional language this is only safe if there are no other pointers to the array extant when the update operation is performed. An array satisfying this property is called *single threaded*, following Schmidt [18].

Consider building an interpreter for a simple imperative language. The abstract syntax for this language is represented by the following data types.

data *Term* = *Var Id* | *Con Int* | *Add Term Term*
data *Comm* = *Asgn Id Term* | *Seq Comm Comm* | *If Term Comm Comm*
data *Prog* = *Prog Comm Term*

Here *Id* is an unspecified type of identifiers. A term is a variable, a constant, or the sum of two terms; a command is an assignment, a sequence of two commands, or a conditional; and a program consists of a command followed by a term.

The current state of execution will be modelled by an array where the indexes are identifiers and the corresponding values are integers.

$$\textbf{type } State = Arr$$
$$\textbf{type } Ix \quad = Id$$
$$\textbf{type } Val \quad = Int$$

Here is the interpreter.

$$eval \qquad\qquad :: Term \rightarrow State \rightarrow Int$$
$$eval\,(Var\,i)\,x \quad = index\,i\,x$$
$$eval\,(Con\,a)\,x \quad = a$$
$$eval\,(Add\,t\,u)\,x \quad = eval\,t\,x + eval\,u\,x$$

$$exec \qquad\qquad :: Comm \rightarrow State \rightarrow State$$
$$exec\,(Asgn\,i\,t)\,x = update\,i\,(eval\,t\,x)\,x$$
$$exec\,(Seq\,c\,d)\,x \quad = exec\,d\,(exec\,c\,x)$$
$$exec\,(If\,t\,c\,d)\,x \quad = \textbf{if } eval\,t\,x = 0 \textbf{ then } exec\,c\,x \textbf{ else } exec\,d\,x$$

$$elab \qquad\qquad :: Prog \rightarrow Int$$
$$elab\,(Prog\,c\,t) \quad = eval\,t\,(exec\,c\,(newarray\,0))$$

This closely resembles a denotational semantics. The evaluator for terms takes a term and a state and returns an integer. Evaluation of a variable is implemented by indexing the state. The executor for commands takes a command and the initial state and returns the final state. Assignment is implemented by updating the state. The elaborator for programs takes a program and returns an integer. It executes the command in an initial state where all identifiers map to 0, then evaluates the given expression in the resulting state and returns its value.

The state in this interpreter is single threaded: at any moment of execution there is only one pointer to the state, so it is safe to update the state in place. In order for this to work, the update operation must evaluate the new value before placing it in the array. Otherwise, the array may contain a closure that itself contains a pointer to the array, violating the single threading property. In semantic terms, one says that *update* is strict in all three of its arguments.

A number of researchers have proposed analyses that determine whether a given functional program uses an array in a single threaded manner, with the intent of incorporating such an analysis into an optimising compiler. Most of these analyses are based on abstract interpretation [1]. Although there has been some success in this area, the analyses tend to be so expensive as to be intractable [2, 7].

Even if such analyses were practicable, their use may be unwise. Optimising update can affect a program's time and space usage by an order of magnitude or more. The programmer must be assured that such an optimisation will occur in order to know that the program will run adequately fast and within the available space. It may be better for the programmer to indicate explicitly that an array should be single threaded, rather than leave it to the vagaries of an optimising compiler.

Again, a number of researchers have proposed techniques for indicating that an array is single threaded. Most of these techniques are based on type systems [6, 19, 22]. This area seems promising, although the complexities of these type systems remain formidable.

The following section presents another way of indicating explicitly the intention that an array be single threaded. Naturally, it is based on monads. The advantage of this method is that it works with existing type systems, using only the idea of an abstract data type.

4.2 Array transformers

The monad of array transformers is simply the monad of state transformers, with the state taken to be an array. The definitions of M, $unit$, $\star$ are as before.

$$
\begin{aligned}
&\textbf{type } M\,a \ = State \to (a, State) \\
&\textbf{type } State = Arr \\[6pt]
&unit \qquad :: a \to M\,a \\
&unit\,a \qquad = \lambda x.\,(a, x) \\[6pt]
&(\star) \qquad :: M\,a \to (a \to M\,b) \to M\,b \\
&m \star k \qquad = \lambda x.\,\textbf{let } (a, y) = m\,x \ \textbf{in} \\
&\qquad\qquad\qquad \textbf{let } (b, z) = k\,a\,y \ \textbf{in} \\
&\qquad\qquad\qquad (b, z)
\end{aligned}
$$

Previously, our state was an integer and we had an additional operation *tick* acting upon the state. Now our state is an array, and we have additional operations corresponding to array creation, indexing, and update.

$$block \quad :: Val \rightarrow M\,a \rightarrow a$$
$$block\,v\,m \;= \textbf{let} \;\; (a,x) = m\,(newarray\,v) \;\; \textbf{in} \;\; a$$
$$fetch \quad :: Ix \rightarrow M\,Val$$
$$fetch\,i \quad = \lambda x.\,(index\,i\,x, x)$$
$$assign \quad :: Ix \rightarrow Val \rightarrow M\,()$$
$$assign\,i\,v = \lambda x.\,((), update\,i\,v\,x)$$

The call *block v m* creates a new array with all locations initialised to v, applies monad m to this initial state to yield value a and final state x, deallocates the array, and returns a. The call *fetch i* returns the value at index i in the current state, and leaves the state unchanged. The call *assign i v* returns the empty value (), and updates the state so that index i contains value v.

A little thought shows that these operations are indeed single threaded. The only operation that could duplicate the array is *fetch*, but this may be implemented as follows: first fetch the entry at the given index in the array, and then return the pair consisting of this value and the pointer to the array. In semantic terms, *fetch* is strict in the array and the index, but not in the value located at the index, and *assign* is strict in the array and the index, but not the value assigned.

(This differs from the previous section, where in order for the interpreter to be single threaded it was necessary for *update* to be strict in the given value. In this section, as we shall see, this strictness is removed but a spurious sequencing is introduced for evaluation of terms. In the following section, the spurious sequencing is removed, but the strictness will be reintroduced.)

We may now make M into an *abstract data type* supporting the five operations *unit*, $\star$, *block*, *fetch*, and *assign*. The operation *block* plays a central role, as it is the only one that does not have M in its result type. Without *block* there would be no way to write a program using M that did not have M in its output type.

Making M into an abstract data type guarantees that single threading is preserved, and hence it is safe to implement assignment with an in-place update. The use of data abstraction is essential for this purpose. Otherwise, one could write programs such as

$$\lambda x.\,(assign\,i\,v\,x, assign\,i\,w\,x)$$

that violate the single threading property.

The interpreter may now be rewritten as follows.

$$
\begin{array}{ll}
eval & :: Term \rightarrow M\,Int \\
eval\,(Var\,i) & = fetch\,i \\
eval\,(Con\,a) & = unit\,a \\
eval\,(Add\,t\,u) & = eval\,t \star \lambda a.\,eval\,u \star \lambda b.\,unit\,(a+b) \\[4pt]
exec & :: Comm \rightarrow M\,() \\
exec\,(Asgn\,i\,t) & = eval\,t \star \lambda a.\,assign\,i\,a \\
exec\,(Seq\,c\,d) & = exec\,c \star \lambda().\,exec\,d \star \lambda().\,unit\,() \\
exec\,(If\,t\,c\,d) & = eval\,t \star \lambda a. \\
& \quad \textbf{if } a = 0 \textbf{ then } exec\,c\,x \textbf{ else } exec\,d\,x \\[4pt]
elab & :: Prog \rightarrow Int \\
elab\,(Prog\,c\,t) & = block\,0\,(exec\,c \star \lambda().\,eval\,t \star \lambda a.\,unit\,a)
\end{array}
$$

The types show that evaluation of a term returns an integer and may access or modify the state, and that execution of a term returns nothing and may access or modify the state. In fact, evaluation only accesses the state and never alters it — we will consider shortly a more refined system that allows us to indicate this.

The abstract data type for M guarantees that it is safe to perform updates in place – no special analysis technique is required. It is easy to see how the monad interpreter can be derived from the original, and (using the definitions given earlier) the proof of their equivalence is straightforward.

The rewritten interpreter is slightly longer than the previous version, but perhaps slightly easier to read. For instance, execution of $(Seq\,c\,d)$ can be read: compute the execution of c, then compute the execution of d, then return nothing. Compare this with the previous version, which has the unnerving property that $exec\,d$ appears to the left of $exec\,c$.

One drawback of this program is that it introduces too much sequencing. Evaluation of $(Add\,t\,u)$ can be read: compute the evaluation of t, bind a to the result, then compute the evaluation of u, bind b to the result, then return $a + b$. This is unfortunate, in that it imposes a spurious ordering on the evaluation of t and u that was not present in the original program. The order does not matter because although $eval$ depends on the state, it does not change it. To remedy this we will augment the monad of state transformers M with a second monad M' of state readers.

4.3 Array readers

Recall that the monad of array transformers takes an initial array and returns a value and a final array.

$$
\begin{array}{ll}
\textbf{type } M\,a & = State \rightarrow (a, State) \\
\textbf{type } State & = Arr
\end{array}
$$

The corresponding monad of array readers takes an array and returns a value. No array is returned because it is assumed identical to the original array.

$$\textbf{type}\ \ M'\,a = State \rightarrow a$$

$$
\begin{aligned}
unit' && &:: a \rightarrow M'\,a \\
unit'\,a && &= \lambda x.\,a \\[4pt]
(\star') && &:: M'\,a \rightarrow (a \rightarrow M'\,b) \rightarrow M'\,b \\
m \star' k && &= \lambda x.\,\textbf{let}\ \ a = m\,x\ \ \textbf{in}\ \ k\,a\,x \\[4pt]
fetch' && &:: Ix \rightarrow M'\,Val \\
fetch'\,i && &= \lambda x.\,index\,i\,x
\end{aligned}
$$

The call $unit'\,a$ ignores the given state x and returns a. The call $m \star' k$ performs computation m in the given state x, yielding value a, then performs computation $k\,a$ in the same state x. Thus, $unit'$ discards the state and $\star'$ duplicates it. The call $fetch'\,i$ returns the value in the given state x at index i.

Clearly, computations that only read the state are a subset of the computations that may read and write the state. Hence there should be a way to coerce a computation in monad M' into one in monad M.

$$
\begin{aligned}
coerce && &:: M'\,a \rightarrow M\,a \\
coerce\,m && &= \lambda x.\,\textbf{let}\ \ a = m\,x\ \ \textbf{in}\ \ (a, x)
\end{aligned}
$$

The call $coerce\,m$ performs computation m in the initial state x, yielding a, and returns a paired with state x. The function $coerce$ enjoys a number of mathematical properties to be discussed shortly.

Again, these operations maintain single threading if suitably implemented. The definitions of $\star'$ and $coerce$ must both be strict in the intermediate value a. This guarantees that when $coerce\,m$ is performed in state x, the computation of $m\,x$ will reduce to a form a that contains no extant pointers to the state x before the pair (a, x) is returned. Hence there will be only one pointer extant to the state whenever it is updated.

A monad is *commutative* if it satisfies the law

$$m \star \lambda a.\,n \star \lambda b.\,o = n \star \lambda b.\,m \star \lambda a.\,o.$$

The scope of a includes n on the right and not on the left, so this law is valid only when a does not appear free in n. Similarly, b must not appear free in m. In a commutative monad the order of computation does not matter.

The state reader monad is commutative, while the state transfomer monad is not. So no spurious order is imposed on computations in the state reader monad. In particular, the call $m\star' k$ may safely be implemented so that m and $k\,a$ are computed in parallel. However, the final result must still be strict in a. For instance, with the annotations used in the GRIP processor, $\star'$ could be defined as follows.

$$
\begin{aligned}
m \star' k = \lambda x.\,&\textbf{let}\ \ a = m\,x\ \ \textbf{in} \\
&\textbf{let}\ \ b = k\,a\,x\ \ \textbf{in} \\
&par\,a\,(par\,b\,(seq\,a\,b))
\end{aligned}
$$

The two calls to *par* spark parallel computations of a and b, and the call to *seq* waits for a to reduce to a non-bottom value before returning b.

These operations may be packaged into two abstract data types, M and M', supporting the eight operations *unit*, $\star$, *unit'*, $\star'$, *block*, *assign*, *fetch'*, and *coerce*. The abstraction guarantees single threading, so *assign* may be implemented by an in-place update.

The interpreter may be rewritten again.

$$
\begin{aligned}
eval &:: Term \rightarrow M' \, Int \\
eval \, (Var \, i) &= fetch' \, i \\
eval \, (Con \, a) &= unit' \, a \\
eval \, (Add \, t \, u) &= eval \, t \star' \, \lambda a. \, eval \, u \star' \, \lambda b. \, unit' \, (a + b)
\end{aligned}
$$

$$
\begin{aligned}
exec &:: Comm \rightarrow M \, () \\
exec \, (Asgn \, i \, t) &= coerce \, (eval \, t) \star \lambda a. \, assign \, i \, a \\
exec \, (Seq \, c \, d) &= exec \, c \star \lambda(). \, exec \, d \star \lambda(). \, unit \, () \\
exec \, (If \, t \, c \, d) &= coerce \, (eval \, t) \star \lambda a. \\
& \quad \textbf{if } a = 0 \textbf{ then } exec \, c \, x \textbf{ else } exec \, d \, x
\end{aligned}
$$

$$
\begin{aligned}
elab &:: Prog \rightarrow Int \\
elab \, (Prog \, c \, t) &= block \, 0 \, (exec \, c \star \lambda(). \, coerce \, (eval \, t) \star \lambda a. \, unit \, a)
\end{aligned}
$$

This differs from the previous version in that *eval* is written in terms of M' rather than M, and calls to *coerce* surround the calls of *eval* in the other two functions. The new types make it clear that *eval* depends upon the state but does not alter it, while *exec* may both depend upon and alter the state.

The excessive sequencing of the previous version has been eliminated. In the evaluation of $(Add \, t \, u)$ the two subexpressions may be evaluated in either order or concurrently.

A *monad morphism* from a monad M' to a monad M is a function $h :: M' \, a \rightarrow M \, a$ that preserves the monad structure:

$$
\begin{aligned}
h \, (unit' \, a) &= unit \, a, \\
h \, (m \star' \lambda a. \, n) &= (h \, m) \star \lambda a. \, (h \, n).
\end{aligned}
$$

It often happens that one wishes to use a combination of monads to achieve a purpose, and monad morphisms play the key role of converting from one monad to another [9].

In particular, *coerce* is a monad morphism, and it follows immediately from this that the two versions of the interpreter are equivalent.

4.4 Conclusion

How a functional language may provide in-place array update is an old problem. This section has presented a new solution, consisting of two abstract data types with eight operations between them. No change to the programming language is required, other than to provide an implementation of these types, perhaps as part of the standard prelude. The discovery of such a simple solution comes as a surprise, considering the plethora of more elaborate solutions that have been proposed.

A different way of expressing the same solution, based on continuation passing style, has subsequently been proposed by Hudak [8]. But Hudak's solution was inspired by the monad solution, and the monad solution still appears to have some small advantages [15].

Why was this solution not discovered twenty years ago? One possible reason is that the data types involve higher-order functions in an essential way. The usual axiomatisation of arrays involves only first-order functions, and so perhaps it did not occur to anyone to search for an abstract data type based on higher-order functions. That monads led to the discovery of the solution must count as a point in their favour.

5 Parsers

Parsers are the great success story of theoretical computing. The BNF formalism provides a concise and precise way to describe the syntax of a programming language. Mathematical tests can determine if a BNF grammar is ambiguous or vacuous. Transformations can produce an equivalent grammar that is easier to parse. Compiler-compilers can turn a high-level specification of a grammar into an efficient program.

This section shows how monads provide a simple framework for constructing recursive descent parsers. This is of interest in its own right, and also because the basic structures of parsing – sequencing and alternation – are fundamental to all of computing. It also provides a demonstration of how monads can model backtracking (or angelic non-determinism).

5.1 Lists

Our representation of parsers depends upon lists. Lists are ubiquitous in functional programming, and it is surprising that we have managed to get by so far while barely mentioning them. Actually, they have appeared in disguise, as strings are simply lists of characters.

We review some notation. We write $[a]$ for the type of a list with elements all of type a, and : for 'cons'. Thus $[1, 2, 3] = 1 : 2 : 3 : []$, and both have type $[Int]$. Strings are lists of characters, so $String$ and $[Char]$ are equivalent, and "monad" is just an abbreviation for $['m', 'o', 'n', 'a', 'd']$.

It is perhaps not suprising that lists form a monad.

$$
\begin{aligned}
&unit &&:: a \rightarrow [a] \\
&unit\, a &&= [a] \\
\\
&(\star) &&:: [a] \rightarrow (a \rightarrow [b]) \rightarrow [b] \\
&[] \star k &&= [] \\
&(a : x) \star k &&= k\, a \,\mathbin{+\!\!+}\, (x \star k)
\end{aligned}
$$

The call $unit\, a$ simply forms the unit list containing a. The call $m \star k$ applies k to each element of the list m, and appends together the resulting lists.

If monads encapsulate effects and lists form a monad, do lists correspond to some effect? Indeed they do, and the effect they correspond to is choice. One can think of a computation of type [a] as offering a choice of values, one for each element of the list. The monadic equivalent of a function of type $a \to b$ is a function of type $a \to [b]$. This offers a choice of results for each argument, and hence corresponds to a relation. The operation *unit* corresponds to the identity relation, which associates each argument only with itself. If $k :: a \to [b]$ and $h :: b \to [c]$, then

$$\lambda a.\, k\, a \star \lambda b.\, h\, b :: a \to [c]$$

corresponds to the relational composition of k and h.

The *list comprehension* notation provides a convenient way of manipulating lists. The behaviour is analogous to set comprehensions, except the order is significant. For example,

$$
\begin{array}{ll}
[\, sqr\, a \mid a \leftarrow [1, 2, 3]\,] & = [1, 4, 9] \\
[\, (a, b) \mid a \leftarrow [1, 2], b \leftarrow \text{``list''}] & = [(1, \text{`}l\text{'}), (1, \text{`}i\text{'}), (1, \text{`}s\text{'}), (1, \text{`}t\text{'}), \\
& \quad\; (2, \text{`}l\text{'}), (2, \text{`}i\text{'}), (2, \text{`}s\text{'}), (2, \text{`}t\text{'})]
\end{array}
$$

The list comprehension notation translates neatly into monad operations.

$$
\begin{array}{ll}
[\, t \mid x \leftarrow u\,] & = u \star \lambda x.\, unit\, t \\
[\, t \mid x \leftarrow u, y \leftarrow v\,] & = u \star \lambda x.\, v \star \lambda y.\, unit\, t
\end{array}
$$

Here t is an expression, x and y are variables (or more generally patterns), and u and v are expressions that evaluate to lists. Connections between comprehensions and monads have been described at length elsewhere [21].

5.2 Representing parsers

Parsers are represented in a way similar to state transformers.

$$
\begin{array}{ll}
\textbf{type } M\, a & = State \to [(a, State)] \\
\textbf{type } State & = String
\end{array}
$$

That is, the parser for type a takes a state representing a string to be parsed, and returns a *list* of containing the value of type a parsed from the string, and a state representing the remaining string yet to be parsed. The list represents all the alternative possible parses of the input state: it will be empty if there is no parse, have one element if there is one parse, have two elements if there are two different possible parses, and so on.

Consider a simple parser for arithmetic expressions, which returns a tree of the type considered previously.

$$\textbf{data } Term = Con\, Int \mid Div\, Term\, Term$$

Say we have a parser for such terms.

$$term :: M\, Term$$

Here are some examples of its use.

$$
\begin{aligned}
term \text{ “23”} &= [(Con\,23,\text{ “ ”})] \\
term \text{ “23 and more”} &= [(Con\,23,\text{ “ and more”})] \\
term \text{ “not a term”} &= [] \\
term \text{ “((1972 ÷ 2) ÷ 23)”} &= [(Div\,(Div\,(Con\,1972)\,(Con\,2))\,(Con\,23)),\text{ “ ”})]
\end{aligned}
$$

A parser m is *unambiguous* if for every input x the list of possible parses $m\,x$ is either empty or has exactly one item. For instance, $term$ is unambiguous. An ambiguous parser may return a list with two or more alternative parsings.

5.3 Parsing an item

The basic parser returns the first item of the input, and fails if the input is exhausted.

$$
\begin{aligned}
item &\;::\; M\,Char \\
item\,[] &= [] \\
item\,(a:x) &= [(a,x)]
\end{aligned}
$$

Here are two examples.

$$
\begin{aligned}
item \text{ “ ”} &= [] \\
item \text{ “monad”} &= [(\text{‘m’},\text{ “onad”})]
\end{aligned}
$$

Clearly, $item$ is unambiguous.

5.4 Sequencing

To form parsers into a monad, we require operations $unit$ and $\star$.

$$
\begin{aligned}
unit &\;::\; a \to M\,a \\
unit\,a\,x &= [(a,x)] \\
(\star) &\;::\; M\,a \to (a \to M\,b) \to M\,b \\
(m \star k)\,x &= [(b,z) \mid (a,y) \leftarrow m\,x,\,(b,z) \leftarrow k\,a\,y]
\end{aligned}
$$

The parser $unit\,a$ accepts input x and yields one parse with value a paired with remaining input x. The parser $m \star k$ takes input x; parser m is applied to input x yielding for each parse a value a paired with remaining input y; then parser $k\,a$ is applied to input y, yielding for each parse a value b paired with final remaining output z.

Thus, $unit$ corresponds to the empty parser, which consumes no input, and $\star$ corresponds to sequencing of parsers.

Two items may be parsed as follows.

$$
\begin{aligned}
twoItems &\;::\; M\,(Char, Char) \\
twoItems &= item \star \lambda a.\,item \star \lambda b.\,unit\,(a,b)
\end{aligned}
$$

Here are two examples.

$$
\begin{aligned}
twoItems \text{ “m”} &= [] \\
twoItems \text{ “monad”} &= [((\text{‘m’},\text{‘o’}),\text{ “nad”})]
\end{aligned}
$$

The parse succeeds only if there are at least two items in the list.

The three monad laws express that the empty parser is an identity for sequencing, and that sequencing is associative.

$$unit\, a \star \lambda b.\, n = n[a/b]$$
$$m \star \lambda a.\, unit\, a = m$$
$$m \star (\lambda a.\, n \star \lambda b.\, o) = (m \star \lambda a.\, n) \star \lambda b.\, o$$

If m is unambiguous and $k\,a$ is unambiguous for every a, then $m \star k$ is also unambiguous.

5.5 Alternation

Parsers may also be combined by alternation.

$$
\begin{aligned}
&zero &&:: M\,a \\
&zero\, x &&= [\,] \\
&(\oplus) &&:: M\,a \rightarrow M\,a \rightarrow M\,a \\
&(m \oplus n)\, x &&= m\, x + \!\!+ \, n\, x
\end{aligned}
$$

The parser $zero$ takes input x and always fails. The parser $m \oplus n$ takes input x and yields all parses of m applied to input x and all parses of n applied to the same input x.

Here is a parser that parses one or two items from the input.

$$
\begin{aligned}
&oneOrTwoItems :: M\,String \\
&oneOrTwoItems = \quad (item \star \lambda a.\, unit\,[a]) \\
&\qquad\qquad\qquad\; \oplus\, (item \star \lambda a.\, item \star \lambda b.\, unit\,[a, b])
\end{aligned}
$$

Here are three examples.

$$
\begin{aligned}
&oneOrTwoItems \text{ ``''} &&= [\,] \\
&oneOrTwoItems \text{ ``m''} &&= [(\,\text{``m''}, \text{``''})] \\
&oneOrTwoItems \text{ ``monad''} &&= [(\,\text{``m''}, \text{``onad''}), (\,\text{``mo''}, \text{``nad''})]
\end{aligned}
$$

The last yields two alternative parses, showing that alternation can yield ambiguous parsers.

The parser that always fails is the identity for alternation, and alternation is associative.

$$zero \oplus n = n$$
$$m \oplus zero = m$$
$$m \oplus (n \oplus o) = (m \oplus n) \oplus o$$

Furthermore, $zero$ is indeed a zero of $\star$, and $\star$ distributes through $\oplus$.

$$zero \star k = zero$$
$$m \star \lambda a.\, zero = zero$$
$$(m \oplus n) \star k = (m \star k) \oplus (n \star k)$$

It is *not* the case that $\star$ distributes rightward through $\oplus$ only because we are representing alternative parses by an ordered list; if we used an unordered bag, then $m \star \lambda a.\, (k\,a \oplus h\,a) = (m \star k) \oplus (m \star h)$ would also hold. An unambiguous parser yields a list of length at most one, so the order is irrelevant, and hence this law also holds whenever either side is unambiguous (which implies that both sides are).

5.6 Filtering

A parser may be filtered by combining it with a predicate.

$$(\triangleright) \quad :: M\,a \to (a \to Bool) \to M\,a$$
$$m \triangleright p = m \star \lambda a.\,\textbf{if }\; p\,a \;\textbf{ then }\; unit\,a \;\textbf{ else }\; zero$$

Given a parser m and a predicate on values p, the parser $m \triangleright p$ applies parser m to yield a value a; if $p\,a$ holds it succeeds with value a, otherwise it fails. Note that filtering is written in terms of previously defined operators, and need not refer directly to the state.

Let *isLetter* and *isDigit* be the obvious predicates. Here are two parsers.

$$letter \;::\; M\,Char$$
$$letter = item \triangleright isLetter$$

$$digit \;::\; M\,Int$$
$$digit \;=\; (item \triangleright isDigit) \star \lambda a.\,unit\,(ord\,a - ord\,\text{`}0\text{'})$$

The first succeeds only if the next input item is a letter, and the second succeeds only if it is a digit. The second also converts the digit to its corresponding value, using $ord :: Char \to Int$ to convert a character to its ASCII code. Assuming that $\triangleright$ has higher precedence than $\star$ would allow some parentheses to be dropped from the second definition.

A parser for a literal recognises a single specified character.

$$lit \quad :: Char \to M\,Char$$
$$lit\,c = item \triangleright (\lambda a.\,a = c)$$

The parser $lit\,c$ succeeds if the input begins with character c, and fails otherwise.

$$lit\,\text{`}m\text{'}\,\text{``}monad\text{''} = [(\,\text{`}m\text{'},\, \text{``}onad\text{''})]$$
$$lit\,\text{`}m\text{'}\,\text{``}parse\text{''} \;= []$$

From the previous laws, it follows that filtering preserves zero and distributes through alternation.

$$zero \triangleright p = zero$$
$$(m \oplus n) \triangleright p = (m \triangleright p) \oplus (n \triangleright p)$$

If m is an unambiguous parser, so is $m \triangleright p$.

5.7 Iteration

A single parser may be iterated, yielding a list of parsed values.

$$iterate \quad :: M\,a \to M\,[a]$$
$$iterate\,m = \quad (m \star \lambda a.\,iterate\,m \star \lambda x.\,unit\,(a : x))$$
$$\oplus unit\,[\,]$$

Given a parser m, the parser $iterate\,m$ applies parser m in sequence zero or more times, returning a list of all the values parsed. In the list of alternative parses, the longest parse is returned first.

Here is an example.

$$iterate\,digit\ ``23\ and\ more" = [([2,3],\ ``\ and\ more"),$$
$$([2],\ ``3\ and\ more"),$$
$$([\,],\ ``23\ and\ more")]$$

Here is one way to parse a number.

$$number\ ::\ M\,Int$$
$$number = digit \star \lambda a.\,iterate\,digit \star \lambda x.\,unit\,(asNumber\,(a:x))$$

Here $asNumber$ takes a list of one or more digits and returns the corresponding number. Here is an example.

$$number\ ``23\ and\ more" = [(23,\ ``\ and\ more"),$$
$$(2,\ ``3\ and\ more")]$$

This supplies two possible parses, one which parses both digits, and one which parses only a single digit. A number is defined to contain at least one digit, so there is no parse with zero digits.

As this last example shows, often it is more natural to design an iterator to yield only the longest possible parse. The next section describes a way to achieve this.

5.8 Biased choice

Alternation, written $m \oplus n$, yields all parses yielded by m followed by all parses yielded by n. For some purposes, it is more sensible to choose one or the other: all parses by m if there are any, and all parses by n otherwise. This is called biased choice.

$$(\oslash) \qquad ::\ M\,a \to M\,a \to M\,a$$
$$(m \oslash n)\,x = \textbf{if}\ m\,x \neq [\,]\ \textbf{then}\ m\,x\ \textbf{else}\ n\,x$$

Biased choice, written $m \oslash n$, yields the same parses as m, unless m fails to yield any parse, in which case it yields the same parses as n.

Here is iteration, rewritten with biased choice.

$$reiterate \quad ::\ M\,a \to M\,[a]$$
$$reiterate\,m = \quad (m \star \lambda a.\,reiterate\,m \star \lambda x.\,unit\,(a:x))$$
$$\oslash unit\,[\,]$$

The only difference is to replace $\oplus$ with $\oslash$. Instead of yielding a list of all possible parses with the longest first, this yields only the longest possible parse.

Here is the previous example revisited.

$$reiterate\,digit\ ``23\ and\ more" = [([2,3],\ ``\ and\ more")]$$

In what follows, $number$ is taken to be written with $reiterate$.

$$number\ ::\ M\,Int$$
$$number = digit \star \lambda a.\,iterate\,digit \star \lambda x.\,unit\,(asNumber\,(a:x))$$

Here is an example that reveals a little of how ambiguous parsers may be used to search a space of possibilities. We use *reiterate* to find all ways of taking one or two items from a string, zero or more times.

$$reiterate\,oneOrTwoItems\,\text{``many''} = [([\,\text{``}m\text{''}, \text{``}a\text{''}, \text{``}n\text{''}, \text{``}y\text{''}], \text{`` ''}),$$
$$([\,\text{``}m\text{''}, \text{``}a\text{''}, \text{``}ny\text{''}], \text{`` ''}),$$
$$([\,\text{``}m\text{''}, \text{``}an\text{''}, \text{``}y\text{''}], \text{`` ''}),$$
$$([\,\text{``}ma\text{''}, \text{``}n\text{''}, \text{``}y\text{''}], \text{`` ''}),$$
$$([\,\text{``}ma\text{''}, \text{``}ny\text{''}], \text{`` ''})]$$

This combines alternation (in *oneOrTwoItems*) with biased choice (in *reiterate*). There are several possible parses, but for each parse *oneOrTwoItems* has been applied until the entire input has been consumed. Although this example is somewhat fanciful, a similar technique could be used to find all ways of breaking a dollar into nickels, dimes, and quarters.

If m and n are unambiguous, then $m \oslash n$ and *reiterate* m are also unambiguous. For unambiguous parsers, sequencing distributes right through biased choice:

$$(m \star k) \oslash (m \star h) = m \star \lambda a.\, k\, a \oslash h\, a$$

whenever m is unambiguous. Unlike with alternation, sequencing does not distribute left through biased choice, even for unambiguous parsers.

5.9 A parser for terms

It is now possible to write the parser for terms alluded to at the beginning. Here is a grammar for fully parenthesised terms, expressed in BNF.

$$term ::= number \mid \text{`('}\,term\,\text{`}\div\text{'}\,term\,\text{`)'}$$

This translates directly into our notation as follows. Note that our notation, unlike BNF, specifies exactly how to construct the returned value.

$$
\begin{array}{ll}
term :: & M\,Term \\
term = & (number \qquad \star\,\lambda a. \\
& unit\,(Num\,a)) \\
\oplus & (lit\,\text{`('} \qquad \star\,\lambda\_. \\
& term \qquad \star\,\lambda t. \\
& lit\,\text{`}\div\text{'} \qquad \star\,\lambda\_. \\
& term \qquad \star\,\lambda u. \\
& lit\,\text{`)'} \qquad \star\,\lambda\_. \\
& unit\,(Div\,t\,u))
\end{array}
$$

(Here $\lambda\_.\,e$ is equivalent to $\lambda x.\,e$ where x is some fresh variable that does not appear in e; it indicates that the value bound by the lambda expression is not of interest.) Examples of the use of this parser appeared earlier.

The above parser is written with alternation, but as it is unambiguous, it could just as well have been written with biased choice. The same is true for all the parsers in the next section.

5.10 Left recursion

The above parser works only for fully parenthesised terms. If we allow unparenthesised terms, then the operator $\div$ should associate to the left. The usual way to express such a grammar in BNF is as follows.

$$term \quad ::= term \text{ '}\div\text{'} factor \mid factor$$
$$factor ::= number \mid \text{'('} term \text{ ')'}$$

This translates into our notation as follows.

$$
\begin{aligned}
term \quad &:: M\,Term \\
term \quad &= \quad (term &&\star\,\lambda t. \\
& \quad\;\; lit \text{ '}\div\text{'} &&\star\,\lambda_-. \\
& \quad\;\; factor &&\star\,\lambda u. \\
& \quad\;\; unit\,(Div\,t\,u)) \\
& \oplus\; factor
\end{aligned}
$$

$$
\begin{aligned}
factor &:: M\,Term \\
factor &= \quad number \\
& \oplus (lit \text{ '('} &&\star\,\lambda_-. \\
& \quad\;\; term &&\star\,\lambda t. \\
& \quad\;\; lit \text{ ')'} &&\star\,\lambda_-. \\
& \quad\;\; unit\,t)
\end{aligned}
$$

There is no problem with *factor*, but any attempt to apply *term* results in an infinite loop. The problem is that the first step of *term* is to apply *term*, leading to an infinite regress. This is called the *left recursion problem*. It is a difficulty for all recursive descent parsers, functional or otherwise.

The solution is to rewrite the grammar for *term* in the following equivalent form.

$$term \quad ::= factor\,term'$$
$$term' ::= \text{'}\div\text{'} factor\,term' \mid unit$$

where as usual *unit* denotes the empty parser. This then translates directly into our notation.

$$
\begin{aligned}
term \quad &:: M\,Term \\
term \quad &= factor \star \lambda t.\,term'\,t \\[4pt]
term' \quad &:: Term \rightarrow M\,Term \\
term'\,t &= \quad (lit \text{ '}\div\text{'} &&\star\,\lambda_-. \\
& \quad\;\; factor &&\star\,\lambda u. \\
& \quad\;\; term'\,(Div\,t\,u)) \\
& \oplus\; unit\,t
\end{aligned}
$$

Here *term'* parses the remainder of a term; it takes an argument corresponding to the term parsed so far.

This has the desired effect.

$$
\begin{aligned}
term \text{ "}1972 \div 2 \div 23\text{"} &= [((Div\,(Div\,(Con\,1972)\,(Con\,2))\,(Con\,23)), \text{ ``"}] \\
term \text{ "}1972 \div (2 \div 23)\text{"} &= [((Div\,(Con\,1972)\,(Div\,(Con\,2)\,(Con\,23))), \text{ ``"}]
\end{aligned}
$$

In general, the left-recursive definition

$$m = (m \star k) \oplus n$$

can be rewritten as

$$m = n \star (closure\, k)$$

where

$$closure \quad :: (a \to M\, a) \to (a \to M\, a)$$
$$closure\, k\, a = (k\, a \star closure\, k) \oplus unit\, a$$

Here $m :: M\, a$, $n :: M\, a$, and $k :: a \to M\, a$.

5.11 Improving laziness

Typically, a program might be represented as a function from a list of characters – the input – to another list of characters – the output. Under lazy evaluation, usually only some of the input need be read before the first part of the output list is produced. This 'on line' behavior is essential for some purposes.

In general, it is unreasonable to expect such behaviour from a parser, since in general it cannot be known that the input will be successfully parsed until all of it is read. However, in certain special cases one may hope to do better.

Consider applying $reiterate\, m$ to a string beginning with an instance of m. In this case, the parse cannot fail: regardless of the remainder of the string, one would expect the parse yielded to be a list beginning with the parsed value. Under lazy evaluation, one might expect to be able to generate output corresponding to the first digit before the remaining input has been read.

But this is not what happens: the parser reads the entire input before any output is generated. What is necessary is some way to encode that the parser $reiterate\, m$ always succeeds. (Even if the beginning of the input does not match m, it will yield as a value the empty list.) This is provided by the function $guarantee$.

$$guarantee \quad :: M\, a \to M\, a$$
$$guarantee\, m\, x = \mathbf{let}\ u = m\, x\ \mathbf{in}\ (fst\, (head\, u), snd\, (head\, u)) : tail\, u$$

Here $fst\, (a, b) = a$, $snd\, (a, b) = b$, $head\, (a : x) = a$, and $tail\, (a : x) = x$.

Here is $reiterate$ with the guarantee added.

$$reiterate \quad :: M\, a \to M\, [a]$$
$$reiterate\, m = guarantee\, (\quad (m \star \lambda a.\, reiterate\, m \star \lambda x.\, unit\, (a : x))$$
$$\oslash unit\, [])$$

This ensures that $reiterate\, m$ and all of its recursive calls return a list with at least one answer. As a result, the behaviour under lazy evaluation is much improved.

The preceding explanation is highly operational, and it is worth noting that denotational semantics provides a useful alternative approach. Let $\bot$ denote a program that does not terminate. One can verify that with the old definition

$$reiterate\, digit\, ('1' : \bot) = \bot$$

while with the new definition

$$reiterate\,digit\,('1'\!:\bot) = (('1'\!:\bot),\bot):\bot$$

Thus, given that the input begins with the character '1' but that the remainder of the input is unknown, with the old definition nothing is known about the output, while with the new definition it is known that the output yields at least one parse, the value of which is a list which begins with the character '1'.

Other parsers can also benefit from a judicious use of *guarantee*, and in particular *iterate* can be modified like *reiterate*.

5.12 Conclusion

We have seen that monads provide a useful framework for structuring recursive descent parsers. The empty parser and sequencing correspond directly to *unit* and $\star$, and the monads laws reflect that sequencing is associative and has the empty parser as a unit. The failing parser and alternation correspond to *zero* and $\oplus$, which satisfy laws reflecting that alternation is associative and has the failing parser as a unit, and that sequencing distributes through alternation.

Sequencing and alternation are fundamental not just to parsers but to much of computing. If monads capture sequencing, then it is reasonable to ask: what captures both sequencing and alternation? It may be that *unit*, $\star$, *zero*, and $\oplus$, together with the laws above, provide such a structure. Further experiments are needed. One hopeful indication is that a slight variation of the parser monad yields a plausible model of Dijkstra's guarded command language.

References

1. S. Abramsky and C. Hankin, *Abstract Interpretation of Declarative Languages*, Ellis Horwood, 1987.
2. A. Bloss, Update analysis and the efficient implementation of functional aggregates. In *4'th Symposium on Functional Programming Languages and Computer Architecture*, ACM, London, September 1989.
3. R. Bird and P. Wadler, *Introduction to Functional Programming*. Prentice Hall, 1987.
4. P. Hudak, S. Peyton Jones and P. Wadler, editors, *Report on the Programming Language Haskell: Version 1.1*. Technical report, Yale University and Glasgow University, August 1991.
5. J.-Y. Girard, Linear logic. *Theoretical Computer Science*, 50:1–102, 1987.
6. J. Guzmán and P. Hudak, Single-threaded polymorphic lambda calculus. In *IEEE Symposium on Logic in Computer Science*, Philadelphia, June 1990.
7. P. Hudak, A semantic model of reference counting and its abstraction (detailed summary). In *ACM Conference on Lisp and Functional Programming*, pp. 351–363, Cambridge, Massachusetts, August 1986.
8. P. Hudak, Continuation-based mutable abstract data types, or how to have your state and munge it too. Technical report YALEU/DCS/RR-914, Department of Computer Science, Yale University, July 1992.
9. D. King and P. Wadler, Combining monads. In *Glasgow Workshop on Functional Programming*, Ayr, July 1992. Workshops in Computing Series, Springer Verlag, to appear.

10. S. Mac Lane, *Categories for the Working Mathematician*, Springer-Verlag, 1971.

11. R. Milner, M. Tofte, and R. Harper, *The definition of Standard ML*. MIT Press, 1990.

12. E. Moggi, Computational lambda-calculus and monads. In *Symposium on Logic in Computer Science*, Asilomar, California; IEEE, June 1989. (A longer version is available as a technical report from the University of Edinburgh.)

13. E. Moggi, An abstract view of programming languges. Course notes, University of Edinburgh.

14. L. C. Paulson, *ML for the Working Programmer*. Cambridge University Press, 1991.

15. S. L. Peyton Jones and P. Wadler, Imperative functional programming. In *20'th Symposium on Principles of Programming Languages*, Charleston, South Carolina; ACM, January 1993.

16. G. Plotkin, Call-by-name, call-by-value, and the λ-calculus. *Theoretical Computer Science*, 1:125–159, 1975.

17. J. Rees and W. Clinger (eds.), The revised[3] report on the algorithmic language Scheme. *ACM SIGPLAN Notices*, 21(12):37–79, 1986.

18. D. Schmidt, Detecting global variables in denotational specifications. *ACM Trans. on Programming Languages and Systems*, 7:299–310, 1985.

19. V. Swarup, U. S. Reddy, and E. Ireland, Assignments for applicative languages. In *Conference on Functional Programming Languages and Computer Architecture*, Cambridge, Massachusetts; LNCS 523, Springer Verlag, August 1991.

20. D. A. Turner, An overview of Miranda. In D. A. Turner, editor, *Research Topics in Functional Programming*. Addison Wesley, 1990.

21. P. Wadler, Comprehending monads. In *Conference on Lisp and Functional Programming*, Nice, France; ACM, June 1990.

22. P.Wadler, Is there a use for linear logic? *Conference on Partial Evaluation and Semantics-Based Program Manipulation (PEPM)*, New Haven, Connecticut; ACM, June 1991.

23. P. Wadler, The essence of functional programming (invited talk). In *19'th Symposium on Principles of Programming Languages*, Albuquerque, New Mexico; ACM, January 1992.

The Design of a Pretty-printing Library

John Hughes

Chalmers Tekniska Högskola, Göteborg, Sweden.

1 Introduction

On what does the power of functional programming depend? Why are functional programs so often a fraction of the size of equivalent programs in other languages? Why are they so easy to write? I claim: because functional languages support software reuse extremely well.

Programs are constructed by putting program components together. When we discuss reuse, we should ask

- What kind of components can be given a name and reused, rather than reconstructed at each use?
- How flexibly can each component be used?

Every programming language worthy of the name allows sections of a program with identical control flow to be shared, by defining and reusing a procedure. But 'programming idioms' — for example looping over an array — often cannot be defined as procedures because the repeated part (the loop construct) contains a varying part (the loop body) which is different at every instance. In a functional language there is no problem: we can define a *higher-order function*, in which the varying part is passed as a function-valued parameter. This ability to name and reuse programming idioms is at the heart of functional languages' power.

Other features contribute to making reused components more flexible. *Polymorphic typing* enables us to use the *same* programming idiom to manipulate data of *different* types. *Lazy evaluation* abstracts away from execution time, and enables us to reuse the same function with many different behaviours. For example, a lazy list can behave like an array (a sequence of elements stored at the same time), or like an imperative variable (a sequence of values stored at different times), or like something in between (say a buffer in which a bounded number of elements are stored at any one time). Regardless of behaviour the same functions can be used to manipulate the list.

Software reuse is plainly visible in functional programs: for example, the Haskell standard prelude contains many higher-order functions such as *map*, *foldr* etc., which are used intensively in many programs. These standard functions capture very general programming idioms that are useful in almost any context. But it is just as important to define and use *application specific* idioms.

The functional programmer, then, should approach a new application by seeking to identify the programming idioms common in that application area, and to define them as (probably higher order) functions. Each particular application program should then be built by so far as possible combining these functions, rather than writing 'new code'. (Perhaps for this reason, such functions are often called *combinators*). The benefits of such an approach are very rapid programming, once the library of idioms is defined, and very often that application programs are correct first time, since they are built by assembling correct components.

One example of an application area whose idioms have been thoroughly studied is parsing: libraries of parsing combinators are described in this volume. Another good example on a much larger scale is Carlsson and Hallgren's *fudget* library, also described here, which enables graphical user interfaces to be constructed very easily.

The question we address in this chapter is: how should libraries of combinators be designed? How do we know which operations to provide? Monads, also explained in this volume, are certainly helpful — but how do we know which monad to use? Must we rely completely on intuition?

Our goal is to show how we can use formal specification of the combinators, and a study of their algebraic properties, to guide both the design and the implementation of a combinator library. Our case study is a library for pretty-printing, which has gone through many iterations and been much improved by a more formal approach. But we hope the methods we present are of wider applicability, and we will also present some smaller examples to justify this claim.

2 A Preview of the Pretty-printing Library

2.1 Why Pretty-printing?

Almost every program which manipulates symbolic data needs to display this data to the user at some point — whether it is a compiler displaying internal structures for debugging, a proof-editor displaying proofs, or a program transformer writing its output. The problem of displaying symbolic, and especially tree structured data, is thus a recurring one.

At the same time, structured data is hard to read unless layout is used to make the structure visible. Take a simple example: a binary tree of type[1].

data *Tree = Node String Tree Tree | Leaf*

The tree *Node* "foo" (*Node* "baz" *Leaf Leaf*) (*Node* "foobaz" *Leaf Leaf*) is much easier to read if it is presented as

Node "foo" (*Node* "baz" *Leaf Leaf*)
    (*Node* "foobaz" *Leaf Leaf*)

A pretty-printer's job is to lay out structured data appropriately.

Pretty-printing is complicated because the layout of a node cannot just be inferred from its form. In the example above, *Nodes* are laid out in two different ways: some horizontally and some vertically. Moreover the correct indentation of the final *Node* depends on the length of the string in the parent node. A pretty-printer must keep track of much contextual information.

Because of this pretty-printers are hard to write, and there is plenty of scope for mistakes. Many programmers simply do not bother — they put up with badly formatted output instead. There is much to be gained by capturing the hard part of pretty-printing in a library.

---

[1] All examples in this chapter use Haskell syntax

Remark Note that we are considering the problem of displaying internal data-structures in a readable form, not the harder problem of improving the layout of an existing text, such as a program. In the latter case we would have to consider questions such as: should we try to preserve anything of the original layout? How should we handle comments? Such problems are outside the scope of this chapter.

2.2 A Sketch of the Design

What kind of objects should pretty-printing combinators manipulate? I chose to work with 'pretty documents', of type *Doc*, which we can think of as documents which 'know how to' lay themselves out prettily. A pretty-printer for a particular datatype is a function mapping any value to a suitable *Doc*. The library provides operations for constructing *Docs* in various ways, and for converting a *Doc* to text at the top level.

We will need to convert literal strings to *Docs*, and it seems reasonable to provide operations that combine *Docs* horizontally and vertically. That suggests we provide operations

$$text :: String \rightarrow Doc$$
$$(\diamond) :: Doc \rightarrow Doc \rightarrow Doc \quad \text{[horizontal composition]}$$
$$(\$\$) :: Doc \rightarrow Doc \rightarrow Doc \quad \text{[vertical composition]}$$

The composition operators ($\diamond$) and ($\$\$$) relieve the user of the need to think about the correct indentation: for example, the pretty tree layout above can be constructed as

$$text \text{ "Node "foo" "} \diamond (text \text{ "Node "baz" } Leaf \, Leaf \text{"} \$\$$$
$$text \text{ "Node "foobaz" } Leaf \, Leaf\text{"})$$

and the last *Node* is automatically indented the right amount.

However, these operations only enable us to construct *Docs* with a fixed layout. We also need to construct *Docs* that choose between alternative layouts depending on the context. We will therefore define

$$sep :: [Doc] \rightarrow Doc$$

which combines a list of *Docs* horizontally or vertically, depending on the context.

With these operations we can write a pretty-printer for the tree type above:

$$pp :: Tree \rightarrow Doc$$
$$pp \; Leaf = text \text{ "Leaf"}$$
$$pp \; (Node \; s \; l \; r) = text \; (\text{"Node "} +\!\!+ s) \diamond sep \; [pp' \, l, pp' \, r]$$
$$pp' \; Leaf = pp \; Leaf$$
$$pp' \; t = text \text{ "("} \diamond pp \; t \diamond text \text{ ")"}$$

The context-dependent choice of layout is entirely hidden in the implementation of the *Doc* type — the only complication is deciding when to insert brackets.

The library provides one further operation,

$$nest :: Int \rightarrow Doc \rightarrow Doc$$

which indents a document a given number of spaces. For example,

$$\textit{text "while x>0 do" \$\$ nest 2 (text "x := x-2")}$$

produces the layout

```
while x>0 do
  x := x-2
```

The difference between using *nest* and inserting spaces is that *nest* indents only where it is appropriate — so for example,

$$\textit{sep [text "while x>0 do", nest 2 (text "x := x-2")]}$$

will appear as above laid out vertically, but without indentation as

```
while x>0 do x := x-2
```

if laid out horizontally.

This choice of combinators was made quite early on in the development of the library, and the first implementation was written from a description more or less like the one just given. But the description is far from satisfactory: although the intention of the design is fairly clear, the precise behaviour of the combinators is certainly not. Not surprisingly, this led to a number of difficulties and strange behaviours.

Later on we will give a precise specification of the combinators' behaviour, and use this to derive several alternative implementations. But before we continue with this larger case study, we'll present some simpler examples to illustrate the methods we will be using.

3 Deriving Functional Programs from Specifications

How can we conveniently use a specification to help develop a functional program? Let us suppose that the specification consists of a *signature*, containing possibly new types such as *Doc* and the names and types of the functions being specified, and properties that the new functions must satisfy. Our task is to invent representations of the new types and definitions of the functions so that the properties are satisfied. We will call functions from the new types to old types *observations*. Observations are important: if there are none then we cannot distinguish between values of the new types, and so we can represent them all by (). We will assume that the specification determines the value of every possible observation — if not, we must strengthen the specification until it does.

The implementations which we are trying to derive consist of equations of a restricted form. We will derive implementations by proving their constituent equations from the specification. By itself this is no guarantee that the implemented functions satisfy the specification (because we might not have proved *enough* equations). But if we also check that the derived definitions are *terminating* and *exhaustive*, then this property is guaranteed.

To see why, consider the case of a single function f. We start from a specification $P(f)$ and derive implementation equations $Q(f)$, both considered as predicates on f.

By construction $P(f) \Rightarrow Q(f)$. But in general, the implementation equations $Q(f)$ might be satisfied by many different functions, of which the *least* is the one that the equations define. Call this least function f_{imp}. Now, if the derived definitions are exhaustive and terminating, then for any argument x, f_{imp}/x is a defined value y and $Q(f) \Rightarrow f\ x = y$. In other words $Q(f) \Rightarrow f = f_{imp}$ — the implementation equations have a unique solution. Now if the specification is satisfied by any f at all, we know that

$$P(f) \Rightarrow Q(f) \Rightarrow f = f_{imp}$$

and therefore $P(f_{imp})$ holds — the implementation satisfies the specification.

Since we will use the specification to derive equations, it will be most convenient if the specification also consists of equations — or laws — that the new functions are to satisfy.

But before we can start deriving implementations of functions we must choose a representation for each new type. We will present two different ways of choosing such a representation. The first is based on representing values by *terms* in the algebra we are working with. The second is based on representing values by *functions* from the context in which the value is placed to the value of the corresponding observation.

4   Designing a Sequence Type

We begin by considering a very simple and familiar example: the design of a representation for sequences. Of course we know how to represent sequences — as lists. The point here is not to discover a new representation, but to see how we could have arrived at the well-known representation of lists starting from an algebraic specification.

We take the following signature as our starting point,

$$nil :: Seq\ a$$
$$unit :: a \to Seq\ a$$
$$cat :: Seq\ a \to Seq\ a \to Seq\ a$$
$$list :: Seq\ a \to [a]$$

where *nil*, *unit*, and *cat* give us ways to build sequences, and *list* is an observation. The correspondence with the usual list operations is

$$nil = []$$
$$unit\ x = [x]$$
$$cat = (\text{++})$$

These operations are to satisfy the following laws[2]:

$$xs\ `cat`\ (ys\ `cat`\ zs) = (xs\ `cat`\ ys)\ `cat`\ zs$$
$$nil\ `cat`\ xs = xs$$
$$xs\ `cat`\ nil = xs$$
$$list\ nil = []$$
$$list\ (unit\ x\ `cat`\ xs) = x : list\ xs$$

---

[2] Haskell allows a binary function to be used as an infix operator if the name is enclosed in backquotes. Thus a `op` b is the same as $op\ a\ b$

4.1 Term Representation

The most direct way to represent values of sequence type is just as terms of the albegra, for example using

$$\textbf{data } Seq\ a = Nil\mid Unit\ a\mid Seq\ a\ \text{'}Cat\text{'}\ Seq\ a$$

But this trivial representation does not exploit the algebraic laws that we know to hold, and moreover the *list* observation will be a little tricky to define (ideally we would like to implement observations by very simple, non-recursive functions: the real work should be done in the implementations of the *Seq* operators themselves). Instead, we may choose a restricted subset of terms — call them simplified forms[3] — into which every term can be put using the algebraic laws. Then we can represent sequences using a datatype that represents the syntax of simplified forms.

In this case, there is an obvious candidate for simplified forms: terms of the form *nil* and *unit x 'cat' xs*, where *xs* is also in simplified form. Simplified forms can be represented using the type

$$\textbf{data } Seq\ a = Nil\mid a\ \text{'}UnitCat\text{'}\ Seq\ a$$

with the interpretation[4]

$$Nil = nil$$
$$x\ \text{'}UnitCat\text{'}\ xs = unit\ x\ \text{'}cat\text{'}\ xs$$

We choose this representation because a definition of *list* is now very simple to derive:

$$
\begin{aligned}
list\ Nil\ &= list\ nil\\
&= []\\
list\ (x\ \text{'}UnitCat\text{'}\ xs)\ &= list\ (unit\ x\ \text{'}cat\text{'}\ xs)\\
&= x : list\ xs
\end{aligned}
$$

We can also derive implementations of the three operators of the algebra by simply applying the algebraic laws:

$$nil = Nil \quad [\text{defn. } Nil]$$

$$
\begin{aligned}
unit\ x\ &= unit\ x\ \text{'}cat\text{'}\ nil\\
&= x\ \text{'}UnitCat\text{'}\ Nil \quad [\text{defn. } UnitCat]
\end{aligned}
$$

$$
\begin{aligned}
Nil\ \text{'}cat\text{'}\ ys\ &= nil\ \text{'}cat\text{'}\ ys\\
&= ys
\end{aligned}
$$

$$
\begin{aligned}
(x\ \text{'}UnitCat\text{'}\ xs)\ \text{'}cat\text{'}\ ys\ &= (unit\ x\ \text{'}cat\text{'}\ xs)\ \text{'}cat\text{'}\ ys\\
&= unit\ x\ \text{'}cat\text{'}\ (xs\ \text{'}cat\text{'}\ ys) \quad [\text{associativity}]\\
&= x\ \text{'}UnitCat\text{'}\ (xs\ \text{'}cat\text{'}\ ys) \quad [\text{defn. } UnitCat]
\end{aligned}
$$

```
data Seq a = Nil | a 'UnitCat' Seq a

nil = Nil

Nil 'cat' ys = ys
(x 'UnitCat' xs) 'cat' ys = x 'UnitCat' (xs 'cat' ys)

list Nil = []
list (x 'UnitCat' xs) = x : list xs
```

Fig. 1. Term representation of sequences.

Collecting the results we obtain the definitions in figure 1. Termination of each function is obvious.

How do we know that every *Seq* term can be expressed as a simplified form? The definitions we have derived are a proof! Since each function maps simplified arguments to simplified results (and always terminates), we can construct a simplified form equal to any term just by evaluating it with these definitions. In more complicated algebras this observation is valuable: when we're choosing a simplified form we need not worry whether all terms can be put into it — we simply try to derive terminating definitions for the operations, and if we succeed, the result follows.

So far we've just derived the usual implementation of lists — *Nil* and *UnitCat* correspond to [] and (:). But notice that it isn't without its problems: the implementation of *cat* is linear in its first argument, and we run into the well known problem that an expression such as

$$(\ldots (unit\ x_1\ 'cat'\ unit\ x_2) \ldots\ 'cat'\ unit\ x_{n-1})\ 'cat'\ unit\ x_n$$

takes quadratic time to evaluate. Using the associative law n times we can obtain the equivalent expression

$$unit\ x_1\ 'cat'\ (unit\ x_2\ 'cat'\ \ldots (unit\ x_{n-1}\ 'cat'\ unit\ x_n))$$

which runs in linear time. We might hope to exploit the associative law in an improved implementation that achieves the better complexity in the first case also. We could try to derive an implementation of *cat* that recognises *cat* in its left argument, and applies the associative law before continuing. But alas, if we are to recognise applications of *cat* then they must be simplified forms, which means that the *cat* operation can do nothing; we are forced back to the trivial representation we started with. In the next section we look at a different approach which can exploit associativity in this case.

---

[3] We avoid the term 'canonical form' because in general there's no reason why a term need have a *unique* simplified form.

[4] Here we really mean the *semantics* of *Nil* and *UnitCat*, and by equality we mean equality in the algebra we are implementing — not necessarily Haskell's equality. Perhaps it would be more conventional to write [*Nil*] and [*UnitCat*] here, but we prefer to identify syntax and semantics in the interests of lightening the notation.

4.2   Context Passing Representation

If we can't apply the associative law by making the outer *cat* recognise that its left argument is a *cat*, perhaps we can make the inner *cat* recognise that it is called in a *cat* context. This idea motivates a representation of sequences as functions from their context to the observation being made.

A *context* is just an expression with a hole, written [•]. For example, [•] 'cat' ys is a context. If $C[•]$ is a context and e is an expression, we write $C[e]$ for the result of replacing the hole with e. In this case ([•] 'cat' ys)[xs] is xs 'cat' ys.

We can describe the contexts we are interested in by a grammar. For example, the following grammar describes all possible contexts of type list for expressions of type *Seq* .

$$C[•] ::= list\ [•]$$
$$|\ \ C[[•]\ 'cat'\ E]$$
$$|\ \ C[E\ 'cat'\ [•]]$$

where E is an expression of *Seq* type. And just as with terms, we can represent contexts by a corresponding Haskell datatype:

data *Cxt a = List | CatLeft (Seq a) (Cxt a) | CatRight (Seq a) (Cxt a)*

where

$$List = list\ [•]$$
$$CatLeft\ E\ C = C[[•]\ 'cat'\ E]$$
$$CatRight\ E\ C = C[E\ 'cat'\ [•]]$$

Notice that the representation of, say, a *CatLeft* context *contains* the representation of the enclosing context; contexts resemble therefore a stack. Notice also that the context type must be parameterised on a because it refers to *Seq a*.

In fact, just as we used the laws to work with a restricted set of terms, we shall use the laws to work with a restricted set of contexts. For our purposes in this example, we will only need to consider contexts of the form

$$C[•] ::= list\ [•]\ |\ list\ ([•]\ 'cat'\ E)$$

represented by the following datatype:

data *Cxt a = List | ListCat (Seq a)*

Now we can represent sequence values by functions from contexts to lists: the value e is represented by the function $\lambda C[•].C[e]$. (So contexts are like continuations whose internal structure can be inspected). For example,

$$nil = \lambda C[•].C[nil]$$

where again we make no notational distinction between the *nil* on the left, which is a representation, and the *nil* on the right, which is a semantic object. When we apply this representation to a context, we derive for example

$$nil \ (ListCat \ zs) = nil \ (list \ ([\bullet] \ `cat` \ zs)) \quad [\text{defn. } ListCat]$$
$$= list \ (nil \ `cat` \ zs) \qquad\qquad [\text{defn. } nil]$$

In future we will switch backwards and forwards between the first and last form in one step, and without comment. We can derive definitions of the operators using the laws of the algebra as before:

$$nil \ List = list \ nil$$
$$= []$$

$$nil \ (ListCat \ zs) = list \ (nil \ `cat` \ zs)$$
$$= list \ zs$$
$$= zs \ List$$

$$unit \ x \ List = list \ (unit \ x)$$
$$= list \ (unit \ x \ `cat` \ nil)$$
$$= x : list \ nil$$
$$= [x]$$

$$unit \ x \ (ListCat \ zs) = list \ (unit \ x \ `cat` \ zs)$$
$$= x : list \ zs$$
$$= x : zs \ List$$

$$(xs \ `cat` \ ys) \ List = list \ (xs \ `cat` \ ys)$$
$$= xs \ (ListCat \ ys)$$

$$(xs \ `cat` \ ys) \ (ListCat \ zs) = list \ ((xs \ `cat` \ ys) \ `cat` \ zs)$$
$$= list \ (xs \ `cat` \ (ys \ `cat` \ zs)) \quad [\text{assoc!}]$$
$$= xs \ (ListCat \ (ys \ `cat` \ zs))$$

Notice that the derived definition of *cat* recognises an enclosing *cat* and applies the associative law — just the optimisation we wanted to capture. Gathering the results together, we obtain the implementation shown in figure 2.

We can show that these definitions terminate, and moreover derive their complexity, by considering a suitable cost measure on terms. We construct the cost measure so that every reduction strictly reduces cost.

Start by observing that terms not containing *cat* or *ListCat* are reduced to a normal form in one step. We'll give such terms a cost of zero. Now notice that the second equations defining *nil* and *unit* eliminate a *ListCat*. If *ListCat* is assigned a cost of one, then these reductions reduce cost. Looking at the definition of *cat*, we see that the first equation converts a *cat* to a *ListCat*. If we assign *cat* a cost of two, then this reduction also reduces cost. The tricky case is the second equation for *cat*, since it neither reduces the number of occurrences of *cat* nor of *ListCat*.

We can obtain a cost reduction in this case also by assigning *different costs* to the occurrences of *cat* on the left and right hand side. We assign *cat* a cost of two in a 'cheap' context, and a cost of three in other contexts. Cheap contexts are defined by the following grammar:

$$Cheap[\bullet] ::= [\bullet] \ List$$
$$| \ \ ListCat \ [\bullet]$$
$$| \ \ Cheap[E \ `cat` \ [\bullet]]$$

data *Cxt a = List | ListCat (Seq a)*
type *Seq a = Cxt a → [a]*

nil List = []
nil (ListCat zs) = zs List

unit x List = [x]
unit x (ListCat zs) = x : zs List

(xs'cat'ys) List = xs (ListCat ys)
(xs'cat'ys) (ListCat zs) = xs (ListCat (ys'cat'zs))

list xs = xs List

Fig. 2. The context passing implementation of sequences.

Now it is easy to verify that the *cat* on the right in the last equation is in a cheap context, while that on the left is not. We also have to check that in every equation, bound variables appear in a cheap context on the left hand side iff they appear in a cheap context on the right hand side — otherwise our implicit assumption that a bound variable contributes the same cost at each occurrence would be false. Having done so, we know that the number of reductions needed to evaluate a term is bounded by its cost. And this is linear in the size of the term.

We have therefore cured the quadratic behaviour that motivated us to consider a context-passing implementation.

4.3 Changing the Representation of Contexts

If we examine the definitions in figure 2, we can see that the *zs* component of *ListCat zs* is only used by applying it to *List*. That is, we are not interested in the value of *zs* itself, only in the value of *list zs*. This suggests that we try changing the representation of contexts to store the latter rather than the former.

The new context datatype will therefore be

$$\textbf{data } Cxt\ a = List\,|\,ListCat\,[a]$$

with the interpretation

$$List = list\ [\bullet]$$
$$ListCat\ (list\ zs) = list\ ([\bullet]\ 'cat'\ zs)$$

Now if we let $\hat{z}s = list\ zs$, we can derive

$$
\begin{aligned}
nil\ (ListCat\ \hat{z}s) &= list\ (nil\ 'cat'\ zs) \\
&= list\ zs \\
&= \hat{z}s
\end{aligned}
$$

$$unit\ x\ (ListCat\ \hat{z}s) = list\ (unit\ x\ `cat`\ zs)$$
$$= x : list\ zs$$
$$= x : \hat{z}s$$

$$(xs\ `cat`\ ys)\ (ListCat\ \hat{z}s) = list\ ((xs\ `cat`\ ys)\ `cat`\ zs)$$
$$= list\ (xs\ `cat`\ (ys\ `cat`\ zs))$$
$$= xs(ListCat\ (list\ (ys\ `cat`\ zs)))$$
$$= xs(ListCat\ (ys(ListCat\ (list\ zs))))$$
$$= xs(ListCat\ (ys(ListCat\ \hat{z}s)))$$

Notice how each time we introduce a *ListCat*, the accompanying application of *list* enables a further simplification.

In each case we have succeeded in maneouvering the right hand side into a form in which zs does not appear — only $\hat{z}s$. We can therefore take the derived equations as definitions, with a formal parameter $\hat{z}s$. Provided, of course, that contexts of the form *ListCat* $\hat{z}s$ always satisfy the invariant $\exists zs.\hat{z}s = list\ zs$, which is easily verified.

In this case we can go a little further still. Noting that

$$list\ xs = list\ (xs\ `cat`\ nil)$$
$$= xs(ListCat\ (list\ nil))$$
$$= xs(ListCat\ [])$$

we can redefine *list* and do without *List* contexts altogether. Now since only one form of context remains we can drop the *ListCat* constructor also, and represent contexts just by lists. The resulting definitions appear in figure 3.

```
type Cxt a = [a]
type Seq a = Cxt a → [a]
nil ẑs = ẑs
unit x ẑs = x : ẑs
(xs `cat` ys) ẑs = xs (ys ẑs)
list xs = xs []
```

Fig. 3. Optimised context passing representation of sequences

Exercise 1. Could we have used a similar trick to eliminate *List* contexts and the *ListCat* constructor in the previous section?

5   Implementing Monads

The ideas in the previous section are applicable when we want to implement a datatype specified by a signature and some equations that the operations in the signature should satisfy. One very interesting class of datatypes specified in this way are *monads*. At its simplest, a monad is a parameterised type M and a pair of operations

$$unit :: a \rightarrow M\ a$$
$$bind :: M\ a \rightarrow (a \rightarrow M\ b) \rightarrow M\ b$$

satisfying the laws

$$unit\ x\ `bind`\ f = f\ x$$
$$m\ `bind`\ unit = m$$
$$m\ `bind`\ \lambda x \rightarrow (f\ x\ `bind`\ g) = (m\ `bind`\ \lambda x \rightarrow fx)\ `bind`\ g$$

See the chapter by Wadler in this volume for an exposition of the uses of monads in functional programming.

With no further operations a monad is rather uninteresting. In reality, we always extend the signature with some additional operations. In particular, there must be some way to observe a monad value — otherwise we could implement the monad by

$$\textbf{type}\ M\ a = ()$$
$$unit\ x = ()$$
$$m\ `bind`\ f = ()$$

which satisfies the monad laws.

We will consider the simplest interesting monad: that with one additional operation

$$value :: M\ a \rightarrow a$$

satisfying the law

$$value\ (unit\ x) = x$$

We'll look at implementations based on simplified terms and on context passing.

5.1 The Term Representation of a Simple Monad

Suppose we try to represent monad values directly by terms:

$$\textbf{data}\ M\ a = Unit\ a\ |\ M\ b\ `Bind`\ (b \rightarrow M\ a)$$

Notice that the type variable b does not occur on the left hand side of this definition! It is an existentially quantified type variable: one may construct an $M\ a$ by applying *Bind* at *any* type b[5]. With this representation *value* can be defined by

$$value :: M\ a \rightarrow a$$
$$value\ (Unit\ x) = x$$
$$value\ (m\ `Bind`\ f) = value\ (f\ (value\ m))$$

---

[5] Such existential type definitions were proposed by Läufer[2] and are not part of standard Haskell, but are accepted by hbc.

which uses polymorphic recursion: the inner recursive call of *value* is at a different type from the enclosing one[6].

However, we can avoid these complications by using a representation based on simplified terms instead. In fact, we can simplify every term to the form *unit x*. Dropping the *Bind* constructor from the monad type, we obtain

$$unit\ x = Unit\ x$$
$$(Unit\ x)\ `bind`\ f = f\ x$$
$$value\ (Unit\ x) = x$$

where the only property of *unit* and *bind* we need to derive these definitions is the first monad law. And now, since *Unit* is the only constructor in the monad type we can drop it too, represent *M a* just by *a*, and obtain the standard identity monad.

5.2 The Context-passing Representation of a Simple Monad

Suppose we instead derive a context-passing implementation. We are interested in contexts which make an observation by applying *value*, and using the monad laws we will be able to put every such context into the form *value ([•] `bind` k)*, because

$$value\ [\bullet] = value\ ([\bullet]\ `bind`\ unit)$$
$$value\ (([\bullet]\ `bind`\ f)\ `bind`\ k) = value\ ([\bullet]\ `bind`\ \lambda x \rightarrow (f\ x\ `bind`\ k))$$

Notice here that if the hole is of type *M a*, the final value computed may be of some other type — call it *ans*. We must therefore represent contexts by a type parameterised on both *a* and *ans*. Consequently we are also obliged to represent monad values by a type parameterised on both *a* and *ans*. For example, we can define

$$\textbf{data}\ Cxt\ a\ ans = ValueBind\ (a \rightarrow M\ ans\ ans)$$
$$\textbf{type}\ M\ a\ ans = Cxt\ a\ ans \rightarrow ans$$

where

$$ValueBind\ k = value\ ([\bullet]\ `bind`\ k)$$

However, it isn't hard to guess that uses of *k* will all take the form *value (k x)* for some *x*. We therefore optimise the representation of contexts to

$$\textbf{data}\ Cxt\ a\ ans = ValueBind\ (a \rightarrow ans)$$

where

$$ValueBind\ (\lambda x.value\ (k\ x)) = value\ ([\bullet]\ `bind`\ k)$$

(If our guess proves to be wrong no harm will be done, we will simply be unable to derive definitions for the monad operations).

Now letting $\hat{k} = \lambda x.value\ (k\ x)$, we can derive

---

[6] Again this is not standard Haskell, but is accepted by hbc provided the type of *value* is explicitly given.

$$unit\ x\ (ValueBind\ \hat{k}) = value\ (unit\ x\ `bind`k)$$
$$= value\ (k\ x) \qquad \text{[1st monad law]}$$
$$= \hat{k}\ x$$

$$(m\ `bind`f)\ (ValueBind\ \hat{k})$$
$$= value\ ((m\ `bind`f)\ `bind`k)$$
$$= value\ (m\ `bind`\lambda x \to (f\ x\ `bind`k)) \qquad \text{[3rd monad law]}$$
$$= m\ (ValueBind\ (\lambda x \to value\ (f\ x\ `bind`k))) \qquad \text{[prop. }ValueBind]$$
$$= m\ (ValueBind\ (\lambda x \to f\ x\ (ValueBind\ \hat{k}))) \qquad \text{[again]}$$

$$value\ m = value\ (m\ `bind`unit) \qquad \text{[2nd monad law]}$$
$$= m\ (ValueBind\ (\lambda x \to value\ (unit\ x))) \qquad \text{[prop. }ValueBind]$$
$$= m\ (ValueBind\ (\lambda x \to x)) \qquad \text{[prop. }value]$$

And now dropping the superfluous constructor *ValueBind*, we obtain the definitions in figure 4 — the standard monad of continuations!

$$\text{type } M\ a\ ans = (Cxt\ a\ ans) \to ans$$
$$\text{type } Cxt\ a\ ans = a \to ans$$
$$unit\ x\ \hat{k} = \hat{k}\ x$$
$$(m\ `bind`f)\ \hat{k} = m\ (\lambda x \to f\ x\ \hat{k})$$
$$value\ m = m\ (\lambda x \to x)$$

Fig. 4. The Optimised Context-passing Monad.

6 Monads for Backtracking

We've seen how we can derive both the identity monad and the monad of continuations from the 'vanilla' monad specification. But in reality we wish to add further operations to the signature — that is the *raison d'être* of monads. As an example, we'll consider operations for backtracking:

$$fail :: M\ a$$
$$orelse :: M\ a \to M\ a \to M\ a$$

The new operations form a monoid,

$$fail\ `orelse`x = x$$
$$x\ `orelse`fail = x$$
$$(x\ `orelse`y)\ `orelse`z = x\ `orelse`(y\ `orelse`z)$$

and we must also specify their interaction with the monad operations[7]:

$$fail\ 'bind'\ f = fail$$
$$(x\ 'orelse'y)\ 'bind'\ f = (x\ 'bind'\ f)\ 'orelse'(y\ 'bind'\ f)$$

Finally, it is no longer appropriate to give *value* the type

$$value :: M\ a \rightarrow a$$

because there is no sensible behaviour for *value fail*. Instead, we give it the type

$$value :: M\ a \rightarrow Maybe\ a$$

where

$$\textbf{data}\ Maybe\ a = Yes\ a \mid No$$

satisfying the laws

$$value\ fail = No$$
$$value\ (unit\ x\ 'orelse'm) = Yes\ x$$

So we can observe whether a backtracking computation succeeds or fails, and if it succeeds we observe the first answer. Let us apply the same methods to derive implementations of this monad.

6.1 The Term Representation of the Backtracking Monad

Rather than start from scratch to develop a term representation for backtracking, observe that if we replace M by *Seq*, *fail* by *nil*, and *orelse* by *cat*, then these operations together with *unit* satisfy exactly the same axioms as in section 4. That suggests that we try to use the same kind of simplified terms as in section 4.1, namely *fail* and *unit x 'orelse'm*. So let us define

$$\textbf{data}\ M\ a = Fail \mid a\ 'UnitOrElse'\ M\ a$$

reuse the previously derived definitions for *unit*, *fail* and *orelse*, and see if we can derive implementations of the remaining operators.

In the case of *bind*, we derive

$$\begin{aligned} Fail\ 'bind'\ f &= fail\ 'bind'\ f \\ &= fail \\ &= Fail \end{aligned}$$

$$\begin{aligned} (x\ 'UnitOrElse'm)\ 'bind'\ f &= (unit\ x\ 'orelse'm)\ 'bind'\ f \\ &= (unit\ x\ 'bind'\ f)\ 'orelse'(m\ 'bind'\ f) \\ &= f\ x\ 'orelse'(m\ 'bind'\ f) \end{aligned}$$

(which is a terminating definition because the recursive call of *bind* has a smaller first argument), and in the case of *value*, we find directly that

$$value\ Fail = No$$
$$value\ (x\ 'UnitOrElse'm) = Yes\ x$$

So as we expected, we can implement the backtracking monad using lists.

---

[7] It is the second equation here which distinguishes backtracking from exception handling.

6.2 Context-passing Implementation of Backtracking

When we develop a context-passing implementation of backtracking we have to consider more complex forms of context than in section 5.2, since of course the new operations *fail* and *orelse* may occur in the context too. But just as we used the monad laws then to express all contexts with a single bind, so here we can use the monoidal properties of *fail* and *orelse* to express all contexts with a single *orelse*. Furthermore, we need not consider contexts with *orelse* nested inside *bind*, because

$$([\bullet] \; `orelse` \; b) \; `bind` \; k = ([\bullet] \; `bind` \; k) \; `orelse` \; (b \; `bind` \; k)$$

It is therefore sufficient to consider contexts of the form

$$value \; (((([\bullet] \; `bind` \; k) \; `orelse` \; b)$$

(Remember that this choice isn't critical. If we make a mistake at this point, we will discover it when we are unable to complete the derivations of the operators.)

Moreover, we may reasonably guess (or discover by doing the derivations) that uses of k will be in the context *value* $(k \; x \; `orelse` \; b)$ for some x and b, and uses of b will be in the context *value* b. We will therefore represent contexts by the type

$$\textbf{data} \; Cxt \; a \; ans = VBO \; (a \to Maybe \; ans \to Maybe \; ans) \; (Maybe \; ans)$$

where

$$(\forall x, b'.\hat{k} \; x \; (value \; b') = value \; (k \; x \; `orelse` b'))$$
$$\Rightarrow VBO \; \hat{k} \; (value \; b) = value \; ((([\bullet] \; `bind` \; k) \; `orelse` b)$$

The antecedent says that uses of k of the form we expect can be represented by applying $\hat{k}$. Since we plan to store only the *value* of b and b' it is natural to require that $\hat{k}$ need only the value. The conclusion says that in that case, the contexts we are interested in can be represented using *VBO*.

Now assuming that $\hat{k}$ has the property in the antecedent and that $\hat{b} = value \; b$, we can derive

$$
\begin{aligned}
unit \; x \; (VBO \; \hat{k} \; \hat{b}) &= value \; ((unit \; x \; `bind` \; k) \; `orelse` b) \\
&= value \; (k \; x \; `orelse` b) & \text{[1st monad law]} \\
&= \hat{k} \; x \; (value \; b) & \text{[prop. } \hat{k}] \\
&= \hat{k} \; x \; \hat{b} & \text{[prop. } \hat{b}]
\end{aligned}
$$

$$
\begin{aligned}
fail \; (VBO \; \hat{k} \; \hat{b}) &= value \; ((fail \; `bind` \; k) \; `orelse` b) \\
&= value \; (fail \; `orelse` b) \\
&= value \; b \\
&= \hat{b}
\end{aligned}
$$

The derivation of *bind* is a little more complicated because of the more complex property that $\hat{k}$ satisfies. We begin in the usual way,

$$
\begin{aligned}
&(m \; `bind` \; f) \; (VBO \; \hat{k} \; \hat{b}) \\
&= value \; (((m \; `bind` \; f) \; `bind` \; k) \; `orelse` b) \\
&= value \; ((m \; `bind` (\lambda x \to f \; x \; `bind` \; k)) \; `orelse` b) & \text{[3rd monad law]} \\
&= m \; (VBO \; \hat{k}' \; \hat{b})
\end{aligned}
$$

provided $\hat{k}'$ satisfies

$$\hat{k}'\ x\ (value\ b') = value\ ((f\ x\ 'bind'\ k)\ 'orelse'\ b')$$

But the right hand side of this equation is equal to

$$f\ x\ (VBO\ \hat{k}\ (value\ b'))$$

and so we can satisfy the condition by taking

$$\hat{k}'\ x\ \hat{b}' = f\ x\ (VBO\ \hat{k}\ \hat{b}')$$

So completing the derivation,

$$(m\ 'bind'\ f)\ (VBO\ \hat{k}\ \hat{b}) = m\ (VBO\ (\lambda x\ \hat{b}' \to f\ x\ (VBO\ \hat{k}\ \hat{b}'))\ \hat{b})$$

The derivation of *orelse* is straightforward:

$$
\begin{aligned}
&(m\ 'orelse'\ n)\ (VBO\ \hat{k}\ \hat{b}) \\
&= value\ (((m\ 'orelse'\ n)\ 'bind'\ k)\ 'orelse'\ b) \\
&= value\ (((m\ 'bind'\ k)\ 'orelse'\ (n\ 'bind'\ k))\ 'orelse'\ b) \\
&= value\ ((m\ 'bind'\ k)\ 'orelse'\ ((n\ 'bind'\ k)\ 'orelse'\ b)) \quad &\text{[associativity]} \\
&= m\ (VBO\ \hat{k}\ (value\ ((n\ 'bind'\ k)\ 'orelse'\ b))) \quad &\text{[prop. } VBO] \\
&= m\ (VBO\ \hat{k}\ (n\ (VBO\ \hat{k}\ (value\ b)))) \quad &\text{[prop. } VBO] \\
&= m\ (VBO\ \hat{k}\ (n\ (VBO\ \hat{k}\ \hat{b})))
\end{aligned}
$$

Finally, we derive *value*:

$$
\begin{aligned}
value\ m &= value\ (m\ 'orelse'\ fail) \\
&= value\ ((m\ 'bind'\ unit\ )\ 'orelse'\ fail) \\
&= m\ (VBO\ \hat{k}'\ (value\ fail)) \\
&= m\ (VBO\ \hat{k}'\ No)
\end{aligned}
$$

provided

$$\hat{k}'\ x\ (value\ b') = value\ (unit\ x\ 'orelse'\ b')$$

But the right hand side here is equal to *Yes x*, so we take $k' = \lambda x\ \hat{b}' \to Yes\ x$ to complete the derivation.

We can simplify the definitions slightly further by dropping the *VBO* constructor and replacing every context argument by two arguments, $\hat{k}$ and $\hat{b}$. Putting the results together, we obtain the definitions in figure 5, a continuation passing implementation of backtracking.

Exercise 2. Consider the *state monad*, with additional operations

$$
\begin{aligned}
&fetch :: M\ St \\
&store :: St \to M\ () \\
&run :: M\ a \to St \to a
\end{aligned}
$$

type M a $ans = (a \to Maybe\ ans \to Maybe\ ans) \to Maybe\ ans \to Maybe\ ans$
$unit\ x\ \hat{k}\ \hat{b} = \hat{k}\ x\ \hat{b}$
$(m\ `bind`\ f)\ \hat{k}\ \hat{b} = m\ (\lambda x\ \hat{b}' \to f\ x\ \hat{k}\ \hat{b}')\ \hat{b}$
$fail\ \hat{k}\ \hat{b} = \hat{b}$
$(m\ `orelse`\ n)\ \hat{k}\ \hat{b} = m\ \hat{k}\ (n\ \hat{k}\ \hat{b})$
$value\ m = m\ (\lambda x\ \hat{b}' \to Yes\ x)\ No$

Fig. 5. A Context-passing Implementation of Backtracking.

satisfying

$$fetch\ `bind`\ \lambda s \to store\ s = unit\ ()$$
$$store\ s\ `bind`\ \lambda() \to fetch = store\ s\ `bind`\ \lambda() \to unit\ s$$
$$store\ s\ `bind`\ \lambda() \to store\ s' = store\ s'$$
$$run\ (unit\ x)\ s = x$$
$$run\ (fetch\ `bind`\ f)\ s = run\ (f\ s)\ s$$
$$run\ (store\ s\ `bind`\ f)\ s' = run\ (f\ ())\ s$$

Derive term and context passing implementations of these operations.

7 Specifying Pretty-printing

Now we shall return to our case study: pretty-printing. Before we can start to derive implementations of the pretty-printing combinators we must develop a specification. But in this case, it isn't intuitively obvious what laws the pretty-printing combinators should satisfy! We need some way to guide our intuition, to lead us to write down the *right* laws for the combinators.

In mathematics, we often guide our intuition with the help of an example. If we are formulating hypothesis about certain topological spaces, we might think about the reals. It is even more important when formulating a new concept, such as a group, to have a concrete model in mind. We are trying to formulate a theory of pretty-printing, but as yet we have no model to guide us. So we shall start off by looking for an abstract model of documents, on which we can agree what the behaviour of the combinators should be. Our model will not be — and is not intended to be — a reasonable implementation, but it can be thought of as a kind of 'denotational semantics' for the combinators. Using the model we can establish algebraic properties which the combinators should satisfy — in *any* implementation. And then once these properties are established, we can use them as in the previous sections to derive implementations.

7.1 Abstract Layouts

We'll begin by looking for an abstract model of a pretty-printer's output — that is, prettily indented text. We could say that the output is just a string, but a string has so little structure that we can derive no intuition from it. Let us say instead, that a *layout* is a sequence of indented lines, which we can model as

$$\textbf{type } Layout = [(Int, String)]^+$$

Notice that we shall allow indentations to be negative: later on this will contribute to a nicer algebra, just as integers have a nicer algebra than natural numbers. But notice also that we restrict layouts to be *non-empty* (we use $[-]^+$ for the type of non-empty lists). We'll return to this point below.

We can now specify *text*, *nest* and ($$) very easily:

$$text\ s = [(0, s)]$$
$$nest\ k\ l = [(i + k, s)|(i, s) \leftarrow l]$$
$$l_1\ \$\$\ l_2 = l_1 \mathbin{+\!\!+} l_2$$

The right definition of horizontal composition ($\diamondsuit$) is not so obvious. The desired behaviour is clear enough when *text s* is placed beside *text t*, but what if both layouts are indented? What if the arguments occupy more than one line each?

Our choice is guided by the following principles:

- The two dimensional structure of each argument should be preserved; that is, the appearance of $x \diamondsuit y$ on the page should consist of some combination of a translation of x and a translation of y.
- Our intention is that a layout is just a pretty way of displaying a string. What string? We define

$$string :: Layout \rightarrow String$$
$$string\ l = foldr1\ (\oplus)\ (map\ snd\ l)$$
$$\textbf{where } s \oplus t = s \mathbin{+\!\!+} `` " \mathbin{+\!\!+} t$$

  (We interpret a line break as white space — equivalent to a single space). Then we expect that $string\ (x \diamondsuit y) = string\ x \mathbin{+\!\!+} string\ y$. This property enables the programmer to predict the string that $x \diamondsuit y$ represents, without thinking about how x and y are laid out.
- Indentation cannot appear in the middle of a line — since our abstract model (fortunately) cannot represent this.

There is really only one choice for ($\diamondsuit$) that meets these three criteria: to translate the second operand so that its first character abuts against the last character of the first operand. Formally,

$$(x \mathbin{+\!\!+} [(i, s)]) \diamondsuit ([(j, t)] \mathbin{+\!\!+} y) = x \mathbin{+\!\!+} [(i, s \mathbin{+\!\!+} t)] \mathbin{+\!\!+} nest\ (i + length\ s - j)\ y$$

To see that the definition is reasonable, consider the following two examples:

So at least in cases where one of the operands is a single line, the result is reasonable and useful.

Now look again at the formal definition of ($\diamondsuit$). It is only defined for non-empty arguments! This is the reason for the restriction to non-empty layouts that we made above: there is simply no sensible definition of ($\diamondsuit$) for empty arguments. The restriction is unfortunate: the empty layout would be a unit for $\$\$$, so improving the combinator algebra, and moreover would be useful in practice. But if we allow empty layouts and simply make some arbitrary choice for the value of $\diamondsuit$ in these cases, many algebraic laws involving $\diamondsuit$ cease to hold. A way out of the dilemma would be to allow empty layouts, and define $\diamondsuit$ to be a partial operator. But since this would complicate the development we have not done so.

7.2 The Algebra of Layouts

Now that we have formal definitions of the layout operators we can study their algebra. The laws in figure 6 are easily proved, although the proofs are not included here.

$$(x \diamondsuit y) \diamondsuit z = x \diamondsuit (y \diamondsuit z)$$
$$(x \ \$\$ \ y) \ \$\$ \ z = x \ \$\$ \ (y \ \$\$ \ z)$$
$$x \diamondsuit text \ ''' = x$$
$$nest \ k \ (x \ \$\$ \ y) = nest \ k \ x \ \$\$ \ nest \ k \ y$$
$$nest \ k \ (x \diamondsuit y) = nest \ k \ x \diamondsuit y$$
$$x \diamondsuit nest \ k \ y = x \diamondsuit y$$
$$nest \ k \ (nest \ k' \ x) = nest \ (k + k') \ x$$
$$nest \ 0 \ x = x$$
$$(x \ \$\$ \ y) \diamondsuit z = x \ \$\$ \ (y \diamondsuit z)$$
$$text \ s \diamondsuit ((text \ ''' \diamondsuit y) \ \$\$ \ z) = (text \ s \diamondsuit y) \ \$\$ \ nest \ (length \ s) \ z$$
$$text \ s \diamondsuit text \ t = text \ (s +\!\!+ t)$$

Fig. 6. Algebraic laws for layout operations.

First, both $\diamondsuit$ and $\$\$$ are associative, and $\diamondsuit$ has $text \ '''$ as a right unit. However, $\diamondsuit$ has no left unit because the indentation of the second operand is always lost. For example,

$$text \ ''' \diamondsuit \boxed{\qquad foo} = \boxed{foo}$$

Since we excluded empty layouts, $\$\$$ has no units at all.

The indentation combinator $nest$ distributes over $\$\$$, and distributes over $\diamondsuit$ on the left. We do not need to indent the right operand of $\diamondsuit$ here, because it is translated to abut against the left operand and so its indentation is lost. For the same reason $nest$ can be cancelled to the right of $\diamondsuit$. Of course consecutive $nests$ can be combined, and $nesting$ by zero is the identity operation.

Moreover $\$\$$ and $\diamondsuit$ are related to one another by a kind of associative law: we may say they 'associate with' one another. For example,

$$\boxed{a} \,\$\$\, \boxed{b} \diamondsuit \boxed{\begin{smallmatrix}c\\d\end{smallmatrix}} = \boxed{\begin{smallmatrix}a\\bc\\d\end{smallmatrix}} = \boxed{a} \,\$\$\, (\boxed{b} \diamondsuit \boxed{\begin{smallmatrix}c\\d\end{smallmatrix}})$$

On the other hand,

$$(x \diamondsuit y) \,\$\$\, z \neq x \diamondsuit (y \,\$\$\, z)$$

Here the indentation of z is different in the two cases: for example,

$$\boxed{a} \diamondsuit \boxed{b} \,\$\$\, \boxed{c} = \boxed{\begin{smallmatrix}ab\\c\end{smallmatrix}} \neq \boxed{\begin{smallmatrix}ab\\\ c\end{smallmatrix}} = \boxed{a} \diamondsuit (\boxed{b} \,\$\$\, \boxed{c})$$

It is the failure of this law to hold that makes the pretty-printing algebra interesting! We have to have some way to transform expressions of the form $x \diamondsuit (y \,\$\$\, z)$, and we can in the special case when we know the position where x ends, and the indentation of the first line of y. For example, when x is just a *text*, and y is of the form *text* "" $\diamondsuit y'$. The following law is sufficient:

$$\text{text } s \diamondsuit ((\text{text "" } \diamondsuit y) \,\$\$\, z) = (\text{text } s \diamondsuit y) \,\$\$\, \text{nest } (\text{length } s)\ z$$

One might say that the difficult part of pretty-printing is transforming expressions so that this law is applicable.

Finally there is a simple law relating $\diamondsuit$ and *text*.

In a sense these laws completely specify the bahaviour of the layout operators: any two closed terms which denote the same layout can be proved equal using these laws.

Exercise 3. Prove this remark, by choosing a canonical form for layout expressions such that every layout is denoted by a unique canonical form, and by deriving implementations of the operators that map canonical forms to canonical forms.

Remark on the benefits of a formal approach: This formal specification of the layout operators is an after-the-fact reconstruction. The first implementation was constructed using seat-of-the-pants intuition, and the combinators' behaviour was very subtly different. The *nest* combinator inserted spaces 'in a vertical context': that is, when used as an operand of $\$\$$ or at the top level.

As a consequence the law

$$\text{nest } k\ x \diamondsuit y = x \diamondsuit y$$

held in the implementation — the context here is 'horizontal'. But since the behaviour of a layout depended on its context, we could not give a simple abstract model such as that in the previous section. Moreover, of the eleven laws in figure 6, four did not hold (which four?) Both the user and the developer of the library were deprived of a useful algebra.

For the user (that is the author of a pretty-printer) each law means one less worry: there is no need to think about whether to write the left or the right hand side. For the developer, each law simplifies optimisation: the original library was very hard to optimise without changing its behaviour. The program we are following now, of deriving implementations from the algebra, would have been extremely difficult to follow.

And all these problems stemmed from a very subtle error that was only revealed by writing a formal specification...

7.3 Abstract Documents

The layout operations enable us to construct individual layouts, but a pretty-printer must of course choose between many alternative layouts. We make a design decision: to separate the construction of alternatives from the choice of the prettiest layout. We represent a collection of alternatives by a set:

$$\textbf{type } Doc = \mathcal{P}(Layout)$$

We will require that every layout in a Doc represent the same string, so that the programmer knows which string is being pretty-printed.

The choice of a particular layout will be made by a function

$$best :: Doc \rightarrow Layout$$

Thus the author of a pretty-printer need only construct a set of alternatives; the hard work of selecting the best alternative is done just by reusing the function $best$.

Since $Docs$ are just sets of layouts, there is a natural way to promote the layout operations to work on $Docs$ too. We just apply the operation to the elements of the operand sets and form a set of the results — for example,

$$d_1 \Diamond d_2 = \{l_1 \Diamond l_2 | l_i \in d_i\}$$

The promoted operations distribute over $\cup$ and preserve $\emptyset$ — for example,

$$(x \cup y) \Diamond z = (x \Diamond z) \cup (y \Diamond z)$$
$$\emptyset \Diamond z = \emptyset$$

Moreover, since the laws of the layout algebra are all *linear* in the sense that no variable appears more than once on either the left or right hand side, then they hold for documents also. So all the laws in figure 6 remain true for $Docs$.

Of course, if we confine ourselves to the layout operations we can only construct $Docs$ with a single element. We must add an operation with multiple possible layouts. Since we require that all layouts in a document represent the same string, union is not an appropriate operator to provide — rather we should define an operation that forms the union of two $Docs$ that are guaranteed to represent the same string. Noting that

$$string (x \,\$\$\, y) = string\ x +\!\!+ "\ " +\!\!+ string\ y$$

it is tempting to define

$$x \Leftrightarrow y = x \Diamond text\ "\ " \Diamond y$$

and define an operator that forms the union of x $\$\$$ y and x <+> y.

However, this isn't quite enough. Sometimes we want to make several choices consistently: for example, we may want to allow

$$\boxed{\text{if e}} \text{ <+> } \boxed{\text{then s1}} \text{ <+> } \boxed{\text{else s2}} = \boxed{\text{if e then s1 else s2}}$$

$$\boxed{\text{if e}} \,\$\$\, \boxed{\text{then s1}} \,\$\$\, \boxed{\text{else s2}} = \boxed{\begin{array}{l}\text{if e}\\ \text{then s1}\\ \text{else s2}\end{array}}$$

as alternatives, without also allowing

$$\boxed{\text{if e}} \text{ <+> } (\boxed{\text{then s1}} \,\$\$\, \boxed{\text{else s2}}) = \boxed{\begin{array}{l}\text{if e then s1}\\ \quad\text{else s2}\end{array}}$$

$$\boxed{\text{if e}} \,\$\$\, \boxed{\text{then s1}} \text{ <+> } \boxed{\text{else s2}} = \boxed{\begin{array}{l}\text{if e}\\ \text{then s1 else s2}\end{array}}$$

We therefore define an n-ary operation, which makes $n-1$ choices consistently:

$$sep :: [Doc]^+ \to Doc$$
$$sep\ xs = foldr1\ (\text{<+>})\ xs \cup foldr1\ (\$\$)\ xs$$

We'll revise this definition slightly below, but first let us observe a pleasing interaction between *sep* and *nest*. Consider for example,

$$sep\ \boxed{\boxed{\text{while x}\geq\text{0 do}},\ nest\ 2\ \boxed{\text{x := x-2}}}$$

The alternative layouts here are

$$\boxed{\text{while x}\geq\text{0 do}} \text{ <+> } nest\ 2\ \boxed{\text{x := x-2}} = \boxed{\text{while x}\geq\text{0 do}} \text{ <+> } \boxed{\text{x := x-2}}$$
$$= \boxed{\text{while x}\geq\text{0 do x := x-2}}$$

and

$$\boxed{\text{while x}\geq\text{0 do}} \,\$\$\, nest\ 2\ \boxed{\text{x := x-2}} = \boxed{\begin{array}{l}\text{while x}\geq\text{0 do}\\ \quad\text{x := x-2}\end{array}}$$

In the horizontal form no unwanted extra indentation appears, because *nest* can be cancelled on the right of (<>).

Now let us consider an example which motivates a slight refinement to the definition of *sep*. Suppose we wish to pretty-print pairs of statements separated by a semicolon, choosing between horizontal and vertical layouts. We might define

$$semic\ x\ y = sep\ [x \diamond text\ \text{";"}, y]$$

Now for example,

$$semic\ \boxed{\text{x:=0}}\ \boxed{\text{y:=0}} = \left\{ \boxed{\text{x:=0; y:=0}}, \boxed{\begin{array}{l}\text{x:=0;}\\ \text{y:=0}\end{array}} \right\}$$

in which both horizontal and vertical layouts look fine. But consider

$$semic \quad \boxed{\begin{array}{c}\text{while x}\geq\text{2 do}\\ \text{x:=x-2}\end{array}} \boxed{\begin{array}{c}\text{while y}\geq\text{2 do}\\ \text{y:=y-2}\end{array}}$$

$$= \left\{ \boxed{\begin{array}{c}\text{while x}\geq\text{2 do}\\ \text{x:=x-2; while y}\geq\text{2 do}\\ \text{y:=y-2}\end{array}}, \boxed{\begin{array}{c}\text{while x}\geq\text{2 do}\\ \text{x:=x-2;}\\ \text{while y}\geq\text{2 do}\\ \text{y:=y-2}\end{array}} \right\}$$

In cases such as this, the horizontal layout is ugly or even misleading. We therefore redefine

$$sep \ xs = fit \ (foldr1 \ (\Leftrightarrow) \ xs) \cup foldr1 \ (\$\$) \ xs$$
$$\textbf{where} \ \ fit \ d = \{l \in d | length \ l = 1\}$$

which restricts the horizontal form of a *sep* to fit on one line.

The algebraic properties of *fit* are very simply stated — see figure 7. The *sep* operator has fewer useful properties, and we will develop them as we need them.

$$fit \ (text \ s) = text \ s$$
$$fit \ (nest \ k \ x) = nest \ k \ (fit \ x)$$
$$fit \ (x \Leftrightarrow y) = fit \ x \Leftrightarrow fit \ y$$
$$fit \ (x \ \$\$ \ y) = \emptyset$$
$$fit \ (x \cup y) = fit \ x \cup fit \ y$$
$$fit \ \emptyset = \emptyset$$

Fig. 7. The *fit* laws.

Exercise 4. Define a type of abstract syntax trees for a simple imperative language, with assignment statements, **if–then–else**, **while–do**, and **begin–end**. Use the combinators to write a pretty-printer for this type.

7.4 Choosing a Pretty Layout

Now that we have designed combinators for constructing documents with many possible layouts, it is time to discuss choosing among those alternatives. Many pretty-printers aim simply to avoid exceeding a given page width. However, we found that using this criterion alone tends to produce layouts such as

$$\boxed{\text{for i} = 1 \text{ to } 100 \text{ do for j} = 1 \text{ to } 100 \text{ do for k} = 1 \text{ to } 100 \text{ do a[i,j,k]} := 0}$$

which fits on a page, but cannot be described as pretty. We therefore impose an additional constraint limiting the number of characters on each line (excluding indentation) to a smaller number. The idea is to avoid placing too much information on a line — even a line that begins at the left margin. Under this constraint the example above might instead be laid out as

```
for i = 1 to 100 do
  for j = 1 to 100 do
    for k = 1 to 100 do a[i,j,k] := 0
```

In general a pretty layout will consist of a ribbon of text snaking across the page. To see that this is reasonable, ask yourself: 'is the prettiest layout on an infinitely wide page really to place everything on one line?'

We will say that a line that meets both constraints is *nice*, and define

$$nice_r^w (i, s) \iff i + length\ s \le w \land length\ s \le r$$

where w is the page width and r is the width of the ribbon.

We might be tempted to specify that the pretty-printer choose a layout all of whose lines are nice, but we must be careful: some documents have no such layout at all. For example, *text* "13 characters" cannot be made to fit within a pagewidth of 12. Even in such cases we want the pretty-printer to produce something, and rather than adopt an ad hoc solution we accept that the niceness criteria will not always be met.

Moreover, even if a nice layout exists we may not want the pretty-printer to choose it! Consider for example the document

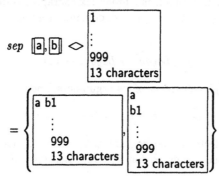

This document has a nice layout on a page of width 14 characters — the second one. But it would be unreasonably inefficient for a pretty-printer to decide whether or not to split the first line of a document on the basis of the contents of the last. An efficient pretty-printer should need only a limited look-ahead, and so we must expect the first layout to be chosen despite the trouble ahead[8]. The question of which layout a pretty-printer chooses is thus trickier than it at first appears. Of course, it could never have been sufficient to say simply that a nice layout is chosen, since even if all layouts are nice, some will be preferable to others. We must instead define an *ordering* on layouts and choose the best.

We begin by defining an ordering $\rhd_r^w$ on individual lines. Our guiding principles are

---

[8] A different design decision is possible: we might choose to 'play safe' and split the first line unless a limited look-ahead shows that it is definitely unnecessary. We have not explored this alternative.

- a nice line is always better than an overflowing line,
- if one cannot avoid overflowing, it is better to overflow by a little than by a lot,
- unnecessary line breaks should be avoided.

We therefore define

$$x \triangleright_r^w y \iff \begin{aligned} &(nice_r^w\ x \wedge \neg nice_r^w y) \\ \vee\ &(\neg nice_r^w\ x \wedge \neg nice_r^w\ y \wedge \#x < \#y) \\ \vee\ &(nice_r^w\ x \wedge nice_r^w\ y \wedge \#x > \#y) \end{aligned}$$

where the length of a line is given by $\#(i, s) = i + length\ s$.

If we know that $\#x > \#y$ then we can test $\triangleright_r^w$ particularly simply:

$$nice_r^w\ x \implies x \triangleright_r^w y$$
$$\neg nice_r^w\ x \implies y \triangleright_r^w x$$

In the first case y must also be nice, but not as nice because it is shorter. In the second case either y is nice (and therefore nicer than x), or it is not nice, but nicer than x because it is shorter. We will use this property in the implementations.

Unfortunately an ordering on lines does not extend in a unique way to an ordering on layouts, and so we must make an arbitrary decision. We choose to order layouts by the lexicographic extension of the ordering on lines, which we will also write as $\triangleright_r^w$. The reason for this choice is simple: lexicographic ordering can be decided left-to-right, and we hope to pretty-print documents from left to right without much look-ahead. We define

$$\nabla_r^w :: Layout \to Layout \to Layout$$

to select the lexicographically nicer of its arguments, and

$$best :: Int \to Int \to Doc \to Layout$$

such that $best\ w\ r$ selects the lexicographically nicest layout in the set. It's also convenient to introduce a unit ∞ for ∇_r^w, representing a layout uglier than any other.

The careful reader will have noticed that $\triangleright_r^w$ is only a *partial* order — if x and y are both lines of equal length, then neither $x \triangleright_r^w y$ nor $y \triangleright_r^w x$ holds, even though x and y need not be equal. Consequently both ∇_r^w and *best* are partial operations. But this will not trouble us, because all the document operations construct sets which are totally ordered by $\triangleright_r^w$. This will become evident when we derive implementations of the library. Consider this: our task is to define when one layout is nicer than another layout *of the same document*; we have no need to (and indeed, we cannot) define when a layout is nicer than a layout of an unrelated document.

Let us now investigate the properties of $\triangleright_r^w$, ∇_r^w and *best*. Since the ordering on layouts is lexicographic,

$$x \triangleright_r^w y \implies \left(\begin{aligned} z\ \$\$\ x &\triangleright_r^w z\ \$\$\ y \\ \wedge\quad x &\triangleright_r^w y\ \$\$\ z \\ \wedge\quad x\ \$\$\ z &\triangleright_r^w y \end{aligned} \right)$$

Moreover,

$$x \triangleright_r^w y \implies nest \; k \; x \triangleright_r^{w+k} nest \; k \; y$$

and therefore

$$nest \; k \; (x \nabla_r^w y) = nest \; k \; x \nabla_r^{w+k} nest \; k \; y$$

Finally, we can reformulate the observation about a simple test for $\triangleright_r^w$ as follows:

$$length \; s > length \; t \implies \left(\wedge \begin{array}{l} length \; s \leq w \; \text{`min`} r \Rightarrow text \; s \triangleright_r^w text \; t \\ length \; s > w \; \text{`min`} r \Rightarrow text \; t \triangleright_r^w text \; s \end{array} \right)$$

From these properties, and from the fact that *best* chooses the nicest element from a set, we can derive the laws in figure 8 for *best*.

$$best \; w \; r \; (x \; \$\$ \; y) = best \; w \; r \; x \; \$\$ \; best \; w \; r \; y$$
$$best \; w \; r \; (nest \; k \; x) = nest \; k \; (best \; {}_r^{w-k} \; x)$$
$$best \; w \; r \; (text \; s) = text \; s$$
$$best \; w \; r \; (x \cup y) = best \; w \; r \; x \nabla_r^w best \; w \; r \; y$$
$$best \; w \; r \; \emptyset = \infty$$

Fig. 8. The *best* laws.

8 Implementing Pretty-printing: A Term Representation

Now that we have developed a collection of algebraic properties of the pretty-printing operators, we can apply the methods presented in the earlier sections of the chapter to construct implementations.

(The reader may be wondering why we can't just use the abstract representation of documents as an implementation, say representing a *Doc* as a list of the possible *Layouts*. Consider for a moment a medium sized syntax tree for an imperative language, which contains 100 occurrences of **if–then–else**, each pretty-printed using *sep*. Ignoring the fact that nesting may force some *seps* to make related choices, such a *Doc* has 2^{100} alternative layouts, and so would be represented by a list with this many elements. There is no reason to expect the best layout to be near the beginning, and so it should be clear that searching for it in such a list is a hopeless exercise.)

We will begin by deriving an implementation based on a term representation of *Docs*. We choose simplified terms to which the *best* laws are easily applicable, which suggests

$$E ::= text \; S \mid nest \; N \; E \mid E \; \$\$ \; E \mid E \cup E \mid \emptyset$$

However, we also want to be sure that we can apply our simplified test for $\rhd_r^w$, and so we will restrict the form of unions further. We can define a class of documents with a 'manifest' first line by

$$M ::= text\ S \mid text\ S \ \$\$ \ E$$

The simplified test is easily applicable to documents of this form provided one has a longer first line than the other. We will therefore only permit unions of the form

$$U ::= M \mid U \cup U$$

and moreover we shall impose an invariant that the first line of every layout in the left operand of $\cup$ must be strictly longer than the first line of every layout in the right operand. Since both operands represent the same string it follows that all layouts in the right operand consist of at least two lines.

Now we can define simplified terms by

$$E ::= U \mid nest\ N\ E$$

We allow $\emptyset$ only at the top level of the result of *fit*,

$$E0 ::= E \mid \emptyset$$

With these restrictions *best* of a union is easily determined.

We can represent *Docs* by the type

$$
\begin{array}{lll}
\textbf{data } Doc = & Text\ String & \text{---} text\ s \\
& \mid String\ 'TextAbove'\ Doc & \text{---} text\ s \ \$\$ \ x \\
& \mid Doc\ 'Union'\ Doc & \text{---} x \cup y \\
& \mid Empty & \text{---} \emptyset \\
& \mid Nest\ Int\ Doc & \text{---} nest\ k\ x
\end{array}
$$

although we must be careful only to construct documents of the form described above.

We can use the same type to represent *Layouts*: a *Doc* not involving *Union* or *Empty* represents a *Layout*.

The definition of *best* is now easy to derive by applying the *best* laws — see figure 9. We'll discuss only the *Union* case. We know from the *best* laws that

$$best\ w\ r\ (x\ 'Union'\ y) = best\ w\ r\ x \nabla_r^w best\ w\ r\ y$$

But since *best* must choose one of the layouts in its argument, the datatype invariant implies that if $best\ w\ r\ x$ is either $text\ s$ or $text\ s \ \$\$ \ x'$, and $best\ w\ r\ y$ is $text\ t \ \$\$ \ y'$, then $length\ s > length\ t$. So the simplified niceness comparison is applicable. If $nice_r^w(text\ s)$ then $text\ s \ \rhd_r^w \ text\ t$, and by the lexicographic properties it follows that $text\ s \ \rhd_r^w \ text\ t \ \$\$ \ y'$ and $text\ s \ \$\$ \ x' \ \rhd_r^w \ text\ t \ \$\$ \ y'$. So in this case ∇_r^w chooses its left operand. If $\neg nice_r^w(text\ s)$ then the opposite holds. So we can implement ∇_r^w in this case by the function *nicest*, which simply inspects the first line of its first operand.

Haskell's lazy evaluation is exploited here, in two ways. Firstly, *shorter xs n* is defined to test whether $length\ xs \leq n$ *without* evaluating all of xs if it is not. Since

$$best \ w \ r \ (Text \ s) = Text \ s$$
$$best \ w \ r \ (s \ 'TextAbove' x) = s \ 'TextAbove' best \ w \ r \ x$$
$$best \ w \ r \ (Nest \ k \ x) = Nest \ k \ (best \ (w - k) \ r \ x)$$
$$best \ w \ r \ (x \ 'Union' y) = nicest \ w \ r \ (best \ w \ r \ x) \ (best \ w \ r \ y)$$

$$nicest \ w \ r \ x \ y = \textbf{if} \ shorter \ (firstline \ x) \ (w \ 'min' r) \ \textbf{then} \ x \ \textbf{else} \ y$$
$$shorter \ xs \ n = null \ (drop \ n \ xs)$$
$$firstline \ (Text \ s) = s$$
$$firstline \ (s \ 'TextAbove' x) = s$$

Fig. 9. The definition of *best*.

some layouts may have very long first lines — for example, the layout produced when all *seps* adopt a horizontal form — this is an important optimisation. Secondly, since *nicest* makes its decision on the basis of the first line of each argument *only*, then when we select the best layout from a *Union* the layout of the unsuccessful branch is evaluated only as far as the first line. Although the *Doc* we apply *best* to may be a large tree, we follow (and therefore evaluate) only a single path through it.

Definitions of *text*, *nest*, $(\diamond)$ and ($\$\$$) are obtained by simple algebraic manipulation. To take just two examples,

$$
\begin{aligned}
(Nest \ k \ x) \ \$\$ \ y &= (nest \ k \ x) \ \$\$ \ y \\
&= (nest \ k \ x) \ \$\$ \ (nest \ k \ (nest \ (-k) \ y)) \\
&= nest \ k \ (x \ \$\$ \ nest \ (-k) \ y) \\
&= Nest \ k \ (x \ \$\$ \ Nest \ (-k) \ y)
\end{aligned}
$$

$$
\begin{aligned}
Text \ s \ \diamond \ (t \ 'TextAbove' x) &= text \ s \ \diamond \ (text \ t \ \$\$ \ x) \\
&= text \ s \ \diamond \ ((text \ "" \ \diamond \ text \ t) \ \$\$ \ x) \\
&= (text \ s \ \diamond \ text \ t) \ \$\$ \ nest \ (length \ s) \ x \quad [\diamond / \ \$\$ \ \text{law}] \\
&= text \ (s + \!\!+ t) \ \$\$ \ nest \ (length \ s) \ x \\
&= (s + \!\!+ t) \ 'TextAbove' Nest \ (length \ s) \ x
\end{aligned}
$$

The remaining equations are derived similarly; the complete definitions appear in figure 10. It is easy to verify that the definitions terminate. We leave it to the reader to check that if the datatype invariant holds for the arguments, it also holds for the result of each these operators.

It is interesting to look at the way *Unions* are treated in these definitions. In almost every case *Unions* in arguments are 'floated upwards' to give a *Union* in the result. The exception is a *Union* in the right argument of ($\$\$$): we do not use the property

$$x \ \$\$ \ (y \cup z) = (x \ \$\$ \ y) \cup (x \ \$\$ \ z)$$

One good reason is that to do so would violate the datatype invariant: the operands of the union on the right hand side have the *same* first lines. Another good reason is efficiency: the *Doc* form we have chosen groups together all layouts with the same first line in a value of the form $s \ 'TextAbove' x$. The *best* function can then reject all these layouts in one go, if s is not nice. Here x may represent many billions of

$text\ s = Text\ s$

$nest\ k\ x = Nest\ k\ x$

$Text\ s \text{ \$\$ } y = s\ \text{`}TextAbove\text{'}\ y$
$(s\ \text{`}TextAbove\text{'}\ x)\ \text{\$\$ } y = s\ \text{`}TextAbove\text{'}\ (x\ \text{\$\$ } y)$
$(Nest\ k\ x)\ \text{\$\$ } y = Nest\ k\ (x\ \text{\$\$ } Nest\ (-k)\ y)$
$(x\ \text{`}Union\text{'}\ y)\ \text{\$\$ } z = (x\ \text{\$\$ } z)\ \text{`}Union\text{'}\ (y\ \text{\$\$ } z)$

$Text\ s \Diamond Text\ t = Text\ (s \mathbin{+\!\!+} t)$
$Text\ s \Diamond (t\ \text{`}TextAbove\text{'}\ x) = (s \mathbin{+\!\!+} t)\ \text{`}TextAbove\text{'}\ Nest\ (length\ s)\ x$
$Text\ s \Diamond (Nest\ k\ x) = Text\ s \Diamond x$
$Text\ s \Diamond (x\ \text{`}Union\text{'}\ y) = (Text\ s \Diamond x)\ \text{`}Union\text{'}\ (Text\ s \Diamond y)$
$(s\ \text{`}TextAbove\text{'}\ x) \Diamond y = s\ \text{`}TextAbove\text{'}\ (x \Diamond y)$
$Nest\ k\ x \Diamond y = Nest\ k(x \Diamond y)$
$(x\ \text{`}Union\text{'}\ y) \Diamond z = (x \Diamond z)\ \text{`}Union\text{'}\ (y \Diamond z)$

Fig. 10. The definitions of $text$, $nest$, ($\Diamond$) and ($\$\$$).

alternative layouts, and if all *Unions* were floated to the top level then *best* would have to reject each one individually. The cost would be prohibitive, and the library simply would not work.

We still need to implement *sep* — recall its specification

$$sep\ xs = fit\ (foldr1\ (\mathbin{<\!+\!>})\ xs) \cup foldr1\ (\$\$)\ xs$$

We can almost use this directly as the implementation, but we must ensure that the *Union* is well-formed. Firstly, if the result of *fit* is $\emptyset$ we must avoid creating a *Union* with an empty operand. Secondly, we must ensure that the first line of the result of the *fit* is strictly longer than the first lines in the second operand. Provided xs consists of at least two documents this is guaranteed, since the longest first line in $(x_1 \text{ \$\$ } x_2 \ldots \text{ \$\$ } x_n)$ is the longest first line in x_1, and the horizontal form contains at least one extra space. But if xs consists of exactly one document then the horizontal and vertical forms are the same, and a *Union* would be badly formed. So we must treat this as a special case. Thirdly, we must avoid constructing a *Union* with nested operands: this can only happen if the first *Doc* in the list is of the form $Nest\ k\ x$. In that case we factor out the *Nest*:

$$
\begin{aligned}
sep\ (nest\ k\ x : xs) &= fit\ (nest\ k\ x \mathbin{<\!+\!>} foldr1\ (\mathbin{<\!+\!>})xs) \cup \\
&\quad (nest\ k\ x \text{ \$\$ } foldr1\ (\$\$)xs) \\
&= nest\ k\ (fit\ (x \mathbin{<\!+\!>} foldr1\ (\mathbin{<\!+\!>})xs)) \cup \\
&\quad nest\ k\ (x \text{ \$\$ } foldr1\ (\$\$)(map\ (nest\ (-k))\ xs)) \\
&= nest\ k(sep\ (x : map\ (nest\ (-k))\ xs
\end{aligned}
$$

The definitions of *sep* and *fit* appear in figure 11. Notice that the datatype invariant lets us define *fit* of a *Union* very efficiently, since we know the layouts in the second operand consist of at least two lines.

$$sep\ [x] = x$$
$$sep\ (Nest\ k\ x : xs) = Nest\ k\ (sep\ (x : map\ (nest\ (-k))\ xs))$$
$$sep\ xs = fit\ (foldr1\ (<+>)\ xs)\ `u`\ foldr1\ (\$\$)\ xs$$
$$\mathbf{where}\ Empty\ `u`\ y = y$$
$$x\ `u`\ y = x\ `Union`\ y$$

$$fit\ (Text\ s) = Text\ s$$
$$fit\ (s\ `TextAbove`\ x) = Empty$$
$$fit\ (Nest\ k\ x) = \mathbf{case}\ fit\ x\ \mathbf{of}$$
$$Empty \rightarrow Empty$$
$$y \quad\ \rightarrow Nest\ k\ y$$
$$fit\ (x\ `Union`\ y) = fit\ x$$

Fig. 11. The definition of *sep*.

To complete the implementation of the library we just need to define a function mapping *Layouts* to appropriate strings. Let us define

$$layout :: Int \rightarrow Doc \rightarrow String$$

such that *layout k x* constructs a string displaying *nest k x*. A suitable definition appears in figure 12.

$$layout\ k\ (Text\ s) = indent\ k\ s$$
$$layout\ k\ (s\ `TextAbove`\ x) = indent\ k\ s + layout\ k\ x$$
$$layout\ k\ (Nest\ k'\ x) = layout\ (k + k')\ x$$

$$indent\ k\ s\ |\ k \geq 8 = `\backslash t` : indent\ (k - 8)\ s$$
$$indent\ k\ s\ |\ k \geq 1 = `\ ` : indent\ (k - 1)\ s$$
$$indent\ 0\ s = s + ``\backslash n"$$

Fig. 12. Mapping layouts to strings.

One or two minor optimisations can be made. For example,

$$best\ w\ r\ ((x\ `Union`\ y)\ `Union`\ z)$$

tests *x* for niceness twice if it is nice — once to reject *y*, and once to reject *z*. This is easily avoided, say by redefining *best* to return a pair of the best layout and a boolean indicating whether the first line is nice. Such measures can bring a useful improvement in performance, but in fact a much more serious problem remains. Consider for example

$$sep\ [sep\ [sep\ [\boxed{\text{hello}}, \boxed{\text{a}}], \boxed{\text{b}}], \boxed{\text{c}}]$$

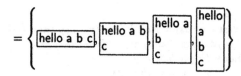

If this document is displayed on a page of width 5 then the last layout must be chosen, but since each layout has a different first line, our implementation must first construct and reject each of the first three. Yet as soon as the length of hello is known it is clear that the innermost *sep*, and therefore all the others, must be laid out vertically. We could therefore go immediately to the fourth layout. For large documents in which *sep* may be nested very deep, this optimisation is important. Without it the complexity of prettyprinters is at least $O(n^2)$ in the depth of *sep* nesting, and in practice they pause for an embarrassingly long time at the beginning of pretty-printing, gradually speeding up as more and more *sep* decisions are resolved.

But to incorporate this optimisation we will need to change our representation of documents.

9 Optimised Pretty-printing: A Term Representation

Looking back at the problematic example, we can see that the three first layouts have a common prefix — "hello a" — and moreover we can tell just from the prefix that none of the layouts has a nice first line. Our goal will be to factor out this common prefix, express the union of the three layouts as

$$\boxed{\text{hello a}} \Diamond (x \cup y \cup z)$$

for suitable x, y and z, and then reject all of them together in favour of the fourth.

But to be able to observe this situation, we must introduce *text* $S \Diamond E$ as a simplified form. At the same time we can replace the simplified forms *text* S by *text* "" and *text* S \$\$ E by *text* "" \$\$ E, because the old forms can be expressed in terms of the new ones as follows

$$\text{text } s = \text{text } s \Diamond \text{text "''}$$
$$\text{text } s \text{ \$\$ } x = \text{text } s \Diamond (\text{text "''} \text{ \$\$ } nest \ (-length \ s) \ x)$$

We will need to allow $\emptyset$ in more places than before, because we intend to use the property

$$\text{fit } (\text{text } s \Diamond x) = \text{text } s \Diamond \text{fit } x$$

where the right hand side is a canonical form with a component (*fit* x) that might very well be empty. We don't want to *test* for an empty set here, of course, because that would make *fit* hyper-strict with disastrous consequences.

Our new simplified forms are therefore given by the grammar

$$E ::= U \mid nest \ N \ E$$
$$U ::= M \mid U \cup U \mid \emptyset$$
$$M ::= text \ \text{"''} \mid text \ \text{"''} \text{ \$\$ } E \mid text \ S \Diamond E$$

We impose the same condition on unions as before: every layout in the first operand must have a longer first line than every layout in the second.

These simplified forms can be represented by the datatype

$$
\begin{array}{lll}
\textbf{data } Doc = & Nil & \text{--- } text \text{ ""} \\
& | \;\; NilAbove \; Doc & \text{--- } text \text{ ""} \; \$\$ \; x \\
& | \;\; String \; 'TextBeside' \; Doc & \text{--- } text \; s \Leftrightarrow x \\
& | \;\; Nest \; Int \; Doc & \text{--- } nest \; k \; x \\
& | \;\; Doc \; 'Union' \; Doc & \text{--- } x \cup y \\
& | \;\; Empty & \text{--- } \emptyset
\end{array}
$$

And now the key problem is to rederive *sep* so as to *delay* introducing a *Union* until after the common prefix of the two branches of the *sep* is produced.

We need an algebraic law permitting us to draw a prefix out of a *sep*. Let us try to prove one. Assuming *xs* is non-empty, then

$$
\begin{aligned}
& sep \; ((text \; s \Leftrightarrow x) : xs) \\
& = fit \; (text \; s \Leftrightarrow x \Leftrightarrow (foldr1 \; (\Leftrightarrow) \; xs)) \cup \\
& \quad ((text \; s \Leftrightarrow x) \; \$\$ \; foldr1 \; (\$\$) \; xs) \\
& = (text \; s \Leftrightarrow fit \; (text \; "" \Leftrightarrow x \Leftrightarrow foldr1 \; (\Leftrightarrow) \; xs)) \cup \\
& \quad (text \; s \Leftrightarrow ((text \; "" \Leftrightarrow x) \; \$\$ \; foldr1 \; (\$\$) \; (map \; (nest \; (-length \; s)) \; xs) \\
& = text \; s \Leftrightarrow sep \; ((text \; "" \Leftrightarrow x) : map \; (nest \; (-length \; s)) \; xs)
\end{aligned}
$$

This last step holds because *nest* can be either cancelled or introduced freely in the horizontal alternative. We have already seen that we can move a *Nest* out of a *sep*, and indeed we can even move a *Union* out of *sep*'s first argument *without* splitting the *sep* into two branches which must be explored separately. In fact the only time that we have to do this is when the first argument is *Nil* — and by that point the horizontal and vertical alternatives differ at the very next character, so there is really no alternative. The derived definition of *sep* is given in figure 13. We have used an auxiliary function specified by

$$
sep' \; x \; k \; ys = sep \; (x : map \; (nest \; k) \, ys)
$$

to avoid repeated applications of *nest* to the remaining arguments.

Implementations of the other four operators can be derived in the usual way — this time we skip the details. The resulting definitions are presented in figure 14. Once again we leave it to the reader to check that the datatype invariant is satisfied.

In fact, these are not quite the implemented definitions. Heap profiling revealed that the derived definition of (\$\$) leaks space: unevaluated calls of (\$\$) and *nest* collect on the heap. These are introduced in the 3rd and 4th equations for (\$\$), and unfortunately passed to a recursive call of (\$\$) which usually introduces still more unevaluated applications. A solution is to avoid constructing these unevaluated applications at all by using an auxiliary function

$$
aboveNest \; x \; k \; y = x \; \$\$ \; nest \; k \; y
$$

instead. This is of course just the specification of *aboveNest*; the derived implementation appears in figure 15. It is important that *aboveNest*s second parameter is

$$sep\ [x] = x$$
$$sep\ (x : ys) = sep'\ x\ 0\ ys$$

$$sep'\ Nil\ k\ ys = fit\ (foldl\ (<\!\!+\!\!>)\ Nil\ ys)\ `Union`\ vertical\ Nil\ k\ ys$$
$$sep'\ (NilAbove\ x)\ k\ ys = vertical\ (NilAbove\ x)\ k\ ys$$
$$sep'\ (s\ `TextBeside`x)\ k\ ys = s\ `TextBeside`sep'\ (Nil \Diamond x)\ (k - length\ s)\ ys$$
$$sep'\ (Nest\ n\ x)\ k\ ys = Nest\ n\ (sep'\ x\ (k - n)\ ys)$$
$$sep'\ (x\ `Union`y)\ k\ ys = sep'\ x\ k\ ys\ `Union`vertical\ y\ k\ ys$$
$$sep'\ Empty\ k\ ys = Empty$$

$$vertical\ x\ k\ ys = x\ \$\$\ nest\ k\ (foldr1\ (\$\$)\ ys)$$

Fig. 13. *sep* optimised to delay *Union*.

$$text\ s = s\ `TextBeside`Nil$$

$$nest\ k\ x = Nest\ k\ x$$

$$Nil \Diamond (Nest\ k\ x) = Nil \Diamond x$$
$$Nil \Diamond x = x$$
$$NilAbove\ x \Diamond y = NilAbove\ (x \Diamond y)$$
$$(s\ `TextBeside`x) \Diamond y = s\ `TextBeside`(x \Diamond y)$$
$$Nest\ k\ x \Diamond y = Nest\ k\ (x \Diamond y)$$
$$(x\ `Union`y) \Diamond z = (x \Diamond z)\ `Union`(y \Diamond z)$$
$$Empty \Diamond z = Empty$$

$$Nil\ \$\$\ x = NilAbove\ x$$
$$NilAbove\ x\ \$\$\ y = NilAbove\ (x\ \$\$\ y)$$
$$(s\ `TextBeside`x)\ \$\$\ y = s\ `TextBeside`((Nil \Diamond x)\ \$\$\ nest\ (-length\ s)y)$$
$$Nest\ k\ x\ \$\$\ y = Nest\ k\ (x\ \$\$\ nest\ (-k)\ y)$$
$$(x\ `Union`y)\ \$\$\ z = (x\ \$\$\ z)\ `Union`(y\ \$\$\ z)$$
$$Empty\ \$\$\ y = Empty$$

Fig. 14. Implementations of *text*, *nest*, ($\Diamond$) and ($\$\$$).

evaluated strictly — otherwise the heap would fill up with unevaluated subtractions instead. We can arrange this using hbc's standard function *seq a b*, which evaluates *a* and returns the value of *b*.

And now we must derive an implementation of *best*.

The trickiest case is *best w r (text s $\Diamond$ x)*. We know that this must be equal to *text s $\Diamond$ y* for some *y* — but what is *y*? It clearly depends on both *x* and *s*, because the length of *s* affects the width of 'ribbon' available to the first line of *x*. Let us introduce a new function *best'*, whose defining property is

$$best\ w\ r\ (text\ s \Diamond x) = text\ s \Diamond best'\ w\ r\ s\ x$$

We can derive a definition for *best'* using the algebra; we present the details this time.

$x \mathbin{\$\$} y = aboveNest\ x\ 0\ y$

$aboveNest\ Nil\ k\ y = NilAbove\ (nest\ k\ y)$
$aboveNest\ (NilAbove\ x)\ k\ y = NilAbove\ (aboveNest\ x\ k\ y)$
$aboveNest\ (s\ \text{‘}TextBeside\text{‘}x)\ k\ y = seq\ k'\ (s\ \text{‘}TextBeside\text{‘}\ aboveNest\ (Nil \diamond x)\ k'\ y)$
$\qquad\qquad\qquad\qquad\qquad\qquad \textbf{where}\ k' = k - length\ s$
$aboveNest\ (Nest\ k'\ x)\ k\ y = seq\ k''\ (Nest\ k'\ (aboveNest\ x\ k''\ y))$
$\qquad\qquad\qquad\qquad\qquad \textbf{where}\ k'' = k - k'$
$aboveNest\ (x\ \text{‘}Union\text{‘}y)\ k\ z = aboveNest\ x\ k\ z\ \text{‘}Union\text{‘}\ aboveNest\ y\ k\ z$
$aboveNest\ Empty\ k\ z = Empty$

Fig. 15. Defining $\$\$$ without a space leak.

$$
\begin{aligned}
text\ s \diamond best'\ w\ r\ s\ Nil &= best\ w\ r\ (text\ s \diamond text\ \text{""}) \\
&= best\ w\ r\ (text\ s) \\
&= text\ s \\
&= text\ s \diamond Nil
\end{aligned}
$$

so we can take $best'\ w\ r\ s\ Nil = Nil$.

$$
\begin{aligned}
&text\ s \diamond best'\ w\ r\ s\ (NilAbove\ s) \\
&= best\ w\ r\ (text\ s \diamond (text\ \text{""}\ \$\$\ x)) \\
&= best\ w\ r\ (text\ s\ \$\$\ nest\ (length\ s)\ x) \\
&= text\ s\ \$\$\ nest\ (length\ s)(best\ (w - length\ s)\ r\ x) \\
&= text\ s \diamond (text\ \text{""}\ \$\$\ best\ (w - length\ s)\ r\ x)
\end{aligned}
$$

so we can take

$$best'\ w\ r\ s\ (NilAbove\ x) = NilAbove\ (best\ (w - length\ s)\ r\ x)$$

For the *TextBeside* case,

$$
\begin{aligned}
&text\ s \diamond best'\ w\ r\ s\ (t\ \text{‘}TextBeside\text{‘}x) \\
&= best\ w\ r\ (text\ s \diamond text\ s \diamond x) \\
&= text\ s \diamond text\ t \diamond best'\ w\ r\ (s \mathbin{++} t)\ x
\end{aligned}
$$

so we can take

$$best'\ w\ r\ s\ (t\ \text{‘}TextBeside\text{‘}x) = t\ \text{‘}TextBeside\text{‘}best'\ w\ r\ (s \mathbin{++} t)\ x$$

The *Nest* case is very simple:

$$
\begin{aligned}
text\ s \diamond best'\ w\ r\ s\ (Nest\ k\ x) &= best\ w\ r\ (text\ s \diamond nest\ k\ x) \\
&= best\ w\ r\ (text\ s \diamond x) \\
&= text\ s \diamond best'\ w\ r\ s\ x
\end{aligned}
$$

so $best'\ w\ r\ s\ (Nest\ k\ x) = best'\ w\ r\ s\ x$. Finally,

$$text\ s \Diamond best'\ w\ r\ s\ (x\ 'Union'y)$$
$$= best\ w\ r\ (text\ s \Diamond (x \cup y))$$
$$= best\ w\ r\ (text\ s \Diamond x)\nabla_r^w best\ w\ r\ (text\ s \Diamond y)$$
$$= (text\ s \Diamond best'\ w\ r\ s\ x)\nabla_r^w(text\ s \Diamond best'\ w\ r\ s\ y)$$
$$= text\ s \Diamond (best'\ w\ r\ s\ x\ \nabla_r^{w'}(s)\ best'\ w\ r\ s\ y)$$

where we have introduced a new operator whose defining property is that

$$text\ s \Diamond (x\ \nabla_r^{w'}(s)\ y) = (text\ s \Diamond x)\nabla_r^w(text\ s \Diamond y)$$

But recall that because of the invariant that *Unions* satisfy, ∇_r^w chooses its left argument if and only if its first line is nice. But if s is already longer than $(w\ 'min'r)$, then no *text* $s \Diamond x$ can have a nice first line. So in this case $\nabla_r^{w'}(s)$ can choose its right argument without looking at either one! This is the optimisation we have been trying to capture: just by looking at the common prefix we can select the right branch, and thereby the vertical form for the *sep* from which the *Union* came. The complete definition of *best* appears in figure 16.

$$best\ w\ r\ Nil = Nil$$
$$best\ w\ r\ (NilAbove\ x) = NilAbove\ (best\ w\ r\ x)$$
$$best\ w\ r\ (s\ 'TextBeside'x) = s\ 'TextBeside'best'\ w\ r\ s\ x$$
$$best\ w\ r\ (Nest\ k\ x) = Nest\ k\ (best\ (w-k)\ r\ x)$$
$$best\ w\ r\ (x\ 'Union'y) = nicest\ w\ r\ (best\ w\ r\ x)\ (best\ w\ r\ y)$$
$$best\ w\ r\ Empty = \infty$$

$$best'\ w\ r\ s\ Nil = Nil$$
$$best'\ w\ r\ s\ (NilAbove\ x) = NilAbove\ (best\ (w-length\ s)\ r\ x)$$
$$best'\ w\ r\ s\ (t\ 'TextBeside'x) = t\ 'TextBeside'best'\ w\ r\ (s \mathbin{+\!\!+}t)x$$
$$best'\ w\ r\ s\ (Nest\ k\ x) = best'\ w\ r\ s\ x$$
$$best'\ w\ r\ s\ (x\ 'Union'y) = nicest'\ w\ r\ s\ (best'\ w\ r\ s\ x)\ (best'\ w\ r\ s\ y)$$
$$best'\ w\ r\ s\ Empty = \infty$$
$$nicest\ w\ r\ x\ y = nicest'\ w\ r\ ""\ x\ y$$

$$nicest'\ w\ r\ s\ x\ y = \textbf{if}\ fits\ (w\ 'min'r)\ (length\ s)\ x\ \textbf{then}\ x\ \textbf{else}\ y$$

$$fits\ n\ k\ x = \textbf{if}\ n < k\ \textbf{then false else}$$

$$\begin{array}{ll}
\textbf{case}\ x\ \textbf{of} & \\
\quad Nil & \to \textbf{true} \\
\quad NilAbove\ y & \to \textbf{true} \\
\quad t\ 'TextBeside'y & \to fits\ n\ (k + length\ t)\ y \\
\quad \infty & \to \textbf{false}
\end{array}$$

Fig. 16. The optimised definition of *best*.

Once again minor improvements can be made to the implementation. Quite a substantial speed-up is obtained by storing strings with their length — that is, strings are represented within the library by a pair of their length and their characters.

String concatenation is used heavily in the library and is performed in constant time: it consists of addition of the lengths and composition of the characters, which are represented by a function as in section 4.2.

This implementation of the library is a major improvement on the previous ones. There are no 'embarrassing pauses'. While the cost of pretty-printing seems to grow slightly faster than linearly, the library is able to produce large outputs (>200K) in little space and reasonable time. On a SPARC ELC a benchmark program with deeply nested *seps* evaluated between 500 and 1000 *seps* per second. Performance is quite acceptable, and far superior to both the earlier term-based implementation (sometimes $O(n^2)$) and the seat-of-the-pants implementation (which was actually sometimes exponential).

10 A Context-passing Pretty-printer

The key observation in the development of the efficient combinators in the last section was that

$$sep\ ((text\ s \diamond x) : xs) = text\ s \diamond sep\ ((text\ "" \diamond x) : map\ (nest\ (-length\ s))\ xs)$$

and so we can 'factor out' all the text in the first element of a *sep* before splitting the computation into a *Union* of two alternatives. We exploited the observation by making *text s* $\diamond$ *x* into a simplified form, and testing for it in *sep*. But we could equally well have derived a context-passing implementation, in which *text* tests for the presence of an enclosing *sep*. Indeed, it seems natural to think of a *Doc* as a function that chooses a layout depending on the context, and this is how the very first implementation of the combinators was constructed.

What kind of contexts should we consider? Certainly observations of the form *best w r* [•] — that is, we should be able to lay out a document with a given page and ribbon width. We will also need to lay out documents with a given indentation, that is consider contexts of the form *best w r* (*nest k* [•]). If we take $k = 0$ then this form subsumes the first.

Now imagine that a union appears in such a context. We can simplify as follows:

$$best\ w\ r\ (nest\ k\ (x \cup y)) = best\ w\ r\ (nest\ k\ x)\nabla_r^w best\ w\ r\ (nest\ k\ y)$$

We expect to continue working on x, so we must be able to represent contexts of the form *best w r* (*nest k* [•])$\nabla_r^w b$ also. We can think of b as the layout to choose if we are forced to backtrack. Once again, the conditions on unions will enable us to decide which of x and b to choose purely on the basis of the value of x.

Of course, in order to apply the key optimisation we must be able to recognise when a document is the first element of an enclosing *sep*. We shall therefore need contexts of the form $C[sep\ [[•], y_1 \ldots y_n]]$. Moreover, the optimisation applies to documents of the form *text s* $\diamond$ *x*. But when such a document appears at the top level, we shall need to evaluate

$$best\ w\ r\ (nest\ k\ (text\ s \diamond x))$$

To do so we must be able to evaluate x, and we therefore need to be able to represent its context in this expression. We shall add contexts of the form $C[text\ s \Leftrightarrow [\bullet]]$ to cover this case.

When we lay out $x \Leftrightarrow y$ and $x\ \$\$\ y$, we shall start by laying out x. We therefore have to represent the contexts $C[[\bullet] \Leftrightarrow y]$ and $C[[\bullet]\ \$\$\ y]$. And when we expand a *sep* into a union of two alternatives, the horizontal alternative appears inside *fit*. We must therefore represent contexts of the form $C[fit\ [\bullet]]$ also.

So we choose contexts of the forms

$$C[\bullet] ::= best\ N\ N\ (nest\ N\ [\bullet])$$
$$|\quad best\ N\ N\ (nest\ N\ [\bullet]) \nabla_r^w E$$
$$|\quad C[text\ s \Leftrightarrow [\bullet]]$$
$$|\quad C[sep\ [[\bullet], E \dots E]]$$
$$|\quad C[fit\ [\bullet]]$$
$$|\quad C[[\bullet] \Leftrightarrow E]$$
$$|\quad C[[\bullet]\ \$\$\ E]$$

where N represents integer expressions, and E represents document expressions. Contexts can be represented by the following Haskell datatype:

$$\textbf{data}\ Cxt\ =\ BestNest\ Int\ Int\ Int$$
$$|\quad BestNestOr\ Int\ Int\ Int\ Doc$$
$$|\quad TextBeside\ String\ Cxt$$
$$|\quad Sep\ [Doc]\ Cxt$$
$$|\quad Fit\ Cxt$$
$$|\quad Beside\ Doc\ Cxt$$
$$|\quad Above\ Doc\ Cxt$$

Must we consider such complex contexts, or can we apply the laws of the pretty-printing algebra to simplify them? Unfortunately, we have been unable to eliminate any of the forms of context given above. Certainly, some context simplifications are possible. In particular, we can always move *TextBeside* up to the top level — this is after all the observation that the key optimisation is based on. But we cannot usefully combine *TextBeside* with the enclosing *BestNest* or *BestNestOr*, because there would then be no way to express a *BestNest* without a *TextBeside*: no instance of

$$best\ w\ r\ (nest\ k\ (text\ s \Leftrightarrow [\bullet]))$$

is equal to

$$best\ w\ r\ (nest\ k\ [\bullet])$$

because $text\ ""\ \Leftrightarrow x \neq x$ in general.

We can also use the facts

$$fit\ (x\ \$\$\ y) = \emptyset$$
$$sep\ ((x\ \$\$\ y) : zs) = x\ \$\$\ y\ \$\$\ foldr1\ (\$\$)zs$$
$$(x\ \$\$\ y)\ \$\$\ z = x\ \$\$\ (y\ \$\$\ z)$$
$$(x\ \$\$\ y) \Leftrightarrow z = x\ \$\$\ (y \Leftrightarrow z)$$

to simplify contexts in which *Above* occurs inside *Fit, Sep, Above* or *Beside*. If we could always move *Above* to the top level, we could apply

$$best \ w \ r \ (nest \ k \ (x \ \$\$ \ y)) = best \ w \ r \ (nest \ k \ x) \ \$\$ \ best \ w \ r \ (nest \ k \ y)$$

But alas, we cannot simplify *text s* $\diamond$ $(x \ \$\$ \ y)$ without knowing more about x.

In fact there is no form of context which can *always* be simplified away, and we must just work with this rather complex set.

Now that the contexts have been chosen, the actual derivation of an implementation follows exactly the same method as in earlier sections. We will not go through the details. We simply remark that, just as in the previous section, the implementation has a space leak. 'Pending' applications of *nest* fill up the heap. And to avoid this, just as in the previous section, we combine an application of *nest* with other operators. In this case we define two forms of context with a 'built-in' *nest*:

$$AboveNest \ k \ y \ C = C[[\bullet] \ \$\$ \ nest \ k \ y]$$
$$SepNest \ k \ ys \ C = C[sep \ ([\bullet] : map \ (nest \ k) \ ys)]$$

In the derived implementation, when we exploit

$$sep \ ((text \ s \ \diamond \ x) : xs) = text \ s \ \diamond \ sep \ ((text \ "" \ \diamond \ x) : map \ (nest \ (-length \ s)) \ xs)$$

and the corresponding property for (\$\$), we just have to change a number in x's context, instead of building applications of *nest*.

Evaluation of the Context-passing Combinators This version of the pretty-printing library is definitely more complex than the term-based versions, as a consequence of the rather complex forms of context we were forced to work with. It is also harder to modify: in particular, a change to the way the best layout is chosen would have far reaching effects. In the term-based libraries, *best* is a separate function and may be replaced with another without altering the rest of the library. But in the context-passing library, every combinator knows how to behave in a *BestNest* context: the criterion for selecting the best layout is distributed throughout the code.

This could be a fair price to pay for better performance. But at least in my implementation, the context passing library is (a little) slower than the term based one, and uses (a little) more space. Its only advantage seems to be that it does not require lazy evaluation, as the term based library does (to make traversing one path through an enormous tree efficient). If one were to reimplement the pretty-printing library in a strict functional language such as ML, the context passing version might prove more efficient than simulating laziness with references and nullary functions.

Relationship to the Original Implementation The first implementation of the pretty-printing combinators was indeed based on context-passing, with contexts represented by a five-tuple containing the page width, ribbon width, length of text to the left (*c.f.* $C[text \ s \ \diamond \ [\bullet]]$), a boolean forcing a one-line layout (*c.f.* $C[fit \ [\bullet]]$), and a boolean indicating whether the surrounding context was horizontal or vertical. Such a design seems natural, if one intuitively expects a pretty-printer just to maintain a little state (the context) to guide layout choices. But as we have seen, this context information is not sufficient to implement the correct behaviour of the combinators — which was an obstacle to the *discovery* of the simple specification they now satisfy.

Moreover the performance of the combinators was poor, at first exponential in the depth of *sep*-nesting, later improved to square. Further optimisations were hard to find, because of the lack of a good algebra, and no doubt also because of the necessary complexity of the solution — the efficient context-passing library described in this section is nothing one would stumble on by accident.

The first implementation was developed rapidly, and its usefulness was certainly an inspiration to develop the solutions presented in this chapter. But in retrospect, the seemingly natural choice of a context-passing implementation was unfortunate. Abandoning that choice, and working with a more abstract specification and systematic program development, led both to better behaviour and much more efficient implementations.

11   A Comparison with Oppen's Pretty-printer

The classic work in 'language independent pretty-printing' is Oppen's pretty-printer [3]. He defined a small language for expressing documents, and an interpreter for the language which generates a pretty layout. The output of a user's pretty-printer is thus intended to be piped through the interpreter. The interpreter is written in an imperative language, and its space requirements are small.

The similarity between Oppen's language and my pretty-printing combinators is striking. Oppen provides equivalents of *text*, *sep*, and *nest*, and his language can also express ($\diamondsuit$), although well-formed documents should not contain it. Oppen also provides a variant of *sep* which places as many elements as will fit on one line, then places more on the next line, and so on. An equivalent combinator could very usefully be added to my pretty-printing library.

On the other hand, Oppen's interpreter is quite large and hard to understand. His paper describes its behaviour for 'well-formed' inputs, but the interpreter accepts a wider class of inputs, and its behaviour on the others is hard to predict. The interpreter defines the meaning of every program, but in a monolithic way — there is no way to describe the meaning of one construct in isolation. Moreover it isn't clear which of the possible layouts the interpreter actually chooses. One way to regard the pretty-printing combinators is as a candidate for a denotational semantics of Oppen's language.

Oppen's interpreter is probably more efficient than our combinators, but on the other hand our libraries are probably easier to modify. For example, to make the pretty-printer look ahead a few lines and avoid imminent line overflows by breaking lines earlier, rather than making decisions only on the basis of the current line, we would just need to redefine the *best* function. At least with the first two implementations we described, the other combinators could be reused as they are. It is not at all clear what changes would need to be made to Oppen's interpreter to achieve the same effect.

Exercise 5. Specify and implement Oppen's *sep*-variant, which allows several elements per line in a vertical layout. *Warning* this is a substantial exercise!

12 Conclusions

In this chapter we have considered the design of combinator libraries. We saw how studying the algebraic properties of the combinators desired can both help to suggest natural choices of representation, and guide the implementation of the operators. We saw several examples — lists, monads, and a pretty-printing library. For this kind of program development we need a language with higher-order functions and lazy evaluation, for which equational reasoning is valid; in other words, Haskell is ideally suited.

In the case of pretty-printing, studying the algebra led to the correction of a subtle error in the combinators' behaviour, and to the development of much more efficient implementations. The pretty-printing algebra is just too intricate to rely on intuition alone: working informally I could not see how to implement the optimisation considered in section 9, nor could I invent the representation used there. The formal approach has been invaluable.

The pretty-printing library itself has proved useable, despite its simplicity. Indeed, versions of it have seen quite extensive use, in program transformation tools, proof assistants, and compilers. All the pretty-printers in both the Chalmers and the Glasgow Haskell compilers are written using variants of this design.

References

1. Lennart Augustsson, *Haskell B. user's manual*, available over WWW from http://www.cs.chalmers.se:80/pub/haskell/chalmers/.
2. Konstantin Läufer, *Combining Type Classes and Existential Types*, Proc. Latin American Informatics Conference (PANEL), ITESM-CEM, Mexico, September 1994.
3. Derek C. Oppen, *Pretty-printing*, in ACM Transactions on Programming Languages and Systems, Vol. 2, No. 4, October 1980.

A The Optimised Pretty-printing Library

```
module NewPP(Doc,(<>),($$),text,sep,nest,pretty) where
import Seq

infixl <>
infixl $$

data Doc = Nil                    -- text ""
          | NilAbove Doc          -- text "" $$ x
          | Str 'TextBeside' Doc-- text s <> x
          | Nest Int Doc          -- nest k x
          | Doc 'Union' Doc       -- x U y
          | Empty                 -- {}
          deriving (Text)

type Str = (Int,String->String)
   -- optimised rep of strings: fast length, fast concat.
len (i,_) = i
(i,s) 'cat' (j,t) = (i+j,s.t)
str s = (length s,(s++))
string (i,s) = s []

text s = str s 'TextBeside' Nil

nest k x = Nest k x

x $$ y = aboveNest x 0 y

aboveNest Nil k y = NilAbove (nest k y)
aboveNest (NilAbove x) k y = NilAbove (aboveNest x k y)
aboveNest (s 'TextBeside' x) k y =
  seq k'
  (s 'TextBeside' (aboveNest (Nil<>x) k' y))
  where k' = k-len s
aboveNest (Nest k' x) k y =
  seq k'' (Nest k' (aboveNest x k'' y))
  where k'' = k-k'
aboveNest (x 'Union' y) k z =
  aboveNest x k z 'Union' aboveNest y k z
aboveNest Empty k x = Empty
```

```
Nil <> (Nest k x) = Nil <> x
Nil <> x = x
NilAbove x <> y = NilAbove (x <> y)
(s 'TextBeside' x) <> y = s 'TextBeside' (x <> y)
Nest k x <> y = Nest k (x <> y)
Empty <> y = Empty
(x 'Union' y) <> z = (x <> z) 'Union' (y <> z)


sep [x] = x
sep (x:ys) = sep' x 0 ys


sep' Nil k ys = fit (foldl (<+>) Nil ys)
                'Union' vertical Nil k ys
sep' (NilAbove x) k ys = vertical (NilAbove x) k ys
sep' (s 'TextBeside' x) k ys =
  s 'TextBeside' sep' (Nil <> x) (k-len s) ys
sep' (Nest n x) k ys = Nest n (sep' x (k-n) ys)
sep' (x 'Union' y) k ys = sep' x k ys 'Union' vertical y k ys
sep' Empty k ys = Empty


vertical x k ys = x $$ nest k (foldr1 ($$) ys)
x <+> y = x <> text " " <> y


fit Nil = Nil
fit (NilAbove x) = Empty
fit (s 'TextBeside' x) = s 'TextBeside' (fit x)
fit (Nest n x) = Nest n (fit x)
fit (x 'Union' y) = fit x
fit Empty = Empty

best w r Nil = Nil
best w r (NilAbove x) = NilAbove (best w r x)
best w r (s 'TextBeside' x) = s 'TextBeside' best' w r s x
best w r (Nest k x) = Nest k (best (w-k) r x)
best w r (x 'Union' y) = nicest w r (best w r x) (best w r y)
best w r Empty = Empty

best' w r s Nil = Nil
best' w r s (NilAbove x) = NilAbove (best (w-len s) r x)
best' w r s (t 'TextBeside' x) =
  t 'TextBeside' best' w r (s 'cat' t) x
best' w r s (Nest k x) = best' w r s x
best' w r s (x 'Union' y) =
  nicest' w r s (best' w r s x) (best' w r s y)
best' w r s Empty = Empty
```

```
nicest w r x y = nicest' w r (str "") x y
nicest' w r s x y = if fits (w 'min' r) (len s) x then x else y

fits n k x = if n<k then False else
                case x of
                  Nil -> True
                  NilAbove y -> True
                  t 'TextBeside' y -> fits n (k+len t) y
                  Empty -> False

layout k (Nest k' x) = layout (k+k') x
layout k x = [' ' | i<-[1..k]] ++ layout' k x

layout' k Nil = "\n"
layout' k (NilAbove x) = "\n" ++ layout k x
layout' k (s 'TextBeside' x) = string s ++ layout' (k+len s) x

pretty w r d = layout 0 (best w r d)
```

Functional Programming with Overloading and Higher-Order Polymorphism

Mark P. Jones

Department of Computer Science, University of Nottingham, University Park, Nottingham NG7 2RD, UK.

Abstract. The Hindley/Milner type system has been widely adopted as a basis for statically typed functional languages. One of the main reasons for this is that it provides an elegant compromise between flexibility, allowing a single value to be used in different ways, and practicality, freeing the programmer from the need to supply explicit type information.

Focusing on practical applications rather than implementation or theoretical details, these notes examine a range of extensions that provide more flexible type systems while retaining many of the properties that have made the original Hindley/Milner system so popular. The topics discussed, some old, but most quite recent, include higher-order polymorphism and type and constructor class overloading. Particular emphasis is placed on the use of these features to promote modularity and reusability.

1   Introduction

The Hindley/Milner type system [6, 19, 3], hereafter referred to as HM, represents a significant and highly influential step in the development of type systems for functional programming languages. In our opinion, the main reason for this is that it combines the following features in a single framework:

- **Type security**: soundness results guarantee that well-typed programs cannot 'go wrong'. This should be compared with the situation in dynamically typed languages like Scheme where run-time tests are often required to check that appropriate types of value are used in a particular context, and the execution of a program may terminate if these tests fail.
- **Flexibility**: polymorphism allows the use and definition of functions that behave uniformly over all types. This should be compared with the situation in monomorphically typed languages where it is sometimes necessary to produce several versions of a particular function or algorithm to deal with different types of values. Standard examples include swapping a pair of values, choosing the minimum of two values, sorting an array of values, etc.
- **Type inference**: there is an effective algorithm which can be used to determine that a given program term is well-typed and, in addition, to calculate its most general (principal) type, without requiring any type annotations in the source program. In practice, even though it is not required, programmers often choose to include explicit type information in a program as a form of

documentation. In this case, the programmer benefits from a useful consistency check that is obtained automatically by comparing the declared types with the results of the type inference algorithm.

- **Ease of implementation**: the type inference algorithm is easy to implement and behaves well in practice. Polymorphism itself is also easy to implement, for example, by using a uniform (or *boxed*) representation that is independent of the type of the values concerned.

As a result, HM has been used as a basis for several widely used functional languages including Hope [2], Standard ML [20], Miranda[1] [27] and Haskell [7].

The features listed above make HM an attractive choice for language designers, but we should also recognize that it has some significant limitations. In particular, while HM polymorphism allows the definition of functions that behave uniformly over all types, it does not permit:

- **Restricted polymorphism/overloading**: the use or definition of functions that are can be used for some, but not necessarily all, types, with potentially different behaviours in each case.
- **Higher-order polymorphism**: the use or definition of functions that behave uniformly over all type constructors.
- **Polymorphic arguments**: the use or definition of functions with polymorphic arguments that can be used at different instances in the body of the function.

These notes describe how the first two of these restrictions can be relaxed, while preserving many of the properties that have made HM so popular. The third item, to permit the use of function arguments with polymorphic components, is a topic of current research. For example, one approach that we are investigating is to use explicit type annotations to supplement the results of type inference. However, for reasons of space, this will not be addressed any further here.

Our main aim is to illustrate practical applications of these extended type systems using a variety of functional programming examples. To this end, we avoid the distraction of long technical discussions about either the underlying type theory or the implementation; these have already been covered in depth elsewhere. We place particular emphasis on the use of these extensions to promote modularity, extensibility and reusability at the level of the core language[2].

The main subjects of these notes are illustrated in Fig. 1. We start with a brief review of the original Hindley/Milner type system (Sect. 2). The first extension of HM that we consider is to support overloading using a system of *type classes*, as described in Sect. 3. Introduced, at least in the form used here, by Wadler and Blott [30], type classes have been adopted as part of the definition of the standard for the functional programming language Haskell [7]. Type classes are

---

[1] Miranda is a is a trademark (TM) of Research Software Limited.

[2] i.e. for programming in the small. These notes do not address the subject of modularity for programming in the large. Such goals are better met by powerful module systems, for example, the structures and functors of Standard ML.

particularly useful for describing the implementation of standard polymorphic operators such as equality, arithmetic and printing. We also include examples to show how they can be used to provide a flexible framework for other applications.

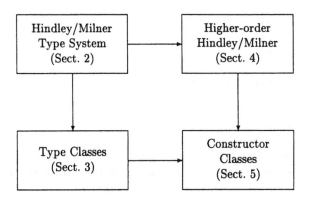

Fig. 1. A summary of the main subjects covered in these notes

Another way to extend HM is to make use of a form of higher-order polymorphism, i.e. polymorphism over type constructors as well as types. This is described in Sect. 4. The generalization to the higher-order case is surprisingly straightforward; it is most useful as a tool for specifying datatypes but it does not significantly increase the expressiveness of the type system as a whole.

However, there is a significant increase in expressiveness when we combine higher-order polymorphism with a class based overloading mechanism, leading to the system of *constructor classes* described in Sect. 5. For example, we show how constructor classes can be used to capture general patterns of recursion of a large family of datatypes, to support the use of monads and to construct modular programming language interpreters.

We assume familiarity with the basic techniques of functional programming, as described by Bird and Wadler [1] for example, and with the concrete syntax and use of Haskell [7] and/or Gofer [12]; these are the languages that were used to develop the examples shown in these notes.

2   The Hindley/Milner Type System

These notes assume that the reader is already familiar with the use of HM in languages like Standard ML or Haskell. However, it seems useful to start with a summary of what we consider the most important features of HM for the purposes of this paper.

The goal of the type system is to assign a type to each part of an input program, guaranteeing that execution of the program will not go wrong, i.e.

that it will not encounter a run-time type error. Terms that cannot be assigned a type will result in a compile-time type error.

One of the most striking differences between HM and many other type systems is the fact that the most general type of a term can be inferred without the need for type annotations. In some cases, the most general type is monomorphic:

```
not        :: Bool -> Bool
not False = True
not True  = False
```

In other cases, the most general type is polymorphic:

```
identity  :: a -> a
identity x = x
```

The type variable a appearing in the type of identity here represents an arbitrary type; if the argument x to identity has type a, then so will the result of identity x. Another simple example is the length function which is used to calculate the length of a list. One way to define length is as follows:

```
length        :: [a] -> Int
length []     = 0
length (x:xs) = 1 + length xs
```

In this example, the appearance of the type variable a in the type of length indicates that this single function length may be applied to any list, regardless of the type of values that it contains.

In some treatments of HM, the types of the identity and length functions about might be written more formally as $\forall a.a \to a$ and $\forall a.[a] \to Int$, respectively, so that polymorphic type variables are explicitly bound by a universal quantifier. These quantifiers are left implicit in the concrete syntax of Haskell. However, it is sometimes convenient to write the types of particular functions using the quantifier notation to emphasize the role of polymorphism.

3 Type Classes

The HM type system is convenient for many applications, but there are some important functions that cannot be given a satisfactory type. There are several well-rehearsed examples, including arithmetic and equality operators, which illustrate this point:

- If we treat addition as a monomorphic function of type Int -> Int -> Int, then it can be used to add integer values, but it is not as general as we might have hoped because it cannot also be used to add floating point quantities. On the other hand, it would not be safe to use a polymorphic type such as a -> a -> a for the addition operator because this allows a to be *any* type, but addition is only defined for numeric types.

– If we treat equality as a monomorphic function of type `T -> T -> Bool` for some type constructor `T`, then it is less general than we might have hoped because it cannot be used to compare values of other types. However, a polymorphic type like `a -> a -> Bool` would not be appropriate because it includes the case where `a` is a function type, and there is no computable equality for functional values.

In both of these examples we find ourselves in a position where monomorphic types are too restrictive and fully polymorphic types are too general. Type classes, described in some detail below, are an attempt to remedy such problems. This is achieved by providing an intermediate step between monomorphic and polymorphic types, i.e. by allowing the definition of values that can be used over a range of types, without requiring that they can be used over *all* types.

3.1 Basic principles

Type classes can be understood and used at several different levels. To begin with, we restrict our attention to the built-in classes of Haskell. Later, we will describe how these classes can be extended, and how new classes can be introduced.

The Haskell *standard prelude* is a large library of useful types, type classes, and functions, that is automatically imported into every Haskell program. The prelude datatypes include Booleans (`Bool`), integers (fixed precision `Int` and arbitrary precision `Integer`), rationals (`Ratio`), complex numbers (`Complex`), floating point values (single precision `Float` and double precision `Double`), characters (`Char`), lists, tuples, arrays, etc.

The prelude also defines a number of *type classes*, which can be thought of as sets of types whose members are referred to as the *instances* of the class. If C is the name of a class and `a` is a type, then we write C `a` to indicate that `a` is an instance of C. Each type class is in fact associated with a collection of operators and this has an influence on the choice of names. For example, the Eq class contains types whose elements can be tested for equality, while the class Ord contains types whose elements are ordered. We will return to this again below, but for the time being, we will continue to think of classes as sets of types.

The instances of a class are defined by a collection of *instance declarations*. For example, the instances of the Eq class are described by the declarations:

```
instance Eq Bool
instance Eq Char
instance Eq Int
instance Eq Integer
instance Eq Float
instance Eq Double
instance Eq a => Eq [a]
instance (Eq a, Eq b) => Eq (a,b)
instance (Eq a, Eq b, Eq c) => Eq (a,b,c)
```

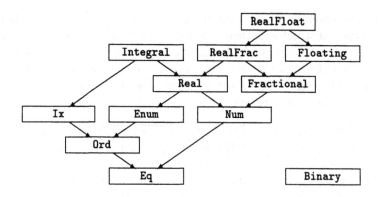

Fig. 2. The hierarchy of standard Haskell type classes

```
instance (Eq a, Eq b, Eq c, Eq d) => Eq (a,b,c,d)
...
```

The first few lines indicate that the types `Bool`, `Char`, `Int`, `Integer`, `Float` and `Double` are instances of `Eq` class. The remaining declarations include a *context* to the left of the `=>` symbol. For example, the `instance Eq a => Eq [a]` declaration can be read as indicating that, if `a` is an instance of `Eq`, then so is the list type `[a]`. The very first declaration tells us that `Bool` is an instance of `Eq`, and hence so are `[Bool]`, `[[Bool]]`, ...

More formally, the effect of these instance declarations is to define `Eq` as the smallest solution of the equation:

$$
\begin{aligned}
\text{Eq} = \ & \{\, \text{Bool, Char, Int, Integer, Float, Double} \,\} \ \cup \\
& \{\, [\tau] \ | \ \tau \in \text{Eq} \,\} \ \cup \\
& \{\, (\tau_1, \tau_2) \ | \ \tau_1, \tau_2 \in \text{Eq} \,\} \ \cup \\
& \{\, (\tau_1, \tau_2, \tau_3) \ | \ \tau_1, \tau_2, \tau_3 \in \text{Eq} \,\} \ \cup \\
& \{\, (\tau_1, \tau_2, \tau_3, \tau_4) \ | \ \tau_1, \tau_2, \tau_3, \tau_4 \in \text{Eq} \,\} \ \cup \\
& \ldots
\end{aligned}
$$

The Haskell prelude defines a number of other classes, as illustrated in Fig. 2. Not all of the standard classes are infinite like `Eq`. For example, the prelude includes instance declarations which defines the classes `Integral` and `RealFloat` of integer and floating point number types, respectively, to be equivalent to:

$$
\begin{aligned}
\text{Integral} \ &= \{\, \text{Int, Integer} \,\} \\
\text{RealFloat} &= \{\, \text{Float, Double} \,\}
\end{aligned}
$$

The prelude also specifies inclusions between different classes; these are illustrated by arrows in Fig. 2. For example, the `Ord` class is a subset of `Eq`: every instance of `Ord` is also an instance of `Eq`. These inclusions are described by a collection of *class declarations* like the following:

```
class Eq a
class (Eq a) => Ord a
class (Eq a, Text a) => Num a
...
```

The last declaration shown here specifies that Num is a subset of both Eq and Text[3]. The inclusions between classes are verified by the compiler, and are of most use in reasoning about whether a particular type is an instance of a given class.

Finally, on top of the type, class, and instance declarations, the standard prelude defines a large collection of primitive values and general purpose functions. Some of the values defined in the prelude have monomorphic types:

```
not      :: Bool -> Bool         -- Boolean negation
ord      :: Char -> Int          -- Character to ASCII code
```

Others have polymorphic types:

```
(++)   :: [a] -> [a] -> [a]      -- List append
length :: [a] -> Int             -- List length
```

There are also a number of functions with restricted polymorphic types:

```
(==)     :: Eq a => a -> a -> Bool   -- Test for equality
min      :: Ord a => a -> a -> a     -- Find minimum
show     :: Text a => a -> String    -- Convert to string
(+)      :: Num a => a -> a -> a     -- Addition
```

We refer to these types as being restricted because they include type class constraints. For instance, the first example tells us that the equality operator, (==), can be treated as a function of type a -> a -> Bool. But the choice for a is not arbitrary; the context Eq a will only be satisfied if a is an instance of Eq. Thus we can use 'a'=='b' to compare character values, or [1,2,3]==[1,2,3] to compare lists of integers, but we cannot use id == id, where id is the identity function, because the class Eq does not contain any function types. In a similar way, the (+) operator can be used to add two integer values or two floating point numbers because these are all instances of Num, but it cannot be used to add two lists, say, because Haskell does not include lists in the Num class; any attempt to add two list values will result in a compile-time type error.

Class constraints may also appear in the types of user-defined functions that make use, either directly or indirectly of prelude functions with restricted polymorphic types. For example, consider the following definitions:

```
> member xs x  = any (x==) xs
> subset xs ys = all (member ys) xs
```

---

[3] This aspect of Haskell syntax can sometimes be confusing. It might have been better if the roles of the expressions on the left and right hand side of => were reversed so that Num a => (Eq a, Text a) could be read as an implication; if a is an instance of Num, then a is also an instance of Eq and Text.

The definition of member takes a list xs of type [a] and a value x of type a, and returns a boolean value indicating whether x is a member of xs; i.e. whether any element of xs is equal to x. Since (==) is used to compare values of type a, it is necessary to restrict our choice of a to instances of Eq. In a similar way, it follows that subset must also have a restricted polymorphic type because it makes use of the member function. Hence the types of these two functions are:

```
> member      :: Eq a => [a] -> a -> Bool
> subset      :: Eq a => [a] -> [a] -> Bool
```

These functions can now be used to work with lists of type [a] for any instance a of Eq. But what if we want to work with user-defined datatypes that were not mentioned in the prelude? In Haskell, this can be dealt with by including a list of classes as part of the datatype definition. For example:

```
> data Day = Sun | Mon | Tue | Wed | Thu | Fri | Sat
>               deriving (Eq, Ord, Text)
```

The second line, deriving (Eq, Ord, Text), is a request to the compiler to extend the three named classes to include the Day datatype, and to generate appropriate versions of any overloaded operators for values of type Day. For example:

```
? member [Mon,Tue,Wed,Thu,Fri] Wed
True
? subset [Mon,Sun] [Mon,Tue,Wed,Thu,Fri]
False
?
```

Instances of a type class that are obtained in this way are described as *derived instances*. In the general case, a derived instance may require a context. For example, the following datatype definition:

```
> data Either a b = Left a | Right b  deriving (Eq, Ord)
```

will result in two derived instances:

```
instance (Eq a, Eq b) => Eq (Either a b)
instance (Ord a, Ord b) => Ord (Either a b)
```

3.2 Defining instances

The simple approach to type classes described above works quite well until you run into a situation where either you want to include a new datatype in a class for which derived instances are either not permitted[4] or not suitable because

---

[4] Haskell only permits derived instances of Eq, Ord, Text, Ix, Enum, and Binary. In some cases, there are additional restrictions on the form of the datatype definition when a derived instance is requested.

the rules for generating versions of overloaded functions do not give the desired semantics. For example, suppose that we define a set datatype using lists to store the members of each set, but without worrying about duplicate values or about the order in which the elements are listed. A datatype definition like:

```
data Set a = Set [a]   deriving (Eq)
```

would result in an implementation of equality satisfying:

```
Set xs == Set ys  =  xs == ys
```

where the equality on the right hand side is the equality on lists. Thus the sets Set [1,2] and Set [2,1,2] would be treated as being distinct because their element lists differ, even though they are intended to represent the same set.

In situations like this, it is possible for a programmer to provide their own semantics for the overloaded operators associated with a particular class. To start with, we need to take a more careful look at the full definition of the Eq class:

```
class Eq a where
     (==), (/=) :: a -> a -> Bool
     x /= y      = not (x == y)
```

This indicates that, to include a type a as an instance of the Eq class, the programmer must supply definitions for the (==) and (/=) functions, both of type a -> a -> Bool. In fact, the final line eases the programmers task a little by providing a *default definition* for (/=) that will be used if the programmer does not give a suitable definition of their own. As a result, all that the programmer has to do is to provide a definition for (==); i.e. to define what it means for two values of type a to be equal.

Returning to the example above, we can define the set datatype as:

```
> data Set a = Set [a]
```

and we use the following in place of a derived instance:

```
> instance Eq a => Eq (Set a) where
>     Set xs == Set ys  =  subset xs ys && subset ys xs
```

This properly captures the intended semantics of set equality, i.e. that two sets are equal precisely when each is a subset of the other, indicating that they have the same members.

It is important to notice that a class can be arbitrarily extended to include new instances, without any modification to the original class definition. This gives a high degree of extensibility and modularity in many cases.

3.3 Defining classes

We have now seen how a programmer can use either derived instances or their own implementations to specify the instances of one the standard Haskell classes. This may be all that some programmers will ever need to know about Haskell type classes. However, for some applications, it is useful for a programmer to be able to define new classes. We will give a number of examples to illustrate this point below.

In defining a new class, the first step is to decide exactly what common properties we expect the instances to share, and to decide how this should be reflected in the choice of the operators listed in the class declaration. However, it is important to recognize that overloading is only appropriate if the meaning of a symbol is uniquely determined by the types of the values that are involved. For instance, some might consider the following example, using classes to describe monoids, as an abuse of the system because monoid structures are not uniquely determined by type.

```
class Monoid a where
  e  :: a
  op :: a -> a -> a

instance Monoid [a] where
  e  = []     -- Empty list
  op = (++)   -- List append

instance Monoid (a -> a) where
  e  = id     -- Identity function
  op = (.)    -- Function composition

instance Monoid Int where
  e  = 0
  op = (+)
```

The final instance declaration here is particularly difficult to justify; there is another equally good way to define a monoid structure on Integers using e=1 and op=(*), i.e. multiplication. There does not seem to be any good reason why we should favour either one of these alternatives over the other.

We hope that the reader will find that most of the applications of type classes in this paper, and of constructor classes in later sections, are well suited to overloading, with a single natural implementation for each instance of a particular overloaded operator.

Trees. From search trees to the representation of parsed terms in a compiler, trees, of one form or another, must rate as one of the most widely used data structures in functional programming. There are many different kinds of tree structure, with variations such as the number of branches out of each node, and the type of values used as labels. The following datatype definitions help to illustrate the point:

- Simple binary trees, with a value of type a at each leaf node.

```
> data BinTree a = Leaf a
>                | BinTree a :^: BinTree a
```

- Labelled trees with a value of type a at each leaf node, and a value of type l at each interior node:

```
> data LabTree l a = Tip a
>                  | LFork l (LabTree l a) (LabTree l a)
```

- Binary search trees, with data values of type a in the body of the tree. These values would typically be used in conjunction with an ordering on the elements of type a in order to locate a particular item in the tree.

```
> data STree a = Empty
>              | Split a (STree a) (STree a)
```

- Rose trees, in which each node is labelled with a value of type a, and may have an arbitrary number of subtrees:

```
> data RoseTree a = Node a [RoseTree a]
```

- Abstract syntax, for example, the following datatype might be used to represent λ-expressions in a simple interpreter. In this case, the leaf nodes correspond to variables while the interior nodes represent either applications or abstractions:

```
> type Name = String
> data Term = Var Name        -- variable
>           | Ap  Term Term   -- application
>           | Lam Name Term   -- lambda abstraction
```

On the other hand, there are some strong similarities between these datatypes, and many familiar concepts, for example, depth, size, paths, subtrees, etc. can be used with any of these different kinds of tree.

Consider the task of calculating the depth of a tree. Normally, it would be necessary to write a different version of the depth calculation for each different kind of tree structure that we are interested in. However, using type classes it is possible to take a more general approach by defining a class of tree-like data types. Starting with the observation that, whichever datatype we happen to be using, every tree has a number of subtrees, we are lead to the following simple characterization of tree-like data structures:

```
> class Tree t where
>     subtrees :: t -> [t]
```

In words, **subtrees** t generates the list of (proper) subtrees of a given tree, t. There are many properties of trees that this does not address, for example, the use of labels, but of course, these are exactly the kind of things that we need to ignore to obtain the desired level of generality.

The following instance declarations can be used to include each of the five tree-like data structures listed above as an instance of the **Tree** class:

```
> instance Tree (BinTree a) where
>     subtrees (Leaf n)  = []
>     subtrees (l :^: r) = [l,r]

> instance Tree (LabTree l a) where
>     subtrees (Tip x)      = []
>     subtrees (LFork x l r) = [l,r]

> instance Tree (STree a) where
>     subtrees Empty        = []
>     subtrees (Split x l r) = [l,r]

> instance Tree (RoseTree a) where
>     subtrees (Node x gts) = gts

> instance Tree Term where
>     subtrees (Var _)   = []
>     subtrees (Ap f x)  = [f,x]
>     subtrees (Lam v b) = [b]
```

With these definitions in place, we can start to construct a library of useful functions that can be applied to any kind of tree that has been included in the **Tree** class. For example, the following definitions can be used to determine the depth and the size (i.e. the number of nodes) in any given tree:

```
> depth  :: Tree t => t -> Int
> depth  = (1+) . foldl max 0 . map depth . subtrees

> size   :: Tree t => t -> Int
> size   = (1+) . sum . map size . subtrees
```

There are more efficient ways to describe these calculations for particular kinds of tree. For example, the definition of **size** for a **BinTree** could be simplified to:

```
  size (Leaf n)  = 1
  size (l :^: r) = size l + size r
```

without constructing the intermediate list of **subtrees**. However, it is entirely possible that this more efficient implementation could be obtained automatically in a compiler, for example, by generating specialized versions of overloaded functions [11].

Another simple example of an algorithm that can be applied to many different kinds of tree is the process of calculating the list of paths from the root node to each of the leaves. In specific cases, we might be tempted to use sequences of labels, or sequences of directions such as 'left' and 'right' to identify a particular path in the tree. Neither of these is possible in our more general framework. Instead, we will identify each path with the corresponding sequence of subtrees. This leads to the following definition:

```
> paths                :: Tree t => t -> [[t]]
> paths t | null br   = [ [t] ]
>         | otherwise = [ t:p | b<-br, p<-paths b ]
>           where br = subtrees t
```

The definitions of depth-first and breadth-first search can also be expressed in our current framework, each yielding a list of subtrees in some appropriate order:

```
> dfs    :: Tree t => t -> [t]
> dfs t   = t : concat (map dfs (subtrees t))

> bfs    :: Tree t => t -> [t]
> bfs     = concat . lev
>   where lev t = [t] : foldr cat [] (map lev (subtrees t))
>         cat   = combine (++)

> combine                   :: (a -> a -> a) -> ([a] -> [a] -> [a])
> combine f (x:xs) (y:ys) = f x y : combine f xs ys
> combine f []      ys    = ys
> combine f xs      []    = xs
```

The depth-first algorithm given here is straightforward. We refer the reader to [8] for further details and explanation of the breadth-first algorithm. It may seem strange to define functions that return the complete list of every subtree in a given tree. But this approach is well-suited to a lazy language where the list produced by the search may not be fully evaluated. For example, if p is some predicate on trees, then we might use the function:

```
head . filter p . dfs
```

to find the first node in a depth first search of a tree that satisfies p, and, once it has been found, there will not be any need to continue the search.

As a final example, we sketch the implementation of a function for drawing character-based diagrams of arbitrary tree values. This might, for example, be useful as a way of visualizing the results of simple tree-based algorithms. The following examples show the output of the function for two different kinds of tree:

```
? drawTree ((Leaf 1 :^: Leaf 2) :^: (Leaf 3 :^: Leaf 4))
--@--@--1
  |  |
  |  '--2
  |
  '--@--3
     |
     '--4

? drawTree (Lam "f" (Ap (Ap (Var "f") (Var "x")) (Var "y")))
--\f--@--@--f
     |  |
     |  '--x
     |
     '--y

?
```

The tree-drawing algorithm is based on a function:

```
> drawTree' :: Tree t => (t -> String) -> t -> [String]
```

The first argument of **drawTree'** is a function of type (t -> String) that produces a text string corresponding to the label (if any) of the root node of a tree of type **t**. The second argument of **drawTree'** is the tree itself. The result of the function is a list of strings, each corresponding to a single line of output, that can be combined using the standard **unlines** function to produce a single string with a newline character after each line.

To save the trouble of specifying a labelling function for **drawTree**, we define a subclass of **Tree** that provides appropriate functions for labelling and drawing:

```
> class Tree t => DrawTree t where
>     drawTree :: t -> String
>     labTree  :: t -> String
>
>     drawTree = unlines . drawTree' labTree
```

For example, the instance declaration that we use for the **Term** datatype is as follows:

```
> instance DrawTree Term where
>     labTree (Var v)   = v
>     labTree (Ap _ _)  = "@"
>     labTree (Lam v _) = "\\"++v
```

We leave the construction of **drawTree'** and the definition of instances of the **DrawTree** class for the other tree types defined above as an exercise for the reader.

Duality and the De Morgan Principle. Our next example is inspired by the work of Turner [26] to extend the concept of duality on Boolean algebras, and the well-known De Morgan principle, to the list datatype. We start by defining a class `Dual` of types with a function `dual` that maps values to appropriate duals:

```
> class Dual a where
>       dual :: a -> a
```

The only property that we will require for an instance of `Dual` is that the corresponding implementation of `dual` is self-inverse:

```
dual . dual = id
```

The easiest way to deal with classes constrained by laws such as this is to treat the laws as proof obligations for each instance of the class that is defined, assuming that the laws are satisfied for each of the subinstances involved.

The first example of duality is the inversion of boolean values given by:

```
> instance Dual Bool where
>       dual = not
```

For example, `dual True = False` and `dual False = True`. It is easy to see that this declaration satisfies the self-inverse property since because `not . not` is the identity on booleans.

To make any further progress, we need to extend the concept of duality to function values:

```
> instance (Dual a, Dual b) => Dual (a -> b) where
>       dual f = dual . f . dual
```

The proof that this satisfies the self-inverse law is straightforward:

```
dual (dual f)
  = { definition of dual, twice }
    dual . dual . f . dual . dual
  = { Assuming dual . dual = id for Dual a, Dual b }
    id . f . id
  = { ((.),id) monoid }
    f
```

The `dual` function distributes over application and composition of functions:

```
dual (f x)    =   (dual f) (dual x)
dual (f . g)  =   dual f . dual g
```

We leave formal verification of these properties as a straightforward exercise for the reader. These laws can be used to calculate duals. For example, consider the definition of conjunction in the Haskell standard prelude:

```
True  && x    = x
False && x    = False
```

Applying `dual` to both sides of each equation and simplifying, we obtain:

```
dual (&&) False x = x
dual (&&) True  x = True
```

which shows that `dual (&&) = (||)`, i.e. that disjunction (or) is the dual of conjunction (and), as we would expect from the standard version of De Morgan's theorem for boolean values.

There are a variety of other applications of duality. Turner's work was motivated by the duality on finite lists that arises from the list reverse function:

```
> instance Dual a => Dual [a] where
>     dual = reverse . map dual
```

If we restrict our attention to finite lists, then `reverse . reverse` is the identity function and it is easy to show that this definition satisfies the self-inverse law. We can make direct use of `dual` in calculations such as:

```
? dual head [1..10]            -- dual head = last
10
? dual tail [1..10]            -- dual tail = init
[1, 2, 3, 4, 5, 6, 7, 8, 9]
? dual (++) [1,2] [3,4]        -- dual (++) = flip (++)
[3, 4, 1, 2]
?
```

The `flip` function referred to in the last example is the Haskell equivalent of the classical W combinator that switches the order of the arguments to a curried function:

```
flip      :: (a -> b -> c) -> (b -> a -> c)
flip f x y = f y x
```

This can also be used to illustrate the use of the duals of the Haskell prelude functions `foldl` an `foldr`, as in the following:

```
? foldl (flip (:)) [] [1..4]
[4, 3, 2, 1]
? dual foldr (:) [] [1..4]
[4, 3, 2, 1]
?
```

In general, the two fold functions are related by the formulae:

```
dual foldr = foldl . flip
dual foldl = foldr . flip
```

We refer the reader to the text by Bird and Wadler [1] for further discussion on the relationship between `foldl` and `foldr`, and on duality for lists.

To conclude our comments about duality, we extend the framework to include integers with unary minus as the `dual` function:

```
> instance Dual Int where
>     dual = negate
```

For example:

```
? dual (+) 3 4      -- dual (+) = (+)
7
? dual max 3 5      -- dual max = min
3
? dual min 3 5      -- dual min = max
5
?
```

Computing with Lattices. A lattice is a partially ordered set with a top and a bottom value in which every pair of elements has a meet (greatest lower bound) and a join (least upper bound). There are many applications for lattices in computer science, particularly in studies of semantics and program analysis. Motivated by the study of *frontiers* and their use in *strictness analysis*, Jones [9] developed a general framework for computing with (finite) lattices using type classes. The result is an elegant system that includes a range of different types of lattice and extends easily to accommodate other kinds of lattice needed for particular applications. This compares very favourably with an earlier implementation of the same ideas that did not use type classes and, because of the limitations imposed by HM, was less robust, more awkward to work with, and harder to extend.

The most important part of Jones' framework is the definition of a class of lattices:

```
> class Eq a => Lattice a where
>     bottom, top :: a
>     meet, join  :: a -> a -> a
>     lt          :: a -> a -> Bool
>     x 'lt' y     = (x 'join' y) == y
```

The lt function, written here as an infix operator, is used to describe the partial order on the elements of the lattice. The default definition for lt shows how it can be defined in terms of the join and equality operators.

The Bool datatype gives one of the simplest examples of a lattice, with meet and join corresponding to conjunction and disjunction, respectively:

```
> instance Lattice Bool where
>     bottom = False
>     top    = True
>     meet   = (&&)
>     join   = (||)
```

Note that we ignore any improper elements of lattice types, in this case, just the bottom element $\bot$ of type Bool, since these values cannot be used without risking abnormal- or non-termination.

As a slightly more complex example, we can define the lattice structure of a product of two lattices using the declaration:

```
> instance (Lattice a, Lattice b) => Lattice (a,b) where
>       bottom             = (bottom,bottom)
>       top                = (top,top)
>       (x,y) 'meet' (u,v) = (x 'meet' u, y 'meet' v)
>       (x,y) 'join' (u,v) = (x 'join' u, y 'join' v)
```

It is possible to extend the Lattice class with other kinds of lattice, such as lattices of subsets, lattices of frontiers, lifted lattices, and lattices of functions.

We will use the problem of defining the least fixed point operator as an illustration of the use of the Lattice class. It is well-known that, if f is a monotonic function[5] on some lattice a, then f has a least fixed point which can be obtained as the limit of the sequence:

```
iterate f bottom = [ bottom, f bottom, f (f bottom), ...
```

Assuming that the lattice in question is finite, the limit will be the first (and only) repeated value in this sequence. This translates directly to an algorithm for calculating the least fixed point, fix f:

```
> fix             :: Lattice a => (a -> a) -> a
> fix f            = firstRepeat (iterate f bottom)

> firstRepeat      :: Eq a => [a] -> a
> firstRepeat (x:xs) = if x==head xs then x else firstRepeat xs
```

Building on examples like these, Jones [9] shows how to define general tools for computing with lattices, including an algorithm to enumerate the elements of a finite lattice. It is beyond the scope of these notes to give any further details of these examples here.

4 A Higher-order Hindley/Milner Type System

We have already seen examples showing how HM allows the programmer to generalize with respect to types, suggesting that a polymorphic function has a uniform implementation for a range of different types. For example, the type of the length function in Sect. 2 is $\forall a.[a] \to Int$; this reflects the fact that the elements of a list do not play a part in the calculation of its length. However, HM does not allow us to generalize with respect to type constructors, for example to define a function:

$$\text{size} :: \forall t. \forall a. t(a) \to Int.$$

that could be used to give some measure of the size of an object of type $(t\ a)$ for any type constructor t, and any type a (for instance, we might expect that

---

[5] In the notation used here, this means that f x 'lt' f y, whenever x 'lt' y.

`length` would be a special case of `size`, using the list type constructor in place of the variable t).

At first glance, we may be concerned that a generalization of HM to support this weak form of *higher-order polymorphism* would quickly run into technical difficulties. For example, standard type inference algorithms require the use of a *unification* algorithm to determine when two types are equal. In the higher-order case, we need to be able to compare type constructors which might seem to imply a need for higher-order unification, known to be undecidable. In fact, the generalization of HM to support higher-order polymorphism that is sketched here is surprisingly straightforward. Many of the technical properties of HM, and their proofs, carry over with little or no change. In particular, there is an effective type inference algorithm, based on a (decidable) kinded, first-order unification process[6]. To the best of our knowledge, the only place where this has been described in the past is as an integral part of the system of constructor classes [10] which is the subject of the next section. Our goal here is to highlight the fact that the higher-order extension is independent of any use of overloading.

The extension rests on the use of a *kind* system:

$$\kappa ::= * \qquad monotypes$$
$$| \quad \kappa_1 \to \kappa_2 \; function \; kinds$$

Kinds are used to identify particular families of type constructors in much the same way as types are used to describe collections of values. The $*$ kind represents the set of all monotypes, i.e. nullary type constructors, while the kind $\kappa_1 \to \kappa_2$ represents constructors that take something of kind κ_1 and return something of kind κ_2. For each kind κ, we have a collection of constructors C^κ (including constructor variables α^κ) of kind κ given by:

$$C^\kappa ::= \chi^\kappa \qquad constants$$
$$| \quad \alpha^\kappa \qquad variables$$
$$| \quad C^{\kappa' \to \kappa} \; C^{\kappa'} \; applications$$

This corresponds very closely to the way that most type expressions are already written in Haskell. For example, `List a` is an application of the constructor constant `List` to the constructor variable `a`. In addition, each constructor constant has a corresponding kind. For example, writing `(->)` for the function space constructor and `(,)` for pairing we have:

```
Int, Float, ()     :: *
List, BinTree      :: * -> *
(->), (,), LabTree :: * -> * -> *
```

The task of checking that a given type expression is well-formed can now be reformulated as the task of checking that a given constructor expression has kind $*$. The apparent mismatch between the explicitly kinded constructor expressions

---

[6] This is possible because the language of constructors is built up from constants and applications; in particular, there are no abstractions.

specified above and the implicit kinding used in examples can be resolved by a process of kind inference; i.e. by using standard techniques to infer kinds without the need for programmer supplied kind annotations [10].

Given this summary of the technical issues, we turn our attention to applications of the extended type system. Here, we find that, by itself, higher-order polymorphism is often too general for practical examples. For example, in the case of the `size` function described above, it is hard to construct a definition for any interesting functions of type $\forall t.\forall \alpha.t(\alpha) \rightarrow Int$[7] because we need a definition that will work for *any* type constructor t, and *any* type a. The only possibilities are functions of the form $\lambda x.n$ where n is an integer constant, all of which can be treated as having the more general type $\forall a.a \rightarrow Int$ without the need for higher-order polymorphism.

Even so, higher-order types are still useful, particularly as a means of specifying new datatypes where we can use a mixture of types and type constructors as parameters.

```
data Mu f   = In (f (Mu f))

data NatF s = Zero | Succ s
type Nat    = Mu NatF

data StateT s m a = STM (s -> m (a,s))
```

The first three examples here can be used to provide a general framework for constructing recursive datatypes and corresponding recursion schemes. The fourth example is used to describe a parameterized state monad. Both of these examples will be described in the following section.

The reader may like to check the following kinds for each of the type constructors introduced above.

```
Mu     :: (* -> *) -> *
NatF   :: * -> *
Nat    :: *
StateT :: * -> (* -> *) -> * -> *
```

All of these kinds can be determined automatically without the use of kind annotations.

As a final comment, it is worth noting that the implementation of this form of higher-order polymorphism is straightforward, and that experience with practical implementations, for example, Gofer, suggests that it is also natural from a programmer's perspective.

---

[7] observation that this argument is based on an implicit assumption that we do not have any extra constants that were not included in HM. Adding suitable constants with types that involve higher-order polymorphism would make the type system described here much more powerful.

5   Constructor Classes

Type class overloading and higher-order polymorphism are independent extensions of HM. In this section, we give a number of examples to illustrate the
expressiveness of a system that combines these two ideas. Previously, we have
used classes to represent sets of types, i.e. constructors of kind *, but in this
section, we will use classes to represent sets of constructors of any fixed kind κ.
We will refer to these sets as *constructor classes* [10], including the type classes
of Sect. 3 as a special case.

5.1   Functors

We begin our discussion of constructor classes with a now standard example.
Consider the familiar map function that can be used to apply a function to each
element in a list of values:

```
map           :: (a -> b) -> (List a -> List b)
map f []     = []
map f (x:xs) = f x : map f xs
```

It is well known that map satisfies the following laws:

```
map id        = id
map f . map g = map (f . g)
```

Many functional programmers will be aware that it is possible to define variants of map, each satisfying very similar laws, for many other datatypes. Such
constructions have also been widely studied in the context of category theory
where the observations here might be summarized by saying that the list type
constructor List, together with the map function correspond to a *functor*. This
is an obvious application for overloading because the implementation of a particular variant of map (if it exists) is uniquely determined by the choice of the
type constructor that it involves.

Overloading map. Motivated by the discussion above, we define a constructor
class, Functor with the following definition:

```
> class Functor f where
>     fun :: (a -> b) -> (f a -> f b)
```

Note that we have used the name fun to avoid a conflict with the prelude map
function. Renaming the 'functor' laws above gives:

```
fun id        = id
fun f . fun g = fun (f . g)
```

The following datatypes will be used in later parts of these notes, and all of them
can be treated as functors:

```
> data Id a     = Id a
> type List     = [ ]
> data Maybe a  = Just a | Nothing
> data Error a  = Ok a | Fail String
> data Writer a = Result String a
> type Read r   = (r ->)
```

The syntax in the final example may need a little explanation; (r->) is just a more attractive way of writing the partial application of constructors ((->) r). The whole declaration tells us that the expression Read r should be treated as a synonym for (r->), and hence that (a->b), ((a->) b), and Read a b are equivalent ways of writing the same type constructor. In this case, the type keyword is something of a misnomer since (r->), and hence also Read r, has kind (*->*) rather than just *.

The functor structures for each of these datatypes are captured by the following definitions:

```
> instance Functor Id where
>     fun f (Id x) = Id (f x)
```

```
> instance Functor List where
>     fun f []    = []
>     fun f (x:xs) = f x : fun f xs
```

```
> instance Functor Maybe where
>     fun f (Just x) = Just (f x)
>     fun f Nothing  = Nothing
```

```
> instance Functor Error where
>     fun f (Ok x)   = Ok (f x)
>     fun f (Fail s) = Fail s
```

```
> instance Functor Writer where
>     fun f (Result s x) = Result s (f x)
```

```
> instance Functor (r->) where
>     fun f g = f . g
```

Again, we would draw special attention to the final example. As functional programmers, we tend to think of mapping a function over the elements of a list as being a very different kind of operation to composing two functions. But, in fact, they are both instances of a single concept. This means that, in future functional languages, we could dispense with the use of two different symbols for these two concepts. We might have, for example:

```
f . (xs ++ ys)  =    (f . xs) ++ (f . ys)
(f . g) . xs    =    f . (g . xs)
id . x          =    x
```

Recursion schemes: Functional programming with bananas and lenses.
Functions like map are useful because they package up a particular pattern of
computation in a convenient form as a higher-order function. Algorithms expressed in terms of map are often quite because they hide the underlying recursion over the structure of a list and may be more useful in program calculation
where standard, but general laws for map can be used in place of inductive proof.
The foldr function is another well known example of this, again from the theory
of lists:

```
foldr              :: (a -> b -> b) -> b -> List a -> b
foldr f z []     = z
foldr f z (x:xs) = f x (foldr f z xs)
```

As with map, there are variants of this function for other datatypes. For example,
the fold function for the RoseTree datatype is:

```
> foldRT                :: (a -> [b] -> b) -> RoseTree a -> b
> foldRT f (Node a xs) = f a (map (foldRT f) xs)
```

Given that foldr and foldRT don't even have the same number of parameters,
it will probably seem unlikely that we will be able to use overloading to view
these two functions as instances of a single concept.

In fact, it is possible to do just this, provided that we are prepared to adopt a
more uniform way of defining recursive datatypes. These ideas have already been
widely studied from a categorical perspective where datatypes are constructed as
fixed points of functors. The general version of a fold function is often described
as a *catamorphism* and there is a dual notion of an *anamorphism*. It is common
to use the notation $(\!|\phi|\!)$ for a catamorphism, and $[\![\psi]\!]$ for an anamorphism.
Inspired by the shape of the brackets used here, the use of these operators has
been described as 'functional programming with bananas and lenses' [17]. The
remainder of this section shows how these ideas can be implemented directly
using constructor classes. These ideas are dealt with in more detail elsewhere
in this volume. A more detailed overview of our implementation can be found
elsewhere [18].

We start by defining a datatype for constructing fixed points of unary type
constructors:

```
> data Mu f  = In (f (Mu f))
```

Ideally, we would like to view the In constructor as an isomorphism of f (Mu f)
and Mu f with the inverse isomorphism given by:

```
> out        :: Mu f -> f (Mu f)
> out (In x) = x
```

Unfortunately, the semantics of Haskell treats In as a non-strict constructor,
so these functions are not actually isomorphisms. We will not concern ourselves
any further with this rather technical point here, except to note that there have

been several proposals to extend Haskell with mechanisms that would allow us to define these functions as true isomorphisms.

Now, choosing an appropriate functor as a parameter, we can use the Mu constructor to build recursive types:

– Natural numbers: the datatype Nat of natural numbers is defined as the fixed point of a functor NatF:

```
> type Nat    = Mu NatF
> data NatF s = Zero | Succ s

> instance Functor NatF where
>     fun f Zero      = Zero
>     fun f (Succ x) = Succ (f x)
```

For convenience, we define names for the zero natural number and for the successor function:

```
> zero   :: Nat
> zero   = In Zero

> succ   :: Nat -> Nat
> succ x = In (Succ x)
```

For example, the number 1 is represented by one = succ zero.

– Lists of integers: Following the same pattern as above, we define the type IntList as the fixed point of a functor IntListF, and we introduce convenient names for the constructors:

```
> type IntList    = Mu IntListF
> data IntListF a = Nil | Cons Int a

> instance Functor IntListF where
>     fun f Nil        = Nil
>     fun f (Cons n x) = Cons n (f x)

> nil      = In Nil
> cons x xs = In (Cons x xs)
```

– Rose trees: Again, we follow a similar pattern:

```
> type RoseTree a    = Mu (RoseTreeF a)
> data RoseTreeF a b = Node a [b]

> instance Functor (RoseTreeF a) where
>     fun f (Node x ys) = Node x (map f ys)

> node    :: a -> [RoseTree a] -> RoseTree a
> node x ys = In (Node x ys)
```

The general definitions of catamorphisms and anamorphisms can be expressed directly in this framework, writing cata phi and ana psi for $(\!|\phi|\!)$ and $[\![\psi]\!]$, respectively:

```
> cata         :: Functor f => (f a -> a) -> Mu f -> a
> cata phi     = phi . fun (cata phi) . out

> ana          :: Functor f => (a -> f a) -> a -> Mu f
> ana   psi    = In . fun (ana psi) . psi
```

To illustrate the use of these recursions schemes, consider the following definitions for arithmetic on natural numbers (addition, multiplication and exponentiation):

```
> addNat n m   = cata (\fa -> case fa of
>                               Zero    -> m
>                               Succ x -> succ x) n
> mulNat n m   = cata (\fa -> case fa of
>                               Zero    -> zero
>                               Succ x -> addNat m x) n
> expNat n m   = cata (\fa -> case fa of
>                               Zero    -> one
>                               Succ x -> mulNat n x) m
```

The same recursion schemes can be used with other datatypes as shown by the following implementations of functions to calculate the length of a list of integers and to append two lists. The final example uses an anamorphism to construct an infinite list of integers:

```
> len         = cata (\fa -> case fa of
>                             Nil         -> zero
>                             Cons z zs -> succ zs)

> append xs ys = cata (\fa -> case fa of
>                             Nil         -> ys
>                             Cons z zs -> cons z zs) xs

> intsFrom    = ana (\n -> Cons n (n+1))
```

5.2 Monads

Motivated by the work of Moggi [21] and Spivey [24], Wadler [29, 28] has proposed a style of functional programming based on the use of *monads*. Wadler's main contribution was to show that monads, previously studied in depth in the context of abstract category theory [16], could be used as a practical method for structuring functional programming, and particularly for modelling 'impure' features in a purely functional setting.

One useful way to think about monads is as a means of representing computations. If m is a monad, then an object of type m a represents a computation that is expected to produce a result of type a. The choice of monad reflects the (possible) use of particular programming language features as part of the computation. Simple examples include state, exceptions and input/output. The distinction between computations of type m a and values of type a reflects the fact that the use of programming language features is a property of the computation itself and not of the result that it produces.

Every monad provides at least two operations. First, there must be some way to return a result from a computation. We will use an expression of the form result e to represent a computation that returns the value e with no further effect, where result is a function:

```
result :: a -> m a
```

corresponding to the unit function in Wadler's presentations.

Second, to describe the way that computations can be combined, we use a function:

```
bind :: m a -> (a -> m b) -> m b
```

Writing bind as an infix operator, we can think of c 'bind' f as a computation which runs c, passes the result x of type a to f, and runs the computation f x to obtain a final result of type b. In many cases, this corresponds to sequencing of one computation after another.

The description above leads to the following definition for a constructor class of monads:

```
> class Functor m => Monad m where
>     result :: a -> m a
>     bind   :: m a -> (a -> m b) -> m b
```

The monad operators, result and bind, are required to satisfy some simple algebraic laws, that are not reflected in this class declaration. For further information, we refer the reader to the more detailed presentations of monadic programming in this volume.

One well-known application of monads is to model programs that make use of an internal state. Computations of this kind can be represented by *state transformers*, i.e. by functions of type s -> (a,s), mapping an initial state to a result value paired with the final state. For the system of constructor classes in this paper, state transformers can be represented using the datatype:

```
> data State s a = ST (s -> (a,s))
```

The functor and monad structures for state transformers are as follows:

```
> instance Functor (State s) where
>     fun f (ST st) = ST (\s -> let (x,s') = st s in (f x, s'))
```

```
> instance Monad (State s) where
>     result x   = ST (\s -> (x,s))
>     m 'bind' f = ST (\s -> let ST m'  = m
>                                (x,s1) = m' s
>                                ST f'  = f x
>                                (y,s2) = f' s1
>                            in  (y,s2))
```

Note that the State constructor has kind * -> * -> * so that, for any state type s, the constructor State s has kind * -> * as required for instances of the Functor and Monad classes. We refer the reader to other sources [28, 29, 10] for examples illustrating the use of state monads.

Many of the datatypes that we described as functors in the previous section can also be given a natural monadic structure:

- The identity monad has little practical use on its own, but provides a trivial base case for use with the monad transformers that are described in later sections.

```
> instance Monad Id where
>     result        = Id
>     Id x 'bind' f = f x
```

- The list monad is useful for describing computations that may produce a sequence of zero or more results.

```
> instance Monad List where
>     result x          = [x]
>     []       'bind' f = []
>     (x:xs)   'bind' f = f x ++ (xs 'bind' f)
```

- The Maybe monad has been used to model programs that either produce a result (by returning a value of the form Just e) or raise an exception (by returning a value of the form Nothing).

```
> instance Monad Maybe where
>     result x        = Just x
>     Just x  'bind' f = f x
>     Nothing 'bind' f = Nothing
```

- The Error monad is closely related to the Maybe datatype, but attaches a string error message to any computation that does not produce a value.

```
> instance Monad Error where
>     result          = Ok
>     Ok x     'bind' f = f x
>     Fail msg 'bind' f = Fail msg
```

- The `Writer` monad is used to allow a program to produce both an output string[8] and a return value.

```
> instance Monad Writer where
>     result x              = Result "" x
>     Result s x 'bind' f = Result (s ++ s') y
>                           where Result s' y = f x
```

- A `Reader` monad is used to allow a computation to access the values held in some enclosing environment (represented by the type `r` in the following definitions).

```
> instance Monad (r->) where
>     result x          = \r -> x
>     x 'bind' f        = \r -> f (x r) r
```

As a passing comment, it is interesting to note that these two functions are just the standard K and S combinators of combinatory logic.

Operations on Monads. From a user's point of view, the most interesting properties of a monad are described, not by the `result` and `bind` operators, but by the additional operations that it supports, for example, to permit access to the state, or to deal with input/output. It would be quite easy to run through the list of monads above and provide a small catalogue of useful operators for each one. For example, we might include an operator to update the state in a `State` monad, or to output a value in a `Writer` monad, or to signal an error condition in an `Error` monad.

In fact, we will take a more forward-thinking approach and use the constructor class mechanisms to define different families of monads, each of which supports a particular collection of simple primitives. The benefit of this is that, later, we will want to consider monads that are simultaneously instances of several different classes, and hence support a combination of different primitive features. This same approach has proved to be very flexible in other recent work [10, 15].

In these notes, we will make use of the following classes of monad:

- **State monads**: The principal characteristic of state based computations is that there is a way to access and update the state. We will represent these two features by a single `update` operator that applies a user supplied function to update the current state, returning the old state as its result.

```
> class Monad m => StateMonad m s where
>     update :: (s -> s) -> m s
```

---

[8] Note that, for a serious implementation of `Writer`, it would be better to use functions of type `ShowS = String -> String` as the output component of the `Writer` monad in place of the strings used here. This is a well-known trick to avoid the worst-case quadratic behaviour of nested calls to the append operator, `(++)`.

The State s monad described above is an obvious example of a StateMonad:

```
> instance StateMonad (State s) s where
>     update f = ST (\s -> (s, f s))
```

Simple uses of a state monad include maintaining an integer counter:

```
> incr     :: StateMonad m Int => m Int
> incr     = update (1+)
```

or generating a sequence of pseudo-random numbers, in this case using the algorithm suggested by Park and Miller [23]:

```
> random  :: StateMonad m Int => Int -> m Int
> random n = update min_stand 'bind' \m ->
>              result (m 'mod' n)

> min_stand  :: Int -> Int
> min_stand n = if test > 0 then test else test + 2147483647
>              where test = 16807 * lo - 2836 * hi
>                    hi   = n 'div' 127773
>                    lo   = n 'mod' 127773
```

— **Error monads**: The main feature of this class of monads is the ability for a computation to fail, producing an error message as a diagnostic.

```
> class Monad m => ErrorMonad m where
>     fail :: String -> m a
```

The Error datatype used above is a simple example of an ErrorMonad:

```
> instance ErrorMonad Error where
>     fail = Fail
```

— **Writer monads**: The most important feature of a writer monad is the ability to output messages.

```
> class Monad m => WriterMonad m where
>     write :: String -> m ()

> instance WriterMonad Writer where
>     write msg = Result msg ()
```

— **Reader monads**: A class of monads for describing computations that consult some fixed environment:

```
> class Monad m => ReaderMonad m r where
>     env    :: r -> m a -> m a
>     getenv :: m r
```

```
> instance ReaderMonad (r->) r where
>       env e c = \_ -> c e
>       getenv  = id
```

To illustrate why this approach is so attractive, consider the following definition:

```
> nxt m = update (m+)   'bind' \n ->
>            if n > 0 then write ("count = " ++ show n)
>                     else fail "count must be positive"
```

The nxt function uses a combination of features: state, error and output. This is reflected in the inferred type:

```
(WriterMonad m, ErrorMonad m, StateMonad m Int) => Int -> m ()
```

In this example, the type inference mechanism records the combination of features that are required for a particular computation, without committing to a particular monad m that happens to meet these constraints[9]. This last point is important for two reasons. First, because we may want to use nxt in a context where some additional features are required, resulting in an extra constraint on m. Second, because there may be several ways to combine a particular combination of features with corresponding variations in semantics. Clearly, it is preferable to retain control over this, rather than leaving the type system to make an arbitrary choice on our behalf.

Monads as substitutions. Up to this point, we have concentrated on the use of monads to describe computations. In fact, monads also have a useful interpretation as a general approach to substitution. This in turn provides another application for constructor classes.

Suppose that a value of type m v represents a collection of terms with 'variables' of type v. Then a function of type w -> m v can be thought of as a substitution, mapping variables of type w to terms over v. For example, consider the representation of a simple language of types constructed from type variables and the function space constructor using the datatype:

```
> data Type v = TVar v                    -- Type variable
>             | TInt                       -- Integer type
>             | Fun (Type v) (Type v)   -- Function type
```

For convenience, we define an instance of the Text class to describe how such type expressions will be displayed:

```
  instance Text v => Text (Type v) where
>     showsPrec p (TVar v)  = shows v
>     showsPrec p TInt      = showString "Int"
>     showsPrec p (Fun l r) = showParen (p>0) str
>       where str = showsPrec 1 l . showString " -> " . shows r
```

---

[9] In fact, none of the monad examples that we have seen so far are instances of all of these classes. The process of constructing new monads which do satisfy all of the class constraints listed here will be described later in these notes.

The functor and monad structure of the Type constructor are as follows:

```
> instance Functor Type where
>     fun f (TVar v)  = TVar (f v)
>     fun f TInt      = TInt
>     fun f (Fun d r) = Fun (fun f d) (fun f r)
```

```
> instance Monad Type where
>     result v         = TVar v
>     TVar v 'bind' f = f v
>     TInt   'bind' f = TInt
>     Fun d r 'bind' f = Fun (d 'bind' f) (r 'bind' f)
```

In this setting, the fun function gives a systematic renaming of the variables in a term (there are no bound variables), while result corresponds to the null substitution that maps each variable to the term for that variable. If t has type Type v and s is a substitution of type v -> Type v, then t 'bind' s gives the result of applying the substitution s to the term t, replacing each occurrence of a variable v in t with the corresponding term s v in the result. In other words, application of a substitution to a term is captured by the function:

```
> apply     :: Monad m => (a -> m b) -> (m a -> m b)
> apply s t = t 'bind' s
```

Note that this operator can be used with any monad, not just the Type constructor that we are discussing here. Composition of substitutions also corresponds to a more general operator, called *Kleisli composition*, that can be used with arbitrary monads. Written here as the infix operator (@@), Kleisli composition can be defined as:

```
> (@@)     :: Monad m => (a -> m b) -> (c -> m a) -> (c -> m b)
> f @@ g   = join . fun f . g
```

```
> join    :: Monad m => m (m a) -> m a
> join xss = bind xss id
```

Apart from its use in the definition of (@@), the join operator defined here can also be used an alternative to bind for combining computations [28].

In most cases, the same type will be used to represent variables in both the domain and range of a substitution. We introduce a type synonym to capture this and to make some type signatures a little easier to read.

```
> type Subst m v = v -> m v
```

One of the simplest kinds of substitution, which will be denoted by v >> t, is a function that maps the variable v to the term t but leaves all other variables fixed:

```
> (>>)        :: (Eq v, Monad m) => v -> m v -> Subst m v
> (v >> t) w  = if v==w then t else result w
```

The type signature shown here is the most general type of the (>>) operator, and could also have been inferred automatically by the type system. The class constraints (Eq v, Monad m) indicate that, while (>>) is defined for arbitrary monads, it can be used only in cases where the values representing variables can be tested for equality.

The following definition gives an implementation of the standard unification algorithm for values of type Type v. This illustrates the use of monads both as a means of describing substitutions and as a model for computations, in this case, in an ErrorMonad:

```
> unify TInt      TInt     = result result
> unify (TVar v)  (TVar w) = result (if v==w then result
>                                             else v >> TVar w)
> unify (TVar v)  t        = varBind v t
> unify t         (TVar v) = varBind v t
> unify (Fun d r) (Fun e s) = unify d e           'bind' \s1 ->
>                             unify (apply s1 r)
>                                   (apply s1 s) 'bind' \s2 ->
>                             result (s2 @@ s1)
> unify t1        t2        = fail ("Cannot unify " ++ show t1 ++
>                                   " with " ++ show t2)
```

The only way that unification can fail is if we try to bind a variable to a type that contains that variable. A test for this condition, often referred to as the *occurs check*, is included in the auxiliary function varBind:

```
> varBind v t   = if (v 'elem' vars t)
>                    then fail "Occurs check fails"
>                    else result (v>>t)
>                 where vars (TVar v)  = [v]
>                       vars TInt      = []
>                       vars (Fun d r) = vars d ++ vars r
```

A Simple Application: A Type Inference Algorithm. To illustrate how some of the classes and functions introduced above might be used in practice, we will describe a simple monadic implementation of Milner's type inference algorithm W. We will not attempt to explain in detail how the algorithm works or to justify its formal properties since these are already well-documented, for example in [19, 3].

The purpose of the type checker is to determine types for the terms of a simple λ-calculus represented by the Term datatype introduced in Section 3.3:

```
> type Name = String
> data Term = Var Name       -- variable
>           | Ap  Term Term  -- application
>           | Lam Name Term  -- lambda abstraction
>           | Num Int        -- numeric literal
```

We will also use the representation of types described above with type variables represented by integer values so that it is easy to generate 'new' type variables as the algorithm proceeds. For example, given the term `Lam x (Var x)`, we expect the algorithm to produce a result of the form `Fun n n :: Type Int` for some (arbitrary) type variable `n = TVar m`.

At each stage, the type inference algorithm maintains a collection of assumptions about the types currently assigned to free variables. This can be described by an environment mapping variable names to types and represented using association lists:

```
> data Env t = Ass [(Name,t)]

> emptyEnv            :: Env t
> emptyEnv            = Ass []

> extend              :: Name -> t -> Env t -> Env t
> extend v t (Ass as) = Ass ((v,t):as)

> lookup              :: ErrorMonad m => Name -> Env t -> m t
> lookup v (Ass as)   = foldr find err as
>   where find (w,t) alt = if w==v then result t else alt
>         err             = fail ("Unbound variable: " ++ v)

> instance Functor Env where
>     fun f (Ass as) = Ass [ (n, f t) | (n,t) <- as ]
```

As the names suggest, `emptyEnv` represents the empty association list, `extend` is used to add a new binding, and `lookup` is used to search for a binding, raising an error if no corresponding value is found. We have also defined an instance of the `Functor` class that allows us to apply a function to each of the values held in the list, without changing the keys.

The type inference algorithm behaves almost like a function taking assumptions a and a term e as inputs, and producing a pair consisting of a substitution s and a type t as its result. The intention here is that t will be the principal type of e under the assumptions obtained by applying s to a. The complete algorithm is given by the following definition, with an equation for each different kind of Term:

```
> infer a (Var v)
>   = lookup v a                              'bind' \t        ->
>       result (result,t)

> infer a (Lam v e)
>   = incr                                    'bind' \b        ->
>       infer (extend v (TVar b) a) e          'bind' \(s,t) ->
>       result (s, s b 'Fun' t)
```

```
> infer a (Ap l r)
>   = infer a l                              'bind' \(s,lt) ->
>       infer (fun (apply s) a) r            'bind' \(t,rt) ->
>       incr                                 'bind' \b      ->
>       unify (apply t lt) (rt 'Fun' TVar b) 'bind' \u      ->
>       result (u @@ t @@ s, u b)

> infer a (Num n)
>   = result (result, TInt)
```

The reason for writing this algorithm in a monadic style is that it is not quite functional. There are two reasons for this; first, it is necessary to generate 'new' variables during type checking. This is usually dealt with informally in presentations of type inference, but a more concrete approach is necessary for a practical implementation. For the purposes of this algorithm, we use a StateMonad with an integer state to represent the next unused type variable. New variables are generated using the function incr.

The second reason for using the monadic style is that the algorithm may fail, either because the term contains a variable not bound in the assumptions a, or because the unification algorithm fails.

Both of these are reflected by the class constraints in the type of infer indicating that an instance of both StateMonad and ErrorMonad is required to use the type inference algorithm:

```
infer :: (ErrorMonad m, StateMonad m Int) =>
            Env (Type Int) ->
              Term ->
                m (Subst Type Int, Type Int)
```

Our problem now is that to make any use of infer, we need to construct a monad m that satisfies these constraints. It is possible to deal with such problems on a case-by-case basis, but it is obviously more attractive to use more general tools if possible. This is the problem that we turn our attention to in the following sections.

Combining Monads. While we can give some nice examples to illustrate the use of one particular set of features, for example, the use of state in a state monad, real programs typically require a combination of several different features. It is therefore quite important to develop systematic techniques for combining groups of features in a single monad.

In recent years, there have been several investigations into techniques for combining monads in functional programming languages[10]. Examples of this include the work of King and Wadler [14], and of Jones and Duponcheel [13]

---

[10] In fact, much of this work is a rediscovery of ideas that have already been developed by category theorists, albeit in a more abstract manner that is perhaps less accessible to some computer scientists.

to investigate the conditions under which a pair of monads m and n can be composed. In the following definitions, we adapt the swap construction of Jones and Duponcheel to the framework used in these notes. For reasons of space, we do not give any formal proof or motivation for these techniques here. We urge the reader not to be too distracted by the formal definitions shown below, focusing instead on the main objective which is to construct composite monads.

To begin with, it is useful to define two different forms of composition; forwards (FComp) and backwards (BComp):

```
> data FComp m n a = FC (n (m a))
> data BComp m n a = BC (m (n a))


> unBC (BC x) = x
> unFC (FC x) = x
```

It may seem strange to provide both forms of composition here since any value of type FComp m n a corresponds in an obvious way to a value of type BComp n m a, and vice versa. However, it is useful to have both forms of composition when we consider partial applications; the constructors FComp m and BComp m are not equivalent.

The functor structure for the two forms of composition are straightforward:

```
> instance (Functor m, Functor n) => Functor (FComp m n) where
>       fun f (FC c) = FC (fun (fun f) c)


> instance (Functor m, Functor n) => Functor (BComp m n) where
>       fun f (BC c) = BC (fun (fun f) c)
```

These two definitions rely on the overloading mechanisms to determine which version of the fun operator is used for a particular occurrence.

Two monads m and n can be 'composed' if there is a function:

```
  swap :: m (n a) -> n (m a)
```

satisfying certain laws set described by Jones and Duponcheel [13]. Fixing the monad m and using n to represent an arbitrary monad, it follows that the forward composition FComp m n is a monad if m is an instance of the class:

```
> class Monad m => Into m where
>       into :: Monad n => m (n a) -> n (m a)
```

and the into function satisfies the laws for swap. We refer to this operator as into because it allows us to push the monad m into an arbitrary computation represented by a monad n. Given this function, the structure of the composite monad is given by:

```
> instance (Into m, Monad n) => Monad (FComp m n) where
>       result x      = FC (result (result x))
>       FC c 'bind' f = FC ((fun join . join . fun f') c)
>                       where f' = into . fun (unFC . f)
```

For example, any forward composition of one of either the `Maybe`, `Error` or `Writer` monads with another arbitrary monad can be obtained using the following instances of `Into`:

```
> instance Into Maybe where
>      into Nothing  = result Nothing
>      into (Just c) = fun Just c

> instance Into Error where
>      into (Fail msg) = result (Fail msg)
>      into (Ok c)     = fun Ok c

> instance Into Writer where
>      into (Result s c) = c 'bind' \x -> result (Result s x)
```

In a similar way, for any fixed monad m and an arbitrary monad n, the backward composition BComp m n is a monad if m is an instance of the class:

```
> class Monad m => OutOf m where
>    outof :: Monad n => n (m a) -> m (n a)
```

and the `outof` operator satisfies the laws for `swap`. In this case, the monad structure can be described by the definition:

```
> instance (OutOf m, Monad n) => Monad (BComp m n) where
>      result x     = BC (result (result x))
>      BC c 'bind' f = BC ((fun join . join . fun f') c)
>                        where f' = outof . fun (unBC . f)
```

For example, any backward composition of a reader monad and another arbitrary monad, yields a monad:

```
> instance OutOf (r ->) where
>    outof c = \r -> c 'bind' \f -> result (f r)
```

Monad Transformers. Notice that, rather than allowing us to combine two arbitrary monads, all of the examples above use one fixed monad to transform another arbitrary monad. In other words, the following constructors can be understood as *monad transformers*, each having kind (* -> *) -> (* -> *) and mapping a monad to a new transformed monad that includes some extra features:

```
> type MaybeT     = FComp Maybe
> type ErrorT     = FComp Error
> type WriterT    = FComp Writer
> type ReaderT r = BComp (r ->)
```

The possibility of using monad transformers had previously been suggested by Moggi [22], leading independently to the use of *pseudomonads* in Steele's work on the construction of modular interpreters [25], and to a Scheme implementation by Espinosa [4, 5]. The problem of implementing monad transformers in a strongly typed language has been addressed by Liang, Hudak and Jones [15] using constructor classes.

We can define a class of monad transformers using the definition:

```
> class MonadT t where
>     lift :: Monad m => m a -> t m a
```

The intention here is that `lift` embeds a computation in the m monad into the extended monad t m, without using any of the extra features that it supports. Partial applications of both forward and backward compositions give rise to monad transformers, including the four examples above as special cases:

```
> instance Into m => MonadT (FComp m) where
>     lift = FC . fun result

> instance OutOf m => MonadT (BComp m) where
>     lift = BC . result
```

There are also examples of monad transformers that are not easily expressed as compositions. A standard example of this is the following definition of a state monad transformer:

```
> data StateT s m a = STM (s -> m (a,s))

> instance Monad m => Functor (StateT s m) where
>     fun f (STM xs) = STM (\s -> xs s 'bind' \(x,s') ->
>                                 result (f x, s'))

> instance Monad m => Monad (StateT s m) where
>     result x       = STM (\s -> result (x,s))
>     STM xs 'bind' f = STM (\s -> xs s 'bind' (\(x,s') ->
>                                 let STM f' = f x
>                                 in  f' s'))

> instance MonadT (StateT s) where
>     lift c = STM (\s -> c 'bind' \x -> result (x,s))
```

In fact, this defines a family of monad transformers, each of which takes the form `StateT s` for some state type s.

Previously, we have defined classes of monads for describing computations involving state, errors, writers and readers, but we have only defined one instance of each with no overlap between the different classes. Using monad transformers, we can extend these classes with new instances, and construct monads that are simultaneously instances of several different classes. We will illustrate this with two examples, leaving the task of extending some of the other classes introduced above to include transformed monads as an exercise for the reader.

- The state monad transformer: The following instance declaration indicates that we can apply StateT s to an arbitrary monad m to obtain a monad with a state component of type s:

```
> instance Monad m => StateMonad (StateT s m) s where
>     update f = STM (\s -> result (s, f s))
```

On the other hand, if m is a monad with a state component of type s, then so is the result of applying an arbitrary transformer to m:

```
> instance (MonadT t, StateMonad m s) => StateMonad (t m) s where
>     update f = lift (update f)
```

These two instance definitions overlap; a monad of the form StateT s m matches both of the monad constructors to the right of the => symbol. In Gofer, these conflicts are dealt with by choosing the most specific instance that matches the given constructor.

- The Error monad transformer: Following a similar pattern to the declarations above, the following definitions tell us that applying ErrorT to any monad or an arbitrary transformer to an ErrorMonad will produce an ErrorMonad:

```
> instance Monad m => ErrorMonad (ErrorT m) where
>     fail msg = FC (result (fail msg))

> instance (MonadT t, ErrorMonad m) => ErrorMonad (t m) where
>     fail msg = lift (fail msg)
```

Now, at last, we have the tools that we need to combine monads to satisfy particular sets of constraints. For example, for the type inference algorithm described above, we need to find a monad m satisfying the constraints:

```
(ErrorMonad m, StateMonad m Int)
```

We have at least two different ways to construct a suitable monad:

- ErrorT (State Int): in this case, m is equivalent to the monad:

```
ES a = Int -> (Error a, Int)
```

With this combination of state and error handling it is possible to return a modified state, even if an error occurs.

- StateT Int Error, in this case, m is equivalent to the monad:

```
SE a = Int -> Error (a, Int)
```

With this combination of state and error handling the final state will only be returned if the computation does not produce an error.

This example shows how monad transformers can be used to combine several different features in a single monad, with the flexibility to choose an appropriate semantics for a particular application.

References

1. R. Bird and P. Wadler. *Introduction to functional programming.* Prentice Hall, 1988.
2. R.M. Burstall, D.B MacQueen, and D.T. Sanella. Hope: An experimental applicative language. In *The 1980 LISP Conference*, pages 136–143, Stanford, August 1980.
3. L. Damas and R. Milner. Principal type schemes for functional programs. In *9th Annual ACM Symposium on Principles of Programming languages*, pages 207–212, Albuquerque, N.M., January 1982.
4. David Espinosa. Modular denotational semantics. Unpublished manuscript, December 1993.
5. David Espinosa. Building interpreters by transforming stratified monads. Unpublished manuscript, June 1994.
6. R. Hindley. The principal type-scheme of an object in combinatory logic. *Transactions of the American Mathematical Society*, 146:29–60, December 1969.
7. P. Hudak, S. Peyton Jones, and P. Wadler (editors). Report on the Programming Language Haskell, A Non-strict Purely Functional Language (Version 1.2). *ACM SIGPLAN Notices*, 27(5), May 1992.
8. Geraint Jones and Jeremy Gibbons. Linear-time breadth-first tree algorithms, an exercise in the arithmetic of folds and zips. Programming Research Group, Oxford, December 1992.
9. Mark P. Jones. Computing with lattices: An application of type classes. *Journal of Functional Programming*, 2(4), October 1992.
10. Mark P. Jones. A system of constructor classes: overloading and implicit higher-order polymorphism. In *FPCA '93: Conference on Functional Programming Languages and Computer Architecture, Copenhagen, Denmark*, New York, June 1993. ACM Press.
11. Mark P. Jones. Dictionary-free overloading by partial evaluation. In *ACM SIGPLAN Workshop on Partial Evaluation and Semantics-Based Program Manipulation, Orlando, Florida*, June 1994. To appear.
12. Mark P. Jones. The implementation of the Gofer functional programming system. Research Report YALEU/DCS/RR-1030, Yale University, New Haven, Connecticut, USA, May 1994.
13. M.P. Jones and L. Duponcheel. Composing monads. Research Report YALEU/DCS/RR-1004, Yale University, New Haven, Connecticut, USA, December 1993.
14. D.J. King and P. Wadler. Combining monads. In *Proceedings of the Fifth Annual Glasgow Workshop on Functional Programming*, Ayr, Scotland, 1992. Springer Verlag Workshops in Computer Science.
15. Sheng Liang, Paul Hudak, and Mark Jones. Monad transformers and modular interpreters. In *Conference record of POPL '95: 22nd ACM SIGPLAN-SIGACT Symposium on Principles of Programming Languages*, San Francisco, CA, January 1995.
16. S. MacLane. *Categories for the working mathematician.* Graduate texts in mathematics, 5. Springer-Verlag, 1971.
17. Erik Meijer, Maarten Fokkinga, and Ross Paterson. Functional programming with bananas, lenses, envelopes and barbed wire. In *5th ACM conference on Functional Programming Languages and Computer Architecture*, pages 124–144, New York, 1991. Springer-Verlag. Lecture Notes in Computer Science, 523.

18. Erik Meijer and Mark P. Jones. Gofer goes bananas. In preparation, 1994.
19. R. Milner. A theory of type polymorphism in programming. *Journal of Computer and System Sciences*, 17(3), 1978.
20. Robin Milner, Mads Tofte, and Robert Harper. *The definition of Standard ML*. The MIT Press, 1990.
21. E. Moggi. Computational lambda-calculus and monads. In *IEEE Symposium on Logic in Computer Science*, Asilomar, California, 1989.
22. E. Moggi. An abstract view of programming languages. Technical Report ECS-LFCS-90-113, Laboratory for Foundations of Computer Science, University of Edinburgh, Edinburgh, Scotland, 1990.
23. Stephen K Park and Keith W Miller. Random number generators: Good ones are hard to find. *Communications of the ACM*, 31(10):1192–1201, Oct 1988.
24. M. Spivey. A functional theory of exceptions. *Science of Computer Programming*, 14(1), 1990.
25. Guy L. Steele Jr. Building interpreters by composing monads. In *Conference record of POPL '94: 21st ACM SIGPLAN-SIGACT Symposium on Principles of Programming Languages*, pages 472–492, Portland, OR, January 1994.
26. D.A. Turner. Duality and De Morgan principles for lists. In W. Feijen, N. van Gasteren, D. Gries, and J. Misra, editors, *Beauty is Our Business, A Birthday Salute to Edsger W. Dijkstra*, pages 390–398. Springer-Verlag, 1990.
27. D.A. Turner. An overview of Miranda. In David Turner, editor, *Research Topics in Functional Programming*, chapter 1, pages 1–16. Addison Wesley, 1990.
28. P. Wadler. Comprehending monads. In *ACM conference on LISP and Functional Programming*, Nice, France, 1990.
29. P. Wadler. The essence of functional programming (invited talk). In *Conference record of the Nineteenth annual ACM SIGPLAN-SIGACT symposium on Principles of Programming Languages*, pages 1–14, Jan 1992.
30. P. Wadler and S. Blott. How to make *ad hoc* polymorphism less *ad hoc*. In *Proceedings of 16th ACM Symposium on Principles of Programming Languages*, pages 60–76, Jan 1989.

Programming with Fudgets

Thomas Hallgren & Magnus Carlsson

Computing Science, Chalmers University of Technology,
S-412 96 Göteborg, Sweden.
E-mail: hallgren, magnus@cs.chalmers.se

1 Introduction

In these notes we present the Fudget Library and the ideas underlying it. The Fudget Library is primarily a toolkit for the construction of Graphical User Interfaces (GUIs) on a high level of abstraction in the lazy functional language Haskell, but it also allows you to construct programs that communicate across the Internet with other programs.

Apart from describing how to use the Fudget Library, we try to describe the underlying ideas in such a way that the reader should be able to use them in his/her own favourite functional language.

The design of the Fudget Library started with the desire to find a good abstraction of GUI building blocks, i.e., an abstraction that makes use of the powerful abstraction mechanisms found in functional languages (higher order functions, polymorphism, etc.) and thereby, hopefully, is better than the abstractions you find in typical GUI toolkits for conventional, imperative languages. We consider an abstraction to be better if it simplifies programming, e.g., by making programs more concise and thereby easier to write, read and maintain.

An additional consideration is that in today's programming language implementations, there usually is a conflict between efficiency and high level of abstraction, so a good abstraction is one that can have a reasonably efficient implementation. If we can not have that, we have lost contact with the real world. To summarise:

> *It is important not to lose contact with the real world, but this does not imply that one must pass around the world explicitly.*

The main abstraction used in the Fudget Library is the *fudget*. A fudget is a process which can, via message passing, communicate with other concurrently running fudgets and with the outside world. A fudget is a first class value of a type that reflects what types of messages the fudget sends and receives. This makes communication type safe. A fudget may have an internal state, which is not visible in the type of the fudget. Fudget programming in this respect resembles object oriented programming, where state information is distributed and hidden within objects rather than centralized and exposed to arbitrary use or misuse. But the encapsulation of state information also makes fudgets easy to compose, like functions in functional languages.

Fudgets are implemented on top of *stream processors*, a simpler kind of process that communicates with its surroundings through an input stream and an output stream of values.

1.1 Overview

We start with a quick recapitulation of some common I/O methods in functional languages (Section 2). In these methods you specify a single-threaded sequence of I/O operations, so the functional program in effect takes the form of a sequential imperative program on the top level.

For reactive programming (Section 2.3), a more attractive program structure is a set of concurrent processes, so we introduce *stream processors* (Section 3). A stream processor is a process that consumes an input stream and produces an output stream. Combinators for serial composition, parallel composition and loops allow programs to be structured as a network of stream processors. Stream processors can be programmed purely functionally.

In addition to communicating with neighbours in a network, in a reactive programming context many stream processors will also need to communicate with external entities through the I/O system. We therefore introduce *fudgets* (Section 4), stream processors which have access to the I/O system in addition to streams for communication with other stream processors or fudgets. Reactive programs can be built as networks of fudgets.

The main use of fudgets is the construction of Graphical User Interfaces (GUIs). The building blocks in GUIs (buttons, menus, sliders, etc.) are reminiscent of physical devices in that they are self-contained units that operate more or less independently and in parallel. The reactive programming model is thus very natural for GUIs. In the Fudget Library, GUI elements are represented as fudgets.[1] Complex user interfaces are built by combining fudgets representing GUI elements and other stream processors (Section 5).

There are two aspects in the design of GUI programs with fudgets: the computational aspect and the visual aspect. The fudget system allows you to worry about them one at a time. Thanks to the automatic layout system you can concentrate on the computational aspect during the initial development stage. You can later add layout information to the program, if the default layout isn't adequate (Section 5.5).

When designing software libraries, e.g., GUI toolkits, there is often a tension between generality and simplicity. Generality is often achieved by using many parameters. Having to give values for a lot of parameters clearly makes library components more difficult to use. In some programming languages there is a mechanism that allows a function parameter to be omitted if the function definition specifies a default value for it. This makes functions easy to use and customizable at the same time. The language that we use (Haskell) does not have such a mechanism, but the scheme used in the fudget library comes pretty close. It uses Haskell's type class system to avoid proliferation of names (Section 5.6).

The second use of fudgets that we cover is the construction of network based client/server programs. A typical server must be able to handle connections from several simultaneous clients, so it is useful to structure a server with a handler process (i.e., a handler fudget) for each client. Programs written in Haskell with the fudget library can communicate with programs written in other languages, but for the case where all programs involved are written in Haskell we show a simple way to make sure that the communication is type safe (Section 6).

1.2 A First Example

As a preview of Graphical User Interface construction with the Fudget Library, Figure 1 shows a small program: a simple counter. The user interface contains a button and a numeric display. When you press the button the number in the display is incremented.

The core of the program is the definition of counterF, where two fudgets implementing the two user interface elements and a stream processor implementing the click counter are connected using the serial composition operator >=<. Data flow from right to left. The button outputs clicks that are fed to the counter. For every click, the counter increments its internal integer state and outputs the new value to the display.

---

1. The word fudget comes from *functional widget*, where widget comes from *window gadget*.

Readers mainly interested in GUI construction may want to skip directly to Section 5 and then go back to the earlier sections to learn more about what stream processors and fudgets really are.

```
module  Main(main) where -- A simple counter

import Fudgets

main :: Dialogue
main = fudlogue (shellF "Counter" counterF)

counterF = intDispF >==< absF countSP >==< incButtonF

incButtonF :: F Click Click
incButtonF = buttonF "Increment"

countSP :: SP Click Int
countSP = putSP startstate $
           mapAccumlSP inc startstate
  where inc n = (n+1,n+1)

startstate = 0
```

Fig. 1. The Counter Example

1.3 Notation

All programs in these lecture notes are written in the pure functional language Haskell [7]. We deviate from Haskell syntax on two points:

- We write → instead of ->.

- We write a+b instead of Either a b, the standard sum type in Haskell, defined as

```
data Either a b = Left a | Right b
```

This proviso aside, the presented examples should compile and run "as is".

To avoid nested bracketing in large expressions we will often use the infix operator $ defined as

```
f $ x = f x
```

$ is right associative and has low precedence, so you can write, e.g.,

```
f $ g $ h $ \x → x+1
```

instead of

```
f (g (h (\x → x+1)))
```

Note that in Haskell, functions can be used as infix operators by placing them in backquotes. For example, parSP (parallel composition of stream processors) is a function taking two arguments. We will write

```
sp1 `parSP` sp2
```

instead of

```
parSP sp1 sp2
```

2   Input/Output in Functional Languages

In this chapter we give a brief introduction to Input/Output in functional languages. Several models of I/O for lazy functional languages have been developed during the years. Good surveys can be found in [3] and [6]. Here, we present Landin's stream model of I/O and the synchronized streams used in Haskell. We present continuation based I/O and monadic I/O as abstractions from streams and note that they are sequential in nature. We note that for some purposes it is more natural to use a set of concurrent processes than a single-threaded sequence of I/O operations to describe the I/O behaviour of a program.

2.1   Referential Transparency and I/O?

In traditional imperative languages Input/Output operations are usually accomplished by calling some predefined procedures that perform the desired operation as a side effect. In functional languages, however, side effects are usually not wanted, since they break *referential transparency*. As an example, suppose there was a function

```
write :: String → String
```

which would take a string and return it unchanged and, as a side effect, print the string on the terminal. Then the program

```
let s = write "Ha"
in (s,s)
```

would probably not produce the same result as

```
(write "Ha", write "Ha")
```

This means that many nice algebraic laws, such as

$$2*a = a+a$$
$$a+b = b+a$$

no longer hold for arbitrary subexpressions a and b.

Still, this is how I/O works in most strict functional languages like LISP and Standard ML. In a lazy language you don't really want to think about *when* or *if* functions are actually called, so specifying I/O in this way is not very useful.

2.2   Programming Styles for Sequential I/O

In order to maintain referential transparency, I/O in functional languages is *not* thought of as something that happens as a side effect of calling certain functions. Instead the program is thought of as a pure function from some input to some output.

2.2.1   Landin's Stream Based I/O model

Suppose the only I/O operations we want in a program are reading from the computer keyboard and writing to the computer screen (Figure 2). Then the program can be a function from a list of characters (the characters read from the keyboard) to a list of characters (the ones printed on the screen).

As an example, a program to read a sequence of numbers and print their sum could look something like

```
show . sum . map read . words
```

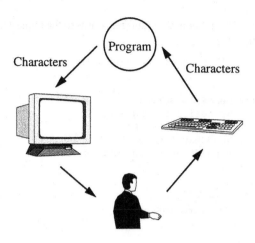

Fig. 2. Landin's Stream I/O model.

where `words` turns a string into a list of words, and `show` and `read` are overloaded functions that convert to and from string representations of data, respectively.

At first it may seem that thinking of programs as functions from input to output only allows you to write programs with batch behaviour: first read all input, then perform the computation and finally print the result. But thanks to *laziness*, I/O and computations can be interleaved. Input is not demanded until it is needed in the computation of the next output. As an example, a program like

```
map toUpper
```

(where `toUpper` converts lower case letters to upper case letters) reads, processes and outputs one character at a time.

The above described I/O method is Landin's streams model of I/O [8].

2.2.2 I/O Based on Synchronized Streams

I/O in Haskell is also based on streams, but to allow more general I/O operations the elements in the streams are not just characters (Figure 3). The output stream contains requests

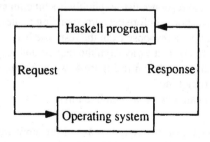

Fig. 3. The I/O model in Haskell.

to the operating system. The input list contains responses to the requests. A program in Haskell is a function of the type

```
type Dialogue = [Response] → [Request]
```

where

```
data Request = ReadFile String
             | WriteFile String String
             | DeleteFile String
             | ReadChan String
             | AppendChan String String
             | ...

data Response = Success
              | Str String
              | Failure IOError
              | ...

data IOError = ...
```

The requests and response streams are synchronized: for each request in the output stream there is a corresponding response in the input stream. A particular request always generates the same kind of response, if the operation succeeds. For example, the response to WriteFile *filename newContents* is Success and the response to ReadFile *filename* is Str *contents*, where *contents* is the contents of the file. If an operation fails, the response is Failure *ioerror*.

For example, to read some lines of text from a file called "forward" and write them in reverse order to a file called "backward" one could write:

```
main responses =
  ReadFile "forward" :
  (case responses of
      Str contents : responses' →
        let revcontents = (unlines.reverse.lines) contents
        in WriteFile "backward" revcontents :
            [])
```

This program doesn't do any error handling.

2.2.3 I/O in Continuation Passing Style

Dealing with the request and response lists explicitly is a bit clumsy. It is easy to make mistakes, like trying to use a response before the corresponding request has been output, or forgetting to inspect and remove a response from the response list.

Fortunately, it is easy to abstract away from the request and response lists. By using the functions doRequest and done shown in Figure 4, we make sure that we do not use the wrong response at the wrong time.

The example program can now be written like this:

```
main2 =
  doRequest (ReadFile "forward") $ \ (Str contents) →
  let revcontents = (unlines.reverse.lines) contents
  in doRequest (WriteFile "backward" revcontents) $ \ Success →
      done
```

This programming style is called *continuation passing style* (CPS). The function doRequest takes a request to perform and a function that defines how the program should *continue* after that.

```
doRequest :: Request → (Response → Dialogue) → Dialogue
doRequest request continuation responses =
  request :
  case responses of
    response : responses → continuation response responses

done:: Dialogue
done[] = []
```

Fig. 4. Abstracting away from the request and response lists.

Using doRequest you can define even more convenient functions for various I/O operations. Here is a function for reading a file with error handling:

```
readFile :: String →
              (IOError→Dialogue) →
              (String→Dialogue) →
              Dialogue
readFile filename failcont continuation =
  doRequest (ReadFile filename) $ \ response →
  case response of
    Str contents → continuation contents
    Failure error → failcont error
```

In Haskell there are predefined functions like readFile for most I/O requests.

2.2.4 I/O in Monadic Style

An abstraction that has proved to be useful for many purposes is the *monad* [14]. An I/O system based on monads is proposed for version 1.3 of Haskell [4].

Monadic style I/O operations can be implemented on top of synchronized streams in much the same way as CPS style I/O. A simple I/O monad (without error handling) is shown in Figure 5. In monadic style, the above example would look like this:

```
main = doIO mainIO

mainIO =
  readFileIO "forward" `bindIO` \ contents →
  let revcontents = (unlines.reverse.lines) contents
  in writeFileIO "backward" revcontents)
```

2.3 Concurrency and GUI Programming

We have seen above how you can use streams, continuations, or monads, to specify a sequence of I/O operations that the program should perform.

For many purposes, a single sequence of I/O operations is an adequate description of the I/O behaviour of a program. But there are other cases. For programs that interact with several external entities (teletype terminals, other computers on a network, elements in a graphical user interface, robotic sensors/motors, etc.) there is usually no predetermined order in which I/O operations will occur. The program must be prepared to *react* to input from any of the external entities. In this situation it can be more attractive to organize the program as a set of concurrent processes. You define one "handler" process per external entity, to deal with the low level aspects of the interaction with the entity. You then add processes that communicate with the handlers on a higher level. Figure 6 shows a simple program with a

```
-- The I/O monad type
type IO a = (a → Dialogue) → Dialogue

doIO :: IO () → Dialogue
doIO io = io (\() → done)

returnIO :: a → IO a
returnIO x = \ cont → cont x

bindIO :: IO a → (a → IO b) → IO b
io1 `bindIO` xio2 =
  \ cont → io1 (\x → xio2 x cont)

-- requestIO: performs one request and returns the response
requestIO :: Request → IO Response
requestIO req =
  \ cont resps →
    req : case resps of
            resp1:resps' → cont resp1 resps'

-- Convenient functions for reading and writing files
readFileIO :: String → IO String
readFileIO filename =
  requestIO (ReadFile filename) `bindIO` \(Str contents) →
  returnIO contents

writeFileIO :: String → String → IO ()
writeFileIO filename contents = ...
```

Fig. 5. Monadic I/O (without error handling) on top of synchronized streams.

graphical user interface structured in this way. The program just shows a button and a numeric display. When you press the button, the number in the display is incremented. The program contains one process per user interface element. They handle the graphical appearance and behaviour of the respective elements. The program also contains a process that does some "useful" work, i.e. counting the button clicks.

To support the above outlined reactive programming model, you need to introduce some kind of process concept in the language. The next chapter describes one way of doing this.

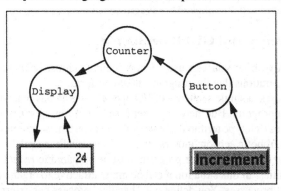

Fig. 6. A program with a graphical user interface, structured according to the reactive programming model.

3 Stream Processors

In this chapter we introduce *stream processors*; a simple but still practical incarnation of the process concept, which can be implemented within a purely functional language. We then define a set of combinators for building networks of stream processors. The stream processors will be first class values, which can be passed around as messages.

First, a *stream* is a potentially infinite sequence of values occurring at different points in time. A stream can be seen as a communication channel, transferring information from one place (a producer) to another (a consumer).

A *stream processor* is a process which consumes some input streams and produces some output streams. A stream processor may have an internal state, i.e., output produced at a certain point in time can depend on all input consumed before that point in time.

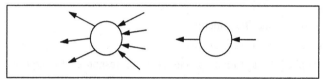

Fig. 7. A general stream processor and a stream processor with a single input stream and a single output stream.

Although stream processors may in general have many input and output streams, in the following we will only consider stream processors with a *single input stream* and a *single output stream* (see Figure 7). This allows us to develop a small set of simple combinators with which it is possible to build complex networks of stream processors. The restriction may seem severe, but the chosen set of combinators allows streams to be merged and split, so a stream processor with many input/output stream can be represented as one with a single input and output stream.

In the following sections, we will present operations used to define atomic stream processors together with a set of combinators for building networks of stream processors. We define three basic compositions: *serial composition, parallel composition* and *loops* (circular connections). These are sufficient to describe any network of stream processors.[2] We will also briefly cover an operational semantics of stream processors, the implementation of stream processors in a lazy functional language and some pragmatical aspects.

3.1 The Stream Processor Type

How should stream processors be represented in a lazy functional language? A first attempt is to represent streams as lists,

```
type Stream a = [a]
```

and stream processors as list functions,

```
type SP input output = [input] → [output] -- First attempt
```

With this definition, the type `Dialogue` in Haskell would be equal to `SP Response Request`.

---

2. We leave the proof as an exercise for the interested reader.

For various reasons, this is not how stream processors are represented in the Fudget library. (We will come back this in Section 3.6.) The Fudget library provides an abstract type for stream processors,

```
data SP input output
```

where input and output are the types of the elements in the input and output streams, respectively (Figure 8).

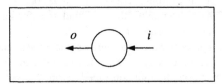

Fig. 8. A stream processor of type SP *i o*.

The library also provides the function

```
runSP :: SP i o → [i] → [o]
```

which, when applied to a stream processor from responses to requests, gives us a Dialogue.

3.2   Atomic Stream Processors in Continuation Style

The behaviour of an atomic stream processor is described by a sequential program. There are three basic actions a stream processor can take:

- it can put a value in its output stream,
- it can get a value from its input stream,
- it can terminate.

The Fudget library provides the following continuation style operations for these actions:

```
putSP :: output → SP input output → SP input output
getSP :: (input → SP input output) → SP input output
nullSP :: SP input output
```

As an example of how to use these in recursive definitions of stream processors, consider the identity stream processor[3]

```
-- The identity stream processor
idSP :: SP a a
idSP = getSP $ \ x → putSP x idSP
```

and the following stream processor equivalents of the well known list functions:

```
mapSP :: (a → b) → SP a b
mapSP f = getSP $ \ x → putSP (f x) $ mapSP f

filterSP :: (a → Bool) → SP a a
filterSP p = getSP $ \ x → if p x
                               then putSP x $ filterSP p
                               else filterSP p
```

---

3. The infix operator $ is just function application. More information about notation is in the introduction.

3.3 Stream Processors with Encapsulated State

A stream processor can maintain an internal state. In practice, this can be accomplished by using an accumulating argument in a recursively defined stream processor. As a concrete example, consider sumSP, a stream processor that computes the accumulated sum of its input stream:

```
sumSP :: Int → SP Int Int
sumSP acc = getSP $ \ n → putSP (acc+n) $ sumSP (acc+n)
```

In this case, the internal state happens to be a value of the type Int, which also happens to be the type of the input and output streams. In general, the type of the state need not be visible in the type of the stream processor.

The Fudget library provides two functions for construction of stream processors with internal state:

```
mapAccumlSP       :: (s → i → (s, o)) → s → SP i o

concatMapAccumlSP :: (s → i → (s, [o])) → s → SP i o
```

Using mapAccumlSP we can define sumSP without recursion like this:

```
sumSP :: Int → SP Int Int
sumSP = mapAccumlSP (\ acc n → (acc+n,acc+n))
```

Representing state information as one or more accumulating arguments is useful when the behaviour of the stream processor is uniform with respect to the state. If a stream processor reacts differently to input depending on its current state, it can be more convenient to use a set of mutually recursive stream processors that define a finite state automaton. As a simple example, consider a stream processor that outputs every other element in its input stream:

```
passOnSP = getSP $ \ x → putSP x $ skipSP
skipSP = getSP $ \ x → passOnSP
```

It has two states: the "pass on" state where the next input is passed on to the output, and the "skip" state where the next input is skipped.

3.4 Plumbing: Composing Stream Processors

3.4.1 Serial Composition

The simplest combinator is the one for serial composition,

```
serCompSP :: SP b c → SP a b → SP a c
```

It connects the output stream of one stream processor to the input of another, as illustrated in Figure 9. Streams flow from right to left, just like values in function compositions, $f_1 . f_2$.

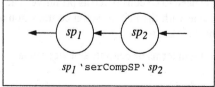

Fig. 9. Serial composition of stream processors.

3.4.2 Parallel Compositions

The combinator for parallel composition in Figure 10 is really the key combinator for

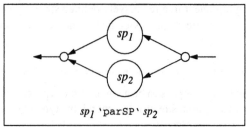

sp_1 `parSP` sp_2

Fig. 10. Parallel composition of stream processors.

stream processors. It allows us to write reactive programs composed by more or less independent, concurrent processes. The idea with parallel composition is that two stream processors should be able to run in parallel, independently of one another. The output streams should be merged in chronological order. We won't be able to achieve exactly this in a functional language, but for stream processors whose behaviour is dominated by I/O operations rather than internal computations we will get close enough for practical purposes.

There is however more than one possible definition of parallel composition. How should values in the input stream be distributed to the two stream processors? How should the output streams be merged? We define two versions:

- Let sp_1 `parSP` sp_2 denote parallel composition where input values are propagated to both sp_1 and sp_2 and output is merged in chronological order. We will call this version *untagged* or *broadcasting* parallel composition.

- Let sp_1 `compSP` sp_2 denote parallel composition where the values of the input and output streams are elements of a disjoint union. Values in the input stream tagged Left or Right are untagged and sent to either sp_1 or sp_2, respectively. Likewise, the tag of a value in the output stream indicates from which component it came. We will call this version *tagged* parallel composition.

The types of the two combinators are:

```
parSP :: SP i o → SP i o → SP i o
compSP :: SP i1 o1 → SP i2 o2 → SP (i1+i2) (o1+o2)
```

where we use a+b as an abbreviation for Either a b, defined as usual in Haskell:

```
data Either a b = Left a | Right b
```

Note that only one of these need to be considered as primitive. The other one can be defined in terms of the primitive one with the help of serial composition and some simple stream processors like mapSP and filterSP.

Exercise 1. Define parSP in terms of compSP, and vice versa!

3.4.3 Circular Connections

Serial composition creates a unidirectional communication channel between two stream processors. Parallel composition splits and merges streams but does not allow the composed stream processors to exchange information. So, with these two operators we can not obtain bidirectional communication between stream processors. Therefore, we introduce combinators that construct loops.

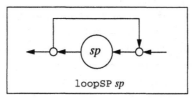

Fig. 11. A simple loop constructor.

The simplest possible loop combinator just connects the output of a stream processor to its input, as illustrated in Figure 11. As with parallel composition, we define two versions of the loop combinator:

- loopSP *sp* – output from *sp* is both looped and propagated to the output.

- loopLeftSP *sp* – output from *sp* is required to be in a disjoint union. Values tagged Left are looped and values tagged Right are output. At the input, values from the loop are tagged Left and values from the outside will be tagged Right.

The types of these combinators are:

```
loopSP :: SP a a → SP a a
loopLeftSP :: SP (loop+input) (loop+output) → SP input output
```

Each of the two loop combinators can be defined in terms of the other, so only one of them need to be considered primitive.

Using one of the loop combinators, one can now obtain bidirectional communication between two stream processors as shown in Figure 12.

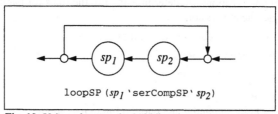

Fig. 12. Using a loop to obtain bidirectional communication.

As another example, using loops and parallel composition we can create fully connected networks of stream processors. With an expression like

```
loopSP (sp₁ `parSP` sp₂ `parSP` ... `parSP` spₙ)
```

we get a broadcasting network. By replacing `parSP` with `compSP` and some tagging/untagging, we get a network with point-to-point communication.

3.5 An Operational Semantics for Stream Processors

Here we give an operational semantics for stream processors in the form of a set of rules for rewriting arbitrary stream processor expressions to canonical form. A stream processor is in canonical form if it is built using only the atomic stream processor constructors nullSP, putSP, and getSP.

- Serial composition:

```
nullSP `serCompSP` sp ⇒ nullSP
(e `putSP` sp₁) `serCompSP` sp₂ ⇒ e `putSP` (sp₁ `serCompSP` sp₂)
getSP xsp₁ `serCompSP` nullSP ⇒ nullSP
getSP xsp₁ `serCompSP` (e `putSP` sp₂) ⇒ xsp₁ e `serCompSP` sp₂
getSP xsp₁ `serCompSP` getSP ysp₂ ⇒
    getSP (\y → getSP xsp₁ `serCompSP` ysp₂ y)
```

- Broadcasting parallel composition:

  `parSP` is meant to be commutative, so we give only the rules for one of two symmetric cases:

```
nullSP `parSP` sp ⇒ sp
(e `putSP` sp₁) `parSP` sp₂ ⇒ e `putSP` (sp₁ `parSP` sp₂)
(getSP xsp₁) `parSP` (getSP xsp₂) ⇒ getSP (\x → xsp₁ x `parSP` xsp₂ x)
```

- Tagged parallel composition

```
nullSP `compSP` nullSP ⇒ nullSP
(e `putSP` sp₁) `compSP` sp₂ ⇒ Left e `putSP` (sp₁ `compSP` sp₂)
sp₁ `compSP` (e `putSP` sp₂) ⇒ Right e `putSP` (sp₁ `compSP` sp₂)

getSP xsp₁ `compSP` getSP ysp₂ ⇒

getSP $ \z → case z of
                Left  x → xsp₁ x `compSP` getSP ysp₂
                Right y → getSP xsp₁ `compSP` ysp₂ y
```

The rules for serial compositions are deterministic, but the rules for parallel compositions are not. For example, the expression

```
(a `putSP` nullSP) `parSP` (b `putSP` nullSP)
```

can be reduced to two canonical forms:

```
a `putSP` b `putSP` nullSP
b `putSP` a `putSP` nullSP.
```

This leaves room for both sequential and parallel implementations.

3.6   Implementation of Stream Processors

Using list functions to represent stream processors, SP i o = [i] → [o], in a sequential language causes some problems. Parallel composition can not be expressed. A reasonable definition would have to look something like this:

```
(sp1 `parSP` sp2) xs = merge (sp1 xs) (sp2 xs)
                       where merge ys zs = ???
```

But what should we replace ??? with so that the first output from the composition is the first output to become available from one of the components? For example, if sp1 $\perp$ = $\perp$ but sp2 $\perp$ = 1:$\perp$, then (sp1 `parSP` sp2) $\perp$ should be 1:$\perp$. But so should (sp2 `parSP` sp1) $\perp$, so ??? must be an expression that chooses the one of ys and zs which happens to be non-bottom. This can clearly not be done in an ordinary purely functional language. We would need a bottom-avoiding operator, like amb, McCarthy's ambivalent operator [9].

So, instead of using lists, we use a data type with constructors corresponding to the actions a stream processor can take (as described in Section 3.2):

```
data SP i o
  = NullSP
  | PutSP o (SP i o)
  | GetSP (i → SP i o)
```

We call this the *continuation-based representation of stream processors*. It differs from the *list-based representation* in that it makes the consumption of the input stream observable, i.e., a stream processor must evaluate to GetSP *sp* each time it wants to read a value from the input stream. It thus comes closer to the operational semantics. It also allows you to make a useful implementation of parallel composition.

With the continuation-based representation, serial composition can be implemented like in Figure 13.

```
sp1 `serCompSP` sp2 =
  case sp1 of
    PutSP y sp1' → PutSP y (sp1' `serCompSP` sp2)
    GetSP xsp1 → xsp1 `serCompSP1` sp2
    NullSP → NullSP

xsp1 `serCompSP1` sp2 =
  case sp2 of
    PutSP y sp2' → xsp1 y `serCompSP` sp2'
    GetSP xsp2 → GetSP (\ x → xsp1 `serCompSP1` xsp2 x)
    NullSP → NullSP
```

Fig. 13. Implementation of serial composition with the continuation-based representation.

An implementation of broadcasting parallel composition is shown in Figure 14. The

```
sp1 `parSP` sp2 =
  case sp1 of
    PutSP y sp1' → PutSP y (sp1' `parSP` sp2)
    GetSP xsp1 → xsp1 `parSP1` sp2
    NullSP → sp2

xsp1 `parSP1` sp2 =
  case sp2 of
    PutSP y sp2' → PutSP y (xsp1 `parSP1` sp2')
    GetSP xsp2 → GetSP (\ x → xsp1 x `parSP` xsp2 x)
    NullSP → GetSP xsp1
```

Fig. 14. Implementation of parallel composition with continuation-based representation.

implementation of tagged parallel composition is analogous. Note that we arbitrarily choose to inspect the left argument sp_1 first. This means that even if sp_2 could compute and output a value much faster than sp_1, it will not get the chance to do so. But at least, we get the property that if a composition can produce more output without consuming more input, it will do so.

Exercise 2.   Implement `runSP :: SP a b → [a] → [b]`.

Exercise 3.   Implement a combinator `startupSP :: i → SP i o → SP i o` that prepends an element to the input stream of a stream processor. Make the implementation independent of the stream processor representation.

Exercise 4.   Implement `loopSP` and `loopLeftSP`.

3.7   More plumbing

3.7.1   Stream processors and Software Re-use

For serious applications programming, it is useful to have libraries of re-usable software components. But in many cases when you find a useful component in a library, you still need to modify it slightly to be able to use it.

A variation of the loop combinators that has turned out to be very useful when re-using stream processors is `loopThroughRightSP`, illustrated in Figure 15. The major difference

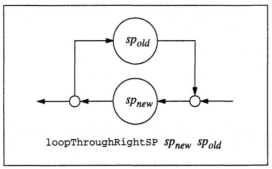

Fig. 15. Encapsulation.

from `loopSP` and `loopLeftSP` is that the loop does not go straight back from the output to the input of a single stream processor. Instead it goes *through* another stream processor.

A typical situation where `loopThroughRightSP` is useful is when you have a stream processor, sp_{old}, that does almost what you want, but you need it to handle some new kind of messages. You can then define a new stream processor sp_{new} which can pass on old messages directly to sp_{old} and handle the new messages in the appropriate way, on its own or by translating them to messages that sp_{old} understands. (See also section 3.1.1 in [11].)

In the composition `loopThroughRightSP` sp_1 sp_2 all communication with the outside world is handled by sp_1. sp_2 is connected only to sp_1 and is in this sense encapsulated inside sp_1.

The type of `loopThroughRightSP` is:

```
loopThroughRightSP :: SP (o2+i1) (i2+o1) → SP i2 o2 → SP i1 o1
```

Exercise 5.   Implement `loopThroughRightSP` using `loopLeftSP` together with parallel and serial compositions as appropriate.

3.7.2 Handling Multiple Input and Output Streams

Although stream processors have only one input stream, it is easy to construct programs where one stream processor receives input from two or more other stream processors. (The case with several outputs is analogous.) For example, the expression

$$sp_1 \text{ `serCompSP` } (sp_2 \text{ `compSP` } sp_3)$$

allows sp_1 to receive input from both sp_2 and sp_3. For most practical purposes, sp_1 can be regarded as having two input streams, as illustrated in Figure 16. When you use `getSP` in

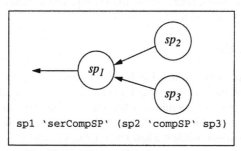

Fig. 16. Handling multiple input streams.

sp_1 to read from the input streams, messages from sp_2 and sp_3 will appear tagged with `Left` and `Right`, respectively. You can not directly read selectively from one of the two input streams, but the Fudget library provides the combinator

```
waitForSP :: (i → Maybe i') → (i' → SP i o) → SP i o
```

which you can use to wait for a selected input. Other input is queued and can be consumed after the selected input has been received. Using `waitForSP` you can define combinators to read from one of two input streams:

```
getLeftSP :: (i1 → SP (i1+i2) o) → SP (i1+i2) o
getLeftSP = waitForSP stripLeft

getRightSP :: (i2 → SP (i1+i2) o) → SP (i1+i2) o
getRightSP = waitForSP stripRight
```

where

```
stripLeft :: a+b → Maybe a
stripLeft (Left x) = Just x
stripLeft (Right _) = Nothing

stripRight :: a+b → Maybe b
stripRight (Left _) = Nothing
stripRight (Right y) = Just y
```

(All of these are provided by the Fudget library.)

Exercises

6. Implement `waitForSP` described above.

7. Implement serial composition using a tagged parallel composition and a loop.

8. Define a *minimal* set of primitive stream processor combinators. Define the remaining combinators in terms of the minimal set and auxiliary atomic stream processors.

4 Fudgets

We have seen how stream processors can be used to structure a program as a set of concurrent processes.

As outlined in Section 2.3, reactive programs that communicate with several external entities typically contain a handler process for each external entity. The handler processes could be implemented as stream processors, but since they need to communicate both with other stream processors and with the outside world we need a special arrangement to give a stream processor convenient access to the I/O system. The special arrangement is called a *fudget*, and was first presented in [1].

4.1 The Fudget Type

A fudget is a stream processor which has *low level streams* for communication with the input/output system and *high level streams* for communication with other fudgets. Fudgets can be composed with a set of combinators like the ones for plain stream processors presented above. A fudget combinator treats the high level streams like the corresponding stream processor combinator, while the low level streams remain connected directly to the I/O system.

The type of a fudget is

F *hi ho*

where *hi* and *ho* are the types of the high level input and output streams, respectively. In order to make types more readable, the types of the low level streams are not parameters of the fudget type. Instead, they are fixed to the request and response types used by the I/O system.

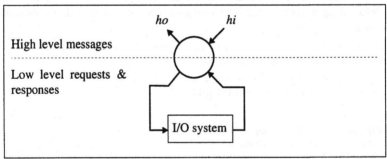

Fig. 17. A fudget of type F *hi ho*

Although fudgets have two input and two output streams, they can be represented as stream processors with one input and one output stream. We will return to this in Section 4.4.

On the top level of a fudget program, you use the function

fudlogue :: F a b → Dialogue

to plug a fudget into the I/O system. fudlogue ignores the high level streams of the fudget, so they can be of any type.

4.2 Fudget Plumbing

As mentioned above, there is a set of fudget combinators directly corresponding to the stream processor combinators described in Section 3. Their names are obtained by replacing the sp suffix with an F. There are also more convenient names for infix use:

```
serCompF, >==< :: F b c → F a b → F a c
compF, >+< :: F i1 o1 → F i2 o2 → F (i1+i2) (o1+o2)
parF, >*< :: F i o → F i o → F i o
listF :: (Eq t) => [(t, F i o)] → F (t, i) (t, o)
loopF :: F a a → F a a
loopLeftF :: F (loop+input) (loop+output) → F input output
loopThroughRightF :: F (o2+i1) (i2+o1) → F i2 o2 → F i1 o1
```

There is one combinator we did not cover in the stream processor section, listF, but from the type it should be clear that this is a variation of tagged parallel composition. The argument is a list of tagged fudgets. The elements in the input and output streams are paired with a tag that says which fudget it is to or from.

Figure 18 illustrates serial and parallel composition of fudgets. The low level streams are

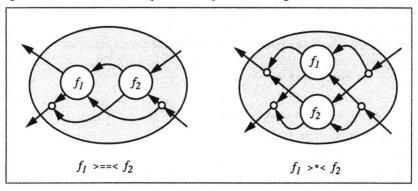

Fig. 18. Serial and parallel composition of fudgets.

treated in the same way in both combinators, i.e., as in parallel stream processor composition, while the high level streams are treated as in the corresponding stream processor combinator. (The tagging of the low level streams is described in Section 4.4.)

4.3 Atomic Fudgets

Fudget programs are built by combining atomic fudgets into more complex ones, using the combinators described above.

In addition to combining fudgets from the library, the application programmer will also need a way to attach his own application specific code. This is done by plugging in *abstract fudgets*.

4.3.1 Abstract Fudgets

An abstract fudget is a fudget that does not use its low level streams. It is simply a stream processor connected to the high level streams of the fudget. The combinator

```
absF :: SP i o → F i o
```

allows you to turn an arbitrary stream processor into an abstract fudget.

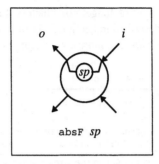

Fig. 19. Abstract Fudgets

Abstract fudgets are often used in serial compositions with other fudgets, i.e., compositions of the form

    absF *sp* >==< *fud*

    fud >==< absF *sp*

are very common. The library provides two operators for these special cases:

```
(>^^=<) :: SP b c → F a b → F a c
sp >^^=< fud = absF sp >==< fud

(>=^^<) :: F b c → SP a b → F a c
fud >=^^< sp = fud >==< absF sp
```

Further, compositions of the form,

    mapSP *f* >^^=< *fud*

    fud >=^^< mapSP *f*

are also common, so the library provides:

```
(>^=<) :: (b→c) → F a b → F a c
(>=^<) :: F b c → (a→b) → F a c
```

The implementations of these operators can be very simple, but by making use of the representation of fudgets and stream processors they can be made more efficient. This has been done in the implementation of the Fudget library.

The next section will show some example uses of these combinators.

4.3.2 Fudgets for I/O from the Library

The Fudget system is implemented on top of the usual stream based I/O system in Haskell, but there are extensions that make fudgets more interesting to use:

1. An interface to X Windows. There is a set of extra requests and corresponding responses that allow you to make calls to the Xlib library. The GUI toolkit described in Section 5 uses this extension.

2. An interface to Unix sockets. This allows fudget programs to communicate with other programs, possibly running on different computers. This extension is used for network communication and client/server programming, as shown in Section 6.

3. A mechanism for asynchronous input and timing, i.e., a way for a program to ask for the next available input from any of a set of sources of input. This allows one fudget to wait for input without blocking other fudgets from doing their work. It also allows fudgets to do something even if no input arrives within a certain time.

The library contains fudgets that provide convenient abstraction from the details of the I/O extensions. These fudgets are described in the sections mentioned above. Below, we just take a quick look at some simple fudgets performing I/O.

Standard I/O Fudgets

To read the standard input (usually the keyboard) and write to the standard output or standard error stream (the screen), you can use the fudgets:

```
stdinF  :: F a String
stdoutF :: F String a
stderrF :: F String a
```

The output from `stdinF` is the characters received from the program's standard input channel. For efficiency reasons, you do not get one character at a time, but larger chunks of characters. If you want the input as a stream of lines, you can use

```
inputLinesSP :: SP String String
```

As a simple example here is a fudget that copies text from the keyboard to the screen with all letters converted to upper case:

```
stdoutF >==< (map toUpper >^=< stdinF)
```

It applies `toUpper` to all characters in the strings output by `stdinF` and then feeds the result directly to `stdoutF`.

Here is a fudget that reverses lines:

```
(stdoutF >=^< ((++"\n").reverse)) >==< (inputLinesSP >^^=< stdinF)
```

The precedences and associativities of the combinators are such that we can write these fudgets as:

```
stdoutF >==< map toUpper >^=< stdinF
stdoutF >=^< (++"\n").reverse >==< inputLinesSP >^^=< stdinF
```

The Timer Fudget

The timer fudget generates output after a certain delay and/or at regular time intervals. Its type is

```
data Tick = Tick

timerF :: F (Maybe (Int, Int)) Tick
```

The timer is initially idle. When it receives `Just (interval,delay)` on its input, it starts ticking. The first tick will be output after `delay` milliseconds and then ticks will appear regularly at `interval` milliseconds intervals, unless `interval` is 0, in which case only one tick will be output. Sending `Nothing` to the timer makes it return to the idle state.

As a simple example, here is a fudget that once a second outputs the number of seconds that have elapsed since it was activated:

```
countSP >^^=< timerF >=^^< putSP (Just (1000,1000)) nullSP

  where countSP = mapAccumlSP inc 0
        inc n Tick = (n+1,n+1)
```

4.4   Implementation of Fudgets

4.4.1   Representing Fudgets as Stream Processors

Although fudgets have more than one input and one output stream, they can be represented as stream processors:

```
type F hi ho = SP (Message TResponse hi) (Message TRequest ho)

data Message low high = Low low | High high
```

We use the type Message instead of the standard disjoint union Either to make programs more readable.

The low level streams carry I/O requests and responses, but when a fudget outputs a request we must be able to send the corresponding response back to the *same* fudget. For this reason, the messages in the low level streams are tagged with a path indicating which fudget in the hierarchy a message is from or to.

```
type TResponse = (Path,Response)
type TRequest  = (Path,Request)

type Path = [Turn]
data Turn = L | R       -- left or right
```

The messages output from atomic fudgets contain an empty path, []. The binary fudget combinators prepend an L or and R onto the path in output messages to indicate whether the message came from the left or the right subfudget. Non-binary combinators can still use a binary encoding of subfudget positions. On the input side, the path is inspected to find out to which subfudget the message should be propagated.

Figure 20 shows an implementation of tagged parallel composition of fudgets. We have re-used tagged parallel composition of stream processors by adding the appropriate tag adjusting pre- and postprocessors. Other fudget combinators can be implemented using similar techniques.

When a request reaches the top level of a fudget program, the path should be detached before the request is output to the I/O system and then attached to the response before it is sent back into the fudget hierarchy. This is taken care of in fudlogue. A simple version of fudlogue is shown in Figure 21. However, to handle asynchronous input you need more than this (see Section 4.4.3).

4.4.2   Writing synchronous atomic fudgets

With the above fudget representation, an atomic fudget which repeatedly accepts a Haskell I/O request, perform it and outputs the response can be implemented as show in Figure 22.

The combinators getHighSP and getLowSP waits for high and low level messages, respectively. They are defined in terms of waitForSP (Section 3.7.2).

```
compF, (>+<) :: F i1 o1 → F i2 o2 → F (i1+i2) (o1+o2)

compF f1 f2 = f1 >+< f2

f1 >+< f2 = mapSP post `serCompSP` (f1 `compSP` f2) `serCompSP` mapSP pre

  where

    post msg =
      case msg of
        Left (High ho1)   → High (Left ho1)
        Right (High ho2)  → High (Right ho2)
        Left (Low (path,req))  → Low (L:path,req)
        Right (Low (path,req)) → Low (R:path,req)

    pre msg =
      case msg of
        High (Left hi1)  → Left (High hi1)
        High (Right hi2) → Right (High hi2)
        Low (L:path,resp) → Left (Low (path,resp))
        Low (R:path,resp) → Right (Low (path,resp))
```

Fig. 20. Tagged parallel composition of fudgets.

```
fudlogue :: F a b → Dialogue
fudlogue mainF = runSP (loopThroughRightSP routeSP (lowSP mainF))

routeSP =
    getLeftSP $ \ (path,request) →
    putSP (Right request) $
    getRightSP $ \ response →
    putSP (Left (path,response)) $
    routeSP

lowSP :: SP (Message li hi) (Message lo ho) → SP li lo
lowSP fud = filterLowSP `serCompSP` fud `serCompSP` mapSP Low

filterLowSP = mapFilterSP stripLow

stripLow (Low  low) = Just low
stripLow (High _  ) = Nothing
```

Fig. 21. A simple version of fudlogue. It does not handle asynchronous input.

```
requestF :: F Request Response
requestF = getHighSP $ \ req →
           putSP (Low ([],req)) $
           getLowSP (_,response) $ \ resp →
           putSP (High response) $
           requestF
```

Fig. 22. An atomic fudget for synchronous I/O.

Some requests should be avoided, because when we evaluate their responses, the program will block. For example, we should not use ReadChan stdin, because its response is a lazy list representing the character streams from the standard input.

Files are usually OK to read, so the fudget readFileF could be useful:

```
readFileF :: F String (IOError + String)
readFileF = post >^=< requestF >=^< ReadFile
   where post (Str s) = Right s
         post (Failure f) = Left f
```

4.4.3 Handling Asynchronous Input

The version of fudlogue in Figure 21 will suffice for programs where the individual fudgets do not block in their I/O requests. If we want to react on input from many sources (e.g. sockets, standard input, the window system, timeout events), this implementation will not be enough. Instead, the library version of fudlogue maintains a table which maps file descriptors and window identifiers to paths. It then issues a request that waits for input on any of these descriptors, or a timeout (using the UNIX select system call). When input becomes available on a descriptor, fudlogue finds the path to the responsible fudget via the table, and sends the input to it.

If the stream model for Haskell I/O is used, the request and response data types need to be extended in order to implement this, something which has been done in the Chalmers Haskell B Compiler.[4] If monadic I/O is used (or rather the C monad, as in Glasgow Haskell [12]), there is no need to change the run-time system.

4.4.4 Fudgets in other I/O models

If we implement fudgets on top of monadic I/O, we might want to perform any monadic I/O operation in a fudget, without the old-fashioned coding in request and response values. What we need then is a function ioF:

```
ioF:: IO a → (a → F b c) → F b c
```

which will take an I/O operation, perform it, and pass the result to the continuation fudget. This can be implemented by modifying the fudget type to be

```
data F hi ho = F (SP hi (IO (F hi ho) + ho))
```

The idea is that if a fudget outputs the value Left ioOp, we should perform the I/O operation ioOp which will yield the continuation fudget. fudlogue would then have the following type and implementation:

```
fudlogue :: F a b → IO ()
fudlogue (F f) = case f of
  NullSP → returnIO ()
  GetSP xf → returnIO ()
  PutSP o f' → case o of
    Left ioOp → ioOp `bindIO` fudlogue
    Right _ → fudlogue (F f')
```

---

4. Or one could have the Haskell program talk to another process which implements the necessary extensions.

Exercises

9. Implement `ioF` and the fudget combinators for the suggested fudget type suitable for monadic I/O.

10. Implement fudgets on top of Clean's I/O system [13]. One approach is to implement monadic I/O first.

5 Fudgets for Graphical User Interfaces

The Fudget concept and the Fudget library was first conceived and designed as a tool for the construction of Graphical User Interfaces (GUIs) in a lazy functional language. Although the Fudget library now supports other kinds of I/O, the biggest part of the library still relates to GUI programming.

In the Fudget library, each GUI element is represented as a fudget. The library provides fudgets for many common basic building blocks, like buttons, popup menus, text boxes, etc. The fudget combinators introduced in Section 4 allow you to combine building blocks into complete user interfaces.

This section starts with a couple of programming examples. They illustrate the basic principles of how to create complete programs from GUI elements and application specific stream processors. After the examples follows a brief presentation some common GUI fudgets from the library. We then describe combinators for layout and a scheme for parameter passing with default values.

5.1 The "Hello, World!" Example

We begin with a simple program that just displays a message in a window (see Figure 23). This example illustrates what the main program should look like, as well as some other practical details.

The Fudgets library contains a fudget[5] for static messages,

```
labelF :: String → F a b
```

It just shows the argument string. It does not use its high level streams.

In the example program we have put the display in a top-level window created with the fudget,

```
shellF:: String → F a b → F a b
```

which given a window title and a fudget, creates a shell window containing the graphical user interface defined by the argument fudget. The fudgets for GUI elements, like `labelF`,

```
module Main where -- The "Hello, World!" program
import Fudgets

main = fudlogue (shellF "Hello" helloF)

helloF = labelF "Hello, World!"
```

Fig. 23. The "Hello World" program.

---

5. To be precise, `labelF` is a function returning a fudget, but for convenience, we will often say "a fudget" when we mean "a function returning a fudget".

can not be used directly on the top level in a program, but must appear inside a shell window.

This illustrates the typical structure of a fudget program. In the `main` function, which in Haskell should have the type `Dialogue`, we call the function `fudlogue`,

```
fudlogue:: F a b → Dialogue
```

which sets up the communication with the window system, gathers commands sent from all fudgets in the program and sends them to the window system, and distributes events coming from the window system to the appropriate fudgets.

Additional things to note with this program is that you do not need to specify the size and placement of the GUI elements. The fudget system automatically picks a suitable size for the label and the size of the shell is adapted to that.

Useful programs of course contain more than one GUI element. The next example will contain two elements!

5.2 The Counter Example

This program is a simple counter. Its user interface consists of a button and a numeric display (see Figure 24). When you press the button, the number in the display is incremented.

In this program we use two basic building blocks,

```
intDispF :: F Int a
```

which is a fudget that displays the numbers it receives on the input, and

```
buttonF :: String → F Click Click
```

which implements command buttons. It outputs clicks,

```
data Click = Click
```

when you press the button. Feeding clicks to its input has the same effect as clicking on the button with the mouse.

When combining fudgets for GUI elements, there are two considerations:

```
module Main(main) where -- A simple counter

import Fudgets

main :: Dialogue
main = fudlogue (shellF "Counter" counterF)

counterF = intDispF >==< absF countSP >==< incButtonF

incButtonF :: F Click Click
incButtonF = buttonF "Increment"

countSP :: SP Click Int
countSP = putSP startstate $
          mapAccumlSP inc startstate
  where inc n Click = (n+1,n+1)

startstate = 0
```

Fig. 24. The Counter Example

1. The data flow aspect: how should they communicate, i.e., should one use a serial, parallel, or some other combinator?

2. The visual aspect: how should the GUI elements be placed on the screen?

These are quite separate concerns, and fortunately the fudget system allows us to worry about them one at a time. Thanks to the automatic layout system, you can concentrate on the data flow aspect during the initial development stage. Later on, if you are not happy with the default layout, you can add layout information in one of the ways described in Section 5.5.

The data flow in this program, illustrated as a circuit diagram in Figure 25, is simple and is implemented by one program line in the definition of `counterF`:

```
dispF >==< absF countSP >==< incButtonF
```

`countSP` contains the application specific code in this program. It starts by outputting the initial state, so that it will be visible in the display when the program starts. It then uses `mapAccumlSP` (Section 3.3) to maintain an internal counter that is incremented for each click received from the button.

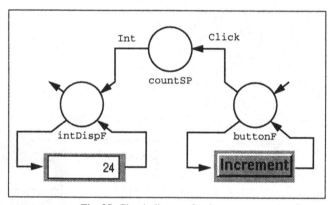

Fig. 25. Circuit diagram for the counter

5.3 Extending the Counter

What if we want an extended counter that can be incremented, decremented and reset?

Starting from the simple counter program above, we obviously have to add two new buttons, but we will also have to change `countSP`. It will now have to deal with three different input messages that have the effect of incrementing, decrementing and resetting the current value of the counter.

There are different ways you can go about this. One way would be to define a data type for the kind of messages we need,

```
data ButtonMsg = Inc | Dec | Reset
```

and then interpret these inside `countSP`. Another way would be to define a general state maintaining stream processor, which receives state modifying functions on the input and delivers the new state on the output after a state modifier has been applied. Here is such a stream processor:

```
stateSP :: state → SP (state→state) state
stateSP state = putSP state $ mapAccumlSP modify state
  where modify state f = (state',state')
          where state' = f state
```

Using `stateSP` instead of `countSP`, all that is left to do to complete the extended counter is to define buttons that output the appropriate state modifying functions,

```
incButtonF   = fButtonF (+1)       "Increment"
decButtonF   = fButtonF (+(-1))    "Decrement"
resetButtonF = fButtonF (const 0) "Reset"

fButtonF f lbl = const f >^=< buttonF lbl
```

and put everything together. The resulting program is shown in Figure 26.

```
module  Main(main) where -- An extended counter

import Fudgets

main :: Dialogue
main = fudlogue (shellF "Counter" counterF)

counterF = intDispF >==<
           absF (stateSP startstate) >==<
           buttonsF

buttonsF :: F a (Int→Int)
buttonsF = incButtonF >*< decButtonF >*< resetButtonF

incButtonF   = fButtonF (+1)       "Increment"
decButtonF   = fButtonF (+(-1))    "Decrement"
resetButtonF = fButtonF (const 0) "Reset"

fButtonF f lbl = const f >^=< buttonF lbl

stateSP :: state → SP (state→state) state
stateSP state = putSP state $
                mapAccumlSP modify state
  where modify state f = (state',state')
          where state' = f state

startstate = 0
```

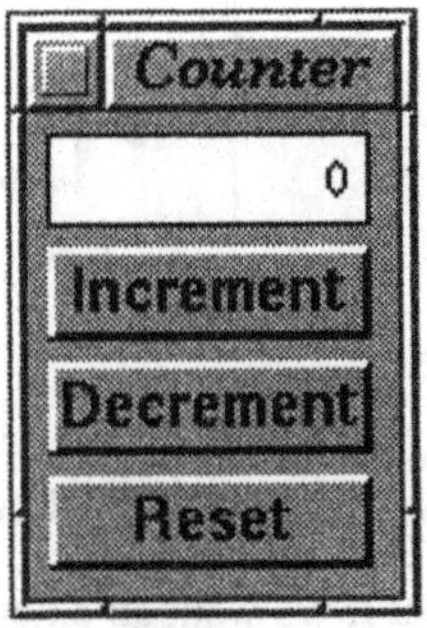

Fig. 26. The Extended Counter Example

Exercises

11. Draw the circuit diagram for the extended counter.

12. Extend the extended counter to a pocket calculator. (Don't worry about the layout of the buttons at this point.)

5.4 More GUI elements

In this section we present some common GUI elements provided by the Fudget Library. For more information, consult the reference manual, which is available via WWW [5].

5.4.1 Buttons

We have already seen `buttonF` in the examples above. It provides *command buttons*, i.e., buttons that you press to trigger some action. The Fudget library also provides toggle buttons and radio groups (Figure 27). Pressing these buttons causes a change that have a lasting visual effect (and probably also some other lasting effect). A toggle button changes between two states (on and off) each time you press it. A radio group allows you to activate one of several mutually exclusive alternatives. The types of these fudgets are

```
toggleButtonF :: String → F Bool Bool
radioGroupF   :: (Eq alt) => [(alt,String)] → alt → F alt alt
```

The input messages can be used to change the setting under program control.

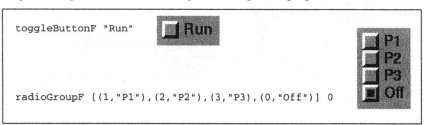

Fig. 27. Toggle buttons and radio groups

5.4.2 Menus and Scrollable Lists

Menus serve much the same purpose as buttons, but they save screen space by appearing only when activated. The fudget `menuF name alts`, where

```
menuF :: String → [(alt,String)] → F alt alt,
```

provides pull-down menus. `name` is the constantly visible name you press to activate the menu and `alts` is the list of menu alternatives.

The fudget

```
popupMenuF :: [(alt,String)] → F i o → F (alt+i) (alt+o)
```

provides pop-up menus, i.e., menus that are activated when a certain mouse button (the third by default) is pressed over the screen area occupied by the argument fudget. The menu fudget and the argument fudget are put in a tagged parallel composition.

As an example, suppose we wanted a compact version of the extended counter in Section 5.3. We could then replace the three buttons with a pop-up menu attached to the display (Figure 28).

When the number of alternatives is large, or when they change dynamically, you can use a scrollable list instead of a menu. The function

```
pickListF :: (a→String) → F [a] a
```

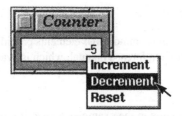

Fig. 28. A Compact Extended Counter

(shown in Figure 29) takes a show function and returns a fudget that displays lists of alternatives received on the high level input. When an alternative is selected, by clicking on it, it will appear in the output stream.

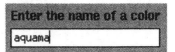

Fig. 29. `pickListF`   **Fig. 30.** `stringF`

Exercises

13. Implement the compact extended counter. *Hint*: a handy combinator is `serCompLeftToRightF`,

```
serCompLeftToRightF :: F (i+a) (a+o) → F i o
```

which turns a tagged parallel composition into a serial composition.

5.4.3   Entering values

Choosing an alternative from a list is usually easier than typing something, e.g., the name of a colour, on the keyboard. But when there is no predefined set of alternatives, you can use fudgets that allow the user to enter values from the keyboard. The library provides

```
stringF :: InF String String
intF    :: InF Int Int
```

for entering strings and integers (see Figure 30). For entering other types of values, you can use `stringF` and attach the appropriate printer and parser functions. The type `InF` is defined as

```
type InF a b = F a (InputMsg b)
data InputMsg b = ...
```

The input fudgets have two kinds of output messages: one that is output whenever the current value changes and one that is output when the user indicates, e.g., by pressing the Return or Enter key, that the value is complete. You can use

```
stripInputMsg :: InputMsg a → a
inputDoneSP :: SP (InputMsg a) a
```

as postprocessors to filter out the messages you are interested in. Use

```
stripInputMsg >^=< stringF
```

if you are interested in all changes made to a string, and

```
inputDoneSP >^^=< stringF
```

if you only want a message when the user has completed a string.

5.4.4 Displaying and editing text

The library provides the fudgets

```
moreF :: F [String] a
moreFileF, moreFileShellF:: F String a
```

which can display longer text.[6] The input to moreF is lines of text to be displayed. The other two fudgets display the contents of file names received on the high level input. moreFile-ShellF in addition appears in its own shell window with a title reflecting the name of the file being displayed.

There also is a text editor fudget:

```
editorF :: F EditCmd EditEvt
```

which supports cut/paste editing with the mouse as well as a small subset of the keystrokes used in GNU emacs. It also has an undo/redo mechanism.

5.4.5 Scroll Bars

GUI elements that potentially can become very large, like pickListF, moreF and editorF have scroll bars attached by default. There are also combinators to explicitly add scroll bars:

```
scrollF, vScrollF, hScrollF :: F a b → F a b
```

The v and h version give only vertical and horizontal scroll bars, respectively. The argument fudget can be any combination of GUI elements.

5.5 Layout

When developing fudget programs, normally we don't have to think about the actual layout of the GUI fudgets if we don't want to. For example, the fudget

```
shellF "Buttons" (buttonF "A Button" >+< buttonF "Another Button")
```

will get some default layout which might look like Figure 30. Sooner or later, we will want to have control over the layout, though. The GUI library lets us do this two different ways:

1. *Fudget Combinator Layout.* This method is based on variants of the fudget combinators >+<, >==<, and listF. It is a quick way of adding layout control to a program. However, the layout possibilities are limited by the structure of the fudget program.

---

6. The names comes from the fact that they serve the same purpose as the UNIX program more.

Fig. 30.

2. *Name Layout.* Here, the layout is specified separately from the fudget structure. GUI fudgets are given names, and these are used to specify layout at one place inside each shellF.

Before describing these, we will present the layout combinators that both of them use.

5.5.1 Boxes, Placers and Spacers

Layout is done hierarchically. Each GUI fudget will reside in a *box*, which will have a certain size and position when the layout is complete. A list of boxes can be put inside a single box by a *placer*, which also defines how the boxes should be placed in relation to each other inside the larger box. The effects of some placers are illustrated in Figure 34. The parameter

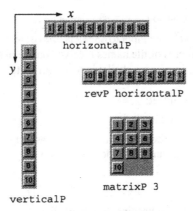

Fig. 31. Different placers.

to matrixP specifies the number of columns the matrix should have. The types of the placers are

```
horizontalP :: Placer
verticalP :: Placer
matrixP :: Int → Placer
revP :: Placer → Placer
```

The effect of applying revP is as if the list of boxes were reversed. Another higher order placer is flipP, which transforms a placer into a mirror symmetric placer, with respect to the line $x = y$:

```
flipP :: Placer → Placer
```

Hence, we can define verticalP as

```
verticalP = flipP horizontalP
```

So, placers are used to specify the layout of a group of boxes. In contrast, *spacers* are used to wrap a box around a single box. Spacers could be used to determine how a box should be aligned if it is given too much space, or to add extra space around a box. Examples of

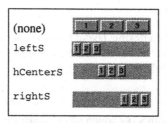

Fig. 32. Spacers for alignment.

spacers that deal with alignment can be seen in Figure 32. On top, the box (placed with `horizontalP`) has to fill up all the available space. The lower three boxes have been placed inside a box, which consumes the extra space. The spacers used are derived from the spacer `hAlignS`, whose argument tells the ratio between the space to the left and the right side of the box:

```
hAlignS :: RealFrac a => a → Spacer
leftS = hAlignS 0
hCenterS = hAlignS 0.5
rightS = hAlignS 1
```

There is a corresponding spacer to `flipP`, namely `flipS`. It too flips the x and y coordinates, and let us define some useful vertical spacers:

```
flipS :: Spacer → Spacer
vAlignS a = flipS (hAlignS a)
topS = flipS leftS
vCenterS = flipS hCenterS
bottomS = flipS rightS
```

By `compS`, we can compose spacers, and define a spacer that centers both horizontally and vertically:

```
compS :: Spacer → Spacer → Spacer
centerS = vCenterS `compS` hCenterS
```

To add extra space to the left and right of a box, we use `hMarginS left right`, where

```
hMarginS :: Distance → Distance → Spacer
type Distance = Int
```

Distances are given in number of pixels.[7] From `hMarginS`, we can derive `marginS`, which adds equally much space on all sides of a box:

```
vMarginS above below = flipS (hMarginS above below)
marginS s = vMarginS s s `compS` hMarginS s s
```

Spacers can be applied to fudgets by means of `spacerF`:

```
spacerF :: Spacer → F a b → F a b
```

`spacerF f` will apply the spacer to all boxes inside `f`.[8] We can also modify a placer by wrapping a spacer around the box that the placer assembles:

```
spacerP :: Spacer → Placer → Placer
```

For example, `spacerP leftS horizontalP` gives a horizontal placer which will left adjust its boxes.

---

7. This is easy to implement, but makes programs somewhat device dependent.
8. It will not apply it recursively to the boxes inside the boxes, however.

5.5.2 Combinator Layout

Combinator layout is good when flexible layout is not a major issue in your program. As an example, we could specify that the two buttons in Figure 30 should have vertical layout by saying that the first button should be above the second:

```
shellF "Buttons"
        ((buttonF "A Button",Above) >+#< buttonF "Another Button")
```

Here, we have replaced `>+<` with `>+#<` which takes an extra layout argument:

```
(>+#<) :: (F a b,Orientation) → F c d → F (Sum a c) (Sum b d)
data Orientation = Above | Below | RightOf | LeftOf
```

The result can be seen in Figure 33. In a similar way, the first button could be placed below,

Fig. 33.

to the right of, or to the left of the second button, by using the corresponding constructor of type `Orientation`.

The same trick can be used on serial composition by using `>==#<`:

```
(>==#<) :: (F a b,Orientation) → F c a → F c b
```

If we want to specify the layout for the fudgets inside a `listF`, we use `listLF` instead:

```
listLF :: (Eq a) => Placer → [(a, F b c)] → F (a, b) (a, c)
```

The first argument to `listLF` is a placer, specifying the layout.

Suppose we have the following fudget, where we have used combinator layout:

```
top = (intDispF >=^^< acc,Above) >==#< buttons

buttons = snd >^=< listLF verticalP (number 1 buttonlist)
buttonlist = [const f >^=< buttonF s | (f,s) <- list]
        where list = [((+1),    "Increment"),
                      ((+(-1)),"Decrement")]

acc = ac 0 where ac n = putSP n $ getSP $ \f → ac (f n)
```

It will have the layout shown in Figure 34a. Now, suppose we want the number display to

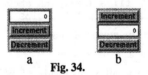

a   **Fig. 34.**   b

appear between the buttons, as in Figure 34b. We can not do that with combinator layout without restructuring the program, because the buttons reside in a `listLF`, whose placer will box them together. By using Name Layout, we get around the problem.

5.5.3 Name Layout

To separate layout from fudget structure, we put unique names on each box (usually corresponding to a simple GUI fudget) whose layout we want to control, by using nameF:

```
type LName = String
nameF :: LName → F a b → F a b
```

The layout of the boxes which have been named in this way is specified using the type NameLayout. Here are the basic functions for constructing NameLayout values:

```
leafNL :: LName → NameLayout
placeNL :: Placer → [NameLayout] → NameLayout
spaceNL :: Spacer → NameLayout → NameLayout
```

The desired layout in Figure 34b has the buttons in a row, so we will use verticalP. To apply the layout to named boxes, we use nameLayoutF:

```
nameLayoutF :: NameLayout → F a b → F a b
```

The names used for the boxes are "bound" by nameLayoutF, by corresponding occurrences of leafNL. Our example becomes

```
top = nameLayoutF $ nameF dispN textF >=^^< acc >==< buttons

buttons = snd >^=< listF (number 1 buttonlist)
buttonlist = [const f >^=< nameF n (buttonF s) | (n,f,s) <- list]
        where list = [(incN,(+1),     "Increment"),
                      (decN,((+(-1)),"Decrement")]

acc = ac 0 where ac n = put1SP n $ getSP $ \f → ac (f n)
-- only layout below
layout = listNL verticalP (map leafNL [incN, dispN, decN])
incN = "inc"
decN = "dec"
dispN = "disp"
```

Now, we can muck around with the layout of the two buttons and the display as much as we want, without changing the rest of the program. The actual strings used for names are not important, as long as they are unique within the part of the fudget structure where they are in scope. So instead we could write

```
(incN:decN:dispN:_) = map show [1..]
```

5.5.4 The placer fudget (the middle way)

Actually, there is a third way of doing layout, which is somewhere in between Fudget Combinator Layout and Name Layout. The fudget

```
placerF :: Placer → F a b → F a b
```

will apply the placer to all boxes in the argument fudget. The order of the boxes is left to right, with respect to the combinators listF, dynListF, >==< and >+<. Actually, when there is no layout specified in a shell fudget with more than one box in it, an implicit placer fudget is applied to obtain one box, which the shell fudget can handle.

With placerF, we can derive the combinators used for Fudget Combinator Layout:

```
listLF placer f = placerF placer (listF f)
place2F (><) (f1,a1) f2 = placerF (placer a1) (f1 >< f2) where
    placer LeftOf = horizontalP
```

```
    placer RightOf = revP horizontalP
    placer Above = verticalP
    placer Below = revP verticalP
(>+#<) = place2F (>+<)
(>==#<) = place2F (>==<)
```

If we take a look at the layout in Figure 34a again, we see that if we write a placer that permutes the first and the second box (cf. revP), we could get the desired layout in b. However, such a layout system would be sensitive for changes in the fudget structure (e.g., if we change $f > + < g$ to $g > + < f$, we have to change the placer. If we use Name Layout, this change does not affect the layout.

Exercises

14. Augment the pocket calculator in exercise 12 with proper layout of the buttons.

5.6 Parameters for Customization

There are many aspects of GUI fudgets that one might want to modify, e.g. the font or the foreground or background colours for displayF. The simple GUI fudgets have some hopefully reasonable default values for these aspects, but sooner or later, we will want to change them. A simple way of doing this would be to have a data type with constructors for each parameter that has a default value. In the case of displayF, it might be

```
data DisplayFParams = Font FontName |
                      ForegroundColor ColorName |
                      BackgroundColor ColorName
```

Then, one could have the display fudget take a list of display parameters as a first argument:

```
displayF :: [DisplayFParams] → F String a
```

Whenever we are happy with the default values, we just use an empty parameter list, and all is fine.

However, suppose we want to do the same trick with the button fudget. We want to be able to customise font and colours for foreground and background, like the display fudget, and in addition we want to specify a "hotkey" that could be used instead of clicking the button:

```
data ButtonFParams =  Font FontName |
                      ForegroundColor ColorName |
                      BackgroundColor ColorName |
                      HotKey (ModState,Key)
```

Now, we are in trouble if we want to customise a button and a display in the same module, because in a given scope in Haskell, no two constructor names should be equal. Of course, we could rename the constructors when importing them, but this is tedious. We could also have different constructor names to start with (ButtonFFont, ButtonFForegroundColor etc.), which is just as tedious.

Our current solution[9] is to not use constructors directly, but to use overloaded functions instead. We will define a class for each kind of default parameter. Then, each customizable fudget will have instances for all parameters that it accepts. This entails some more work

---

9. The basics of this design are due to John Hughes.

when defining customizable fudgets, but the fudgets become easier to use, which we feel more than justifies the extra work.

5.6.1 A Mechanism for Default Values

Let us return to the display fudget example, and show how to make it customizable. First, we define classes for the customizable parameters:

```
type Customiser a = a → a

class HasFont a where
    setFont :: FontName → Customiser a

class HasForegroundColor a where
    setForegroundColor :: ColorName → Customiser a

class HasBackgroundColor a where
    setBackgroundColor :: ColorName → Customiser a
```

Then, we define a data type for the parameter list to `displayF`:

```
data DisplayF = Pars [DisplayFParams]
```

and add the instance declarations

```
instance HasFont DisplayF where
    setFont p (Pars ps) = Pars (Font p:ps)

instance HasForegroundColor DisplayF where
    setForegroundColor p (Pars ps) = Pars (ForegroundColor p:ps)

instance HasBackgroundColor DisplayF where
    setBackgroundColor p (Pars ps) = Pars (BackgroundColor p:ps)
```

The type of `displayF` will be

```
displayF :: (Customiser DisplayF) → F String a
```

We put these declarations inside the module defining `displayF`, making `DisplayF` abstract. When we later use `displayF`, the only thing we need to know about `DisplayF` is its instances, which tell us that we can set font and colours. For example:

```
myDisplayF = displayF (setFont "fixed" . setBackgroundColor "green")
```

If we want to have `buttonF` customizable the same way, we define the additional class:

```
class HasKeyEquiv a  where
    setKeyEquiv :: (ModState,Key) → Customiser a
```

The button module defines

```
data ButtonF = Pars [ButtonFParams]
```

and makes it abstract, as well as defining instances for font, colours and hotkeys.[10] We can now customise both the display fudget and the button fudget, if we want:

```
myFudget = displayF setMyFont >+< buttonF (setMyFont.setMyKey) "Quit"
    where setMyFont = setFont "fixed"
          setMyKey = setKeyEquiv ([Meta],"q")
```

---

10. Note that the instance declarations for font and colours will look exactly the same as for the display parameters!

If we do not want to change any default values, we use standard, which doesn't modify anything:

```
standard :: Customiser a
standard p = p

standardDisplayF = displayF standard
```

5.6.2 The Customizable GUI Fudgets

The GUI fudget library is designed so that when you start writing a fudget program, there should be as few distracting parameters as possible. Default values will be chosen for colour, fonts, layout, etc. But a customizable fudget must inevitably have an additional argument, even if it is standard. We use short and natural names for the standard versions of GUI fudgets, without customization argument. So we have

```
buttonF :: String → F Click Click
buttonF = buttonF' standard
buttonF' :: Customiser ButtonF → String → F Click Click

displayF :: F String a
displayF = displayF' standard
displayF' :: Customiser DisplayF → F String a
```

and so on.[11] This way, a programmer can start using the toolkit without having to worry about the customization concept. Later, when the need for customization comes, just add an apostrophe and the parameter.

Most parameters can in fact be changed *dynamically*, if needed. Therefore, each customizable fudget comes in a third variant, which is the most expressive:

```
type CF p a b = F (Customiser p + a) b
buttonF'' :: Customiser ButtonF → String → CF ButtonF Click Click
displayF'' :: Customiser DisplayF → CF DisplayF String a
```

etc.

Exercises

15. Use different colours for different kinds of buttons in the pocket calculator from exercise 12 and 14.

6   Client/Server Programming & Typed Sockets

In this section, we will see how fudgets can be suitable for other kind of I/O than graphical user interfaces. We will write client/server applications, where a fudget program acts as a server on one computer. The clients are also fudget programs, and they can be run from other computers if desired.

The server is an example of a fudget program which may not have the need for a graphical user interface. However, the server should be capable of handling many clients simultaneously. One way of organising the server is to have a *client handler* for each connected

---

11. One could also have the apostrophe on the standard versions, something that sounds attractive since apostrophes usually stand for omitted things (in this case the customizer). But then a programmer must learn which fudgets are customizable (and thus need an apostrophe), even if she isn't interested in customization.

client. Each client handler communicates with its client via a connection (a socket), but it will probably also need to interact with other parts of the server. This is a situation where fudgets come in handy. The server will dynamically create fudgets as client handlers for each new client that connects.

We will also see how the type system of Haskell can be used to associate the address (a host name and a port number) of a server with the type of the messages that the server can send and receive. If the client is also written in Haskell, and imports the same specification of the typed address as the server, we know that the client and the server will agree on the types of the messages, or the compiler will catch a type error.

6.1 Fudgets for Internet Stream Sockets

The type of sockets that we consider here are Internet stream sockets. They provide a reliable, two-way connection, similar to pipes, between any two hosts on the Internet. They are used in Unix tools like telnet, ftp, finger, mail, Usenet and World Wide Web.

6.1.1 Clients

Fig. 35. A client about to connect to a server.

To be able to communicate with a server, a client must know where the server is located. The location is determined by the name of the host (a computer on the network) and a port number. A typical host name is www.cs.chalmers.se. The port number distinguishes different servers running on the same host. Standard services have standard port numbers. For example, WWW servers are usually located on port 80.

The Fudget library uses the following types:

```
type Host = String
type Port = Int
```

The simple fudget

```
socketTransceiverF :: Host → Port → F String String
```

allows a client to connect to a server and communicate with it (Figure 35).[12] Chunks of characters appear in the output stream as soon as they are received from the server (c.f. stdinF in Section 4.3.2).

The simplest possible client you can write is perhaps a telnet client:

```
telnetF host port = stdoutF >==< socketTransceiverF host port
                            >==< stdinF
```

---

12. The library also provides combinators that gives more control over error handling and the opening and closing of connections.

This simple program doesn't do the option negotiations required by the standard telnet protocol [RFC854,855], so it doesn't work well when connected to the standard telnet server (on port 23). However, you can use it to talk to many other standard servers, e.g., mail and news servers.

6.1.2 Servers

Whereas clients actively connect to a specific server, servers passively wait for clients to connect. When a client connects, a new communication channel is established, but the server typically continues to accept connections from other clients as well (Figure 36).

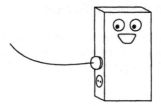

Fig. 36. A communication socket is created.

A simple fudget to create servers is

```
simpleSocketServerF :: Port → F (Int,String) (Int,String)
```

The server allows clients to connect to the argument port on the host where the server is running. A client is assigned a unique number when it connects to the server. The messages to and from `simpleSocketServerF` are strings tagged with a client number. Empty strings in the input and output streams mean that a connection should be closed or has been closed, respectively.

This simple server fudget does not directly support a program structure with one handler fudget per client. A better combinator is shown below.

Exercise 16.   Write a chat client and a chat server. The chat client allows a user to exchange messages with other users running the chat client. A message entered by a user is sent to all other users.

6.2   Typed Sockets

Many Internet protocols use messages that are human readable text. When implementing these, the natural type to use for messages is `string`. However, when we write both clients and severs in Haskell, we may want to use an appropriate data type for messages sent between clients and server, as you would do if the client and server were fudgets in the same program. In this section we show how to abstract away from the actual representation of messages on the network.

We introduce two abstract types for typed port numbers and typed server addresses. These types will be parameterised on the type of messages that we can transmit and receive on the sockets. First, we have the typed port numbers:

```
data TPort c s
```

The client program needs to know the typed address of the server:

```
data TServerAddress c s
```

In these types, c and s stand for the type of messages that the client and server transmit, respectively.

To make a typed port, we apply the function tPort on a port number:

```
tPort :: (Text c, Text s) => Port → TPort c s
```

The context Text in the signature tells us that not all types can be used as message types. Values will be converted into text strings before transmitted as a message on the socket. This is clearly not very efficient, but it is a simple way to implement a machine independent protocol.

Given a typed port, we can form a typed server address by specifying a computer as a host name:

```
tServerAddress :: TPort c s → Host → TServerAddress c s
```

For example, suppose we want to write a server that will run on the host animal, listening on port 8888. The server should accept integer messages, and will send strings to the clients. This can be specified by

```
thePort :: TPort Int String
thePort = tPort 8888
theServerAddr = tServerAddress thePort "animal"
```

A typed server address can be used in the client program to open a socket to the server by means of tSocketTransceiverF:

```
tSocketTransceiverF ::
        (Text c, Text s) => TServerAddress c s → F c (Maybe s)
```

Again, the Text context appears, since this is where the actual conversion from and to text strings occurs. tSocketTransceiverF will output an incoming message m as Just m, and if the connection is closed by the other side, it will output Nothing.

In the server, we will wait for connections, and create client handlers when new clients connect. This is accomplished with tSocketServerF:

```
tSocketServerF :: (Text c, Text s) => TPort c s →
        (F s (Maybe c) → F a (Maybe b)) → F (Int,a) (Int,Maybe b)
```

So tSocketServerF takes two arguments, the first one is the port number to listen on for new clients. The second argument is the client handler function. Whenever a new client connects, a socket transceiver fudget is created and supplied to the client handler function, which yields a client handler fudget. The client handler is then spawned inside tSocketServerF. From the outside of tSocketServerF, the different client handlers are distinguished by unique integer tags. When a client handler emits Nothing, tSocketServerF will interpret this as the end of a connection, and kill the handler.

The idea is that the client handlers should use the transceiver argument for the communication with the client. Complex handlers can be written with loopThroughRightF, if desired. In many cases though, the supplied socket transceiver is good enough as a client handler directly. A simple socket server can therefore be defined by:

```
simpleTSocketServerF :: TPort c s → F (Int,s) (Int,Maybe c)
simpleTSocketServerF port = tSocketServerF port id
```

6.3   Avoiding Type Errors Between Client and Server

By using the following style for developing a client and a server, we can detect when the client and the server disagree on the message types:

First, we define a typed port to be used by both the client and the server. We put this definition in a module of its own. Suppose that the client sends integers to the server, which in turn can send strings:

```
module MyPort where
myPort :: TPort Int String
myPort = tPort 9000
```

We have picked an arbitrary port number. Now, if the client is as follows:

```
module Main where -- Client
import MyPort
...
main = fudlogue (... tSocketTransceiverF myPort ...)
```

and the server

```
module Main where -- Server
import MyPort
...
main = fudlogue (... tSocketServerF myPort ... )
```

then the compiler can check that we don't try to send messages of the wrong type. Of course, this is not foolproof. There is always the problem of having inconsistent compiled versions of the client and the server, for example. Or one could use different port declarations in the client and the server.

Now, what happens if we forget to put a type signature on myPort? Is it not possible then that we get inconsistent message types, since the client and the server could instantiate myPort to different types? The answer is no, and this is because of a subtle property of Haskell, namely the monomorphism restriction. A consequence of this restriction is that the type of myPort can not contain any type variables. If we forget the type signature, this would be the case, and the compiler would complain. It is possible to circumvent the restriction by explicitly expressing the context in the type signature, though. When defining typed ports, it defeats the purpose, of course:

```
module MyPort where
myPort :: Text a => TPort a String -- No no, don't do this!
myPort = tPort 9000
```

6.4 Example: Calendar

Outside the lunch room in our department, there is a whiteboard where the week's activities are registered. We will look at an electronic version of this calendar, where people can get a view like this on their workstation (Figure 37).

The entries in the calendar can be edited by everyone. When that happens, all calendar clients should be updated immediately.

The calendar consists of a server maintaining a database, and the clients, running on the workstations.

6.4.1 The Calendar Server

The server's job is to maintain a database with all the entries on the whiteboard, to receive update messages from clients and then update the other connected clients. The server con-

	Måndag	Tisdag	Onsdag	Torsdag	Fredag
8					
9					
10					
11					
12					
13	Problemlösning			Doktorandkurs:	Doktorandkurs: Datorstödd
14				Temporal Logic	utveckling av bevis & pgm
15				Multimöte:	Kakprat: Erland
16				Magnus C & Kent K	SUPA JÄRNET!

Fig. 37. The calendar client.

sists of the stream processor databaseSP, and a tSocketServerF, where the output from the stream processor goes to tSocketServerF, and vice versa (Figure 38).

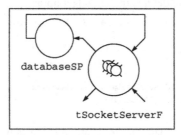

Fig. 38. The structure of server. The small fudgets are client handlers created inside the socket server.

databaseSP maintains two values: the client list cl, which is a list of the tags of the connected clients, and the database db, organised as a list of (key,value) pairs. This database is sent to newly connected clients. When a user changes an entry in her client, it will send that entry to the server, which will update the database and use the client list to broadcast the new entry to all the other connected clients. When a client disconnects, it is removed from the client list. The client handlers (clienthandler) initially announce themselves with NewHandler, then they apply HandlerMsg to incoming messages.

Here is a complete listing of the server:

```
module Main where -- Server
import Fudgets
import MyPort(myPort) -- also used in the client

main = fudlogue (server myPort)

data HandlerMsg a = NewHandler | HandlerMsg a
server port = loopF (databaseSP [] [] >^^=<
                     tSocketServerF port clienthandler) where
  clienthandler transceiver =
      -- New client - announce myself,
      -- convert Just a → Just (HandlerMsg a)
    put1SP (Just NewHandler) (mapSP (mapMaybe HandlerMsg))
    >^^=< transceiver
databaseSP cl db =
```

```
getSP $ \(i,e) →
let clbuti = filter (/= i) cl
in case e of
        -- A message from client number i:
        Just handlermsg -> case handlermsg of
            -- A new client, send the database to it,
            -- and add to client list:
            NewHandler -> putSP [(i,d) | d <- db] $
                          databaseSP (i:cl) db
            -- Update entry in the database...¹³
            HandlerMsg s -> let db' = replace s db in
                -- ... and tell the other clients
                            putSP [(i',s) | i' <- clbuti] $
                            databaseSP cl db'
        -- A client disconnected, remove it from
        -- the client list:
        Nothing -> databaseSP clbuti db
```

`replace` and `mapMaybe` are defined in the Fudget library:

```
replace :: (Eq a) => (a,b) → [(a,b)] → [(a,b)]
replace p [] = [p]
replace (t, v) ((t', v') : ls') | t == t' = (t, v) : ls'
replace p (l : ls') = l : replace p ls'

mapMaybe:: (a → b) → Maybe a → Maybe b
mapMaybe f Nothing = Nothing
mapMaybe f (Just x) = Just (f x)
```

The type of the (key,value) pairs in the database is the same as the type of the messages received and sent, and is defined in the module `MyPort`:

```
module MyPort where
import Fudgets
type SymTPort a = TPort a a
myPort :: SymTPort ((String,Int),String)
    --            e.g. (("Torsdag",13),"Doktorandkurs:")
port = tPort 8888
```

Exercises

17. Implement the calendar client.

7   Conclusions

Stream processors and fudgets make it possible to structure programs as networks of concurrent processes in purely functional languages, like Haskell. This is a useful program structure when a program interacts with several external entities and all the time has to be prepared to react to input from any external source. We have shown two concrete examples of this. In Graphical User Interface programming the external entities that the program interacts with are the GUI components. In Client/Server programming the server usually interacts with several clients.

---

13. Unfortunately, the update will not take place until a new client connects, resulting in a space leak. It can be eliminated by inserting `seq (force db')` $ after `let db' = replace s db in`.

Rather than being a new mechanism for I/O, the Fudget concept is an abstraction that can be implemented on top of many existing I/O systems, e.g., stream based I/O, monadic I/O, or the I/O model used in Clean. Although fudgets can be implemented on top of sequential I/O models, fudgets give the feeling of programming in a parallel language.

The Fudget combinators allow programs to be built in a hierarchical way. The basic building blocks are fudgets. Complete programs are fudgets too. This makes it easy to use existing applications as components when writing new, larger applications.

Polymorphism and higher order functions are valuable features of functional languages that allow libraries of re-usable software components to be both flexible and type safe. The Fudget library clearly benefits from this.

7.1 More Information on Fudgets

There are lots of things we didn't write about (because of time and space constraints). For example, these notes don't say much about the implementation of the Fudget GUI toolkit or how to write new GUI elements. We haven't said anything about parallel implementations of stream processors. We have not shown any large programming examples.

The WWW home page for Fudgets is located at URL

```
http://www.cs.chalmers.se/Fudgets/
```

There you can find pointers to more information on fudgets. You can also run demo programs and browse the hypertext version of the Fudget Library Reference Manual.

The Fudget library is distributed free of charge by anonymous ftp from ftp.cs.chalmers.se (for more info, see the Fudgets home page).

7.2 Acknowledgements

Thanks to Johan Jeuring, Andrew Moran and Jan Sparud for comments on these notes. Jan Sparud also implemented the first version of Name Layout, described in Section 5.5.3. John Hughes came up with the idea of default parameters (Section 5.6).

References

[1] M. Carlsson & T. Hallgren, Fudgets - A Graphical User Interface in a Lazy Functional Language, in *FPCA 93' - Conference on Functional Programming Languages and Computer Architecture*, pages 321--330, June 1993.

[2] M. Carlsson & T. Hallgren, The Fudget distribution,
     See ftp://ftp.cs.chalmers.se/pub/haskell/chalmers/

[3] A. D. Gordon, *Functional Programming and Input/Output*, Cambridge University Press, 1994. ISBN 0-521-47103-6.

[4] A. D. Gordon et al, *Haskell 1.3 Monadic I/O Definition*.
     At http://www.cl.cam.ac.uk/users/adg/io.html

[5] T. Hallgren & M. Carlsson, *The Fudgets Home Page*.
     At http://www.cs.chalmers.se/Fudgets/

[6] P. Hudak & R. S. Sundaresh. *On the expressiveness of purely functional I/O systems*. Research Report YALEU/DCS/RR-665, Yale University Department of Computer Science, March 1989.

[7] Paul Hudak et al., *Report on the Programming Language Haskell: A Non-Strict, Purely Functional Language*, March 1992. Version 1.2. Also in Sigplan Notices, May 1992.

[8] P.J. Landin. A correspondence between ALGOL 60 and Church's lambda-notation: Parts I and II. *Communications of the ACM*, 8(2,3):89-101, 158-165, February and March 1965.

[9] J. McCarthy. A basis for a mathematical theory of computations. In P. Brattort and D. Hirschberg, editors, *Computer Programming and Formal Systems*, pages 33–70. North-Holland, 1963.

[10] R. Milner, *Communication and concurrency*, Prentice-Hall International, 1989. ISBN 0-13-114984-9.

[11] R. Noble & C. Runciman, *Functional Languages and Graphical User Interfaces – a review and a case study*, Technical report YCS-94-223, Dept. of Comp. Sci., Univ. of York, Heslington, York, Y01 5DD, England, 1994.
At ftp://minster.york.ac.uk/reports/YCS-94-223.ps.Z

[12] Simon L. Peyton Jones, Cordelia V. Hall, Kevin Hammond, Will Partain, and Philip Wadler "The Glasgow Haskell compiler: a technical overview" In *Proc. UK Joint Framework for Information Technology (JFIT) Technical Conference*, July 93.
At ftp://ftp.dcs.gla.ac.uk/pub/glasgow-fp/papers/grasp-jfit.ps.Z

[13] R. Plasmeijer, *Cleans' Home Page*. At http://www.cs.kun.nl/~clean/

[14] P. Wadler, "Monads for functional programming". In *Lecture Notes on Advanced Functional Programming Techniques* (i.e., this volume), LNCS, Springer-Verlag 1995.

Constructing Medium Sized Efficient Functional Programs in Clean

Marko C.J.D. van Eekelen, Rinus (M.) J. Plasmeijer
Computing Science Institute, University of Nijmegen
Toernooiveld 1, 6525 ED Nijmegen, The Netherlands
e-mail: marko@cs.kun.nl, rinus@cs.kun.nl

Abstract

As functional programming comes of age, writing medium sized functional programs (i.e. programs in the range of 10.000 to 100.000 lines of source code) becomes a realistic task. As a test case for development techniques for medium sized efficient functional program these notes describe the experience with writing in the functional language Clean a functional spreadsheet, i.e. a spreadsheet which has as its cell expression language a lazy functional programming language with the ability for the user to define lazy higher-order recursive functions.

An important aim of the design was to reuse existing functional software as much as possible. The resulting application uses about 25000 lines of Clean combining general components such as a window-based text editor, a symbolic evaluator and a high-level I/O library.

The design of the spreadsheet application (FunSheet) is shortly introduced, experience with development techniques for this application is discussed and some examples are given of general techniques for writing medium-sized functional programs that may be used in future experiments.

1 Introduction

Traditionally, the only way to create an interface between a functional language and the imperative world was to give the functional input via a single, special input parameter and to interpret the result of the program (the output) as a sequence of commands for the outside world (Turner (1990)). In principle it is possible to do window-based I/O in this way. Due to the strong separation of input and output however it becomes a very tedious task to program a realistic application. Furthermore, the required efficiency is in many cases hard to achieve. Several proposals have addressed these issues (Monads (Peyton Jones & Wadler (1993)), Fudgets (Carlsson & Hallgren (1993)), Clean I/O (Achten & Plasmeijer (1995))). This has given rise to the opinion that functional programming comes of age (Pountain (1994)). The spreadsheet project of which the results are described in this paper was set out to gather evidence to support this opinion.

In the lazy, functional graph rewriting language Clean (Brus *et al.* (1987), Nöcker *et al.* (1991), Plasmeijer & van Eekelen (1994)), uniqueness typing (Barendsen &

Smetsers (1993)) which is based on the underlying graph rewriting model (Barendregt *et al.* (1987), Plasmeijer & van Eekelen (1993)) can be used to guarantee that upon its evaluation a function will hold the only reference to a certain (sub)argument. So, such a function can destructively use this unique argument (Smetsers *et al.* (1993)). Uniqueness also makes it possible to address system functions directly from within a purely functional program without loss of efficiency. The only required addition is that within the functional program uniqueness is maintained (this can be done e.g. by adding an extra unique dummy parameter to the Clean equivalent of the system functions that read/write the same globals; in this way the order of the calls of the system functions is determined by the standard function application mechanism).

Section 2 introduces the test case spreadsheet application (called **FunSheet**). The used development techniques for increasing efficiency and for writing medium sized functional programs are discussed in section 3. Some examples of techniques for writing efficient medium-sized functional programs that may be used in the future, are given in section 4 after which conclusions are drawn in section 5.

2 FunSheet: a Spreadsheet Application

The spreadsheet application FunSheet is constructed by combining and adapting existing software components written in the lazy functional programming language Clean (version 0.8). The project described here consisted of designing and implementing the sheet and cell manipulation part (performed by an M.Sc. student) and improving and extending the symbolic evaluator part (performed by a Ph.D. student). Taken together the project took about 10 student months. The project could be finished within this period partly because the lack of side-effects made debugging relatively straightforward.

In this section we introduce the reader to this application and its implementation since it has formed (and will form in the future) as a test case for techniques for writing efficient medium sized functional programs. For more information and motivation the reader is referred to De Hoon *et al.* (1995).

2.1 Design

An important overall intention of the design was to reuse as much available software as possible in order to keep the scope of the design and implementation within a six-month computer science Masters thesis project (de Hoon (1993)). Candidates for reuse were a symbolic evaluator written by L. Rutten to prove the correctness of the application of transformation rules on functional programs, a high-level machine-independent window-based I/O library written by P. Achten to increase the level of abstraction available for functional window-based software (Achten & Plasmeijer (1995)), a window-based editor written by H. Huitema as a first test of the effectiveness of this I/O library, and a small help tool written by H. Huitema to make it easier to add help facilities to functional software. All of these components were written in Clean (version 0.8).

The most important choice of the design was to use a functional language as the spreadsheet cell expression language (see section 2.2). An interesting aspect of the chosen functional language is its capability for symbolic evaluation and for applying normalisation rules on symbolic expressions including equations. This enables the proof of symbolic equality for a large class of expressions.

Basic Idea of the FunSheet Application

Each sheet has a window in which the evaluated values and the entries are displayed. The values are contained in *cells*, indicated by squares separated by horizontal and vertical lines. Index and column information is constantly displayed in the window. Figure 1 gives a typical user's view of the program.

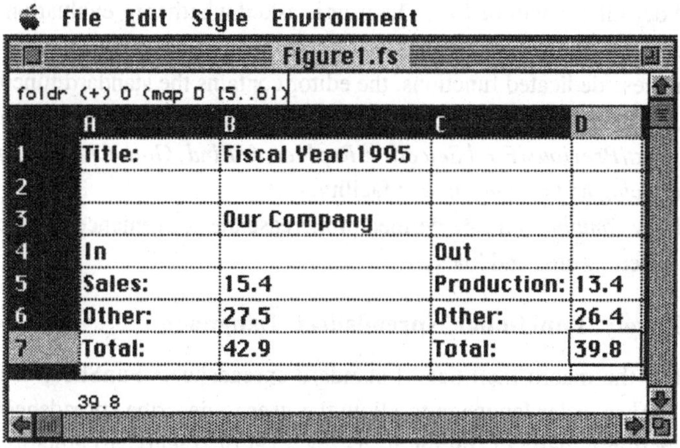

Fig. 1. A user's view of FunSheet

FunSheet is menu driven, which means that various actions from the menu (consisting of **File, Edit, Style** and **Environment** functions) can be applied to the (contents of the topmost) sheet. The design includes *sheet manipulation* actions, *sheet editing* actions, *remote values* defined in other sheets, manipulation actions for *labels* as verbose synonyms for references to a (block of) cell(s), *formatting* actions, a facility to *select* (user-defined or predefined) *functions* and an on-line *Help* facility.

An important aspect of the design is the built-in *function editor* with which the possibility is created to *define new functions* by switching to this function editor with which for each sheet a separate set of user-defined functions can be created.

Classical spreadsheets offer lots of additional features among which hiding, adding and deleting rows and columns, and the ability to make, import and export all kinds of *diagrams*, *print* and *report* facilities based on the information in the sheet. These functions are not included in the basic design. They are intended to be added later to extend the capabilities of the application.

The Function Editor

To enable the user to define functions, a function editor can be called which has a *separate user interface* that temporarily replaces the spreadsheet user interface. It starts up a window based editor with some extensions in the menu to perform a *Syntax Check* of the new functions and to try an *Expression Test* to test the function by evaluating various expressions. Initially, a window is opened which shows the functions which are already defined (by the user). When a new function is added to the environment, its syntax can be checked. If the function is syntactically correct, the environment is updated with the new definition.

When from the editor a *Return to Spreadsheet* is performed, the adapted function environment is passed and the user interface of the spreadsheet is re-established. Unchecked definitions will be lost. The user is asked whether re-evaluation of all cells is required.

Besides these dedicated functions, the editor contains the standard functions a window-based editor must have such as *Undo, Cut/Copy/Paste, Clear, Tab/Font Changes, Find/Find Next/Previous/Find Selection/Replace & Find, Goto Cursor/Line* and also *Bracket Balancing* and an *Auto-indent* facility.

Several *key combinations* are defined to increase the convenience of editing and selecting characters, words and lines.

2.2 A Purely Functional Spreadsheet Language

In contrast to the macro-facilities of standard spreadsheets FunSheet uses a *purely functional higher order* language to allow the user to describe spreadsheet computations. A function is defined (by the user) via a set of (recursive) equations with the usual *rewrite semantics*: upon evaluation of an expression, the equations are used as rewrite rules where the left-hand side of an equation serves as a pattern to determine whether the rule is applicable and the right-hand side is used to determine the result of the corresponding reduction. The order of the rules is important: they are considered as candidates for rewriting proceeding textually from top to bottom.

The design of the spreadsheet chooses to model each column of cells as a function of indexes to values such that each cell expression in fact forms the right-hand side of one of the alternatives of this column function. For example, an alternative of some column function A may be A 1 = e. The right-hand side e of this alternative defines the contents of cell A1, i.e. the application of column function A to the index 1. These *column functions* are *first-class citizens* in the spreadsheet language. They can be used in a curried way (i.e., a column function can be used while its argument is not yet supplied). Column functions can occur as arguments and as results of functions in any cell expression.

Since symbolic evaluation will be performed and since the types of the values of cells in the same column are not necessarily the same, it was decided that the spreadsheet language should be *untyped* (no type checking at all was implemented: 'c' + 1 is not disallowed: it is just an irreducible expression).

FunSheet Language Syntax

The syntax of the language describes a simple language (essentially function definitions with pattern matching and guards extended with special syntax for lists, tuples, local definitions, range expressions (denoted using ..), and ZF-expressions). Most expressions would be specified similarly in commonly available functional languages. Denotations are included for integers, reals, booleans, characters and strings. Special cell range expressions (denoted using ... instead of ..) are available to denote blocks of cells. Lists are a predefined data structure. Besides using the notation hd : tl for a list, the equivalent notation [hd l tl] is also allowed. Algebraic data structures can be defined. Most standard operators on these data structures have been included in the language. A number of standard functions is predefined. The language does not have an off-side rule. For more information on the language the reader is referred to (de Hoon *et al.* (1994)).

Cell References and Dependencies

The design uses absolute references only. It distinguishes two kinds of cell references: references via *column functions* and references via *labels*. A *label* is an identifier referring to a (block of) cell(s).

Cells are referred to via applications of *column functions*. As an abbreviation of the application of a column function to an index (e.g. A 1) the possibility is introduced to collapse such an application into a single identifier when the index is an integer literal (A1) which is more in conformity with classical spreadsheet references. Column functions can be curried and they can be used just as any other function in cell expressions.

The spreadsheet design avoids having to update the whole sheet when the entry of a cell changes by maintaining dependency information. For a curried application of a column function or an application of a column function to an expression which is not an integer denotation, it is not possible to statically determine all dependencies. So, they have to be approximated safely. This is done by considering such expressions to depend on *all* cells in the column.

Using references to other cells creates the possibility of defining cells with a cyclic dependency structure. In many cases however such cycles correspond to erroneously non-terminating evaluation. Therefore, as in classical spreadsheets, a *cycle detector* is included which prohibits definitions that may lead to such cyclic dependencies of cells. The cycle detector guarantees that non-termination cannot be caused by cyclic dependencies of cells. It operates on partly evaluated cell expressions.

When the cell expression is parsed, standard functions and remote values are also evaluated. For reasons of efficiency the result of this is used as the expression to evaluate when a change occurs of other cell expressions on which this expression depends (e.g.: the partly evaluated cell expression of foldr (+) 0 (map D [5..6]) is D5 + D6).

The cycle detector does allow the standard examples with e.g. sub-totals and totals in the same column. It can, however, require certain expressions that heavily use curried column functions to be put in a different column (the expression map (twice (twice A)) [1..4] would be allowed in a cell in column B but not in column A: its partly evaluated expression is [A(A(A(A1))), A(A(A(A2))), A(A(A(A3))), A(A(A(A4)))] which may be cyclic if put in a cell of column A).

Symbolic Evaluation

The evaluation of expressions in the language is done *symbolically* using rewrite semantics. Essentially there is no difference between functions and constructors. In definitions they can both occur at any position in a left-hand side of an equation (e.g. besides the usual arithmetic equations, one of the rules of the predefined basic function + is that a + (b + c) = (a + b) + c. In this rule, the function + occurs twice in the left-hand side, which is typically only allowed if rewrite semantics are used).

Evaluation of a single cell expression is chosen to correspond to evaluation of an initial term in a standard lazy functional language. So, evaluation of a single cell expression is always performed to *normal form*.

Symbolic values can either be symbolic *variables* or *references to cells which are (still) empty*. The evaluation mechanism treats both cases in the same way.

When a symbolic equation cannot be solved, the equation itself, reduced as much as possible, is returned as the result. When instead of symbolic values, basic values are used in the same equation (this can be done by manual substitution, by adding local definitions (in the case of a symbolic variable) or by defining a cell (in the case of a reference to an undefined cell) the equation may be solved depending on the actual values.

For several pre-defined operators which exhibit properties like associativity, commutativity and distributivity, the symbolic evaluator includes normalisation rules. This makes it possible to symbolically solve simple algebraic equations (e.g. (x-y)*(x+y) == x^2 - y^2 will yield True).

In the symbolic evaluator it has been chosen to implement the common associativity, commutativity and distributivity rules for the arithmetic operators not excluding finite precision integers and floating point numbers. It has to be noted however that when these rules are applied on such numbers, due to (rounding) errors differences can occur between symbolically deduced results and concrete results. This anomaly can be removed when solutions for exact real arithmetic (Cartwright & Boehm (1990), Vuillemin (1987)) become practical.

The symbolic evaluator can also be used to check properties with *lists* containing symbolic values (e.g. sum of one list is symbolically equal to sum of another). Such a list may not only contain symbolic values but it may be generated using symbolic values in a dot-dot expression.

Predefined Functions

Apart from the basic arithmetic functions like + and *, over 60 standard functions are predefined. These do not only include classical spreadsheet functions like sum or average but also functions that are most often used in the functional programming community, e.g. map and foldr. The definitions of the *standard* functions (the non-basic predefined functions) are contained in the *Help* files. They could have been given in exactly the same way by the user of the spreadsheet by using the ability to define a set of functions in a dedicated environment for each separate sheet.

Besides the well-known standard functions, the FunSheet application supports some special functions and constructors. There are functions to convert column indications to integers (e.g. A is converted to 1) and vice-versa. There is a function to generate blocks of cells. There is a special constructor $ which acts as a prefix of a number which is maintained during arithmetic operations (useful for financial calculations). There is a function to perform lambda-abstraction (\) of which the definition is such that $x_1\ x_2\ ...\ x_n\ \backslash\ e$ corresponds with the lambda term $\lambda x_1.\lambda x_2\ ....\ \lambda x_n.\ e$. It is also used internally to implement ZF-expressions. Furthermore, there is a function to simplify equations in which list expressions occur, by performing induction on the length of lists.

The Use of FunSheet

Apart from being used in a way which is standard for a spreadsheet, the FunSheet application offers new opportunities to explore the use of the symbolic evaluator.

An important way to avoid spreadsheet errors is offered by the symbolic evaluation mechanism: the system can try to symbolically *prove* certain *properties* by simplifying equations.

An example of a commutativity diagram proof is the case in which the sheet is set up such that while the cells that are referred to are still empty, symbolically the sum of the sums of rows is checked to be equal to the sum of the sums of columns. This shows how a user can *prove* that a particular set-up of a spreadsheet has a required property by adding symbolic equations.

It is clear that such general, automatically performed proofs can greatly improve a spreadsheet's reliability. However, the power of such a symbolic evaluator is inherently limited: the equations which it can prove are determined by the transformation rules it knows (this holds for every proof system).

Another area in which FunSheet offers new opportunities is an area which is a kind of *reverse engineering*. The property that, when an equation is to be solved, the system returns an equivalent equation simplified as much as possible, can be used to inform the user what the requirements are to satisfy a certain property.

2.3 Implementation

Since the design sets out to re-use existing software as components in the implementation, the implementation will have to be modular and highly structured. The main components (user-interface, editor, symbolic evaluator, spreadsheet structures) access each other only through interface modules defining abstract data structures with access functions.

Input/Output

The Clean I/O library makes it possible to write efficient event-based interactive programs in a purely functional language. Essentially, an interactive Clean program gets a representation of the world as an extra parameter. This world is given as an argument to a driver together with a specification of the required I/O devices which specifies what kind of device it is and what the call-back functions are for each possible event. This driver is the library function StartIO which repeatedly takes an event from the event queue and calls the corresponding call-back function. The I/O specification is an algebraic data structure which must be an instance of the algebraic data type defined in the library. Uniqueness types (indicated by *) guarantee that an object will be privately accessed. This enables an efficient and realistic implementation of the I/O functions using destructive screen and file updates. For more information on the Clean I/O System the reader is referred to (Achten and Plasmeijer (1995)).

To show how such an abstract device definition is used in the spreadsheet program, figure 2 gives an example of the *File* menu definition as it occurs in the code for the spreadsheet user interface. This definition of an algebraic data structure is an instance of the general algebraic data type which can be used in Clean to specify Menu-devices. The picture next to the definition shows the concrete device in the case of the menu definition being mapped to a Macintosh system.

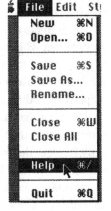

```
PullDownMenu FileId "File" Able [
    MenuItem NewId    "New"     (Key 'n') Able    New,
    MenuItem OpenId   "Open…"   (Key 'o') Able    Open,
    MenuSeparator,
    MenuItem SaveId   "Save"    (Key 's') Unable  Save,
    MenuItem SvAsId   "Save As…" NoKey    Unable  SaveAs,
    MenuItem RenId    "Rename…" NoKey     Unable  Rename,
    MenuSeparator,
    MenuItem CloseId  "Close"   (Key 'w') Unable  Close,
    MenuItem ClsAllId "CloseAll" NoKey    Unable  ClsAll,
    MenuSeparator,
    MenuItem HelpId   "Help"    (Key '/') Able    Help,
    MenuSeparator,
    MenuItem QuitId   "Quit"    (Key 'q') Able    Quit ]
```

Fig. 2.   FunSheet's File-menu definition

Although the spreadsheet has been written in Clean version 0.8, in the Clean program examples 1.0 syntax (which is similar to the syntax of most other functional languages) is used in order to avoid unnecessary distraction of the reader.

The type of each call-back function must be an instance of :: *s *(IOState *s) -> (*s, *IOState *s), in which IOState is a polymorphic I/O library type representing the external I/O status of the program and its event-queue. Each call-back function is a state transition function with two arguments. The first argument is the specific state of the program (for the spreadsheet program this is the type State). The second argument (of type IOState State) represents the world with which input and output is performed. Each call-back function (New, ... , Quit) delivers a tuple with a new program state and a new IOState.

```
:: *IO   = IOState State

New      :: State   IO   ->    (State,IO)
...
Quit     :: State   IO   ->    (State,IO)
```

An event-handling driver is started (usually as the main function executed by the program) with the function StartIO. As the type of StartIO shows, it takes an I/O specification, an initial program state, an initial I/O action, and the event queue. When it is finished, it delivers the final program state and event queue.

```
StartIO :: (IOSystem *s) *s (InitIO *s) *Events -> (*s, *Events)
```

Expressions and Function Definitions

For evaluation of function definitions and expressions several environments are important.

The following two environments are the same for all sheets. The *Basic* environment contains function definitions concerning values of basic type. These definitions include transformation rules for employing the associativity and distributivity laws of basic operators. These rules employ functions that are internal to the evaluator. Therefore it has not been made possible for the user to change or extend these definitions although they are put in a standard text file which was helpful for the ease of the development process. The *Standard* environment contains the predefined standard functions. These definitions are predefined for reasons of efficiency and user convenience.

Each sheet has its own instance of the following environments. The *User-defined* function environment contains the definitions that are given by the user employing the built-in editor. The *Label* definition environment contains the definitions of labels, which are effectively just synonyms for particular cells. For each column function, the *Column* function environment contains the set of rule alternatives that correspond to the cells of the column.

Evaluation of functions from the user's environment is generally an order of magnitude less efficient than evaluation of functions from the standard environment since the user's functions are interpreted instead of compiled. So, for reasons of efficiency the predefined function definitions are given to a special Clean application which uses the spreadsheet language parser and generates a Clean definition and implementation module for each predefined function. These modules are compiled and linked in the standard way together with all other modules from which the spreadsheet application is built. An advanced user with access to all Clean sources can easily take his or her own function definitions and compile and link them to achieve a better efficiency.

Apart from the optimised compilation process (see section 3.8) there is no difference in the evaluation mechanism for the various environments mentioned above. Evaluation is done entirely symbolically.

Parsing

Lexical analysis and parsing of expressions and definitions is relatively straightforward. It was already available in the symbolic evaluator. Compound expressions adhere to an operator grammar. Cell references can be formulated as A 1 (an application of a column function to a row index), but also as A1. For the latter case, a few adjustments had to be made to the lexical analysis present in the symbolic evaluator.

Representation of Expressions, Function Definitions and Environments

The symbolic evaluator implements a purely functional language which supports symbolic values. Semantically, a symbolic expression may contain one ore more *free variables*. A free variable is an identifier which is not defined as a function, constant, or constructor. To explain the meaning of functions written in the FunSheet language, we will consider their translations to Clean. The translated functions operate on arguments of type Value. Values are evaluated using the definitions from the environments rewriting their subgraphs in the same way as standard combinator graph rewriting is performed.

```
:: Value   = EV                    // Empty value
           | F Id [Value]          // Application of a function without
                                   // definition or of a free variable
                                   // to a list of arguments
           | C Id [Value]          // Application of a constructor to
                                   // a list of arguments
           | INT   Int             // Basic values
           | REAL  Real
           | CHAR  Char
           | BOOL  Bool
           | Msg   String          // Error message
           | A Id  [Alt] [Value]   // Application of a function with
                                   // definition to a list of arguments
           | B Id Fns [Value]      // Application of a compiled function
```

```
                                        // to  a list of arguments
:: Fns       = Fn0 Value                // Nullary function; Value is the type
                                        // of the result
             | Fn1 (Value -> Value)     // Unary function
             | FnL ([Value] -> Value)   // N-ary function with
                                        // arguments in a list
:: Id        :==   String
```

Example: 1+1 is represented as   A "+" {alternatives of +} [INT 1, INT 1]

A function environment is represented as a list of constructor and function definitions.

```
:: Env   :==   [Rule]                   // Environment is a list of rules
:: Rule  =     Cn Id [Value]            // Constructor definition
         |     Fn Id [Alt]              // Function definition
:: Alt   :==   ([Value], Value)         // Tuple with a list of patterns
                                        // and a right-hand side
```

Interpreted Symbolic Evaluation of Expressions

When an expression is to be interpreted, it is given as an argument to an interpreter that also takes an environment and substitutes the definitions for the function applications, reducing the expression to normal form employing symbolic evaluation lazily.

To simplify this evaluation process, all local definitions of an environment are transformed to global definitions using lambda lifting.

In order to easily deal with recursion, the choice was made to let recursive applications of function definitions refer directly to their definitions. The way in which this is achieved is similar to the way recursion in combinator rewriting is usually dealt with. There, a Y-combinator is used which in an implementation is optimised by creating a cyclic graph for it (so-called knot-tying). Since Clean is a graph rewriting language, cyclic graph expressions can be expressed directly (see the definition of MakeRecursive). So, recursive applications in an environment are made effective by explicitly replacing them (this is done by the function DistRule) by references to the root of the environment (hence creating a cyclic reference).

```
MakeRecursive:: Env -> Env
MakeRecursive env = e    where   e =: Map (DistRule e) env
```

The function MakeRecursive uses this method to replace all applications of identifiers of functions (F ...) by applications of the corresponding function with its definition (A ...) or by a direct call to a standard function (B ...). Lazy evaluation ensures that this process is applied only when necessary.

The Main Data Structures of the Spreadsheet

The spreadsheet data structures contain information that has to do with the efficiency of the program as well as information concerning the contents of the cells and the visual aspects of the sheet.

Cell

The most important information stored in the cells are the *entries*. These are the input strings given by the user. The user must be able to adjust these entries and in order to access them they have to be saved in the cells.

The *parsing information* of the entries is also stored in the cells after partial evaluation is performed on it as follows. The entry is first parsed and evaluated using the standard environment of the interpreter. This results in an expression (of type Value) that is evaluated as far as possible using standard functions only. Then, this partly evaluated cell expression is further evaluated to its result (also of type Value), using all information available. Because it might use references, it is possible (and very likely) that some of these values will change and therefore will affect the result. When one of these references changes, the entry does not have to be parsed and partly evaluated again since the *partly evaluated expression* is saved in the cell. Also when cells are evaluated again after the user has changed function definitions, this partly evaluated expression is taken as the starting point of re-evaluation. In the environment (of type Env) the final result is saved in the right-hand side of the corresponding alternative of the corresponding column function.

Changing the entry of a certain cell may affect a large group of cells in the sheet. Other cells can refer to this particular cell with labels or direct references. To increase efficiency, avoiding having to check the entire sheet for references to this particular cell, a list of *used-by* references is retained in the cell. This list is also used by the cycle detector. For efficient adjustment of these references, the list of cell references and label names which the entry of a certain cell *uses*, is also stored in the cell. These lists are determined from the partly evaluated cell expression.

Sheet

Sheet is an abstract type, corresponding to a concrete type which is a tuple of several components. The set of cells is represented as a *Matrix of Cells*, where Matrix is defined as a list of lists since proper arrays were not available when the program was written.

Since it is possible to open more than one sheet, one must have some *identification* information for each sheet.

Each sheet, has a *local function environment*. This environment actually consists of two environments. The first one contains the *column-functions* and the second one contains the *user-defined functions*. To be able to save the latter, the actual *text of the user-defined functions* is also added to the sheet (the text of the column functions is saved in the cells).

Furthermore, a sheet contains *format information,* i.e. information about the *format of groups of cells* (rows and columns). The height and width of rows and columns can be adjusted. The corresponding properties are stored in separate lists defined in the sheet.

A sheet also has a part which contains information concerning the *interactions* between the user and the program. This information includes the *frame* (i.e. a rectangle in window co-ordinates) that is selected by the mouse, and the *input* tuple that is being edited in the cell. The input tuple contains a boolean indicating whether something has been changed, the input text, and the selected cell *block* (i.e. a rectangle in cell matrix co-ordinates).

Finally, it contains information about the *labels.* The labels are also added to the environment, but when the user needs information about (one of) the defined labels, he or she can not get this information from the environment. Therefore this information has to be extracted from the sheet.

```
:: Sheet
   :== (Ident,Matrix Cell,Interaction,Row,Col,[Label],ParseEnv,Font)
```

State

Finally, there is the abstract program state State, containing all global information needed by the spreadsheet. This state is uniquely typed (a * is used to indicate uniqueness of the type it precedes) and it is used by all call-back functions that handle events that are generated by the user. Besides a list of sheets (as defined above), the state contains information that is sheet-independent. So, the state contains the *files-*environment needed for file-IO (reading and saving files) and the *clipboard* containing a list of the entries of the copied cells.

```
:: *State       :==  (!MyFiles, [Sheet], Clipboard)
:: *MyFiles     =    NOFILES
                |    FILES !Files
:: Clipboard    :==  [CopiedCell]
:: CopiedCell   :==  Entry
```

In the State definition above, the tuple-component MyFiles is defined as a strict component (which itself is defined with a strict Files part). When you write a sheet to a file (make a backup of it) you want to make sure this is done right away so that power failures will not result in losing all information. For this reason, the MyFiles component is forced to be evaluated each time a call-back function delivers a new state.

2.4 Performance

With respect to I/O the efficiency is about the same as the efficiency of Excel: there are no delays in editing cell or function definitions nor in 'walking' across the spreadsheet using arrow keys, and scrolling the spreadsheet when necessary.

The function evaluation efficiency of the spreadsheet language is about the same as Miranda[TM][1] (varying from approximately twice as fast for standard function applications to five times as slow for user-defined function applications). The efficiency is good if one considers that symbolic evaluation is employed on untyped expressions. However, the sheet evaluation mechanism which deals with computing all effects of a cell change is an order of magnitude slower than Excel. The used representation of the matrix of cells as a list of lists is probably the main cause of this. The function evaluation mechanism could not be compared with Excel since Excel only has a macro facility which is defined in such a way that the parameters are in fact global variables, giving rise to unwanted semantics when recursion is used.

2.5 Code Sizes

The source code of FunSheet is organised in six major parts: sheet and cell manipulation, editor, symbolic evaluator, I/O library, help tool, and standard environment (including the basic environment). The standard environment is written in the spreadsheet language. It takes about 560 lines, or about 15 kilobytes (kB). When the system is compiled, the files of the standard environment are translated to Clean modules, which are then compiled to object code. The generated implementation modules take about 99 kilobytes and the generated definition modules take about 9 kilobytes. The size of the standard environment is about 14% of the size of the corresponding generated Clean modules.

The size of the combined implementation and definition modules is about 29400 lines, or about 1100 kilobytes. When the spreadsheet application was implemented, the editor and I/O library were already available. The size of their implementation modules is about 67% of the size of all spreadsheet implementation modules. Of course, for the required functionality of the spreadsheet it would have been possible to use many fewer lines if existing code was not reused (the editor and the I/O library are quite general). With the conversion to Clean 1.0, the number of lines is expected to decrease significantly due to the larger expressive power of the high level syntactical constructs present in Clean 1.0 (e.g. a single ZF-expression or record definition can replace several function definitions for construction, filtering, access and update of the data structures).

The application size itself is approximately 1 Megabyte.

---

[1]Miranda[TM] is a trademark of Research Software Limited.

2.6 Availability and applicability

The FunSheet application runs on a Macintosh only since for the use of non-scrolling margins in windows, a small extension was made to the library which is not yet ported to the other platforms. This extension will be incorporated in the new library that is being made with the Clean 1.0 system.

To execute FunSheet 4 Megabytes of free memory is required. This is quite huge for such a program. It will be possible to decrease the amount of necessary memory greatly when efficient code generation for general uniqueness types becomes available in Clean 1.0.

The spreadsheet application and the stand-alone version of the editor are freely available for non-commercial use via FTP (pub/Clean at ftp.cs.kun.nl) or WWW (www.cs.kun.nl/~clean).

2.7 Future Improvements/Extensions

It is the intention to include in a future version of FunSheet diagram, print and report facilities and an explicit method to provide capabilities similar to relative addressing as present in standard spreadsheets.

The code (Clean 0.8) will be converted to Clean 1.0 not just by using the automatic conversion facility but by employing the new features available in Clean 1.0. Apart from more readable code due to the availability of more syntactic sugar, an important advance is expected due to the use of observation types (which simplify the definition of read-access on unique data structures) and of user-defined unique data structures. The use of a destructive array (defined with uniqueness types) for the cell matrix instead of a list of lists is expected to greatly improve the overall efficiency. Due to the propagation property of uniqueness (Smetsers *et al.* (1993)), the type for Sheet must then also be unique since it contains a unique component (destructing the component will destruct the surrounding structure too).

The interfaces between the different components are intended to be redesigned using the techniques in section 4 in such a way that the interface to a component will be fully contained in one definition module while compiling the corresponding implementation module separately will yield a stand alone application of the component. In practice, this will make it easier to guarantee that the interface is kept stable while the component changes.

Finally, it is our intention to develop a distributed version in which different parts of a sheet can be changed and updated on different processors.

3 Experience with Development Techniques for FunSheet

The application was developed with version 0.8 of Clean. Intended as an intermediate language, the syntax of this version was rather poor. One of the reasons to start this project was to gain insight into the essential extensions that were needed towards an upgrade of Clean to a proper programming language.

Obviously, programming was hampered by the absence of well-known goodies such as local function definitions, infix expressions, overloading, ZF-expressions, pattern match wild cards and a lay-out rule. Furthermore, there were no design rules for time and space efficiency of different language constructs. When writing an industry standard efficient application it may prove to be vital for the designer to know the influence of the used language constructs on the time and space behaviour.

The required functionality for the spreadsheet served as an important test case in various stages of the design. Many of the critiques have been input to the design process of the Clean language version 1.0 and the new I/O library version 1.0.

3.1 Modular Design

Since the design was set out to re-use existing software as components in the implementation, the implementation is modular and highly structured.

The main components access each other only through interface modules defining abstract data structures with access functions. When in the development process such a type which was defined as a tuple (e.g. Sheet and State, see section 2.3) was extended, all functions that use pattern matching on this tuple had to be changed since the number of tuple elements changed. The presence of records in the language would have had a significant benefit on the development process.

It has proven to be good practice to present a design technically by producing the required definition modules. The module structure containing the definitions of the data types with the type definitions of the defined functions gives a good insight in the set-up of the design.

However, the implicit import facility (which imports all definitions known in a module and can be applied recursively) in definition modules made it be hard to keep track of the definitions that are available within a certain module since when the implicit import mechanism is used not only all definitions contained in the definition module of an imported module are imported but also all definitions that are imported by the imported module.

The module structure had to be changed during the development process for technical reasons: the Macintosh linker has a limit size of 32K for an object file to be linked into an application. It is a pain having to split up a module just because the linker cannot deal with the size of the generated code.

The Clean programming environment has only limited support for larger programs consisting of many modules (all it has is a search facility which enables the user to open quickly definition or implementation modules or to find quickly the definition or the implementation of a selected function identifier). For larger projects, more programming environment support is required (see section 4.4).

Adding Process Structure

The ability to define interleaved processes with a separate I/O interface as described in Achten and Plasmeijer (1994) would allow the programmer to give more structure to the program.

In FunSheet the Help facility for example could then be redesigned in such a way that it could be always visible and run in a separate window with a separate menu bar accessible just by clicking on its window. In a similar way the function editor could be used side-by-side to the sheet itself.

3.2 Higher Order Functions

Higher order functions were used throughout the implementation. The I/O library (with its algebraic data structure describing the I/O components and containing call-back functions for the possible events) could not have been written without the availability of higher order functions. Its *definition* modules contain many higher order functions.

Of course, there were also several cases in *implementation* modules of the use of (variants of) standard functions like fold and map with (curried applications of) functions as arguments where this was felt needed (in particular in the symbolic evaluator this occurred rather often). It is our experience that overall efficiency was not hampered by such use of higher-order functions (with the exception of the use of foldr which is inherently rather inefficient).

3.3 Lazy Evaluation and Graph Rewriting

At many points in the implementation, lazy evaluation and explicit sharing were used. The most important use of the combination of these two techniques has already been treated in section 2.3 (in dealing with recursion in the symbolic evaluator).

An example of the use of lazy evaluation in the spreadsheet is the following. When a cell is changed, in principle all cells that depend on it have to be recalculated. However, for cells that are not visible in the window and of which the value is not used by cells that are visible, such recalculation is not necessary yet. Depending on the use, this recalculation will be required later (when the window is scrolled) or never (when the same cell is changed again). Lazy evaluation can take care of that with hardly any programming effort. The only thing which is required is that on the top-most level of interaction, the list of frames to be updated is restricted to the visible ones. Due to lazy evaluation, the calculations corresponding to invisible cells will then be delayed automatically. This will not lead to a continuous accumulation of space consumption (sometimes referred to as a space leak) because the list of update frames can never be larger than the number of cells in the sheet (which is finite).

3.4 Strictness

Lazy evaluation is turned *by the programmer* into strict evaluation at several points for various reasons. The *required behaviour* can be inherently strict (see the discussion on saving files in section 2.3) or the *interface to the outside world* can require arguments to be evaluated before they are passed (needed in many places in the I/O library) or the *memory management* of the resulting application would otherwise turn out to be unsatisfactory (used internally in the editor to avoid certain space leaks).

In several cases the use of the basic function foldl instead of foldr proved useful to create efficient left-recursive *derived* strict evaluation.

3.5 Uniqueness

The Clean 0.8 version has relatively primitive support for uniqueness typing. Uniqueness types are checked but not inferred. There are no ways to define, via a projection function, a read-only access on a (part of) a unique data structure without having to produce a tuple with the unique data structure and its projection. In other words, the concept of observation of a unique typed object is not present. Furthermore, for data structures that are defined by the user as being unique, the code generator does not generate code that makes use of this information.

The Clean 1.0 design has incorporated the suggested changes in this section.

3.6 Clean I/O

The advantage of Clean I/O is its direct way of interfacing to system calls. In particular for the relatively I/O intensive parts like scrolling (in the sheet or in the editor), this was important in order to achieve a proper efficiency of interaction.

It is our impression that, due to referential transparency and the use of higher order functions, using Clean I/O it is easier to modify and read I/O programs than using an imperative language.

However, all I/O functions have the full program state as their argument. In many cases a large part of the state is needed only locally to the I/O function itself each time it is called. The Clean 1.0 library will support local state in I/O components.

The user can relatively easily define higher levels of abstraction. This can be done both on a small scale defining useful higher order extensions of the I/O library (e.g. for often used dialogues) as well as on a large scale on which a user could define a new style of I/O.

3.7 Debugging

A large part of the debugging of FunSheet was done by someone other than the original programmer.

Due to referential transparency it was relatively easy to correct a bug as soon as it was identified as a wrong definition of a particular function: only the definition of the function itself had to be considered and all required information was present via the arguments of the function. The absence of side-effects proved to be very useful for debugging the program. The programming environment facility to open the definition or the implementation module of a selected function (displaying the type or the full definition correspondingly) proved to be indispensible in this context. No need was felt for special debugging facilities.

3.8   Replace Interpretation by Compilation

For reasons of efficiency, the predefined function definitions are given to a special Clean application which translates FunSheet functions to Clean code which is linked into the application so that they can be evaluated efficiently.

As free variables are not allowed in Clean, treatment of these symbolic values by compiled FunSheet functions has to be coded explicitly. A FunSheet function alternative which has a non-variable pattern in its left hand side is translated to two Clean alternatives. The first alternative is employed to catch unwanted matchings of free variables with non-variable patterns. The second alternative corresponds directly with the original alternative.

As a simple example, let us consider the following alternative.

```
f 0 = 0
```

It will be translated to the following two Clean alternatives (in which variable is a function defined below).

```
f v       | variable v = F "f" [v]
f (INT 0)            = INT 0
```

Let us consider the more general case of an alternative of a function f, printed as "f", with n arguments,

```
f p1 ... pn = r
```

This alternative will be translated to the following two (schematically written) Clean alternatives

```
f v1 ... vn   | condition = F "f" [v1, ..., vn]
f p1 ... pn              = r
```

The *condition* is an expression over the free variables $v_1 \ldots v_n$. If $f\, x_1 \ldots x_n$ is evaluated for some expressions $x_1 \ldots x_n$, *condition* is True if and only if matching some x_i with a p_i would involve matching a free variable with a non-variable pattern. The *condition* can be expressed as a function of $p_1 \ldots p_n$ and $v_1 \ldots v_n$. Its implementation follows below. From the implementation it can be inferred that evaluation of a *condition* does not have an effect on the strictness (and hence termination) properties of the translated function in which the *condition* occurs, if the function is applied to arguments which do not contain free variables.

```
condition:: [Value]  [Value] -> Value
condition [F f a:ps] [v:vs] = ncondition ps vs
condition [p:ps]     [v:vs] = or (pat_cond p v) (condition ps vs)
condition []         []     = F "False" []

pat_cond:: Value    Value -> Value
pat_cond p=:(C f a) v =  or (F "variable" [v])
                            (and  (F "same_structure" [p, v])
                                  (condition a (select_args a 1 v)))
pat_cond p          v = F "variable" [v]

select_args:: [Value] Int Value -> [Value]
select_args []       i v = []
select_args [a : as] i v
   = [F "nth_argument" [F (ToString i) [],v]:select_args as (i+1) v]
```

The or and and functions below are used to simplify the *condition* if possible.

```
or ::   Value       Value          -> Value
or      x           (F "False" [])  = x
or      x           y               = F "||" [x, y]

and ::  Value       Value          -> Value
and     x           (F "False" [])  = F "False" []
and     x           y               = F "&&" [x, y]
```

The functions below will only be used at the run-time of a compiled FunSheet program. They are linked with the Clean code which is (partly) generated by the functions above.

```
variable :: Value -> Bool
variable (F f a) = True
variable x       = False

same_structure :: Value Value -> Bool
same_structure (C f a)  (C g b) = f == g && # a == # b
same_structure x        y       = False

nth_arg :: Int Value -> Value
nth_arg n (C f a)  = select n a

select :: Int [Value] -> Value
select n [a : as] | n == 1     = a
                  | otherwise = select (n - 1) as
```

As a more complicated example, let us consider the following alternative.

```
f [0] = 0
```

It will be translated to the following two Clean alternatives.

```
f v
| variable v ||
  (same_structure (C ":" [INT 0, C "[]" []]) v &&
  (variable (nth_arg 1 v) || variable (nth_arg 2 v))) =  F "f" [v]
f (C ":" [INT 0, C "[]" []])                          =  INT 0
```

Here, || and && are infix operators in Clean for the "or" and "and" functions respectively.

It is possible that a non-trivial Value *value* occurs more than once in a *condition*, or that it occurs in a left hand side pattern and in the condition of the corresponding right hand side. Then in the final translated code a node identifier will be defined as *value* in a where-expression, and the original occurrences of *value* will be replaced with that node identifier. For example, if *condition* looks like ... *value* ... *value* ..., it will be translated to ... *v* ... *v* ... where *v* = *value*, *v* being a node identifier. This obviously saves space. It also saves time since values do not have to be rebuilt.

An example where node identifiers are generated is the following. Consider the alternative

```
f [[0]] = 0
```

It will be translated to the following two Clean alternatives:

```
f v
| variable v ||
  (same_structure (C ":" [n1, C "[]" []]) v &&
  ((variable n2 ||
    (same_structure n1 n2 &&
      (variable (nth_arg 1 n2) || variable (nth_arg 2 n2)))) ||
   variable (nth_arg 2 v)))                      = F "f" [v]
where
     n1 = C ":" [INT 0, C "[]" []]
     n2 = nth_arg 1 v
f (C ":" [C ":" [INT 0, C "[]" []], C "[]" []]) = INT 0
```

Apart from generating conditions from patterns, the translation of the FunSheet language to Clean is quite straightforward. One aspect of the translation still needs to be addressed. If the set of alternatives of a FunSheet function is not exhaustive, then one extra alternative is generated at the end of its translated counterpart in Clean. If the function, say f, expects n arguments, then this extra alternative looks like

```
f v₁ ... vₙ  =  F "f" [v₁, ..., vₙ]
```

where $v_1 \ldots v_n$ are node identifiers. By adding this alternative a head normal form will be yielded when the other generated alternatives do not match.

Efficiency of Interpreted and Compiled FunSheet Programs

The standard environment is translated to Clean code to increase its execution efficiency. Let us take the nfib function which produces as its result the number of times the function was called in the recursion as an example to serve as a 'poor man's benchmark' of the number of functional calls per second (the nfib number).

On a 33 MHz 68030 Macintosh, the nfib number of the interpreted definition (defined by the user) is about 700.

If the definition is made part of the standard environment, it will be translated to Clean code when the FunSheet application is built. Then, on the same machine the nfib number of the translated definition is about 7000, an order of magnitude faster than the interpreted definition.

Because the spreadsheet language is untyped, the translated definition is strewn with type tags. Therefore it is still two orders of magnitudes slower than the nfib function when written directly in Clean. Then, its nfib number on the same machine is about 700.000, three orders of magnitude faster than the interpreted definition.

3.9 Combining Interactive Applications

Event-handling drivers can be nested with the library function NestIO which is similar to StartIO. It takes an I/O specification, an initial program state, an initial I/O action to start with and it takes its parent's IOState (which represents the world including the event-queue). NestIO delivers its own final program state and the original parent's IOState to continue. Effectively, this means that at any point in a program a sub-program can be called with its own user-interface.

```
NestIO::(IOSystem *t) *t (InitIO *t) *(IOState *s) ->(*t,*IOState *s)
```

The spreadsheet program uses this nesting when calling the window-based editor of new functions with its own user interface. Since a nested I/O system returns its own program state, the IOState of the editor had to be slightly extended in order to return the new function environment. Of course, the editor's user interface (the algebraic data structure describing the main menu and its call-back functions) was also extended with a facility to check and test functions and the state of the editor had to be extended with an environment (of type Env) to be aware of function definitions. However, due to the use of NestIO, all other function definitions of the editor program could remain unchanged. So, the function NestIO played a vital role in re-using the editor program. It dealt with switching I/O interfaces when switching from the sheet to the editor and it dealt with passing the required information about the functions between them.

Below, the definition of the call-back function SwitchToEditor is given. This call-back function is called when the user of the spreadsheet performs the command *Define/Test Function* from the Environment menu. It employs NestIO and some access functions to transfer the definitions of the user-defined functions from the editor to the spreadsheet and vice-versa.

```
SwitchToEditor:: State IO -> (State, IO)
SwitchToEditor shstate io   = (newshstate, nio)
where
    newshstate      = AdaptShFunctionEnv  newfunenv shstate
    newfunenv       = GetEdFunctionEnv edstate
    (edstate,nio)   = NestIO IOSystemEd (InitEdState funenv) InitIOEd io
    funenv          = GetShFunctionEnv sheetstate
```

It is interesting to compare the definition above with the initial expression of the original stand-alone editor application which is given below (note that the definitions of the arguments of StartIO were changed as described above to be able to deal with functions).

```
StartIO IOSystemEd InitEdState InitIOEd io
```

Extending Interactive Applications With Re-compilation

With the nesting scheme above, in Clean 0.8 it was necessary to change the editor's program state which was a tuple. It had to be extended with an extra field containing the function environment.

```
::*Ed -> (Disk,Defaults,Clipbrd,FindInfo,EditWdIds,EditWndws,Env)

// old definition:
//::*Ed  -> (Disk,Defaults,Clipbrd,FindInfo,EditWdIds,EditWndws)

InitEdState:: Files Env -> Ed;
InitEdState files funenv
    = (files,defs,InitClipbrd,InitFindInfo,InitWdIds,InitEdWds,funenv)
where
    defs        =   (DefTabWidth,(ft,sz),DefAutoIndent)
    (ft,_,sz)   =   DefaultFont

GetFunEnv:: Ed -> (Ed, Env)
GetFunEnv ed:(fls,ds,cb,fi,is,ws,env) = (ed,env)

SetFunEnv:: Env Ed -> Ed
SetFunEnv funenv (fls,ds,cb,fi,is,ws,env)
```

```
      = (fls,ds,cb,fi,is,ws,funenv)

GetDefaults:: Ed -> (Ed, Defaults)
GetDefaults ed:(_,defaults,_,_,_,_,_) = (ed,defaults)

SetDefaults:: Defaults Ed -> Ed
SetDefaults deflts (fls,_,cb,fi,is,ws,env)
  = (fls,deflts,cb,fi,is,ws,env)
```

All access functions (including initialisation and closing down) that were used by the editor had to be changed. Since the editor's program state was implemented as an abstract data type, the rest of the editor's definitions could remain unchanged (they just had to be recompiled) with the exception of the definition of the menu system which had to be changed in order to incorporate the new functions for checking and testing function definitions. An interesting aspect of the new menu system definition is that it contains many of the unchanged old definitions which effectively only operate on the old part of the extended state.

```
menus:: DeviceSystem Editor IO
menus = MenuSystem [file, edit, search]
where
 file
  = PullDownMenu MFileID "File" Able
    [MenuItem IHelpID "Help..."    (Key '/') Able      SSHelp, // new
     MenuSeparator,
     MenuItem CKID "Syntax Check" (Key 'S') Able CheckFunction,// new
     MenuItem TestID "Expression Test" (Key 'E')   Able Test, // new
     MenuSeparator,
     MenuItem IQuitID "Return to Sheet" (Key 'W') Able SSClose // new
     ]                                              // no quit anymore
 edit
  = PullDownMenu MEditID "Edit" Unable
    [MenuItem IUndoID  "Undo"     (Key 'Z') Able      Undo, // old
     MenuSeparator,
     MenuItem ICutID   "Cut"      (Key 'X') Unable  Cut,    // old
     MenuItem ICopyID  "Copy"     (Key 'C') Unable  Copy,   // old
     MenuItem IPasteID "Paste"    (Key 'V') Unable Paste,   // old
     MenuItem IClearID "Clear"      NoKey   Unable Clear,   // old
     MenuSeparator,
     MenuItem IBalanID "Balance" (Key 'B') Able Balance,    // old
     MenuSeparator,
     MenuItem IFormaID "Format"  (Key 'J') Able  Format     // old
     ]
 search
  = PullDownMenu MSearcID "Search" Unable
    [MenuItem IFindID  "Find..."  (Key 'F') Able      Find,    //old
     MenuItem IFindNID "Find Next" (Key 'G') Unable FndNext,  //old
     MenuItem IFindSID "Find Selection" (Key 'H') Unable FndSel,//old
```

```
MenuItem IReplID "Replace&Find" (Key 'T') Unable Repl&Find,//old
MenuSeparator,
MenuItem IGotoCID "Goto Cursor" (Key 'L') Able GotoCursor, //old
MenuItem IGotoLID "Goto Line..."  NoKey Able GotoLine    //old
]
```

So, for the extension of a text editor to a function editor changes were done in only two modules: the module that defined the abstract program state and the module that defined the I/O system and started the interaction. The rest was recompiled.

A disadvantage of this recompilation is that a copy has to be made if both editors co-exist on the same machine. This requires version management if changes are made in the future.

4 Development Techniques for Efficient Medium-Sized Functional Programs

In this section for several important development techniques that could have been used in the FunSheet project or may be used in future projects, examples are given of the way they can be applied in a functional language.

All program examples in this section are written in Clean 1.0. Below some general remarks are made about the Clean 1.0 and the differences with respect to Clean 0.8. The key constructs used in the examples are explained briefly. For further reference on the syntax and semantics of the constructs available in Clean 1.0 the reader is referred to FTP (pub/Clean at ftp.cs.kun.nl) or WWW (www.cs.kun.nl/~clean) where the system is freely available for non-commercial use.

About Concurrent Clean 1.0

Compared with the previous version of Clean a lot of new features are added based on experience with writing complex applications. Many of the added language constructs are similar to those commonly found in other modern lazy functional languages (such as Miranda (Turner, 1985), SML (Harper *et al.*, 1986), Haskell (Hudak *et al.*, 1992) and Gofer (Jones, 1993)). People familiar with these languages should have no difficulty to program in Clean and we hope that they enjoy the compilation speed and quality of the produced code.

In addition Clean offers a couple of very special features. Of particular importance for practical use is Cleans' uniqueness typing enabling the incorporation of *destructive updates* of arbitrary objects *within a pure functional framework* and the creation of *direct interfaces with the outside world.*

Cleans "unique" features have made it possible to predefine (in Clean) a sophisticated and efficient I/O library. The Clean I/O library enables a Clean programmer to *specify interactive window based I/O* applications on a *very high level of abstraction.* The library forms a platform independent interface to window systems which makes it possible to port window based I/O applications written in Clean without modification of source code.

In Clean it is possible to create *processes*. The new Clean I/O library takes advantage of this feature such that it is now also has become possible to develop *distributed executing interactive applications* running on several PC's/workstations connected in a network. The applications can communicate via *asynchronous as well as synchronous message passing*. Such a distributed application can be developed on one processor on which the processes will run in an *interleaved* fashion. This is very handy for testing.

The new Clean compiler still combines *fast compilation* with the generation of *efficient code* and is available on an increasing number of platforms (Mac, PC, Sun).

Major differences with Clean 0.8

Compared with the previous release (0.84b) many important changes have been made (there is a noticeable difference between an intermediate language and a programming language).

The most important changes in the language are:

❑ various syntactic sugar is added (infix operators, a case construct, local function definitions, lamda-abstractions, list comprehensions, lay-out rule, CAF's etc.);

❑ overloaded functions, type classes and type constructor classes can be defined;

❑ records and arrays are added as predefined data structure with handy operations (such as an update operator for arrays and records, array comprehensions etc.);

❑ a more refined control of strictness is possible (partially strict data structures can be defined for any type, in particular for recursive types, there is strict let construct);

❑ existentially quantified types can be defined;

❑ the uniqueness typing is refined (now polymorphic and inferred, observation of uniquely typed objects is made easier);

❑ there is support for destructive updates of predefined and user defined data in a pure functional context;

❑ the semantics for parallel evaluation is adapted for uniqueness typing and its use is simplified as well;

❑ the module structure is improved;

❑ the macro facility is extended.

Also the Clean I/O library has been changed:

❑ the I/O library is improved (with respect to orthogonality, modularity, extendibility, portability);

❑ the I/O library is extended allowing to define interactive processes running interleaved inside one application which can communicate via files, shared data, (a)synchroneous message passing, remote procedure call;

❑ one can define interactive processes which run distributed on workstations connected via a network.

The compiler and code generator have been extended and are partly rewritten.

Furthermore,

❑ the code generator is extended for parallel and distributed evaluation;
❑ the code generator is improved;
❑ more platforms are supported.

Some remarks on the new Clean syntax

Compared with the 0.84 version we have made a lot of syntactic changes to the language. The complete redesign of Clean has as consequence that Clean version 1.0 is *not* compatible with its predecessors. A Clean application is available to transform programs written in old Clean into new Clean.

The new Clean syntax is similar to the notation found in most other modern functional languages. So people familiar with these languages will have no difficuluties with programming in Clean. However, there are a couple of small differences we want to point out here for people who don't like to read language reports.

In Clean the arity of a function is reflected in its type. When a function is defined its uncurried type is specified (to avoid any confusion we want to explicitly state here that in Clean there is no restriction whatsoever on the curried use of functions).

The standard map function (arity 2) is specified in Clean as follows:

```
map::(a -> b) [a] -> [b]
map f []     = []
map f [x:xs] = [f x : map f xs]
```

In types funny symbols can appear like ., u:, *, ! which can be ignored and left out if one is not interested in uniqueness typing or strictness.

Each predefined structure such as a list, a tuple, a record or array has its own kind of brackets: lists are *always* denoted with square brackets [...], for tuples the usual parenthesis are used (... , ...), curly braces are used for records { ... }, and arrays look like this { : ... : }. There are only a few keywords in Clean leading to a heavily overloaded use of : and = symbols:

```
function::argstype -> restype  // type specification of a function
function pattern | guard = rhs // definition of a function

selector = graph                // definition of a constant/ CAF/graph

::type args    =     type       // an algebraic type definition
::type args    :==   type       // a type synonym definition
::type args                     // an abstract type definition
```

```
macro args    :==    rhs        // a macro definition (function synonym)
```

Defining algebraic data types with existentially quantified variables

Clean incorporates the extension of the Hindley/Milner type system with the possibility of algebraic types to be existential. An *existential algebraic data type definition* is an algebraic type definition in which *existentially quantified variables* are used. These special variables are marked with "E.". Existential types are useful if one wants to create (recursive) data structures in which objects of *different types* are being stored (e.g. a list with elements of different types). Such kind of data structures are for instance used internally in Cleans' I/O library to store (program and I/O) states of different types and state transition functions defined on these states in one data structure.

```
// Existential algebraic type definition and its use

::Tree E.a = NilTr
           | NodeTr (a, a, a a -> a) (Tree Void) (Tree Void)

F :: Tree Void
F = NodeTr (3,5,(+)) (NodeTr (3.5,5.4,(+)) NilTr NilTr) NilTr

G :: (Tree Void) -> Tree Void
G (NodeTr (obj1,obj2,func) l r)=NodeTr (func obj1 obj1,obj2,func) l r
```

There are severe limitations imposed on the use of data structures of *existential types*. Once a data structure of existential type is created and is passed to another function it is generally statically not possible to determine what the actual type is of those components of the constructor that correspond to the existential quantified variables.

- Therefore, it is *not* allowed to pass such objects to other functions as argument or result *if* these functions either require or deliver this actual type. In other words, for the type inference system an existentially quantified type variable is treated as a type variable that can be unified with a concrete type (= not a type variable) *only* at the explicit creation of a data structure of this type with its defining data constructor. In all other contexts an existentially quantified type variable can only be unified with non concrete types (type variables).
- For software engineering reasons it is required that an existentially quantified type variable is instantiated with the predefined type Void (see the example above).

Components that correspond to the *same* existentially quantified type variable will have the *same* type. So, it is allowed to apply these components in expressions that yield an ordinary type. It is also allowed to use the components to create a new object of existential type. Furthermore, it is allowed to pass the existentially quantified type variable to polymorphic functions.

Apart from the restrictions mentioned above existential algebraic types are not different from standard algebraic types. They can be used e.g. as the basis of record types, synonym types and abstract types.

Defining record types

A *record type* is basically an algebraic data type in which exactly one constructor is defined. Special about records is
* that a *field name* is attached to each of the arguments of the data constructor;
* that they cannot be used in a curried way.

Compared with ordinary algebraic data structures the use of records gives a lot of notational convenience because the field names enable *selection by field name* instead of *selection by position*. When a record is created *all* arguments of the constructor have to be defined but one can specify the arguments in *any* order. Furthermore, when pattern matching is performed on a record, one only has to mention those fields one is interested in. Existentially quantified type variables are allowed in record types. The arguments of the constructor can optionally be annotated as being strict. The specification of uniqueness attributes is also optional.

As data constructor for a record the name of the record type is used internally.
* The semantic restrictions which apply for algebraic data types also hold for record types.
* The field names inside one record all have to be different. It is allowed to use the same field name in different records.

```
// A record definition:

::Complex  = {  re :: Real,
                im :: Real }
```

Defining overloaded function types and concrete instances

With an *overloaded function type definition* one defines the *type scheme* of the overloaded function. The type of a concrete function must be an instance of this type scheme. The special *type scheme variable* defines in which variable the scheme can vary. With an *instance* declaration one defines an overloaded function c.q. operator name to be a *synonym* for some *concrete function* or *operator*. In the instance definition it is specified which concrete function is ment and for which *concrete type* an instance of the overloaded function is created. The type of the concrete function must be equal to the overloaded type after uniform substitution of the specified concrete type for the type scheme variable. For a concrete function one can refer to a function which has already been defined elsewhere or one can define a new function right on the spot.

One can define as many instances as one like. Instances can be added in any module. One and the same concrete function can be used as instance for different overloaded functions (as long as the types match).
```
/*
```

```
Defining an overloaded operator and instantiations with existing
concrete operators: The types of the concrete operators +^ and +.
need to be instances of the type scheme of + (take for the type
scheme variable a of the overloaded operator + respectively Int and
Real)
*/
overload (+) infixl 6 a :: a a -> a

instance + Int  = +^
instance + Real = +.

(+^) infixl 6 :: !Int  !Int    -> Int
(+.) infixl 6 :: !Real !Real   -> Real
```

When an overloaded name is encountered in an expression, the compiler will determine which of the corresponding concrete functions/operators is meant by looking at
the concrete type of the expression. From this type the concrete function to apply is
determined. All concrete functions/operators of an overloaded function/operator must
therefore be defined on *different* instances of the type scheme (with exception of the
default instance, see below). If it is clear from the type of the expression which one of
the concrete function is ment the compiler will in principle substitute the concrete
function application for the overloaded one such that no efficiency is lost.

A concrete function is substituted for an overloaded one: given the definitions
above the function

```
inc n = n + 1
```

It will be internally transformed into

```
inc n = n +^ 1
```

If it is not clear from the type of the expression which concrete function is ment
(more than one of the concrete functions fit type technically) the compiler will make
specialized versions of the function of which the expression is part of. In principle
one version is made for each concrete possible substitution. However, the compiler
will avoid making versions which are not being used or which are not important in
terms of efficiency and in any case it will avoid code explosion.

As an example of the creation of specialized versions for overloaded functions:
assume the following function definition and Start rule:

```
sumlist [x:xs] [y:ys]  = [x + y:sumlist xs ys]
sumlist x y            = []

Start = sumlist [1..10] [11..20]
```

From the context of sumlist it is not clear which concrete instantiation of + to be used. So the compiler will in principle generate a special version of sumlist for all possible versions which are needed. In this example sumlist is only applied to integer lists. So the compiler will only generate a version of sumlist for Ints as follows:

```
sumlistI [x:xs] [y:ys]    = [x +^ y:sumlistI xs ys]
sumlistI x y          =  []

Start = sumlistI [1..10] [11..20]
```

It is possible to specify a function as *default instance* (no concrete type instance is specified for the type scheme variable in the instance declaration in that case) which will be taken when none of the other defined instances happens to be applicable. Since such a function must work for *any* instance the type of the default function must be equivalent to the type of the overloaded function. The default function provides the possibility to define a standard interpretation for an overloaded function.

An example of defining a default instance indicating that objects are by default unequal unless specified otherwise is given below:

```
overload (==) infix 2 a :: a a -> Bool

instance ==   = DefaultEqual

(DefaultEqual) infix 2 :: a a -> Bool
(DefaultEqual) x y = False
```

An alternative equivalent solution avoiding the introduction of a new function name:

```
overload (==) infix 2 a :: a a -> Bool

instance ==
where
   (==) x y = False
```

When one exports instances of an overloaded function or operator in a definition module one may wish to hide the actual function/operator name (in the implementation module). In this way one can ensure that always the overloaded name is being used outside.

An example of defining an instance of an overloaded operator in a definition module hiding the actual operator name:

```
instance ==
```

The following restrictions apply:

- The type of a concrete function or operator must exactly match the overloaded type scheme after uniform substitution of the type scheme variable by the type as specified in the corresponding type instance declaration.
- A type instance of an overloaded type must be a *flat type*, i.e. a type of the form T a_1 ... a_n where a_i are type variables which are *all* different.
- It is not allowed to use a type synonym as instance.
- All instances other than the default instance of a given overloaded type must differ from each other (be ununifyable with each other).
- If a default instance is specified the type of the corresponding concrete default function must be identical to the type of the overloaded function or operator.
- If the concrete function or operator is not specified in a definition module, it has to be defined in the corresponding implementation module.
- The start rule cannot have an overloaded type.
- Ambiguously overloading is not permitted.

Type classes

When a function is defined in terms of an overloaded function it can occur that the type system cannot decide which one of the corresponding concrete functions to apply. The new function then becomes overloaded as well. This has as consequence that an additional restriction must be imposed on the use of such a function. This is reflected in the type of the function.

For instance, the function

```
add x y = x + y
```

becomes overloaded as well because any concrete instance can be applied. So, add can be applied to arguments of any type, as long as addition (+) is defined on them.

In a *type class definition* one gives a name to a *set of overloaded functions* (this set actually defines a type class record, see above). The definition of the overloaded functions themselves can be directly specified in the type class definition itself but one can also refer to overloaded functions type definitions declared elsewhere. One and the same overloaded function can be a *member* of different type classes. Instances of the overloaded functions are created as described above. There is no hierarchy in type classes.

An example of a definition of a type class:

```
class Arith a
where
    (+) infixl 6 :: a a -> a
    (-) infixl 6 :: a a -> a
```

An equivalent definition:

```
class Arith a
where +; -

overload (+) infixl 6 a :: a a -> a
overload (-) infixl 6 a :: a a -> a
```

In the definition of the type of a function that has become overloaded one can now refer to a type class to impose a restricted context on the instantiation of a type variable
of the function. Such a context imposes a condition (predicate) under which type variables is allowed to be instantiated. So one obtains a kind of *bounded polymorphism*.
The function can only be applied if for the corresponding concrete type the indicated
type classes have been instantiated.

```
/*
Use of a type class to impose a restriction on the instantiation of
type variable: the function add can only be applied on arguments for
which an instance of the class Arith is defined.
*/
add :: a a -> a | Arith a
add x y = x + y
/*
Instance declaration of which type is depending on same type class:
the function sumlist itself can also be defined as an instance for
the overloaded operator + working on arbitrary list for which the
type class Arith is defined on the list elements. sumlist must now be
defined as operator because this is expected from an instance of +.
With this definition + is defined on lists, and list of lists etc.
*/
instance + [a] | Arith a = sumlist

(sumlist) infixl 6 :: [a] [a] -> [a] | Arith a
(sumlist) [x:xs] [y:ys]  = [x + y:xs + ys]
(sumlist) x y            = []
```

An equivalent definition:

```
instance + [a] | Arith a
where
    (+) [x:xs] [y:ys]  = [x + y:xs + ys]
    (+) x y            = []
```

Cleans type system will infer contexts automatically. It will however *not* express this
in terms of type classes but simple summarize the collection of functions on which
the overloaded function is depending. This is caused by the fact that it is allowed that
one function is defined as a member of several type classes. If a type class is specified
as restricted context the type system will check the correctness of the specification (as
always a type specification can be more restrictive than is deduced by the compiler).

- For an overloaded function which is exported the type (including the context) has to be defined explicitly by the programmer.
- The type checker will complain if a concrete application cannot be applied due to the fact that certain instances of type classes have not been declared.

```
//      Equality class.

class Eq a
where
    (==) infix 2 :: a a -> Bool

instance ==                = DefaultEq    //    by default, see above
instance ==    Int    = ==^              //    on integers (primitive)

instance ==    [a] | Eq a                //    on lists
(==) [x:xs] [y:ys]  = x == y && xs == ys
(==) []        []       = True
(==) _         _        = False

instance ==    (a,b) | Eq a & Eq b       //    on tuples of arity two
(==) (x1,x2) (y1,y2) = x1 == y1 && x2 == y2
```

The members of a class consists of a set of functions or operators which logically belong to each other. It is often the case that the effect of some members (*derived members*) can be expressed in others. For instance <> can be seen as synonym for not (==). For software engineering (the fixed relation is made explicit) and efficiency (one does not need to include derived members in the class record) reasons it is good to make this relation explicit. In Clean macro definitions can be used for this purpose.

```
// Classes with derived members.

definition module overloaded

class Eq a
where
    (==) infix 2 :: a a -> Bool

    (<>) infix 2 :: a    a  ->    Bool | Eq a
    (<>) x y :== not (x == y)

class Ord a
where
    (<) infix  2 :: a a     ->    Bool

    (>) infix  2 :: a a     ->    Bool | Ord a
    (>) x y :== y < x
```

```
(<=) infix  2 :: a a   ->    Bool | Ord a
(<=) x y :== not (y<x)

(>=) infix  2 :: a a   ->    Bool | Ord a
(>=) x y :== not (x<y)

min :: a a -> a | Ord a
min x y :== if (x<y) x y

max :: a a -> a | Ord a
max x y :== if (x<y) y x
```

When an overloaded function is exported a type class record has to be constructed as explained in the introduction. However, for efficiency reasons it would be nice to know which instances of the type class are known in the implementation module. When a type class is exported one can explicitly define the minimal *set of instances* which exist for this type class. For any function defined on such a type class one can now deduce that at least these instances are known.

```
// Classes with derived members.

definition module StdOverloaded

overload == a :: a a -> Bool

definition module StdInt

import overloaded

instance == Int

definition module StdReal

import overloaded

instance == Real

definition module example

import StdInt, StdReal

class Eq a
where    ==
instances Int, Real
```

4.1 Extending Interactive Applications Without Re-compilation

The use of type classes in Clean 1.0 makes it possible to extend interactive applications without the need for re-compilation of the part that is extended.

It makes it even possible to write higher order functions that extend (parts of) menus without knowing the names of the actual call-back functions that are present in the definitions.

For the extension of the function editor in the FunSheet project as described in section 3.9 this would mean that the old call-back functions would operate on the old editor state and that a general function could be used that takes any menu definition with call-back functions for the old editor and extends that to a menu definition with call-back functions for the function editor. This would be applicable for the pulldown menus for editing and searching.

```
module ExtStdEditor

Start = genexcbf cbf { e = Ex, r = { s = E, io = IO E}}

//    standard definitions for an editor

::Editor    = E
::IOState x = IO x

::State =   {  s ::Editor,
               io::IOState    Editor}

cbf::State -> State
cbf s = s

// added definitions for a state extension

class XState sup
where
   ToState ::sup -> (State,sup)
   FromState::(State,sup) -> sup

// general definition of a state extension including the extension of
// a state-transition function

instance XState ExState
where
   ToState     sup          = (sup.r,sup)
   FromState (state,sup)  = {sup & r = state}

::Extension = Ex
::ExState = { e::Extension,
              r::State }
```

```
excbf::s -> s | XState s
excbf s = FromState (nstate,s1)
where
   (state,s1) = ToState s
   nstate = cbf state
```

```
// higher order function to extend a standard call-back-function to
// the extended state
```

```
genexcbf::(State -> State) s -> s | XState s
genexcbf cbf s = FromState (nstate,s1)
where
   (state,s1) = ToState s
   nstate     = cbf state
```

4.2   Object-oriented Programming Techniques

Object-oriented programming can be useful when large software components are to be combined. Important aspects of object-oriented programming such as abstraction, encapsulation and multiple inheritance can be modelled in a functional language.

Modelling Objects

An object-oriented style of programming can be used in a functional programming language by modelling an object by a record which contains the state of the object and the methods that can be applied on the object. The use of existential types can make such a way of modelling quite general allowing functions to operate on lists of objects with different internal states as is shown in the example below.

```
module object

::Object E.x  =   {  state     ::x,
                     get       ::x -> Int,
                     set       ::x Int -> x
                  }
MyObject::Object Void
MyObject = {state = [], get = myget, set = myset}
where
   myget::[Int] -> Int
   myget [i:is] = i
   myget []     = 0

   myset::[Int] Int  -> [Int]
   myset is i = [i:is]

Get::(Object Void) -> Int
Get {state,get} = get state

Set::(Object Void) Int -> Object Void
```

```
Set o=:{state,set} i = {o & state = set state i}

Start = Get (Set (Set MyObject 1) 2)
```

Modelling Multiple Inheritance

Using type classes and conversion functions combined with overloading an expressive power can be obtained which is similar to the expressive power of subtyping. Multiple inheritance as is present in many object-oriented languages can be modelled using these facilities.

The classic example of combinations of points, colour and lines is given below.

```
module point
import StdEnv

Start   = (moveX {cpp={x=1.0,y=2.4},cpc={c=23}} (1.5,2.5),
            mirrorlX {cplp={x=1.0,y=2.4},
                      cplc={c=23},
                      cpll={f=(0.0,1.0),
                      t=(1.0,2.0)}}})

//     layer 1

::Point  =  {  x::Real,
                y::Real }
::Color  =  {  c::Int   }
::Line   =  {  f::(Real,Real),
               t::(Real,Real)   }
::Dist   :==   (Real,Real)

move::Point Dist -> Point
move {x,y} (dx,dy) = {x=x+dx,y=y+dy}

moveX::spoint Dist -> spoint | XPoint spoint
moveX rec dist = cPoint (np,nrec)
where
    (p,nrec)   = sPoint rec
    np         = move p dist

invcol::Color -> Color
invcol {c} = {c=0-c}

mirrorl::Line -> Line
mirrorl {f=(xf,yf),t=(xt,yt)} = {f=(xf,yt),t=(xt,yf)}

mirrorlX rec = cLine (np,nrec)
where
    (p,nrec)   = sLine rec
    np         = mirrorl p
```

```
// Point
class XPoint su
where
   sPoint :: su -> (Point,su)
   cPoint :: (Point,su) -> su

instance sPoint Point = PtoP_P
instance cPoint Point = P_PtoP
PtoP_P::Point -> (Point,Point)
PtoP_P x = (x,x)
P_PtoP::(Point,Point) -> Point
P_PtoP (p,v) = p

// Color
class XColor su
where
   sColor ::su -> (Color,su)
   cColor ::(Color,su) -> su

instance sColor (Color) = CtoC_C
instance cColor (Color) = C_CtoC
CtoC_C::Color -> (Color,Color)
CtoC_C x = (x,x)
C_CtoC::(Color,Color) -> Color
C_CtoC (p,v) = p

// Line
class XLine su
where
   sLine ::su -> (Line,su)
   cLine ::(Line,su) -> su

instance sLine Line = LtoL_L
instance cLine Line = L_LtoL
LtoL_L::Line -> (Line,Line)
LtoL_L x = (x,x)
L_LtoL::(Line,Line) -> Line
L_LtoL (p,v) = p

// layer2: combinations of the records of layer1

::ColorPoint = { cpc::Color,cpp::Point }

class XColorPoint su
where
   sColorPoint ::su -> (ColorPoint,su)
   cColorPoint ::(ColorPoint,su) -> su
```

```
instance sColorPoint ColorPoint = CPtoCP_CP
instance cColorPoint ColorPoint = CP_CPtoCP
CPtoCP_CP::ColorPoint -> (ColorPoint,ColorPoint)
CPtoCP_CP x = (x,x)
CP_CPtoCP::(ColorPoint,ColorPoint) -> ColorPoint
CP_CPtoCP (p,v) = p

instance sPoint ColorPoint = CPtoP_CP
instance cPoint ColorPoint = P_CPtoCP
CPtoP_CP::ColorPoint -> (Point,ColorPoint)
CPtoP_CP rec=:{cpc,cpp} = (cpp,rec)
P_CPtoCP::(Point,ColorPoint) -> ColorPoint
P_CPtoCP (p,rec) = { rec & cpp=p }

instance sColor ColorPoint = CPtoC_CP
instance cColor ColorPoint = C_CPtoCP
CPtoC_CP::ColorPoint -> (Color,ColorPoint)
CPtoC_CP rec=:{cpc,cpp} = (cpc,rec)
C_CPtoCP::(Color,ColorPoint) -> ColorPoint
C_CPtoCP (c,rec) = { rec & cpc=c }

// layer3: combinations of the records of layer1 and 2

::ColorPointLine = { cplc::Color,cplp::Point,cpll::Line }

class XColorPointLine su
where
    sColorPointLine ::su -> (ColorPointLine,su)
    cColorPointLine ::(ColorPointLine,su) -> su

instance sLine ColorPointLine = CPLtoL_CPL
instance cLine ColorPointLine = L_CPLtoCPL
CPLtoL_CPL::ColorPointLine -> (Line,ColorPointLine)
CPLtoL_CPL rec=:{cpll} = (cpll,rec)
L_CPLtoCPL::(Line,ColorPointLine) -> ColorPointLine
L_CPLtoCPL (l,rec) = { rec & cpll=l }
```

Introducing more Locality in I/O Definitions

The use of existential types with the power of overloading as it is defined in Clean 1.0 makes it possible to define a new version of the I/O library which has a facility to keep a local state in a part of the graphical user interface.

An example of the application of call-back functions on objects with local state in a time-sliced manner is given below.

```
module locstate
import StdEnv

::State E.a ls = {  ps::a,
```

```
                    ms::(a,ls) -> (a,ls) }

Apply::((State Void ls),ls) -> ((State Void ls),ls)
Apply (rec=:{ps,ms},ls) = (nrec,nls)
where
   (na,nls) = ms (ps,ls)
   nrec     = { rec & ps = na }

TimeSlice::([State Void ls],ls) -> ([State Void ls],ls)
TimeSlice ([rec:rest],state) = ([nrec : nrest],endstate)
where
   (nrest,endstate)    = TimeSlice (rest,nstate)
   (nrec,nstate)       = Apply (rec,state)
TimeSlice final = final

NTimes::!([State Void ls],ls) Int -> ([State Void ls],ls)
NTimes state 0 = state
NTimes state n = NTimes (TimeSlice state) (n-1)

Start = NTimes ([MyRec1,MyRec2],0) 20

::LocalState :== Int

MyRec1 = { ps = 1.0, ms = mycbf }
where
   mycbf::(Real,Int) -> (Real,Int)
   mycbf (a,b) = (a+1.5,b+1)

MyRec2 = { ps = 'a', ms = mycbf }
where
   mycbf::(Char,Int) -> (Char,Int)
   mycbf (a,b) = (toChar ((toInt a) + 1),b+1)
```

4.3 Monads

Monads form a programming style which can be useful when higher order functions are combined in a particular pattern.

An example of a state monad is given below. It is important to note that single-threadedness of the definitions is not a supposition but it is derived by Clean's uniqueness type inference scheme.

```
module monad  //state monad

::St s a :== s -> (a,s)

return::u:a -> u:(St .s u:a)
return x = \s -> (x,s)

(`bind`) infix 0:: u:(St .s .a) u:(a -> .(St .s .b)) -> u:(St .s .b)
```

```
(`bind`) f_sta a_fstb = stb
where
   stb st = a_fstb a nst
   where
      (a,nst)  =  f_sta st

Start::[.Char]
Start = result
where
   (result,s) =  (  f `bind` (\a ->
                     g `bind` (\b ->
                     return [a,b] ))) S

::S = S    // concrete state with one possible value: S

f::.a -> (.Char,.a)
f s = ('f',s)

g::.a -> (.Char,.a)
g s = ('g',s)
```

4.4 Programming Environment Support

The fact that functions have no side-effects seems to lead to a much more refined module structure than is the case in imperative programming. Therefore more demands are put on the programming environment to support tools for modular programming. A few examples of such tools to improve modular software productivity are given below.

Adding structure to the project defining layers in which definition modules can depend on each other might also be very helpful.

It can be very important to know quickly which modules use a certain function. Without such a facility easily many almost equivalent function definitions emerge since 'to be safe' new functions are made instead of changing or generalising existing functions.

It can be very useful to have a special facility to change a definition module of a library in a 'benign' way, i.e. just changing the comments or the layout or extending it with one or more new functions. In the latter case all modules that depend on that the definition module do not have to be recompiled completely but just checks on name clashes and possibly the generation of new code labels have to be performed. This may save a lot of development time.

Strictness could be exported automatically. A warning could be given for specified strictness that cannot be inferred by the system.

Facilities should be available to perform editing and formatting operations on groups of modules that form a project. Changing a module name or a function name all over a project or printing all (definition) modules that are used in a project are important examples of the use of such tools.

5 Conclusions

- The functional spreadsheet design served as an interesting *test case* for techniques for developing efficient medium sized functional programs.
- In the FunSheet project reuse and adaptation of *existing software components* (I/O library, help tool, editor and symbolic evaluator) turned out to be possible with a functional language. Considering the relatively small scale of the project its *software productivity* was quite high. Considering the functionality and the facts that huge parts of the software were reused and that code generation for unique data types was not available yet the *efficiency* is satisfactory.
- However, the experience with the project did yield a number of important aspects of the language Clean and its programming environment (version 0.8) that *hampered the software development*. The experience of this project showed the importance of incorporating these aspects in future versions of the language. Clean 1.0 incorporates most of them.
- Several *well-known techniques* for writing larger programs can be *modelled* in a relatively straightforward manner in a functional language (Clean 1.0). This makes these techniques also applicable for functional languages.
- The *support* for medium sized functional programs is still low both in programming languages as well as in programming environments. There are ample opportunities for improvement.

Exercises

The first exercise is an introductory exercise to get acquainted with Clean and with the I/O library. The second exercise is a larger exercise with more demands with respect to re-use of existing software.

1. Extend using the I/O library a given pocket-calculator program with a number of extra buttons for extra functionality.
2. Use the described text editor, help facility and I/O library to create a HTML editor with support for defining hypertext links and hypertext layout. Preferably, the sources of the existing modules remain unchanged and do not even have to be re-compiled.

References

Achten, P.M., and Plasmeijer, M.J. 1994. A Framework for Deterministically Interleaved Interactive Programs in the Functional Programming Language Clean. In Bakker E. ed. *Proc. Computing Science in the Netherlands, CSN'94*. Jaarbeurs Utrecht. The Netherlands. Stichting Mathematisch Centrum, Amsterdam. pp. 30-41.

Achten, P.M., and Plasmeijer, M.J. 1995. The Ins and Outs of Clean I/O, *Journal of Functional Programming*. **5** (1).

Barendregt, H.P., Eekelen van, M.C.J.D., Glauert, J.R.W., Kennaway, J.R., Plasmeijer, M.J., and Sleep, M.R. 1987. Term Graph Rewriting. In Bakker, J.W. de, Nijman, A.J., and Treleaven, P.C. (editors), *Proceedings of Parallel Architectures and Languages Europe*, Eindhoven, The Netherlands, LNCS **259**, Vol.II., pp. 141-158. Springer-Verlag.

Barendsen, E., and Smetsers, J.E.W. 1993. Conventional and Uniqueness Typing in Graph Rewrite Systems (extended abstract). In Shyamasundar, R.K. (editor), *Proceedings of the Thirteenth Conference on the Foundations of Software Technology and Theoretical Computer Science*, Bombay, India,, December 15-17, 1993. LNCS **761**, pp. 41-51. Springer-Verlag.

Brus, T., Eekelen, M.C.J.D. van, Leer, M.O. van, and Plasmeijer, M.J. 1987. Clean: A Language for Functional Graph Rewriting. In Kahn. G. (editor), *Proceedings of the Third International Conference on Functional Programming Languages and Computer Architecture*, Portland, Oregon, USA, LNCS **274**, pp. 364-384. Springer-Verlag.

Carlsson, M., and Hallgren, Th. 1993. Fudgets - A Graphical User Interface in a Lazy Functional Language. In *Proceedings of the Conference on Functional Programming Languages and Computer Architecture*. Copenhagen, Denmark, June 9-11, 1993, pp. 321-330. ACM Press.

Cartwright, R., and Boehm, B. 1990. Exact Real Arithmetic, formulating real numbers as functions. In Turner, D.A. (editor), *Research Topics in Functional Programming*. University of Texas at Austin Year of Programming Series, pp. 43-64. Addison Wesley Publishing Company. ISBN 0-201-17236-4.

Harper, R., D. MacQueen and R. Milner (1986). 'Standard ML'. Edinburgh University, Internal report ECS-LFCS-86-2.

Hoon, W.A.C.A.J. de 1993. Designing a spreadsheet in a pure functional graph rewriting language, Computer Science Master Thesis nr. 300, University of Nijmegen, The Netherlands.

Hoon, W.A.C.A.J. de, Rutten, L.M.W.J., and Eekelen, M.C.J.D. van 1994. FunSheet: A Functional Spreadsheet. *Proceedings of the Sixth International Workshop on the Implementation of Functional Languages*, Norwich, UK, September 1994, pp. 11.1-11.24.

Hoon, W.A.C.A.J. de, Rutten, L.M.W.J., and Eekelen, M.C.J.D. van 1995. Implementing a Functional Spreadsheet in Clean. *Journal of Functional Programming*, Vol **3**, 1995, to appear.

Hudak, P. , S. Peyton Jones, Ph. Wadler, B. Boutel, J. Fairbairn, J. Fasel, K. Hammond, J. Hughes, Th. Johnsson, D. Kieburtz, R. Nikhil, W. Partain and J. Peterson (1992). 'Report on the programming language Haskell'. *ACM SigPlan notices*, **27**, 5, pp. 1-164.

Jones, M.P. (1993). *Gofer - Gofer 2.21 release notes*. Yale University.

Nöcker, E.G.J.M.H., Smetsers, J.E.W., Eekelen, M.C.J.D. van, and Plasmeijer, M.J. 1991. Concurrent Clean. In Aarts, E.H.L., Leeuwen, J. van, Rem, M.

(editors), *Proceedings of Parallel Architectures and Languages Europe*, June 1991, Eindhoven, The Netherlands. LNCS **506**, pp. 202-219. Springer-Verlag.

Peyton Jones, S.L., and Wadler, Ph. 1993. Imperative Functional Programming. In *Proceedings of the Twentieth Annual ACM SIGACT-SIGPLAN Symposium on Principles of Programming Languages*, Charleston, South Carolina, January 10-13, 1993, pp. 71-84.

Plasmeijer, M.J., and Eekelen, M.C.J.D. van 1993. *Functional Programming and Parallel Graph Rewriting*. Addison Wesley Publishing Company. ISBN 0-201-41663-8.

Plasmeijer, M.J., and Eekelen, M.C.J.D. van 1995. Clean 1.0 Reference Manual. Technical Report, in preparation. University of Nijmegen, The Netherlands.

Pountain D. 1994. Functional Programming Comes of Age. *Byte Magazine*, **19**(8): pp. 183-184.

Smetsers, J.E.W., Barendsen, E., Eekelen, M.C.J.D. van, and Plasmeijer, M.J. 1993. Guaranteeing Safe Destructive Updates through a Type System with Uniqueness Information for Graphs. In Schneider H.J., and Ehrig H. (editors), *Proceedings Workshop Graph Transformations in Computer Science*, Schloss Dagstuhl, January 4-8, 1993. LNCS **776**, Springer-Verlag.

Turner, D.A. 1990. An Approach to Functional Operating Systems. In Turner, D.A. (editor), *Research topics in Functional Programming*, pp. 199-217. Addison-Wesley Publishing Company, ISBN 0-201-17236-4.

Turner, D.A. (1985). 'Miranda: a non-strict functional language with polymorphic types'. In: *Proc. of the Conference on Functional Programming Languages and Computer Architecture*, ed. J.P. Jouannaud, Nancy, France. LNCS **201**, Springer Verlag, 1-16.

Vuillemin (1987). Arithmétic réelle exacte par les fractions continues. Technical Report 760. Institute National de Recherche en Informatique et en Automatique. Domaine de Voluceau, Roquencourt, BP105, 78153 Le Chesnay Cedex, France.

Merging Monads and Folds for Functional Programming

Erik Meijer
Department of Computer Science, Utrecht University
PO Box 80.089, NL-3508 TB Utrecht, The Netherlands
email: erik@cs.ruu.nl

Johan Jeuring
Chalmers University of Technology and University of Göteborg
S-412 96 Göteborg, Sweden
email: johanj@cs.chalmers.se

Abstract. These notes discuss the simultaneous use of generalised fold operators and monads to structure functional programs. Generalised fold operators structure programs after the decomposition of the value they consume. Monads structure programs after the computation of the value they produce. Our programs abstract both from the recursive processing of their input as well as from the side-effects in computing their output. We show how generalised monadic folds aid in calculating an efficient graph reduction engine from an inefficient specification.

1 Introduction

Should I structure my program after the decomposition of the value it consumes or after the computation of the value it produces?

Some [Bir89, Mee86, Mal90, Jeu90, MFP91] argue in favour of structuring programs after the decomposition of the value they consume. Such *syntax directed* programs are written using a limited set of recursion functionals. These functionals, called catamorphisms or *generalised fold operators* are naturally derived from the recursive structure of recursive datatypes. Fold operators satisfy a number of laws that support *calculating* with programs. Using these laws efficient implementation programs can be calculated from inefficient specification programs.

Others [Wad90, Wad95, Mog91, Pat95] argue in favour of structuring programs after the computation of value they produce. Such *semantics directed* programs are composed by gluing together computations using a limited set of operators. These *monad* operators are naturally derived from the plumbing structures that arise when computing values of monadic types. Programming with monads provides a uniform means of integrating effects such as I/O, updatable state, exceptions, nondeterminism, etc., into a purely functional language.

As we show in this paper, syntax directed programming and semantics directed programming neatly combine. This means that it is possible to abstract both from the recursive processing of the input as well as from the side-effects in computing the output. The resulting programs often are of an astonishing clarity and conciseness.

1.1 Overview

This paper is organised as follows. Section 2 shows that many functions defined on lists can be defined by folding using the standard function foldr, and it shows how one can calculate programs using properties of function foldr. Section 3 generalises function foldr to other algebraic datatypes. Section 4 introduces monads. Section 5 introduces generalised monadic folds. Section 6 shows how properties of monadic folds can be used to calculate an efficient lazy monadic interpreter from an inefficient one. Section 7 concludes the paper.

2 Folding is replacing constructors by functions

Just as in imperative languages where it is preferable to use structured iteration constructs such as **while**-loops and **for**-loops instead of unstructured gotos, it is advantageous to use structured recursion operators instead of unrestricted recursion when using a functional language. Programs that are similar in content and behaviour should be expressed in similar form [SJW79]. Structured programs are easier to reason about and more amenable to (possibly automatic) optimisations than their unstructured counterparts.

Consider the following functions from the Gofer prelude. Each of them is defined by explicit recursion over lists. We will show that they all follow the same recursive pattern. Thus, they can be written in such a way that this similarity can readily be recognised and exploited.

Function head returns the first element of a nonempty list, so head [3, 2, 4] = 3.

```
head        :: [a] -> a
head (a:_)  = a
```

Function filter takes a predicate p and a list as, and returns those elements of list as that satisfy p. For example, filter even [2,3,4] = [2,4].

```
filter             :: (a -> Bool) -> ([a] -> [a])
filter p []        = []
filter p (a:as)    = let as' = filter p as
                     in if p a then a:as' else as'
```

Function take takes an integer n and a list as, and returns the list consisting of the first (at most) n elements of list as, for example take 2 [4,2,6,7] = [4,2].

```
take            :: Int -> [a] -> [a]
take 0     _    = []
take _     []   = []
take (n+1) (a:as) = a:take n as
```

Given a binary function f, an accumulator b, and a list as, for example as = [4,1,5], the expression foldl f b as denotes the value ((b 'f' 4) 'f' 1) 'f' 5. (Note: in Gofer one can write a function f :: a -> b -> c in between its arguments by using quotes.)

```
foldl            :: (b -> a -> b) -> b -> ([a] -> b)
foldl f b []     = b
foldl f b (a:as) = foldl f (b 'f' a) as
```

Function foldr takes a binary function f, a value b, and a list as and returns the value obtained by replacing in list as the nil constructor [] by the value b, and the constructor (:) by the operator f. For example, foldr f b [3,2,6] = 3 'f' (2 'f' (6 'f' b)).

```
foldr            :: (a -> b -> b) -> b -> ([a] -> b)
foldr f b []     = b
foldr f b (a:as) = a 'f' (foldr f b as)
```

Each of these examples is defined by induction over lists and follows the recursive pattern of foldr. The only difference is in the value b that is returned for the empty list, and the function f that is used to combine the head of the list with the result of the recursive call of the function on the tail of the list. For example for head we have that head [] = error "head []" and head (a:as) = a 'f' (head as) where f = \ a _ -> a. As a result we conclude that we can write function head using function foldr.

$$\text{head} = \text{foldr} (\backslash a \_ \to a) (\text{error "head []"})$$

For function filter p we have that filter p [] = [] for the empty list and filter p (a:as) = a 'f' (filter p as) for a nonempty list a:as, where function f is defined by f = \ a as' -> if p a then a:as' else as', hence

$$\text{filter } p = \text{foldr} (\backslash a \text{ as'} \to \text{if } p \text{ a then } a:as' \text{ else as'}) []$$

Expressing the other two example functions, take and foldl, in terms of foldr is slightly more involved.

Consider the function take n :: [a] -> a. In contrast to function filter, the first parameter of take is not fixed, i.e., take (n+1) (a:as) is defined in terms of take n as. This makes it impossible to define take n in terms of foldr directly. The trick then is to swap the two arguments of function take:

```
take'            :: [a] -> Int -> [a]
take' []         = \ _ -> []
take' (a:as)     = \ n -> case n of 0 -> []; n+1 -> a : take' as n
```

Now we see that we can express take in terms of foldr as follows

```
take n as
  = foldr (\ a h -> \ n -> case n of 0 -> []; n+1 -> a : h n)
          (\ _ -> []) as n
```

To express foldl in terms of foldr we use the same method. Swap the last two arguments of foldl:

```
foldl'           :: (b -> a -> b) -> [a] -> b -> b
foldl' f []      = \ b -> b
foldl' f (a:as)  = \ b -> foldl' f as (b 'f' a)
```

and conclude that we can express foldl in terms of foldr as follows:

```
foldl f b as  =  foldr (\ a h -> \ b -> h (b 'f' a)) (\ b -> b) as b
```

The advice for defining a function h :: [a] -> b using foldr (\ a b -> a 'f' b) b is to think inductively in the following way: "suppose I have obtained the value b :: b by recursively applying function h to the tail of a list a:as. How do I combine this via a function f :: a -> b -> b with the head a of the list to obtain the result of computing h (a:as)?". Finding an appropriate operation f is often suggested by typing considerations; given values a :: a and b :: b there often is only one obvious choice to construct a result a 'f' b :: b. Remember also that the result of recursively applying h might be a function. In that case the sought operation f has type a -> (c -> d) -> (c -> d) and constructs a function given a value and a function. After all, functional programming is programming with functions.

Exercise The list selection operation as !! n selects the n-th element of the list as, for example, [1,9,9,5] !! 3 = 5. Using explicit recursion it reads:

```
(!!)             :: [a] -> Int -> a
(a:_ )!!0        = a
(_:as)!!(n+1)    = as!!n
```

Give an equivalent definition of (!!) using foldr. (*end of exercise*)

2.1 Using foldr allows programs to be optimised

The functional foldr satisfies three fundamental laws. The first law seems rather obvious. It states that folding a list with the constructors functions [] and (:) is the identity on lists.

```
    foldr (:) []
=      (Id)
    id
```

The identity law for lists can be proved by induction over lists. The second law for function foldr is known as the *Fusion law*. The fusion law gives conditions under which intermediate values *produced* by folding can be eliminated.

```
    h . foldr f b = foldr g (h b)
⇐      (Fusion)
    h (a 'f' b) = a 'g' (h b)
```

Fusion is the free theorem [Wad89] of the functional foldr. It can also be proved using induction over lists. If we allow partial or infinite lists we get the extra requirement that h be strict. In this paper we will mostly consider finite lists.

As a simple application of fusion we prove that multiplication distributes over summing the elements of a list:

$$(n*) . \text{foldr } (+) \ 0 \ = \ \text{foldr } ((+) . (n*)) \ 0 \tag{1}$$

This example is somewhat perverse as the expression on the left needs fewer multiplications than the expression on the right; sometimes it is useful to *introduce* intermediate values instead of removing them.

To prove equality (1) we calculate as follows:

```
    (n*) . foldr (+) 0 = foldr ((+) . (n*)) 0
⇐      (Fusion)
    n*(a + m) = n*a + n*m ∧ n*0 = 0
≡      arithmetic
    True
```

The condition n*0 = 0 is obtained by matching the folds in the example with the folds in (Fusion).

The third law is known as the *Acid Rain Theorem* [TM95], or foldr/build-rule [GLPJ93]. The acid rain theorem gives conditions under we can eliminate an intermediate value *consumed* by folding. Thus we get 'deforestation for free', which explains the name of the theorem.

```
    foldr f b . g (:) [] = g f b
⇐      (Acid Rain)
    g :: (A -> b -> b) -> b -> (C -> b)
    for some fixed types A and C
```

Acid rain follows from the free theorem of the list producing function g. It formalises the intuition that first building an intermediate list using g (:) [] and then replacing each constructor (:) by a function f and each constructor [] by a value b, yields the same effect as building the resulting value using function f and value b directly. The polymorphic type of function g enforces that the constructors (:) and [] are actually used in building a list using g (:) []. Acid rain is related to *deforestation* [Wad88] and *virtual data structures* [SdM93].

As a simple application of acid rain we prove that mapping a function over a list does not change the length of that list.

$$\text{length . map h = length} \qquad (2)$$

The functions map h and length can both be defined in terms of foldr as follows:

```
map    :: (a -> b) -> ([a] -> [b])
map h  =  foldr ((:) . h) []

length :: [a] -> Int
length =  foldr (\ _ n -> n+1) 0
```

To prove equality (2) we observe that map h = g h (:) [] where g h f b = foldr (f . h) b and g h :: (a -> b -> b) -> b -> ([c] -> b) whenever h :: c -> a. The actual proof is now a routine calculation:

```
  length . map h
=     definition of length, observation
  foldr (\ _ n -> n+1) 0 . g h (:) []
=     observation, (Acid Rain)
  g h (\ _ n -> n+1) 0
=     definition of g and length
  length
```

Equality (2) can also be proved with the fusion law.

2.2 Constructive algorithmics is calculating with programs

Fusion and Acid Rain are useful in calculating programs from their specification. Engineers often solve problems by applying differential and integral calculus. Similarly, in 'Constructive Algorithmics' computer programs are constructed by means of a program calculus. The central idea is to calculate *with* programs. Specifications and programs are considered to be formal objects in the same theoretical framework and subject to the same calculation rules. The issue of program correctness is reduced to the correct application of simple laws in a calculation:

```
    specification
  =    law
      . . .
  =    law
    implementation
```

Most of the usual approaches to program correctness consist of a method to reason *about* programs. Thus one needs two languages: a programming language, and a language in which one can reason about programs. Program calculation requires just one language.

In order to apply calculation rules they should be easy to remember and easy to manipulate with. This is the reason why surface aspects (emphasis on suitable *notation*) play an important rôle in the field of constructive algorithmics. A rich set of laws is indispensable for effectively calculating with progams. This is where foundational aspects (emphasis on suitable *theory*) come into play.

3 Folding can be generalised to other types

Folding is not unique to lists. Other datatypes can be folded too by replacing their constructor functions by functions of the appropriate type.

3.1 Snoc-lists

The name `foldr` means 'folding from the right' and reflects the fact that `foldr` processes the elements of its argument list from right-to-left. The name `foldl` means 'folding from the left' and reflects the fact that `foldl` processes the elements of its argument list from left-to-right. This is often convenient because the result of processing the first $i-1$ elements of the list is available when processing the i-th element. As we have seen, the function `foldl` is not the natural fold operator over lists; rather it corresponds to a function that folds so called *snoc-lists*. Snoc-lists are lists that are built from left-to-right.

```
data Snoc a  =  II | (Snoc a) :%: a
```

To fold a snoc-list we recursively replace the constant constructor II :: Snoc a by a constant nil :: b and the constructor function (:%:) :: Snoc a -> a -> Snoc a by a function snoc :: b -> a -> b. We pack the functions snoc and nil that replace the constructor functions into a tuple to stress that they belong together.

```
foldS :: (b, b -> a -> b) -> (Snoc a -> b)
foldS (nil,snoc)
  = fS
```

```
where
    fS II         = nil
    fS (as :%: a) = (fS as) 'snoc' a
```

Just like the fold operator on cons-lists it is the case that folding using the constructor functions is the identity on snoc-lists.

$$\text{foldS (II,(:\%:))} = \text{id}$$

Function foldS also satisfies a fusion law and an acid rain theorem. Again these follow from "theorems for free!". The fusion law for snoc-lists is given by

```
h . foldS (b,f)  =  foldS (h b,g)
⇐    (Fusion)
h (b 'f' a)  =  (h b) 'g' a
```

while the acid rain theorem is given by

```
foldS (b,f) . g (II,(:%:))  =  g (b,f)
⇐    (Acid Rain)
g :: (b, b -> A -> b) -> (C -> b) for fixed types A and C
```

Exercise Define (using foldr) a coercion function c2s :: [a] -> Snoc a that transforms ordinary lists into snoc-lists. Then show (using fusion or acid rain for snoc-lists) that foldS (b,f) . c2s = foldl f b. (*end of exercise*)

The moral of the above exercise is that we may consider the standard notation for lists [a,...,z] to be an abbreviation for (...(II:%:a):%:...):%:z when processing a list from left-to-right using foldl, while at the same time we may consider it to be an abbreviation for a:(...:(z:[])...) when processing a list from right-to-left using foldr.

There remains a nasty problem with this approach of treating cons-lists as if they were snoc-lists, namely when we want to return a cons-list as the result of folding a list from the left. Simulating snoccing a value a at the right end of a list as by concatenation as ++ [a] leads to a quadratic time complexity. This can be circumvented by returning a real snoc-list and later coercing the intermediate list into a cons-list via a function s2c :: Snoc a -> [a].

Exercise Define a function s2c :: Snoc a -> [a] and show how in general the intermediate list that arises in a composition s2c . f can be eliminated. (*end of exercise*)

3.2 Peano numerals

There are numerous ways of viewing natural numbers as inductively defined types, even though they are not explicitly defined as such in Gofer. One possible view of the naturals is the *Peano* view; a number is either zero, 0, or the successor n+1 of a number n. Folding a number n with a constant zero and a function succ boils down to the n-fold application of function succ to the constant zero, thus foldN (zero,succ) n = succ (...(succ zero)).

```
foldN :: (a,a -> a) -> (Int -> a)
foldN (zero,succ)
  = fN
    where
        fN 0     = zero
        fN (n+1) = succ (fN n)
```

The fusion law for folding integers foldN is defined as

$$f \ . \ \text{foldN} \ (a,g) \ = \ \text{foldN} \ (f \ a,h)$$
$$\Leftarrow \qquad \text{(Fusion)}$$
$$f \ (g \ a) \ = \ h \ (f \ a)$$

The acid rain theorem for function foldN is defined as

$$\text{foldN} \ (a,f) \ . \ g \ (0,(+1)) \ = \ g \ (a,f)$$
$$\Leftarrow \qquad \text{(Acid Rain)}$$
$$g \ :: \ (a,a \ \text{-> } a) \ \text{-> } (B \ \text{-> } a) \ \text{for some fixed type } B$$

Together with the identity axiom for numbers foldN (0,(+1)) = id, fusion implies induction over numbers. Let p :: Int -> Bool be a predicate over the natural numbers, then

$$\backslash \ n \ \text{-> } (n, \ p \ n)$$
$$= \qquad \text{(Id)}$$
$$(\backslash \ n \ \text{-> } (n, \ p \ n)) \ . \ \text{foldN} \ (0, \ (+1))$$
$$= \qquad \text{(Fusion), assume } p \ (n+1) \ = \ p \ n \ || \ p \ (n+1)$$
$$\text{foldN} \ ((0,p \ 0), \backslash \ (n,b) \ \text{-> } (n+1, \ b \ || \ p \ (n+1)))$$
$$= \qquad \text{(Fusion), assume } p \ 0 \ = \ \text{True}$$
$$(\backslash \ n \ \text{-> } (n,\text{True})) \ . \ \text{foldN} \ (0, \ (+1))$$
$$= \qquad \text{(Id)}$$
$$\backslash \ n \ \text{-> } (n,\text{True})$$

Hence we can conclude that a predicate p is true for all natural numbers if p is true for number 0 and p (n+1) follows from p n.

$$p \ = \ \backslash \ n \ \text{-> True}$$
$$\Leftarrow \qquad \text{(Induction)}$$
$$(p \ (n+1) \ = \ p \ n \ || \ p \ (n+1)) \ \wedge \ (p \ 0 \ = \ \text{True})$$

Many familiar arithmetic functions on natural numbers can be defined by folding. For example, here are definitions for addition and multiplication:

```
(<+>), (<*>) :: Int -> Int -> Int

n <+> m  =  foldN (m,(+1)) n
n <*> m  =  foldN (0,(<+> m)) n
```

Adding a number n to a number m starts with m and then increments this number n times. Multiplying a number m by a number n starts with 0 and then increments this number n times with steps of size m.

The proof that multiplication distributes over addition nicely breaks down into two steps, one that follows from fusion and one that follows from acid rain.

```
    (n <+> m) <*> k
=     (Acid Rain)
    foldN (m <*> k, (<+> k)) n
=     (Fusion)
    (n <*> k) <+> (m <*> k)
```

The second step immediately follows from fusion, using the assumption that addition (<+>) is commutative. The first step is more interesting since it shows that the premise of the acid rain theorem can sometimes be somewhat counter intuitive.

```
    (n <+> m) <*> k
=     rearrange, definition of (<+>)
    (<*> k) (foldN (m, (+1)) n)
=     define: g = \ (a,f) -> foldN (foldN (a,f) m, f) n
    (<*> k) (g (0,(+1)))
=     definition of (<*> k)
    foldN (0,(<+> k)) (g (0,(+1)))
=     (Acid Rain)
    g (0,(<+> k))
=     definition of g
    foldN (foldN (0,(<+> k)) m, (<+> k)) n
=     definition of (<*>)
    foldN (m <*> k, (<+> k)) n
```

Exercise Show that addition (<+>) is associative, and then prove using fusion that foldN (m, (<+> k)) n = n <+> (m <*> k). (*end of exercise*)

Exercise Define the predicate even :: Int -> Bool that tests whether or not a natural number is even by means of function foldN. (*end of exercise*)

Exercise Express exponentiation as a foldN. (*end of exercise*)

Exercise Write function take by folding over the naturals instead of over lists, i.e., use function foldN rather than function foldr. (*end of exercise*)

3.3 Binary trees

All example datatypes we have seen so far have a linear structure. Our first example of a type which exhibits a branching structure is *binary trees*. A binary tree consists of either a leaf that contains a value of type a or a node comprising a left and a right subtree.

```
data Tree a = Leaf a | Node (Tree a) (Tree a)
```

Folding a tree follows the pattern set by folding lists and numbers, namely replace the constructors by functions.

```
foldB :: (a -> b, b -> b -> b) -> (Tree a -> b)
foldB (leaf,node)
 = fB
   where
       fB (Leaf a)      =  leaf a
       fB (Node as as') =  node (fB as) (fB as')
```

Just as with foldr and foldN we can define many functions in terms of folding trees with foldB instead of using explicit recursion.

Exercise Using function foldB, write a function tips :: Tree a -> [a] that returns the list of values that occur in the leaves of a tree. (*end of exercise*)

Exercise Function foldB satisfies a fusion law and an acid rain theorem too. Formulate the fusion law and the acid rain theorem for binary trees. (*end of exercise*)

3.4 Rose trees (Rhododendrons)

Things get a bit more interesting when a datatype is defined using another datatype, such as for example the datatype Rose of multiway branching trees. A node in such a tree has a list of subtrees.

```
data Rose a = Fork a [Rose a]
```

The datatype Rose uses the datatype of lists, [], in its definition. The main idea in the definition of folding rose trees is to use map to apply foldR recursively to the elements in the list of subtrees.

```
foldR :: (a -> [b] -> b) -> (Rose a -> b)
foldR (fork)
 = fR
   where
      fR (Fork a ts)  =  fork a (map fR ts)
```

An example fold over rose trees is function postOrder :: Rose a -> [a] that enumerates the values of a tree in postorder:

```
postOrder  :: Rose a -> [a]
postOrder  =  foldR (\ a ass -> (concat ass) ++ [a])
```

Exercise Define a function depth :: Rose a -> Int that returns the length of the longest path from the root in a rose tree. (*end of exercise*)

3.5 Typed Lambda Expressions

This section defines a fold for a slightly more complicated datatype: typed lambda expressions and types [Set89, page 441].

A simple *type* is either a variable or a function type.

```
data Type  =  TVar String | Type :->: Type
```

A *typed lambda expression* is either a variable, an application, or a typed abstraction which associates a type with the bound variable.

```
data Expr  =  Var String | Expr :@: Expr | (String,Type) ::: Expr
```

Folds on the datatypes Type and Expr are now defined as follows.

```
foldT :: (String -> a,a -> a -> a) -> (Type -> a)
foldT (tvar,arrow)
 = fT
   where
      fT (Tvar s)    =  tvar s
      fT (s :->: t)  =  arrow (fT s) (fT t)

foldE :: (String -> b, b -> b -> b, (String,Type) -> b -> b) ->
         (Expr -> b)
foldE (var,apply,lambda)
 = fE
   where
      fE (Var x)        =  var x
      fE (f :@: a)      =  apply (fE f) (fE a)
      fE ((x,t) ::: b)  =  lambda (x,t) (fE b)
```

3.6 Mutual recursive datatypes

Folds can be defined for mutually recursive datatypes too. An example pair of mutually recursive datatypes is the pair of types Zig and Zag. These types can be used to implement lists in which the type of the elements alternate. We will see an alternative way to implement this kind of lists in the next subsection.

```
data Zig a b  =  Nil | Cins a (Zag b a)
data Zag a b  =  Nal | Cans a (Zig b a)
```

The folds on the datatypes Zig and Zag are mutually recursive too. The folds for Zig and Zag take as arguments two pairs: one corresponding to the Zig type, and one corresponding to the Zag type.

```
foldZig :: (c,a -> d -> c) -> (d,b -> c -> d) -> (Zig a b -> c)
foldZig (nil,cins) (nal,cans)
 = fZig
   where
      fZig Nil         =  nil
      fZig (Cins a z)  =  cins a (fZag z)

      fZag  =  foldZag (nil,cins) (nal,cans)

foldZag :: (c,a -> d -> c) -> (d,b -> c -> d) -> (Zag b a -> d)
foldZag (nil,cins) (nal,cans)
 = fZag
   where
      fZag Nal         =  nal
      fZag (Cans a z)  =  cans a (fZig z)

      fZig  =  foldZig (nil,cins) (nal,cans)
```

3.7 Other types

Even for datatypes containing function spaces, such as the datatype D defined below, it is possible to define folds, [Fre90, Pat94, MH95].

```
data D  =  Func (D -> D)
```

It is however unknown how to construct folds for *non regular* datatypes, datatypes in which the recursive uses of the datatype at the right-hand side of the definition have arguments differing from the left-hand side. An example of such a datatype is the type of ropes:

```
data Rope a b  =  Nil | Twist a (Rope b a)
```

A working, but not very elegant, approach would be to define a fold for each form of recursive use. This corresponds to replacing the type Rope a b by the types Zig a b and Zag a b. But this approach does not always apply. Consider for example the datatype ListTree.

```
data ListTree a  =  Leaf a | Branch (ListTree [a]) (ListTree [a])
```

4   Monads separate values and computations

So much for programming using folds. We now turn our attention to structuring programs in a complementary way, namely after the *computation* of their result value.

4.1   Exceptions

Suppose we are required to write a function that computes the resistance of a list of resistors put in parallel [PBM82, page 52].

```
resistance  :: [Float] -> Float
resistance  =  (1 /) . foldr (\ r r' -> 1/r + r') 0
```

If function resistance is applied to the empty list, or if any of the resistors in the list is zero, execution of the whole program in which resistance is called is aborted and a program error is reported by the Gofer interpreter: Program error: {primDivInt 13 0}. This behaviour will certainly not be appreciated by the users of the program. Since it is our mission to spread the use of functional programming something must be done about this.

A more graceful approach is to let resistance signal an exception when a division by zero occurs. This is similar to what the Gofer interpreter does itself; we don't get a core dump when evaluating the Gofer expression 13/0.

To record exceptions in computing a value of type a we use the type Maybe.

```
data Maybe a  =  No | Yes a
```

The type of the function resistance is enhanced to resistance :: [Float] -> Maybe Float. This makes explicit that the computation may either fail and return an exception No or succeed and return a proper value Yes r. Since the type of function resistance has changed, its definition should be changed as well. At each recursive application of resistance, the form of the result is now checked by a case distinction on Maybe Float. Moreover an exception is raised if a division by zero occurs.

```
resistance :: [Float] -> Maybe Float
resistance
 = (\ mr -> case mr of
               No    -> No
               Yes r -> if r == 0 then No else Yes (1/r)
   )
   .foldr (\ r mr' -> case mr' of
                         No    -> No
                         Yes r' -> if r == 0
                                   then No
                                   else Yes (1/r + r')
          )
          (Yes 0)
```

There are four patterns that occur a number of times: raising an exception by return-ing No, returning a proper value by injecting it into type Maybe using the constructor function Yes (three times), dispatching on the two alternatives of type Maybe (twice), and a test on the second operand of division (twice). We name these recurring pat-terns zeroM, resultM, bindM and divM respectively.

```
zeroM  :: Maybe a
zeroM  = No

resultM    :: a -> Maybe a
resultM a  = Yes a

bindM          :: Maybe a -> (a -> Maybe b) -> Maybe b
ma 'bindM' f   = case ma of No -> No; Yes a -> f a

divM         :: Float -> Float -> Maybe Float
r 'divM' r'  = if r' == 0 then zeroM else resultM (r/r')
```

Using these functions, exception handling becomes well structured: clumsy case-distinctions are expressed once and for all and need not be repeated throughout the program text at each application of an exceptional function.

```
resistance :: [Float] -> Maybe Float
resistance rs
 = foldr (\ r mr' -> mr'                    'bindM' \ r'  ->
                     1 'divM' r             'bindM' \ r'' ->
                     resultM (r'' + r')
         )
         (resultM 0)
         rs 'bindM' \ r -> 1 'divM' r
```

4.2 Substituting leaves of a tree

An *association list* is a list of key/value-pairs. The value bound to a key is found using function lookup. In case a key has no associated value function lookup raises an exception.

```
data Assoc a b  =  a := b

lookup              :: Eq a => a -> [Assoc a b] -> Maybe b
a 'lookup' table  =  case [ b | a' := b <- table, a' == a] of
                         []      -> zeroM
                         (a:_) -> resultM a
```

Consider now the following problem. Given a binary tree and an association list, replace the values in the tree by their associated values. Since we have to traverse the tree recursively to substitute the leaves it is natural to define the substitution function by folding with foldB. Since the substitution might fail due to the fact that some of the leaves have no associated value in the table it is natural to make use of the operations resultM and bindM on exceptions (you may try yourself to write function subst using explicit recursion and without the exception handling operators).

```
subst :: Tree a -> ([Assoc a b] -> Maybe (Tree b))
subst
 = foldB (\ a
             -> \ table -> a 'lookup' table      'bindM' \ b ->
                           resultM (Leaf b)
         ,\ mbs mbs'
             -> \ table -> mbs table             'bindM' \ bs  ->
                           mbs' table            'bindM' \ bs' ->
                           resultM (Node bs bs')
         )
```

But here is yet another recurring pattern that can be abstracted away: the table is passed down the recursive calls of function subst explicitly. Our next goal is therefore to hide the plumbing of the table table through the function subst. For this purpose we define two new operations resultR and bindR that extend the previous operations resultM and bindM by passing along an extra argument. For completeness we also lift function zeroM to accept an argument. To enhance readability we abbreviate r -> Maybe a as ReaderM r a.

```
type ReaderM r a  =  r -> Maybe a

resultR    :: a -> ReaderM r a
resultR a  =  \ _ -> resultM a
```

```
bindR          :: ReaderM r a -> (a -> ReaderM r b) -> ReaderM r b
ma 'bindR' f  = \ r -> ma r 'bindM' \ a -> f a r

zeroR  :: ReaderM r a
zeroR  = \ _ -> zeroM
```

Rewriting function subst using the above operations gives us nearly the conciseness
we are after.

```
subst :: Tree a -> ReaderM [Assoc a b] (Tree b)
subst
= foldB (\ a          -> lookup a              'bindR' \ b ->
                         resultR (Leaf b)
         ,\ mbs mbs' -> mbs                    'bindR' \ bs  ->
                        mbs'                    'bindR' \ bs' ->
                        resultR (Node bs bs')
        )
```

In section 5.1 we return to this example in order to transform it into an even more
compact form. Right now we continue looking for some more monads.

Exercise Define a version of function subst such that the table is not passed down
the tree as an explicit argument [WM91]. Hint: de-lambda-lift function subst. Explain why this trick does not work for the type checking example in the next section.
(*end of exercise*)

4.3 Type checking

A typed lambda expression is *type correct* if the types specified for the bound variables of the expression agree with the types demanded by the ways in which the
bound variables are used. Function flip (|-) :: Expr -> ReaderM [Assoc Var
Type] Type attempts to synthesise the type of an expression given a *basis* that
associates variables with their declared types.

When checking an abstraction, the basis is extended to record the type associated
with the bound variable of the abstraction. For this purpose we introduce the functions fetchR and restoreR that respectively return the basis as the result and
resume a computation using a new basis.

```
fetchR  :: ReaderM r r
fetchR  = \ r -> resultM r

restoreR      :: r -> ReaderM r a -> ReaderM r a
restoreR r ma = \ _ -> ma r
```

To check the type of a variable we look up its type in the basis. To typecheck an
abstraction (x,s) ::: b, we typecheck the body b assuming that variable x has

type s. If the resulting type is t, then the whole abstraction has type s :->: t. To typecheck an application f :@: a we ensure that the type of f is a function type s :->: t and that the type s' of a is the same as the argument type s expected by f. The result of applying f to a then has type t.

```
env |- expr
= foldE (\ x        -> lookup x
        ,\ f a      -> f                          'bindR' \ s ->
                       case s of
                         (s :->: t) -> a          'bindR' \ s' ->
                                       if s == s'
                                       then resultR t
                                       else zeroR
                         _          -> zeroR
        ,\ (x,s) b -> fetchR                      'bindR' \ env ->
                       restoreR (x := s : env) b 'bindR' \ t    ->
                       resultR (s :->: t)
        ) expr env
```

4.4 Chopping trees, marking vertices

A directed graph with vertices of type a can be represented by a value of type Rose a. For example, a small graph with nine vertices labelled with strings is given below: (note that this is a situation where lists are cyclic).

```
root = Fork "root" [a,b,c,d,e,f,g,h,i,j]
       where
           a = Fork "a" [g,j];   b = Fork "b" [a,i]
           c = Fork "c" [e,h];   d = Fork "d" []
           e = Fork "e" [d,h,j]; f = Fork "f" [i]
           g = Fork "g" [f,b];   h = Fork "h" []
           i = Fork "i" [];      j = Fork "j" []
```

The task of function dff ('depth first forest') is to eliminate all edges to vertices that have been visited earlier during a depth-first search of the graph, leaving a spanning forest of the original graph. For the above graph function dff would return the graph:

```
root = Fork "root" [a,c]
       where
           a = Fork "a" [g,j]; b = Fork "b" []
           c = Fork "c" [e];   d = Fork "d" []
           e = Fork "e" [d,h]; f = Fork "f" [i]
           g = Fork "g" [f,b]; h = Fork "h" []
           i = Fork "i" [];    j = Fork "j" []
```

Function dff is defined using an auxiliary function chop. While traversing the graph function chop maintains a list of vertices that have already been visited. To ensure that the updated list of visited nodes is threaded through the computation, function chop returns the augmented list of visited nodes as part of the answer. Since subtrees might not appear in the depth first forest, function chop returns an exceptional tree as the other half of its answer. So function chop has type Rose a -> ReaderM [a] (Maybe (Rose a),[a]). Function dff :: Rose a -> Rose a calls chop with an empty list of visited vertices and throws away the final list of all reachable vertices returned by function chop.

```
dff g  =  g' where Yes (Yes g',_) = chop g []
```

We don't even attempt to first write function chop using ReaderM-operations. Instead, we abbreviate type ReaderM s (a,s) as StateM s a and lift the operations resultR, bindR, and zeroR in advance to work on type StateM s a. To manipulate the list of visited vertices we provide the operations peekS and pokeS.

```
resultS    :: a -> StateM s a
resultS a  =  fetchR 'bind' \ s -> resultR (a,s)

bindS          :: StateM s a -> (a -> StateM s b) -> StateM s b
ma 'bindS' f  =  ma 'bindR' \ (a,s) ->  restoreR s (f a)

zeroS  :: StateM s a
zeroS  =  zeroR

peekS    :: (s -> a) -> StateM s a
peekS f  =  fetchR 'bindR' \ s -> resultR (f s,s)

pokeS    :: (s -> s) -> StateM s ()
pokeS f  =  fetchR 'bindR' \s -> resultR ((),f s)
```

To chop a node, we first check whether this node has been visited before. If so, the node is pruned. If not, we mark the node as visited, recursively chop the subtrees of the node and return a node that keeps only non-pruned subtrees as children.

```
chop :: Rose a -> StateM [a] (Rose a)
chop
= foldR (\ a mts
          -> peekS (a 'elem')                    'bindS' \ v ->
             if v then
               resultS No
             else
               pokeS (a:)                         'bindS' \ _ ->
               accumulateS mts                    'bindS' \ ts ->
               resultS (Yes (Fork a [t | Yes t <- ts]))
       )
```

Function accumulateS :: [StateM s a] -> StateM s [a] collects the results of chopping a list of subtrees from left-to-right into a result list.

```
accumulateS :: [StateM s a] -> StateM s [a]
accumulateS = foldr (\ mt mts -> mt            'bindS' \ t ->
                                 mts           'bindS' \ ts ->
                                 resultS (t:ts)
                     )
                     (resultS [])
```

An example use of function dff is *topological sorting*, which is treated in more depth in Launchbury's notes [Lau95].

```
topSort :: Rose a -> [a]
topSort = reverse . postOrder . dff
```

For example topSort root = ["root", "c", "e", "h", "d", "a", "j", "g", "b", "f", "i"].

Exercise Derive using acid rain (or fusion) a version of function topSort that does not create intermediate values. It is easiest to start with reverse . postOrd. (*end of exercise*)

4.5 Monads generalise bind and result

Let m be a type constructor (such as Maybe). A function of type f :: a -> b can be generalised to a *monadic* function f :: a -> m b that accepts an argument of type a and returns a result of type b with a possible side-effect (such as raising an exception) captured by type constructor m.

To effectively use monadic functions we need an operation bind to apply a function f of type f :: a -> m b to an argument ma of type m a and a function result :: a -> m a to construct a result of type m a. The expression ma 'bind' \ a -> f a reads as "evaluate ma, name the result a, and then evaluate f a". A type constructor m that comes equipped with these two operations is called a *monad*. The requirement on type constructor m can be captured by a constructor class as follows:

```
class  Monad m  where
   result  ::  a -> m a
   bind    ::  m a -> (a -> m b) -> m b
```

The components of a monad should satisfy a number of laws. The left-unit law and right-unit law say how to remove occurrences of function result from an expression.

$$\text{result a 'bind' k} = \text{k a}$$
$$\text{k 'bind' result} = \text{k}$$

Furthermore, bind has to be associative. For each instance of the class Monad we have to verify these laws, but as usual we omit the proofs.

4.6 Exceptions

Datatype `Maybe` is an instance of class `Monad` as witnessed by the following instance declaration.

```
instance  Monad Maybe  where
   result a     =  Yes a
   ma 'bind' f  =  case ma of No -> No; Yes a -> f a
```

As an aside we note that `bindM` can be defined by folding over the type `Maybe`. In fact, for many monads `m` the `bind` operation can be defined as a generalised fold over `m a` in a canonical way.

Exercise Define folding over type `Maybe` and then write `bindM` in terms of `foldM`. (*end of exercise*)

Exceptions are an example of a monad with a zero; a value `zero :: Monad m => m a` such that `zero 'bind' f = zero`.

```
class  Monad m => Monad0 m  where
   zero  ::  m a
```

```
instance  Monad0 Maybe  where
   zero = No
```

Exceptions are also an example of a monad with a plus; a binary operator `(++)` `:: Monad0 m => m a -> m a -> m a` such that the laws `zero ++ ma = ma` and `ma ++ zero = ma` hold.

```
class  Monad0 m => MonadPlus m  where
   (++)  ::  m a -> m a -> m a
```

```
instance  MonadPlus Maybe  where
   ma ++ ma'  =  case ma of No -> ma'; _ -> ma
```

The value `zero` is used to throw an exception that can be caught using `(++)`.

4.7 Readers

The monad of *state readers* passes an extra argument on top of a base monad. We repeat the type of `Reader`.

```
type Reader m r a  =  r -> m a
```

```
instance  Monad m => Monad (Reader m r)  where
```

```
    result a    =  \ _ -> result a
    ma 'bind' f =  \ r -> ma r 'bind' \a -> f a r

  instance  Monad0 m => Monad0 (Reader r m)  where
    zero =  \ _ -> zero

  instance  MonadPlus m => MonadPlus (Reader m r)  where
    ma ++ ma'  =  \ r -> ma r ++ ma' r
```

The reader monad provides two extra operations to fetch and replace the argument passed under water, respectively.

```
  fetch  :: Monad m => Reader m r r
  fetch  =  \ r -> result r

  restore    :: Monad m => r -> Reader m r a -> Reader m r a
  restore r  =  \ ma -> \ _ -> ma r
```

4.8   State transformers

The monad of *state transformers* can be considered as an extra layer on top of the reader monad to thread around global state.

```
  type State m s a  =  Reader m s (a,s)

  instance  Monad (Reader m s) => Monad (State m s)  where
    result a    =  fetch 'bind' \ s -> result (a,s)
    ma 'bind' f =  ma 'bind' \ (a,s) -> restore s (f a)

  instance  Monad0 (Reader m s) => Monad0 (State m s)  where
    zero =  zero

  instance  MonadPlus (Reader m s) => MonadPlus (State m s)  where
    (++)  =  (++)
```

Two additional operations on the state monad are peek and poke. These operations are used to inspect and modify the state.

```
  peek   :: Monad (Reader m s) => (s -> a) -> State m s a
  peek f =  fetch 'bind' \ s -> result (f s,s)

  poke   :: Monad (Reader m s) => (s -> s) -> State m s ()
  poke f =  fetch 'bind' \ s -> result ((),f s)
```

Exercise Simplify the operations bind and result of the state transformer monad as much as possible. In most texts on monads, state transformers are defined using these simplified operations. (*end of exercise*)

Exercise The identity monad is based on the type constructor **type Id a = a**. Give the instance declaration **Monad Id** for the identity monad. (*end of exercise*)

4.9 Do-notation

One advantage of being able to overload the monad operations **result** and **bind** (and **zero**) is that we can use special syntactic sugar for monadic programs. The do-notation as originally proposed by Launchbury [Lau93] and implemented in Gofer [Jon93] provides the following additional form of expressions:

$$
\begin{aligned}
expr &::= \text{do}\{qualifier; \ldots; qualifier; expr\} \\
qualifier &::= pat \text{ <- } expr \\
&\quad | \quad expr \\
&\quad | \quad \text{if } expr
\end{aligned}
$$

The do-notation can be removed by repeatedly applying the following rules where e ranges over expressions, p over patterns, and qse over sequences of qualifiers ending in an expression.

$$
\begin{aligned}
\text{do}\{e\} &= e \\
\text{do}\{p \text{ <- } e; \; qse\} &= e \text{ `bind` } f \text{ where } f \; p = \text{do}\{qse\}; \; f \; \_ = \text{zero} \\
\text{do}\{e; \; qse\} &= e \text{ `bind` } \backslash \_ \text{ -> do}\{qse\} \\
\text{do}\{\text{if } e; \; qse\} &= \text{if } e \text{ then do}\{qse\} \text{ else zero}
\end{aligned}
$$

Rewritten using the do notation, the typechecker starts to look comprehensive at last.

```
env |- expr
= foldE (\ x         -> lookup x
        ,\ f a       -> do{ (s :->: t) <- f
                          ; s' <- a
                          ; if s == s'
                          ; result t
                          }
        ,\ (x,s) b -> do{ env <- fetch
                          ; t <- restore (x := s : env) b
                          ; result (s :->: t)
                          }
        ) expr env
```

Exercise Formulate the three monad laws in terms of the do-notation. (*end of exercise*)

5 Monadic folds

In the previous sections we have discussed folds and monads and we have shown how to write programs of type Monad m => [a] -> m b (or any other recursive type instead of lists [a]) that use both concepts at once. If such functions process the results of their recursive calls in a fixed way we can make yet another abstraction step. Let's look at two example functions to see how this works.

The function mapr maps a monadic function over a list starting from the right. In contrast to the normal map, the order in which the applications are carried out does matter when computing in a monad.

```
mapr :: Monad m => (a -> m b) -> ([a] -> m [b])
mapr f
= foldr (\a mbs -> do{bs <- mbs; b <- f a; result (b:bs)})
        (result [])
```

Recall the function resistance defined in Section 4.1. Written using the do notation this function reads as follows.

```
resistance :: [Float] -> Maybe Float
resistance rs
= do{ s <- foldr (\ r mr' -> do{ r' <- mr'
                               ; r'' <- 1 'divM' r
                               ; result (r'' + r')
                               }
                 )
                 (result 0)
                 rs
   ; 1 'divM' s
   }
```

The correspondence between functions mapr and resistance is that both the operations used for folding the construction function (:) first bind the value of their recursive call. They are of the form:

```
\ a mb -> do{b <- mb; mcons a b}
```

To capture this specific pattern of folding lists within a monad we define a *monadic fold* on lists:

```
mfoldr :: Monad m => (a -> b -> m b) -> m b -> ([a] -> m b)
mfoldr mcons mnil
= foldr (\ a mb -> do{b <- mb; mcons a b}) mnil
```

Programs become more structured and modular by identifying monadic folds as a distinguished pattern of recursion. Moreover we can specialise the basic fold laws for monadic folds so that the number of mechanical steps in proofs is reduced.

The identity law for monadic folds states that monadically folding a list with monadic constructors is equivalent to injecting the list into the monad directly.

```
    mfoldr (\ a as -> result (a:as)) (result []) as
=     (Id)
    result as
```

The monadic fusion law states that the monadic composition of a function that distributes monadically over the function that replaces constructor function cons with a monadic fold, is again a monadic fold.

```
    do{b <- mfoldr f mb as; h b}  =  mfoldr g (do{b <- mb; h b}) as
⇐     (Fusion)
    do{c <- mc; b <- f a c; h b}  =  do{c <- mc; b <- h c; g a b}
```

The monadic acid rain theorem states that it is not necessary to first build a list within a monad and then fold that list, provided the function that builds the list is polymorphic enough.

```
    do{as <- g (\ a as -> result (a:as)) (result []) c
      ; mfoldr f n as
      } = g f n c
=     (Acid Rain)
    g :: Monad m => (A -> b -> m b) -> m b -> C -> m b
    for some fixed types A and C.
```

From a categorical point of view, monadic folds naturally arise from an adjunction between the category of algebras and homomorphisms and another category of algebras and homomorphisms built upon the Kleisli category [Fok94]. This is the approach taken in the language ADL [KL95] too. A disadvantage of monadic folds is that they are in some sense too specific and hence not all functions of type [a] -> m b can be written as a monadic fold.

An example of a function that cannot (easily) be written using a monadic fold is function map1. The function map1 maps a monadic function over a list starting from the left.

```
    map1 :: Monad m => (a -> m b) -> ([a] -> m [b])
    map1 f
      = foldr (\ a mbs -> do{b <- f a; bs <- mbs; result (b:bs)})
              (result [])
```

The problem with function map1 f is that it does not bind the result of its recursive call on the tail of its argument list before using the head of the list. When we view the argument list of mapl as a snoc-list and rewrite function mapl as a fold left, binding the result of the recursive call happens first.

```
mapl :: Monad m => (a -> m b) -> ([a] -> m [b])
mapl f
  = foldl (\ mbs a -> do{bs <- mbs; b <- f a; result (bs ++ [b])})
        (result [])
```

This specific pattern of folding lists within a monad is captured by the *monadic fold left* on lists:

```
mfoldl :: Monad m => (b -> a -> m b) -> m b -> ([a] -> m b)
mfoldl msnoc mnil
  = foldl (\ mb a -> do{b <- mb; msnoc b a}) mnil
```

Now we can define function mapl as a monadic fold: mapl f = mfoldl (\ bs a -> do{b <- f a; result (bs ++ [b])}) (result []).

Exercise Formulate the fusion law and acid rain theorem for function mfoldl. (*end of exercise*)

In the rest of this section we give some more examples of monadic folds on lists. The function accumulate collects the results of executing a list of computations from left-to-right.

```
accumulate :: Monad m => [m a] -> m [a]
accumulate = foldr (\ ma mas -> do{ a <- ma
                                  ; as <- mas
                                  ; result (a:as)
                                  }
                   )
                   (result [])
```

Using function mfoldl, function accumulate is defined as follows.

```
accumulate :: Monad m => [m a] -> m [a]
accumulate = mfoldl (\ as ma -> do{a <- ma; result (as ++ [a])})
                    (result [])
```

The function ignore evaluates its argument only for its side-effect and throws away the result

```
ignore :: Monad m => m a -> m ()
ignore ma = do{ma ; result ()}
```

The function sequence is used to execute a list of computations from left-to-right only for their side effects.

```
sequence  :: Monad m => [m a] -> m ()
sequence  =  ignore . accumulate
```

Exercise Using fusion and the monad laws calculate and efficient version of function sequence that does not built an intermediate list. (*end of exercise*)

5.1 Substituting leaves revisited

Just as function `mfoldr` on lists, function `mfoldB` captures passing on the monad through the recursive parts of the type.

```
mfoldB :: Monad m => (a -> m b, b -> b -> m b) -> (Tree a -> m b)
mfoldB (mleaf, mnode)
 = foldTree (\ a       -> mleaf a
            ,\ mb mb' -> do{b <- mb; b' <- mb'; mnode b b'}
            )
```

Note that evaluating the recursive calls to function `mfoldB` in the opposite order results in a different function.

Using the monadic fold over trees `mfoldB`, function `subst` can be written as:

```
subst  =  mfoldB (\ a      -> do{b <- lookup a; result (Leaf b)}
                 ,\ bs bs' -> result (Node bs bs')
                 )
```

Compare this definition with the definition of the same function in Section 4.2.

5.2 Renaming Lambda Expressions

Here are the monadic folds over expressions and types.

```
mfoldT :: Monad m => (String -> m a,a -> a -> m a) -> Type -> m a
mfoldT (mtvar,marrow)  =  foldT (mtvar
                                ,\ ms mt -> do{ s <- ms
                                              ; t <- mt
                                              ; s 'marrow' t
                                              }
                                )

mfoldE :: Monad m =>
         (String -> m a
         ,a -> a -> m a
         ,(String,Type) -> a -> m a
```

```
          ) -> (Expr -> m a)
mfoldE (mvar, mapply, mlambda)
= foldE (\ x          -> mvar x
        ,\ mf ma      -> do{f <- mf; a <- ma; mapply f a}
        ,\ (x,t) ma   -> do{a <- ma; mlambda (x,t) a}
        )
```

The typechecker (|-) is a good example of a function that cannot be expressed (simply) as a monadic fold. The problem is that the body of an abstraction can only be checked *after* the basis is extended with an additional type assumption. An example that does conform to the recursion pattern of function mfoldE is Wadler's rename function for lambda expressions [Wad90]. This functions uses the state monad to supply a source of new variable names. The function call substv x y b replaces all free occurrences of variable x in b by variable y.

```
rename :: Expr -> State Id String Expr
rename
  = mfoldE (\ x        -> result (Var x)
           ,\ f a      -> result (f :@: a)
           ,\ (x,t) b  -> do{ y <- new_name
                            ; result ((x,t) ::: (substv x y b))
                            }
           )
```

Exercise Write a renamer rename :: Expr -> Reader (State Id String) [Assoc String String] Expr that does the substitution substv x y b on the fly. Can you write this function as a monadic fold over expressions? (*end of exercise*)

6 Calculating abstract machines

Until now we have mainly concentrated on using monadic folds for defining toy functions. This section exemplifies calculating a more involved program in this style. The example discussed in this section is taken from [Joh95], in which Johnsson calculates an efficient but complex functional interpreter (or abstract machine) from a simple, evidently correct, and inefficient interpreter. The calculation in [Joh95] uses unfold-fold transformations. Here we redo the same calculation, using monadic folds and fusion instead, resulting in a shorter calculation, in which the focus is on the important steps.

6.1 A state monad

In the definition of the G-machine in Section 6.3 we use a special instance of the state monad of Section 4.8. Sharing and graph manipulation that goes on in a real graph reduction implementation can be modelled using the state monad. Suppose we have a type Graph, then the state monad we need is defined as follows.

```
type St a  =  Graph -> (a,Graph)
```

We obtain the same type if we define St a as State Id Graph a. For concreteness
sake we simplify the result and bind we obtain from State Id Graph a.

```
instance  Monad St  where
   result a    = \ g -> (a,g)
   ma 'bind' f = \ g -> let (a,g1) = ma g in f a g1
```

A graph g :: Graph contains nodes (of type Node) linked by pointers (of type
Pointer). Folding a node means replacing constructor functions by arbitrary functions.

```
data Node =  Nint Int
          |  Nadd Pointer Pointer
          |  Napp Name [Pointer]

foldNode :: (Int -> a
            ,Pointer -> Pointer -> a
            ,Name -> [Pointer] -> a
            ) -> (Node -> b)
foldNode (nint,nadd,napp)
 = fNode
   where
      fNode (Nint i)    =  nint i
      fNode (Nadd p q)  =  nadd p q
      fNode (Napp n ps) =  napp n ps
```

The types Graph and Pointer are not relevant in this context. They are provided as
abstract types with three operations. Function store stores a node in a graph, and
returns a pointer to where it is stored. Function get fetches a node from the graph
given a pointer. Function update stores a node at a given location.

```
store   ::  Node -> St Pointer
get     ::  Pointer -> St Node
update  ::  Node -> Pointer -> St ()
```

These functions satisfy a number of useful, and more or less straightforward, laws
that we assume as axioms. The first law is the *store-get law* and says that storing
a value and then immediately fetching it to use it in some other function, can be
replaced by storing the value *and* passing it on for use in the other function, so
without fetching it from the state.

```
    do{p <- store v; w <- get p; f w}
 =      (Store-Get)
    do{p <- store v; f v}
```

The second law is a kind of dual of the first law. The *get-store* law says that fetching a node and then immediately storing it is the identity.

```
    do{p <- f; n <- get p; store n}
=       (Get-Store)
    f
```

The third law is the *store-update law* and says that a store followed by an update with value w of the same pointer can be replaced by just storing value w.

```
    do{p <- store v; update w p; f}
=       (Store-Update)
    do{p <- store w; f}
```

The fourth law, the *move-store law*, says that if p does not occur free in f, and a does not appear free in v, then storing node v and computing value a can be swapped.

```
    do{p <- store v; a <- f; k}
≅       (Move-Store)
    do{a <- f; p <- store v; k}
```

The left-hand side and right-hand side are not equal, since they do different things to the store, but apart from that they are equivalent in the sense that in all contexts do{p <- store v; x <- f; k}, simply using k produces the same result.

Exercise The function new :: St Pointer allocates a new unused pointer in the graph. Define function store in terms of function new and update. (*end of exercise*)

6.2 A tiny first order language

We consider a tiny first order language in which all values are integers, and the only operator is addition. Formal parameters are encoded by de Bruijn indices. The expressions are elements of the datatype Expr, which is slightly different from the datatype Expr defined in Section 3.5.

```
data Expr  =  Var Int
           |  Con Int
           |  Add Expr Expr
           |  App Name [Expr]

foldEx :: (Int -> a
          ,Int -> a
          ,a -> a -> a
          ,Name -> [a] -> a
```

```
             ) -> (Expr -> a)
foldEx (var,con,add,app)
  = fEx
    where
       fEx (Var i)     =  var i
       fEx (Con n)     =  con n
       fEx (Add e e')  =  add (fEx e) (fEx e')
       fEx (App f es)  =  app f (map fEx es)
```

A program is represented as an association list in which each pair consists of a function name and a right-hand side expression for that function name. For example, the concrete program

```
f x y  =  y + 1
g x    =  g x
main   =  f (g 2) 3
```

is represented by the following table.

```
["f"     := Add (Var 2) (Int 1)
,"g"     := App "g" [Var 1]
,"main" := App "f" [App "g" [Int 2],Int 3]
]
```

Given a global program environment **definitions** in which names are bound to expressions (the right-hand sides in a program), function **rhs** takes a name, and returns the right-hand side of the function.

```
rhs f  =  e where (Yes e) = lookup f definitions
```

The naive G-machine builds a graph from an expression. The graph is built bottom-up, so the program can be structured after the structure of its input. This is a perfect opportunity to exploit a monadic fold over expressions.

```
mfoldEx :: Monad m =>
           (Int -> m a
           ,Int -> m a
           ,a -> a -> m a
           ,Name -> [a] -> m a
           ) -> (Expr -> m a)
mfoldEx (var,con,add,app)
  = foldEx (var
           ,con
           ,\ ms mt -> do{s <- ms; t <- mt; add s t}
           ,\ f mas -> do{as <- accumulate mas; app f as}
           )
```

Note that function `accumulate` threads the state from left to right through the list of results. Threading the state from right to left gives another definition of a monadic expression fold.

6.3   The G-machine

In the naive G-machine, evaluating a function application is done by instantiating the right-hand side of the function definition given the actual arguments of the function application. A graph is built for the right-hand side, given a stack of pointers into the argument graphs, and the resulting graph is evaluated. Function `build` builds a graph given a stack of pointers and an expression.

```
build :: [Pointer] -> Expr -> St Pointer
build actuals
  = mfoldEx (\ i     -> result (actuals!!i)
            ,\ n     -> store (Nint n)
            ,\ p p' -> store (Nadd p p')
            ,\ f ps -> store (Napp f ps)
            )
```

Function `eval` evaluates a graph with root p and updates p with the resulting value. Note the intricate mutual recursion between functions `eval` and `evalNode`.

```
eval     :: Pointer -> St Pointer
eval p   =  do{ n <- get p
              ; r <- evalNode n
              ; update r p
              ; result p
              }

evalNode :: Node -> St Node
evalNode
 = foldNode
     (\ n      -> result (Nint n)
     ,\ p1 p2 -> do{ q1 <- eval p1
                   ; q2 <- eval p2
                   ; Nint n1 <- get q1
                   ; Nint n2 <- get q2
                   ; result (Nint (n1+n2))
                   }
     ,\ f ps  -> do{ ts <- accumulate (map eval ps)
                   ; p <- build ts (rhs f)
                   ; q <- eval p
                   ; get q
                   }
     )
```

The G-machine evaluates an expression e by first building a graph for expression e and then evaluating the resulting graph.

```
machine      :: [Pointer] -> Expr -> St Pointer
machine ps e = do{p <- build ps e; eval p}
```

Evaluating an expression thus is rather inefficient: function `build ps` builds a complete graph, which is subsequently consumed by function `eval`. Since `build ps` is a monadic fold expression, we can try to apply fusion for monadic expression folds to avoid building the graph.

The above definitions slightly differ from Johnsson's. The difference lies in the fact that `eval` returns a `St Pointer` instead of a `St Node`. To obtain Johnsson's machine it suffices to bind function `get` to the above machine. Fusion applies to the above definitions, but not to Johnsson's definitions.

6.4 Fusion for monadic expression folds

Since a monadic expression fold is defined in terms of a normal expression fold, we can apply fusion for expression folds to obtain a fusion law for monadic expressions folds. Fusion for monadic expression folds reads as follows.

```
    do{r <- mfoldEx f g h j x; k r}
=      (Fusion)
    mfoldEx f' g' h' j' x
```

provided four conditions hold. The first two conditions can be seen as definitions of the functions `f'` and `g'`.

$$do\{x <- f\ y;\ k\ x\} = f'\ y$$
$$do\{x <- g\ y;\ k\ x\} = g'\ y$$

The third condition requires that function k distributes over function h in a monadic way.

```
    do{s <- ms; t <- mt; r <- h s t; k r}
  =
    do{s <- ms; p <- k s; t <- mt; q <- k t; h' p q}
```

The fourth and last condition requires that function k distributes over function j, again taking account of the monad.

```
    do{t <- accumulate ts; p <- j n t; k p}
  =
    do{t <- accumulate (map ('bind' k) ts); j' n t}
```

6.5 Fusion applies to the G-machine

We apply the monadic expression fold fusion law to the composition of functions `do{p <- build ps x; eval p}`. We have

$$do\{p <- build\ ps\ x;\ eval\ p\} \ = \ mfoldEx\ f'\ g'\ h'\ j'\ x$$

provided the components of the folds satisfy the conditions of the fusion law. We verify these conditions in turn.

The first condition

The first condition of the monadic expression fold fusion law can be seen as a definition of function `f'`. This function can be simplified slightly.

```
    do{p <- result (ps!!n); eval p}
=      left-unit law
    eval (ps!!n)
```

So we define function `f'` by

```
f' n  =  eval (ps!!n)
```

The second condition

The second condition of the monadic expression fold fusion law can be used as a definition too, now of function `g'`. Again, function `g'` can be simplified.

```
    do{p <- store (Nint i); eval p}
=      definition of eval
    do{p <- store (Nint i); n <- get p; r <- evalNode n;
       update r p; result p}
=      store-get law
    do{p <- store (Nint i); r <- evalNode (Nint i); update r p;
       result p}
=      definition of evalNode
    do{p <- store (Nint i); r <- result (Nint i); update r p;
       result p}
=      left-unit law
    do{p <- store (Nint i); update (Nint i) p; result p}
=      store-update law
    do{p <- store (Nint i); result p}
=      right-unit law
    store (Nint i)
```

So we define function **g'** by

```
g' i = store (Nint i)
```

The first two steps of the above derivation can be used in the subsequent derivations too. We name the equality obtained the *eval-store law.*

```
    do{p <- store v; eval p}
=       (Eval-Store)
    do{p <- store v; r <- evalNode v; update r p; result p}
```

The third condition
The third condition of the monadic expression fold fusion law is a real condition, and requires a more involved calculation.

```
    do{s <- ms; t <- mt; p <- store (Nadd s t); eval p}
=       eval-store law
    do{s <- ms; t <- mt; p <- store (Nadd s t);
       r <- evalNode (Nadd s t); update r p; result p}
=       definition of evalNode
    do{s <- ms; t <- mt; p <- store (Nadd s t); p1 <- eval s;
       p2 <- eval t; Nint n1 <- p1; Nint n2 <- p2;
       r <- result (add n1 n2); update r p; result p}
≅       move-store law
    do{s <- ms; t <- mt; p1 <- eval s; p2 <- eval t;
       n1 <- get p1; n2 <- get p2; r <- result (add n1 n2);
       p <- store (Nadd s t); update r p; result p}
≅       rearrange terms
    do{s <- ms; p1 <- eval s; t <- mt; p2 <- eval t;
       n1 <- get p1; n2 <- get p2; r <- result (add n1 n2);
       p <- store (Nadd s t); update r p; result p}
```

The last step is justified by the same reasoning as the move-store law: the two expressions do different things to the store, but the result of the expressions is the same. We have calculated an expression of the desired form, i.e., a function that first evaluates the arguments and then processes them. So we can define function **h'** as the last two lines of the last expression in the above calculation. This expression can be simplified as follows.

```
    do{n1 <- get p1; n2 <- get p2; r <- result (add n1 n2);
       p <- store (Nadd s t); update r p; result p}
```

= left-unit law

```
do{n1 <- get p1; n2 <- get p2; p <- store (Nadd s t);
   update (add n1 n2) p; result p}
```

= store-update law

```
do{n1 <- get p1; n2 <- get p2; p <- store (add n1 n2);
   result p}
```

= right-unit law

```
do{n1 <- get p1; n2 <- get p2; store (add n1 n2)}
```

So we define function h' by

```
h' p q  =  do{m <- get p; n <- get q; store (add m n)}
```

The fourth condition

Finally, for the fourth condition of the monadic expression fold fusion law we calculate as follows.

```
do{t <- accumulate ts; p <- store (Napp n t); eval p}
```

= eval-store law

```
do{t <- accumulate ts; p <- store (Napp n t);
   r <- evalNode (Napp n t); update r p; result p}
```

= definition of evalNode

```
do{t <- accumulate ts; p <- store (Napp n t);
   t' <- accumulate (map eval t); s' <- build t' (rhs n);
   s <- eval s'; r <- get s; update r p; result p}
```

$\cong$ move-store law

```
do{t <- accumulate ts; t' <- accumulate (map eval t);
   s' <- build t' (rhs n); s <- eval s'; r <- get s;
   p <- store (Napp n t); update r p; result p}
```

$\cong$ law for accumulate and eval below

```
do{t <- accumulate (map ('bind' eval) ts);
   s' <- build t (rhs n); s <- eval s'; r <- get s;
   p <- store (Napp n t); update r p; result p}
```

The law for accumulate and eval applied above reads:

```
do{ts' <- accumulate ts; t <- accumulate (map eval ts'); k}
```
$\cong$
```
do{t <- accumulate (map ('bind' eval) ts); k}
```

This law can be proved by induction over the actual arguments ts. The last expression of the above calculation is an expression of the desired form. For the definition of j' we simplify the composition of all but the first functions.

```
    do{s' <- build t (rhs n); s <- eval s'; r <- get s;
        p <- store (Napp n t); update r p; result p}
=   definition of machine
    do{s <- machine t (rhs n); r <- get s; p <- store (Napp n t);
        update r p; result p}
=   store-update law
    do{s <- machine t (rhs n); r <- get s; p <- store r; result p}
=   right-unit law
    do{s <- machine t (rhs n); r <- get s; store r}
=   get-store law
    machine t (rhs n)
```

So we define function j' by

```
    j' n t  =  machine t (rhs n)
```

The result
Using fusion for monadic expression folds, we have derived the following optimised version for machine ps.

```
    machine ps
    = mfoldEx (\ i     -> eval (ps!!i)
              ,\ n     -> store (Nint i)
              ,\ p p'  -> do{ Nint m <- get p
                           ; Nint n <- get p'
                           ; store (Nint (m+n))
                           }
              ,\ f ps -> machine ps (rhs f)
              )
```

In a lazy functional language, binding get to this abstract machine results in the same machine as Johnsson derives. To derive this machine, Johnsson used about fifty percent more calculation steps.

7 Conclusion

Imperative languages such as C provide a fixed set of control structures such as **while**- and **for**-loops. These kind of loops are convenient for processing iterative structures such as arrays and files but are less useful for processing other (branching) structures such as trees. On the other hand, *generalised fold operators* are custom made control structures that exactly match the datatypes one wants to traverse. Folding structures functions by the way they consume their arguments.

Imperative languages such as C (or logic languages such as Prolog) provide a fixed set of computations such as state-based computations (or non-deterministic computations). On the other hand *monads* are custom made notions of computations that exactly match the particular computation one wants to perform. Monads structure functions by the way they compute their results.

We have shown that is is possible to use both ideas at once, leading to concise and clear programs. Sometimes processing the recursive calls of folding a datatype within a monad follows a fixed pattern. In that case we can even take a larger notational shortcut by using a *generalised monadic fold* operator. Generalised monadic fold operators are the natural lifting of normal generalised fold operators to the Kleisli category. Despite their mathematical elegance, the recursion patterns captured by generalised monadic fold operators are often too specific to be useful.

Acknowledgements
We thank Doaitse Swierstra for stimulating functional programming in Utrecht, Maarten Fokkinga for his rigorous explanation of monadic folds and maps, and Graham Hutton, Luc Duponcheel, Jeroen Fokker, Thomas Johnsson, and Doaitse Swierstra for their helpful comments and remarks.

References

[Bir89]   R.S. Bird. Lectures on constructive functional programming. In M. Broy, editor, *Constructive Methods in Computing Science*, volume F55 of *NATO ASI Series*, pages 151–216. Springer–Verlag, 1989.

[Fok94]   M.M. Fokkinga. Monadic maps and folds for arbitrary datatypes. Memoranda Informatica 94-28, University of Twente, June 1994.

[Fre90]   P. Freyd. Recursive types reduced to inductive types. In *Proceedings Logic in Computer Science LICS90*, pages 498–507, 1990.

[GLPJ93]   A. Gill, J. Launchbury, and S.L. Peyton Jones. A short cut to deforestation. In *Proceedings Functional Programming Languages and Computer Architecture FPCA93*, pages 223–232, 1993.

[Jeu90]   J. Jeuring. Algorithms from theorems. In M. Broy and C.B. Jones, editors, *Programming Concepts and Methods*, pages 247–266. North-Holland, 1990.

[Joh95]   Thomas Johnsson. Fold-Unfold Transformations on State Monadic Interpreters. In *Proceedings of the Glasgow Functional Programming Workshop, Ayr 1994*, Workshops in Computing. Springer Verlag, 1995. (To appear).

[Jon93]   Mark P. Jones. Release notes for Gofer 2.28. Included as part of the standard Gofer distribution, February 1993.

[KL95]   R.B. Kieburtz and J. Lewis. Programming with algebras. In J. Jeuring and E. Meijer, editors, *Lecture Notes on Advanced Functional Programming Techniques*, LNCS. Springer-Verlag, 1995.

[Lau93]   J. Launchbury. Lazy imperative programming. In *Proceedings ACM Sigplan Workshop on State in Programming Languages*, 1993. YALEU/DCS/RR-968, Yale University.

[Lau95]   J. Launchbury. Graph algorithms with a functional flavour. In J. Jeuring and E. Meijer, editors, *Lecture Notes on Advanced Functional Programming Techniques*, LNCS. Springer-Verlag, 1995.

[Mal90]   G. Malcolm. Data structures and program transformation. *Science of Computer Programming*, 14:255–279, 1990.

[Mee86]   L. Meertens. Algorithmics—towards programming as a mathematical activity. In J.W. de Bakker, M. Hazewinkel, and J.K. Lenstra, editors, *Proceedings of the CWI Symposium on Mathematics and Computer Science*, volume 1 of *CWI Monographs*, pages 289–334. North–Holland, 1986.

[MFP91]   E. Meijer, M. Fokkinga, and R. Paterson. Functional programming with bananas, lenses, envelopes, and barbed wire. In J. Hughes, editor, *Proceedings of the 5th ACM Conference on Functional Programming Languages and Computer Architecture FPCA91, Cambridge, Massachusetts*, pages 124–144, 1991.

[MH95]   E. Meijer and G. Hutton. Bananas in space: Extending fold and unfold to exponential types. In S. Peyton Jones, editor, *Proceedings Functional Programming Languages and Computer Architecture FPCA95*, 1995.

[Mog91]   E. Moggi. Notions of computation and monads. *Information and Computation*, 93(1):55–92, 1991.

[Pat94]   R. Paterson. Control structures from types. rap@doc.ic.ac.uk, 1994.

[Pat95]   R. Paterson. Notes on computational monads. rap@doc.ic.ac.uk, 1995.

[PBM82]   G.N. Franz P.B. Brown and H. Moraff. *Electronics for the Modern Scientist*. Elsevier Science Publishing Co., Inc., 1982.

[SdM93]   S.D. Swierstra and O. de Moor. Virtual datastructures. In Helmut Partsch Berhard Möller and Steve Schuman, editors, *Formal Program Development*, LNCS 755, pages 355–371. Springer-Verlag, 1993.

[Set89]   R. Sethi. *Programming Languages: Concepts and Structures*. Addison-Wesley, 1989.

[SJW79]   W. Strunk Jr. and E.B. White. *The Elements of Style*. MacMillan Publishing Co., Inc., 1979. Third Edition.

[TM95]   A. Takano and E. Meijer. Shortcut deforestation in calculational form. In S. Peyton Jones, editor, *Proceedings Functional Programming Languages and Computer Architecture FPCA95*, 1995.

[Wad88]   P. Wadler. Deforestation: transforming programs to eliminate trees. In *Proceedings European Sytmposium on Programming, ESOP88*, pages 344–358. Springer-Verlag, 1988. LNCS 300.

[Wad89]   P. Wadler. Theorems for free! In *Proceedings Functional Programming Languages and Computer Architecture FPCA89, Imperial College, London*, pages 347–359. ACM Press, 1989.

[Wad90]   P. Wadler. Comprehending monads. In *Proceedings 1990 ACM Conference on Lisp and Functional Programming*, pages 61–78, 1990.

[Wad95]   P. Wadler. Monads for functional programming. In J. Jeuring and E. Meijer, editors, *Lecture Notes on Advanced Functional Programming Techniques*, LNCS. Springer-Verlag, 1995.

[WM91]   J. van der Woude and L. Meertens. A tribute to attributes. *The Squiggolist*, 2(1):20–26, 1991.

Programming with Algebras[*]

Richard B. Kieburtz and Jeffrey Lewis

Pacific Software Research Center
Oregon Graduate Institute
of Science & Technology
P.O. Box 91000
Portland, OR 97291-1000 USA
http://www.cse.ogi.edu/PacSoft/

1 Introduction

From the early days of computing, many individuals have recognized that algebras provide interesting mathematical models for at least some aspects of programs. In mathematics, an algebra consists of a set (called the carrier of the algebra), together with a finite set of total functions that have the carrier set as their common codomain. The algebras we learn in school, however, are usually those derived from number theory and programs are more diverse, if not richer, than operations on numbers. A somewhat more abstract notion, called signature algebras, has been used for some time to to model abstract data types [GTW78]. A signature defines a set of typed operator symbols without specifying functions that would be the actual operators. Thus a signature defines a class of algebras, namely the algebras whose operators conform to the typing constraints imposed by the signature. Signature algebras have been helpful in understanding the issues involved in abstract data types, type classes, program modularity and other software interface issues.

There is an even more abstract notion of algebras that has its origins in category theory. This notion, called *structure algebra*, emphasizes properties of morphisms, or structure-preserving maps. What is meant by structure in this context is that determined by a functor on the category of sets[2]. Because this notion of what constitutes an algebra is so general, it encompasses a huge variety of morphisms, or functions on sets.

A particularly interesting class of structure algebras occurs when the functors that specify the structure are chosen to correspond to the signatures that

---

[*] The research on which this chapter is based was supported by the USAF Materiel Command.

[2] Technically, we should say a functor *Set* → *Set*, where *Set* is the category whose objects are sets and whose arrows are (total) functions. We trust no confusion will arise from referring to such a functor as acting "on the category of sets".

define signature algebras. The set of functions that can be characterized as morphisms of this class of structure algebras is vast—it appears to cover the space of functions that can be computed by functional programs provably terminating in Peano arithmetic. This chapter is about how to specify computable functions in terms of structure algebras, rather than by the more traditional, but less disciplined use of recursive equations. Some of the techniques are already familiar in functional programming—the higher-order functions *fold*, *reduce* or *catamorphisms* defined by various authors construct homomorphisms of structure algebras. The algebra of lists [Bir86] is actually a class a structure algebras.

There are several important advantages to specifying functions in terms of structure algebras, rather than recursive equations:

- Patterns of control can be formally specified and explicit, rather than informal and implicit. Control is derived from a specified signature.
- Termination conditions for a function defined as a structure-algebra morphism can also be derived from a specified signature.
- Algebraic programs have a semantic interpretation over sets and do not require a cpo interpretation.
- Proof rules for algebraic programs are inductive. Verification conditions necessary to prove a hypothesized property of a computation can be automatically derived.

There are also obligations imposed upon an algebraic functional programmer to ensure that a function specified in an algebraic formalism actually exists. The most stringent obligation is to prove totality of the function over a prescribed domain. In conventional functional languages, whose programs are specified by recursive equations, the only obligation is to prove type correctness, which is usually established by an automated type reconstruction algorithm.

In this chapter the reader will be introduced to ADL—an Algebraic Design Language—in which functions are defined in terms of a family of type-parametric combinators, rather than through explicitly recursive, equational declarations. ADL is based upon the categorical notion of structure algebras and coalgebras, although only the algebraic part is discussed here [KL94]. Data types in ADL are the carriers of its free algebras. They correspond closely to the data types of conventional functional programming languages such as ML, Haskell or Miranda. Just as the structure of an algebra is determined from a signature declaration, the data types of ADL are also extracted from its signature declarations.

ADL is an implemented language. Its initial implementation has been built as an extension to Standard ML, and supports interactive use. The initial application for ADL has been in a system that calculates program generators from specifications given in a domain-specific mini-language [B+94, KB+95].

The concept of algebras as they are used in ADL is discussed informally in Section 2. The concepts are more rigorously defined in Section 3, which provides the mathematical background for the rest of the chapter. Although many of the concepts have arisen from category theory, only a superficial knowledge of categories is assumed of the reader. In Sections 4 and 5, structure algebras become elements of programs. A catamorphism combinator provides implicitly recursive control structures and a system of proof rules is introduced. Section 6 extends the scope of algebraic control structures to include functions whose underlying structure is less obvious, functions that are not catamorphisms. With its extended scope, algebraic programming now supports the definition of a huge space of total functions, without recourse to explicit recursion. Verification conditions are also discussed in this section. The type system of ADL is given an abbreviated treatment in 7. Section 8 demonstrates how monads fit naturally into an algebraic framework. The chapter concludes by illustrating the formulation of an algorithm for contraction of lambda-calculus terms.

There are related studies of the use of higher-order combinators (including catamorphism) in theoretical programming [MFP91, Fok92], however, none has previously been incorporated into a practical system for program development. The origin of such techniques appears to lie in the work of the *Squiggol* school [Bir86, Bir88, Mee86], subsequently influenced by a thesis by Hagino [Hag87] in which morphisms of data types are generalized in a categorical framework. A categorical programming language called *Charity* [CS92] embodies inductive and coinductive control structures based upon a categorical framework. The characterization of data types as structure algebras (and coalgebras) [Mac71] can be attributed to Hagino.

2 Algebras, Types and signatures

ADL is a higher-order, typed functional language whose type system is inspired by concepts from the theory of order-sorted algebras, from Martin-Löf's type theory and from the Girard-Reynolds second-order lambda calculus. While ADL does not provide the full generality of the second-order lambda calculus, it uses a constrained form of abstraction on types and it contains combinators that are indexed by the names of type constructors. Its type system is sufficiently rich that type-checking is not decidable.

Nevertheless, the ADL type system is amenable to an abstract interpretation that is similar to the Hindley-Milner system with consistent extensions. Type inference in the Hindley-Milner system, while of exponential complexity in the worst case, has been shown to be feasible in practice through years of experience with its use in several functional programming languages. The Hindley-Milner system, which embodies a structural notion of type, guarantees the slogan

"Well-typed programs don't go wrong".

This means that programs that satisfy the structural typing rules respect the signatures of multi-sorted algebras—integer data are never confused with floating-point numbers or with functions, for instance. ADL adds to the structural typing restrictions the further requirement that

"Well-typed programs always terminate".

This implies that the type system accommodates the precise description of sets that constitute the domains of functions definable in ADL. Accurate type-checking in ADL requires the construction of proofs of propositions. This task is made substantially easier than it would be in an untyped linguistic framework by the underlying approximation furnished by structural typing.

In Standard ML and related languages, the Hindley-Milner type system is extended with data type declarations. A data type declaration names a type and specifies a finite set of data constructors. An ML data type name may have one or more type variables as parameters, and thus actually names a type constructor. A type variable introduced as a parameter in a data type declaration is bound by abstraction. Application of a type constructor to a type expression can be understood syntactically, as the substitution of the argument expression for all occurrences of the type variable in the data type declaration.

In ADL, data type declarations are generalized to signature declarations that specify algebraic varieties[3]. Following the conventions of multi-sorted algebras, we call the names of types and type constructors *sorts*. The generalization can be summarized in the following table:

Parameterized data types	Varieties
type	algebra
type constructor	sort
data constructor	operator

The *arity* is a syntactic property of a sort. The arity indicates how to form type expressions from sorts. A sort with nullary arity, designated by $*$, is said to be *saturated*. A sort with non-nullary arity, designated by $* \to *$, is said to be *unsaturated*. A saturated sort expression is either a saturated sort or an unsaturated sort applied to a saturated sort expression. A saturated sort expression denotes a type in ADL.

ADL departs significantly from functional programming languages such as ML by providing signature declarations that introduce varieties of both signature and structure algebras, not simply data types. The signature of an algebraic variety consists of a finite set of operator names, together with the type of the domain of each operator. The codomain of an operator is the carrier type for the particular algebra to which the operator belongs. In computing, we often need to work with algebras in which there are several carrier types, although such complications are rarely of interest in mathematics. To describe a variety of algebras with several carriers, the operators that have a common codomain are grouped into sets. These sets are called sorts and the sorts are named in a signature declaration.

To determine a signature algebra of a given variety, a carrier type is specified for each sort of the variety, and a well-typed function is specified for each operator of each sort. We shall sometimes refer to a particular signature algebra as being "concrete", to distinguish it from an unspecified algebra of its variety.

---

[3] A variety is a class of algebras having a common signature.

If all that we got from a signature was a variety of signature algebras, then we would be hard-pressed to claim any novelty for ADL. Signature algebras have been thoroughly explored as a basis for the OBJ family of languages [GT79, GW88]. However, signatures can also be modeled abstractly by a particular class of functors in the category of sets. These functors have fixed points which are objects in the same category, i.e. sets. This fact has long been known and exploited to define (recursively) data types in functional programming languages. It is less well known that the fixed points of these functors define whole categories of algebras, called structure algebras, which have useful interpretations for programming. This is the topic of our discourse.

2.1 Some familiar algebras

Signature declaration in ADL generalizes data type declaration in ML. Where we would declare a *list* data type in Standard ML by writing

```
datatype 'a list = nil | cons of ('a *  'a list)
```

the corresponding declaration of a variety of *List*D- signature-algebras is written in ADL as:

```
signature List(a){type c; list/c = {$Nil, $Cons of (a * c)}}
```

A signature algebra is characterized by a carrier and a set of typed operators. A variety of signature algebras specifies neither the carrier nor the operators, but only their typings, in terms of the carrier type variables, the type parameter of the variety. and possibly some constant types or type constructors.

The above declaration asserts $List(a)$ to be the name of a variety of algebras that is parameterized on a single type (designated by the type variable a) and further declares a name for a single sort, *list*. The sort is unsaturated because the variety has a type parameter; thus $list : * \rightarrow *$. The type variable c stands for the carrier type. The signature declares two operator symbols of sort *list*, with typings:

$$\$Nil : c \qquad \$Cons : a \times c \rightarrow c$$

To emphasize that $\$Nil$ is an operator, it could have been given a function type, $1 \rightarrow c$ (where 1 is the type of a singleton set), by declaring it as "$\$Nil$ **of** 1". Since 1 denotes a singleton set, every function in the type $1 \rightarrow c$ is isomorphic to an element in c.

Operator names always begin with '$\$$' to distinguish them from other identifiers. A concrete algebra is specified by providing bindings for the carrier type and for each operator of the algebra.

Each signature declaration implicitly defines one specific algebra. This is the algebra of free terms, whose operators are unconstrained. The equational theory of this algebra is empty; syntactically distinct terms are semantically distinct. The operators of the free term algebra are commonly called *data constructors* and the set of terms constructed by well-typed applications of these operators is called a (free) data type.

The names of the data constructors of a free term algebra definable in ADL are derived from the names of operators in a signature, by dropping the initial '$' symbol. The name of a free data type is taken from a sort name. In case the sort is unsaturated, it names a *type constructor* of free data types, rather than a data type.

Here are the declarations of some other signatures that define useful varieties of algebras in ADL:

```
signature Nat{type c; nat/c = {$Zero, $Succ of c}}
signature Tree(a){type c; tree/c = {$Tip of a, $Fork of (c * c)}}
signature Bush(a){type c; bush/c = {$Leaf of a, $Branch of list(c)}}
```

Note that *nat* is a saturated sort, while *tree* and *bush* are both unsaturated.

The use of signatures to declare free data types is a familiar aspect of typed, functional languages. However, signatures also induce control structures, and that is the main point we wish to make. We shall see in Section 4 how powerful control structures can be derived from signature declarations.

3 Mathematical preliminaries

Before proceeding further, we shall give some essential definitions of mathematical concepts that underlie algebraic programming.

3.1 Signatures and functors

We begin with definition of a signature as a syntactic entity, sufficiently rich for our purposes.

Definition 1. Signatures
Let TC be a set, called type constructors. A signature is an indexed set of sets, possibly abstracted on a parameter, a,

$$\Sigma(a) = (S, \{\Sigma_s \mid s \in S\})$$

and has the following structure:

> S is a finite set of identifiers called sorts.
> Each Σ_s is a triple, $(c_s, I_s, \{\kappa_i \text{ of } \sigma_i \mid i \in I_s\})$, where
> > c_s is an identifier, unique in $\{a\} \cup \{c_t \mid t \in S\}$,
> > I_s is a finite set of indices,
> > each κ_i is an identifier, unique in $\{\kappa_j \mid j \in I_s\}$,
> > each σ_i is a term derived from the following grammar:

$$\sigma ::= c_t \qquad t \in S$$
$$\mid g(\sigma) \qquad g \in TC$$
$$\mid a$$
$$\mid \sigma * \sigma \qquad (*) \text{ is associative}$$
$$\mid 1$$

□

The interpretation intended for a signature is that a and c_s (for $s \in S$) denote sets (i.e. types of ADL), while the elements of TC denote functors in the category of sets (i.e. type constructors of ADL). For each sort s, the κ_i in Σ_s are operator symbols of the sort and denote functions. The domain of the function denoted by κ_i is given by the interpretation of σ_i. The codomain of κ_i is the carrier of sort s, which is the interpretation of c_s. The symbol $(*)$ denotes the operator forming the product of two sets.

Given the interpretation described above, it is straightforward to associate with a signature, a sort-indexed family of multi-functors on the category of sets[4]. The component functor associated with a sort s is derived from the s-sorted component of the signature,

$$\Sigma_s = (c_s, [1..n_s], \{\kappa_1 \text{ of } \sigma_1, \ldots, \kappa_{n_s} \text{ of } \sigma_{n_s}\})$$

The object parameters of the associated multi-functor are the several variables of the signature that have interpretations as types, namely, a and c_t for each $t \in S$. Let us call this set V. Then the multi-functor indexed by sort s is defined to be

$$E_s(V) = F_1(V) + \ldots + F_{n_s}(V)$$

where each of the F_i is also multi-functor and $(+)$ denotes the coproduct bifunctor on the category Set. For each index $i \in [1..n_s]$, the term σ_i is of the form

$$\sigma_i = \sigma_{i,1} * \ldots * \sigma_{i,m_i}$$

where none of the $\sigma_{i,j}$ contains the operator $(*)$. Thus each of the $\sigma_{i,j}$ is either a variable from V or 1 or an expression of the form $g(\sigma')$, where $g \in TC$ is a type constructor and σ' is a term over V. From this expansion, we determine the form of each component multi-functor,

$$F_i(V) = \bar{\sigma}_{i,1} \times \ldots \times \bar{\sigma}_{i,m_i}$$

in which $(\times)$ denotes the set product and $\bar{\sigma}_{i,j}$ denotes the interpretation of $\sigma_{i,j}$. The multi-functor E_s derived from each sort of a signature has the form of a sum of products.

Example 1. The signature *List* has a single sort and a parameter. The bifunctor derived from this signature by the process described above is:

$$E_{List}(a, c) = 1 + (a \times c)$$

For the signatures *Nat*, *Tree* and *Bush* specified in Section 2.1 the derived sum-of-products functors are:

$$E_{Nat}(c) = 1 + c$$
$$E_{Tree}(a, c) = a + (c \times c)$$
$$E_{Bush}(a, c) = a + list(c)$$

---

[4] By a multi-functor, we mean a functor parametric on multiple object variables. A bifunctor is a multi-functor of rank 2, for instance.

□

An important fact is that a sum-of-products functor has a fixed point in $\mathcal{S}et$ [Mal90]. That is, given a sum-of-products functor E_s, there is a set s' such that $E_s(s') \cong s'$, where ($\cong$) denotes the relation of (natural) isomorphism[5]. In case the signature from which the functor is derived takes a parameter, the result still holds but the fixed point is indexed by the parameter. For example, if E_s is a bifunctor, then holding the first parameter constant, we look for a fixed point in the second parameter. The fixed point is then indexed by the (fixed) first parameter, i.e. $E_s(a, s'(a)) \cong s'(a)$. A sort-indexed family of functors also has a fixed point, which is a sort-indexed set of sets.

It is customary to designate the elements of the fixed point of the family of multi-functors derived from a signature by the sort names that index them. For example, we designate by nat the fixed point of E_{Nat}, and by $list(a)$ the fixed point of the bifunctor E_{List} at the point a. These are categorical models of the familiar data types of the same names.

The natural isomorphism at the fixed point of a functor is designated by

$$\mathbf{in}_s : E_s(s') \rightarrow s'$$

The natural isomorphism has an obvious interpretation in the context of a functional programming language. It is the ensemble of data constructors associated with the sort s. These data constructors correspond to the operators of a free term algebra defined by the signature. Thus, for the free nat-algebra, the isomorphism is $\mathbf{in}_{nat} = [Zero, Succ] : 1 + nat \rightarrow nat$ and for the free $list$-algebras it is $\mathbf{in}_{list} = [Nil, Cons] : 1 + a \times list(a) \rightarrow list(a)$. The inverse isomorphism corresponds to a case analysis on the freely constructed terms, discriminating terms by the data constructor whose application is outermost. Naturality of the isomorphism in the parameter, a, implies that the data constructors of the corresponding data type constructor have types that are polymorphic with respect to a.

When E_s is a bifunctor, its fixed point is also a functor. Specifically, if $s(a)$ is the object at the fixed point, that is, $s(a) = \mathbf{in}_s(E_s(a, s(a)))$, then there is a higher-order function, $map\_s : (a \rightarrow b) \rightarrow s(a) \rightarrow s(b)$, that satisfies the equations

$$map\_s\ id_a = id_{s(a)}$$
$$map\_s\ (f \circ g) = map\_s\ f \circ map\_s\ g$$

where id_a denotes an identity function on the type a and $f : b \rightarrow c$, $g : a \rightarrow b$ for types a, b and c. These properties have long been known by programmers to hold for the data type constructor $list$. The function map_s corresponds to the morphism mapping part of the functor s.

---

[5] The fixed points of interesting sum-of-products functors are unique up to isormorphism. There are, however, functors whose fixed points are not even principal. The identity functor, I, is an example, as every set is a fixed point of I. We do not have a characterization of the interesting functors.

As a consequence of the fact that the fixed point of a bifunctor (with respect to one of its arguments) is a functor in the remaining argument, the morphism mapping associated with freely constructed data type has the following characterization:

Corollary 2. *map*—the morphism mapping of a sort-indexed family of functors
Let $\Sigma(a) = (S, \{\Sigma_s \mid s \in S\})$ be a parameterized signature and let $f : a \to b$.
Let

$$\Sigma_s = (c_s, [1..n_s], \{\kappa_1 \text{ of } \sigma_1, \ldots, \kappa_{n_s} \text{ of } \sigma_{n_s}\})$$

for $s \in S$. Then for each sort $s \in S$, $map\_s f : s(a) \to s(b)$ satisfies an equation:

$map\_s f = \lambda x.$ **case** x **of**

$$\vdots$$

$$\kappa_i(x_1, \ldots, x_{m_i}) \Rightarrow \kappa_i(y_1, \ldots, y_{m_i})$$

where $y_j =$
$$\begin{cases} f\,x_j & \text{if } x_j : a \\ map\_s'f\,x_j & \text{if } x_j : s'(a) \quad \text{where } s' \in S \\ map\_t\,(map\_s'f)\,x_j & \text{if } x_j : t(s'(a)) \text{ where } t \text{ is an unsaturated} \\ & \qquad\qquad\qquad\quad \text{sort of a signature } \Sigma' \neq \Sigma \\ & \qquad\qquad\qquad\quad \text{and } s' \in S \end{cases}$$

$\square$

3.2 Structure algebras

The fundamental concept of structure algebras is quite simple. Structure algebras comprise varieties whose structure is induced by a functor on the category *Set* [Mac71]. The functor determines the structure. The following definitions have been specialized, for simplicity, to the case of single-sorted algebras.

Definition 3. Structure algebra
Let t be a functor on the category *Set*. A *t-structure algebra* (or t-algebra, for short) is a pair (c, h), where c is a type called the *carrier* of the algebra and $h : t(c) \to c$ is called its structure function.
$\square$

Definition 4. A *t-algebra morphism* is a function that maps one t-algebra into another. Let $\Sigma(a)$ be a signature with a single sort, t. (Recalling that an unsaturated sort denotes a functor.) A *t-algebra morphism* is a function $f : a \to b$ that satisfies the commuting diagram below:

$$\begin{array}{ccc} t(a) & \xrightarrow{\;map\_t\,f\;} & t(b) \\ {\scriptstyle h}\downarrow & & \downarrow{\scriptstyle k} \\ a & \xrightarrow{\quad f \quad} & b \end{array}$$

The diagram displays the equation

$$f \circ h = k \circ map\_t\, f$$

Note that both h and k are structure functions of t-algebras.

□

Example 2. A *list*-algebra morphism. Let $exp2 = \lambda n.\, 2^n$, and let *sum* and *product* be the functions that reduce a list of non-negative integers to a single integer by addition and multiplication, respectively. Then the following diagram illustrates $exp2$ as a morphism of *list*-algebras:

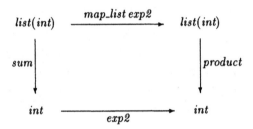

□

The following theorem summarizes an important property of varieties of signature algebras.

Theorem 5. Homomorphism
Let Σ be a signature with a single sort, t, and let E_t be the functor derived from Σ. There is a set, $\bar{t}$, and a natural isomorphism $in_t : E_t(\bar{t}) \rightarrow \bar{t}$ which together define a free algebra, $(\bar{t}, in_t)$.

Let (a, h) be a E_t-algebra. Then there is a unique E_t-algebra morphism, k, from the free algebra to (a, h). The conclusion is summarized in the following commuting square:

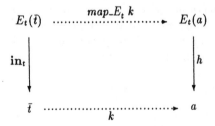

□

The dotted arrows indicate that the function, k, that makes the diagram commute is uniquely determined from the other data in the diagram.

4 Algebras and catamorphisms

A signature algebra provides a set of operators that can be used in constructing terms that represent calculations in the carrier type, as the familiar arithmetic operators do for integers. It also provides exactly the data needed to specify a function that calculates a value from a data-structure representation of a term in the free algebra of the signature. For example, the arguments that must be furnished to a *fold* function to reduce a list are the operators specified in a *list*-signature algebra.

The *list*-algebras that we shall see in Example 3 induce functions that sum a list of integers, calculate the length of a list, and catenate two lists, respectively. A combinator to calculate these functions from the *list*-algebra specifications will be introduced in the next section. First, we shall see how algebras are specified in ADL.

A signature introduces names for the carriers and operators of a (multi-sorted) variety of signature algebras. To define a specific algebra of the variety, the carriers must be bound to types and the operators must be bound to functions in an algebra specification. In ADL, the symbol (:=) is used to designate the binding of either a carrier or an operator.

Example 3. : Three different *List*-algebras are:

```
List(int){c := int; list{$Nil := 0, $Cons := (+)}}
List(a){c := int; list{$Nil := 0, $Cons := \(x,y) 1+y}}
List(a){c := list(a) -> list(a);
        list{$Nil := id,
             $Cons := \(x,f) \y Cons(x,f y)}}
```

where *id* is the polymorphic identity function, here instantiated with the type *list(a)*. The operator (+) belongs to a concrete algebra of integer arithmetic, which is predefined in ADL.
□

When a signature in ADL has only a single sort, as does *List*, an algebra specification may be abbreviated by omitting the inner set of curly braces and the sort name that is prefixed to the opening brace. Thus we could abbreviate the first algebra in the list of examples above, as

```
List{c := int; $Nil := 0, $Cons := (+)}
```

The free term algebra for the sort *list* can also be specified, although this specification is redundant, as its operators are the data constructors for *list* and these are implicitly defined when its signature is declared.

```
List(a){c := list(a); $Nil := Nil, $Cons := Cons}
```

It is important to keep in mind the distinction between data constructors in the free term algebra and operators in the signature of an algebra. The operators bound to the same operator symbol, but in different algebras of the same variety may have different types. The data constructors are a special case of the operators for a specific algebra, and their types are fixed, up to variation in the type parameter of the variety.

4.1 The catamorphism combinator

If t is a sort of a parameterized signature $\Sigma(a)$, a structure function of the class of t-algebras is any function $h : t(a) \to a$. Theorem 5 asserts that if $\Sigma(a)$ has a free term algebra, then h is also the unique -algebra morphism from $(E\$t(a), \mathbf{in}_t)$ to (a, h), and we call it a *homomorphism*. (Recall that the meaning of "morphism" is "form-preserving". Here the form that is preserved is the underlying structure of the algebra.) More generally, the composition of a t-algebra morphism $f : a \to b$ with a homomorphism, i.e. $g = f \circ h : t(a) \to b$, is a t-algebra morphism from the free term algebra, and is uniquely determined by the algebra of its codomain. A function whose domain is the free term algebra of a signature is called a *catamorphism*, borrowing the prefix "*cata*"="down" from Greek [MFP91].

ADL defines a combinator, *red*, that takes an algebra specification to a catamorphism[6] of the algebraic variety. The *red* combinator obeys a homomorphism condition for each algebra on which it is instantiated. For the algebras we have considered, the homomorphism equations are given below. The bindings of operators in the combinator expressions are required to be correctly typed.

Let $R\_nat(z, s) = red[nat]\ Nat\{c := \tau;\ \$Zero := z,\ \$Succ := s\}$
Then $R\_nat(z, s)\ Zero = z$
$\quad R\_nat(z, s)\ (Succ\ n) = s\ (R\_nat(z, s)\ n)$

Let $R\_list(n, f) = red[list]\ List\{c := \tau;\ \$Nil := n,\ \$Cons := f\}$
Then $R\_list(n, f)\ Nil = n$
$\quad R\_list(n, f)\ (Cons\ (x, y)) = f\ (x,\ R\_list(n, f)\ y)$

Let $R\_tree(t, f) = red[tree]\ Tree\{c := \tau;\ \$Tip := t,\ \$Fork := f\}$
Then $R\_tree(t, f)\ (Tip\ x) = t\ x$
$\quad R\_tree(t, f)\ (Fork\ (l, r)) = f\ (R\_tree(t, f)\ l,\ R\_tree(t, f)\ r)$

Let $R\_bush(l, b) = red[bush]\ Bush\{c := \tau;\ \$Leaf := l,\ \$Branch := b\}$
Then $R\_bush(l, b)\ (Leaf\ x) = l\ x$
$\quad R\_bush(l, b)\ (Branch\ y) = b\ (map\_list\ (R\_bush(l, b))\ y)$

The function *map_list*, referred to in the last equation above, is defined below.

Examples of *list*-algebra catamorphisms Here are some examples of *List*-algebra catamorphisms constructed with *red*[list] and the algebra specifications given in Example 3:

---

[6] Other authors [MFP91] have used "banana" brackets, $(\_)$, to designate the cata-morphism combinator.

```
sum_list = red[list] List(int){c := int; $Nil := 0, $Cons := (+)}
length = red[list] List(a){c := int; $Nil := 0, $Cons := \(x,y) 1+y}
append = red[list] List(a){c := list(a) -> list(a);
                           $Nil := id,
                           $Cons := \(x,f) \y Cons(x, f y)}
```

Further examples of *List*-algebra morphisms are:

```
map_list f = red[list] List(a){c := list(b);
                               $Nil := Nil,
                               $Cons := \(x,y) Cons(f x, y)}
```

where f has the type a -> b, and

```
flatten_list = red[list] List(list(a)){c := list(a);
                                       $Nil := Nil,
                                       $Cons := append}
```

The typings of the constants defined by these equations are:

```
sum_list : list(int) -> int
length : list(a) -> int
append : list(a) -> list(a) -> list(a)
map_list : (a -> b) -> list(a) -> list(b)
flatten_list : list(list(a)) -> list(a)
```

Examples of *nat*-algebra catamorphisms: Catamorphisms of *nat*-algebras are enumerations of a carrier type. The function *ntoi* translates natural numbers from a representation in the free term algebra (i.e. a *Succ* representation) to a representation as positive integers.

```
ntoi = red[nat] Nat{c := int; $Zero := 0, $Succ := \n 1+n}
add_nat x = red[nat] Nat{c := nat; $Zero := x, $Succ := Succ}
```

with typings

```
ntoi : nat -> int
add_nat : nat -> nat -> nat
```

Examples of *tree* catamorphisms:

```
sum_tree = red[tree] Tree(int){c := int;
                               $Tip := id,
                               $Fork := (+)}

list_tree = red[tree] Tree(a){c := list(a);
                              $Tip := \x Cons(x,Nil),
                              $Fork := \(x,y) append x y}
```

```
map_tree f = red[tree] Tree(a){c := tree(b);
                               $Tip := \x Tip(f x),
                               $Fork := Fork}

flatten_tree = red[tree] Tree(tree(a)){c := tree(a);
                                        $Tip := id,
                                        $Fork := Fork}
```

with typings

```
sum_tree : tree(int) -> int
list_tree : tree(a) -> list(a)
map_tree : (a -> b) -> tree(a) -> tree(b)
flatten_tree : tree(tree(a)) -> tree(a)
```

Examples of *bush* morphisms:

```
sum_bush = red[bush] Bush(int){c := int;
                               $Leaf := id,
                               $Branch := sum_list}

list_bush = red[bush] Bush(a){c := list(a);
                              $Leaf := \x Cons(x,Nil),
                              $Branch := flatten_list}

map_bush f = red[bush] Bush(a){c := bush(b);
                               $Leaf := \x Leaf(f x),
                               $Branch := Branch}

flatten_bush = red[bush] Bush(bush(a)){c := bush(a);
                                        $Leaf := id,
                                        $Branch := Branch}
```

with typings

```
sum_bush : bush(int) -> int
list_bush : bush(a) -> list(a)
map_bush : (a -> b) -> bush(a) -> bush(b)
flatten_bush : bush(bush(a)) -> bush(a)
```

Exercise 6. Reverse of a list

A. Specify a *list*-catamorphism to compute the reverse of a list.
B. Specify a second *list*-catamorphism with carrier type $list(a) \rightarrow list(a)$ to define a function $rev : list(a) \rightarrow list(a) \rightarrow list(a)$ that satisfies the equation

$$rev\ x\ Nil = reverse\ x$$

4.2   Primitive recursion and case analysis

Recall Kleene's primitive recursion scheme to define functions on natural numbers:

$$f\,(Zero, x_1, \ldots, x_n) = g\,(x_1, \ldots, x_n)$$
$$f\,((Succ\ n), x_1, \ldots, x_n) = h\,(Succ\ n,\ f\,(n, x_1, \ldots, x_n),\ x_1, \ldots, x_n)$$

where $g\ :\ t_1 \times \ldots \times t_n\ \rightarrow\ a$ and $h\ :\ nat \times a \times t_1 \times \ldots \times t_n\ \rightarrow\ a$. Although the primitive recursion scheme can be represented as a nat-catamorphism, the representation is unnatural and if implemented directly, can result in algorithms with worse-than-expected performance. For instance, the **case** expression for type nat when expressed as a nat-catamorphism is

$$
\begin{array}{ll}
\textbf{case } x \textbf{ of} & = snd(red[nat]\ Nat\{c := nat \times a; \\
\quad Zero \Rightarrow g & \qquad \$Zero := (Zero,\ g), \\
\quad |\ Succ(x') \Rightarrow h\ x' & \qquad \$Succ := \lambda(x, y)\,(Succ\ x,\ h\ x)\}) \\
\textbf{end}
\end{array}
$$

Evaluation of the nat-catamorphism explicitly traverses the entire structure of a term to construct the argument needed in the successor instance of the case analysis. This takes time linear in the size of a nat term, whereas the $case$ primitive is a constant time function.

To avoid the problem of introducing a computation time penalty for a primitive control structure, **case** has been adopted as a control combinator in ADL, with syntax similar to that of Standard ML for the benefit of familiarity. The domain of a **case** combinator is the free data type generated by an algebraic variety.

A primitive recursive function is, however, a structure function of nat-algebras, one in which the carrier always has the form $nat * a$ for some type a. A function definable by primitive recursion can be calculated by taking the second projection of a pair calculated by a Nat-catamorphism.

Example 4. A factorial function is easy to define by primitive recursion. However, since the primitive recursion scheme is defined over natural numbers and we would prefer to do arithmetic in the domain of integers, some conversion is needed. The factorial function defined in this way has the typing $fact : nat \rightarrow int$. It can be expressed in ADL as

```
fact = snd o red[nat] Nat{c := nat * int;
            $Zero := (Zero,1),
            $Succ := \(m,n) (Succ m, ntoi(Succ m) * n)}
```

In a later section we shall return to this example to obtain an integer-typed factorial function.

To define a general primitive recursion scheme for natural numbers, declare a combinator, Pr, by

$$Pr(g, h) = snd \circ red[nat] \, Nat\{c := nat * \tau;$$
$$\$Zero := (Zero, \, g),$$
$$\$Succ := \langle Succ \circ fst, \, h \rangle\}$$

in which the angle brackets designate a functional pair, $\langle f, g \rangle \, x = (f \, x, \, g \, x)$. This defines a family of nat algebras, with structure functions $Pr(g, h) \; : \; nat \to \tau$, for each pair $(g : \tau, \, h : nat * \tau \to \tau)$. In terms of this scheme, the factorial function can be defined more succinctly:

$$fact = Pr(1, \, \lambda(m, n) \, ntoi(Succ \, m) * n)$$

where the codomain type has been instantiated to int.

Generalized primitive recursion The primitive recursive control scheme can be generalized to algebras of other varieties. There is no special combinator in ADL for primitive recursion, but a primitive recursion combinator can be composed for each variety. For example, we shall define a primitive recursion for $List$-algebras,

$$Pr\_list(g, h) \; : \; list(a) \to \tau$$
$$Pr\_list(g, h) = snd \, (red[list] \, List(a)\{c := list(a) \times \tau; \; \$Nil := (Nil, \, g), \; \$Cons := h\})$$

where $g : \tau$ and $h : (a \times (list(a) \times \tau)) \to \tau$.

Exercise 7. Splitting a list

Define $splitat \; : \; char \to list(char) \to list(char) \times list(char)$
The function $splitat$ is specified as follows: If the list xs contains an occurrence of the character, c, then $splitat \, c \, xs$ yields the pair of the prefix and suffix of the first occurrence of c in xs. Otherwise, it yields the pair (xs, Nil). Hint: Use primitive recursion for $list$.

4.3 Proof rules for catamorphisms

Inference rules for reasoning about catamorphisms of varieties of signature algebras can be calculated from their signatures. The form of each rule is an induction over the structure expressed by the signature. The proof rule for Nat-algebras is natural induction. Rules for the varieties introduced in Section 2.1 are summarized below. Notice that induction is not a structural rule of the logic. Rather, an inductive proof rule is introduced for each algebraic variety to account for the computational content of its catamorphisms. This has been noted previously by Goguen [Gog80] and others.

In the following rules, τ designates a type expression. In the last rule, the notation $y \in ys$ is the assertion that y is an element of the list ys.

$$\frac{f : \tau \qquad P(Zero, f)}{g : \tau \rightarrow \tau \qquad n : nat \qquad \forall x : \tau. P(n, x) \Rightarrow P(Succ\, n, g\, x)}{\forall n : nat.\ P(n,\ red[nat]\ Nat\{c := \tau;\ \$Zero := f,\ \$Succ := g\}\, n)}$$

$$\frac{f : \tau \qquad P(\$Nil, f)}{g : a \times \tau \rightarrow \tau \qquad xs : list(a) \qquad \forall x : a.\forall y : \tau. P(xs, y) \Rightarrow P(Cons(x, xs), g(x, y))}{\forall xs : list(a).\ P(xs,\ red[list]\ List(a)\{c := \tau;\ \$Nil := f,\ \$Cons := g\}\, xs)}$$

$$\frac{f : a \rightarrow \tau \qquad \forall x : a. P(Tip(x), f\, x)}{g : a \times \tau \rightarrow \tau \quad u, v : tree(a) \quad \forall y, z : \tau. P(u, y) \wedge P(v, z) \Rightarrow P(Fork(u, v), g(y, z))}{\forall y' : tree(a).\ P(y',\ red[tree]\ Tree(a)\{c := \tau;\ \$Tip := f,\ \$Fork := g\}\, y')}$$

5 Multi-sorted signatures

It is often convenient to define a signature that has several sorts. ADL supports the declaration of signatures comprised of a finite set of sorts. The analogy in terms of ML-style data types would be a mutually recursive set of data type declarations.

For example, the types that correspond to the syntactic phyla[7] of a context-free grammar may be mutually recursive. When expressed as a signature, each phylum of an abstract grammar corresponds to a distinct sort. The signature of each sort is comprised of operators that correspond to the productions for a single phylum.

Example 5. Given an abstract grammar specifying arithmetic terms, we shall derive a variety of signature algebras that have the structure of these terms. Suppose the grammar of terms is stratified into additive and multiplicative terms. We define two phyla to represent these term classes,

phyla: *TERM, FACTOR*

The productions for each of these phyla consist of syntactic operators that take as arguments, terms from the indicated phyla:

Additive operators—*TERM*	
Add	*TERM, TERM*
Neg	*TERM*
Prim	*FACTOR*

Multiplicative operators–*FACTOR*	
Mpy	*FACTOR, FACTOR*
Subterm	*TERM*
Ident	*string*

---

[7] A phylum is a grouping in the top level of a classification hierarchy. By syntactic phyla we refer to a classification of terms of an abstract grammar.

The following two-sorted signature is derived from the grammar of terms by substituting a carrier for each phylum and substituting algebraic operator symbols for the syntactic operators. The primitive syntactic phylum, *string*, is generalized to an indeterminate parameter of the signature.

```
signature TermGram(a){type c, d;
                term/c = {$Add of c*c,
                          $Neg of c,
                          $Prim of d}
              factor/d = {$Mpy of d*d,
                            $Subterm of c,
                            $Ident of a}}
```

The operators *$Prim* and *$Subterm* coerce a value from a representation in one carrier to a representation in the other.
□

The catamorphism combinator accommodates multi-sorted signatures by using the sort names as an index set. It takes a sort and a sort-indexed signature-algebra specification as its arguments and it yields a structure function for the specified sort in the induced structure algebra. The sort given as the first argument of the combinator determines the typing of the combinator expression. For example, the two catamorphism forms of *TermGram* algebras have typings:

$$red[term] \; TermGram(a)\{c := \tau_1, \; d := \tau_2; \; term\{\ldots\} \; factor\{\ldots\}\} : term(a) \to \tau_1$$
$$red[factor] \; TermGram(a)\{c := \tau_1, \; d := \tau_2; \; term\{\ldots\} \; factor\{\ldots\}\} : factor(a) \to \tau_2$$

Example 6. To define an arithmetic calculator for terms, where the parameter *a* is specialized to the type *string*, apply *red[term]* to the following *TermGram*-algebra:

```
TermGram(string){c := int; d := int;
    term{$Add := (+), $Neg := (~), $Prim := id},
    factor{$Mpy := (*), $Subterm := id, $Ident := string_to_int}}
```

where **string_to_int** is a conversion function that has not been defined here.
□

Exercise 8. Printing the image of a term

Define a function to translate values of type *term(string)* into strings of **ascii** characters, with infix operator symbols for *$Add* and *$Mpy*, using an implicit operator precedence and with the minimum number of parentheses necessary to avoid incorrect associations. Assume that *$Add* and *$Mpy* are associative operators.

6 Functions that are not catamorphisms

While catamorphisms are elegant constructions, they do not solve all problems of programming. There are many instances of functions whose control is determined by a structure that is not visible in the domain. For instance, a recursive-descent parser is contolled by the structure of a grammar for the language being parsed. That structure is discovered in the list of input tokens by the action of the parser; it is not manifest. A divide-and-conquer algorithm such as Quicksort is controlled by the structure of a binary tree, yet it is applied to lists, not to trees. Such examples abound.

In this section we shall examine functions that can be defined as morphisms of a structure algebra, although they are not catamorphisms. We shall introduce a combinator to construct such functions from a t-algebra specification and a new constituent, a partition relation that analyzes its argument to find a t-algebraic structure. The ability to construct such functions has led us to the idea that algebraic structures are sufficiently general to write most programs of interest. Recall the diagram in terms of which a t-algebra morphism is defined:

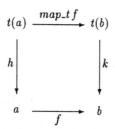

The catamorphisms illustrated in the diagram are h, k, $map\_t\,f$ and the diagonal composition (upper left to lower right) arrow. The homomorphism condition of the diagonal composition is the commutation condition for the diagram,

$$f \circ h = k \circ map\_t\,f \qquad (1)$$

Each catamorphism can be expressed in terms of the combinator red and the appropriate t-algebra. However, f in the diagram above is also a t-algebra morphism, and under certain conditions, it may be expressed in terms of a combinator.

Suppose there were a function $p : a \to t(a)$ such that $p \circ h = id_{t(a)}$. This function need not be a right inverse for h on a, but it is a right inverse when restricted to a domain that is the h-image of $t(a)$,

$$h \circ p = id_{a \downarrow h} \qquad (2)$$

where the notation $a \downarrow h$ means the set a restricted to the codomain of h. Post-composing both sides of (1) with p and making use of (2) gives an equation that is satisfied when the domain of f is restricted to the h-image of $t(a)$:

$$f = k \circ map\_t\,f \circ p \qquad (3)$$

This equation suggests a way to realize f as the composition of a catamorphism with a function that analyzes the domain $a \downarrow h$.

Let $E\$t$ be a sum-of-products bifunctor and let $t(a)$ be a fixed point of the functor with respect to its second argument. Let $E\#t$ be the functor obtained by binding the second argument of $E\$t$ at its fixed point, i.e.

$$E\#t(a) = E\$t(a, t(a))$$

Notice that $e\#t$ is a sum-of-products functor. Thus $E\#t(a) = \text{in}_t^{-1} t(a)$ represents an explicit, one-level unfolding of the structure of terms in the set $t(a)$. Now suppose there is a function $p' : a \to E\#t(a)$ that is isomorphic to a left inverse for h as described in the preceding paragraph. With this nomenclature, an isomorphic relative of equation (3) given above can be summarized in the diagram below, which reveals the structure more clearly:

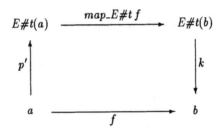

The function p' can be expressed by a case analysis on the data constructors of its argument.

Following the suggestion outlined above, ADL provides a combinator with which to construct morphisms whose domains are t-algebras that are not free. We call this combinator hom. It takes three parameters;

1. the sort of the structure function that is to be mapped,
2. the structure algebra in the codomain of the morphism and
3. a partition relation that is "inverse" to the structure function of its domain algebra.

The partition relation is typically expressed as a conditional or a *case* expression that tests a value of type a to reveal the structure of the algebra. The codomain of the partition relation is $E\$t(a, c)$, where c is an unspecified type parameter. This object has the structure of a disjoint union of the domain types of the set of operators of a signature Σ, to which the sort t belongs.

Thus we write $hom[t] \, T\{b; k\} \, p$, where $k : t(b) \to b$ and $p : a \to E\#t(a)$. Here is an example that illustrates a t-algebra morphism constructed using hom.

Example 7. : Calculate the largest power of 2 that factors a given positive integer. Consider the *Nat*-signature algebra defined by:

$$Nat \, \{c := int; \, \$Zero := m, \, \$Succ := \lambda n \, 2 \times n\}$$

in which the free variable m represents an odd, positive integer. The carrier of this algebra is the set consisting of $\{m, 2m, 4m, 8m, \ldots\}$.

From this algebra, we construct a catamorphism that defines a structure function for a *nat*-structure algebra,

$$h \; : \; nat \rightarrow int$$
$$h = red[nat]\, Nat\{c := int;\; \$Zero := m,\; \$Succ := \lambda n\, 2 \times n\}$$

To invert this structure function (up to isormorphism of types), construct a function that recovers the natural number giving the power of two that multiplies m in forming any element of the carrier. Let

$$p = \lambda n\, \textbf{if } n \bmod 2 <> 0 \textbf{ then } \$Zero$$
$$\textbf{else } \$Succ(n \textbf{ div } 2)$$

Then p is given the typing

$$p \; : \; int \rightarrow E\$nat\, int$$

where $E\$nat$ is a derived, unsaturated type constructor. This type constructor belongs to no declared signature, thus cannot form the type of the domain or codomain of explicitly defined functions.

Notice that in the above definition, the operators of the *Nat*-algebra, $\$Zero$ and $\$Succ$, assume specific types by binding the carrier as *int*. These occurrences of $\$Zero$ and $\$Succ$ represent the operators of the particular *Nat*-algebra that structures the *int*-typed domain of the *Nat*-algebra morphism being defined.

To complete the solution of the problem, we need to specify a *Nat*-algebra that yields an integer representation of a power of 2. To give an exponent of two, we can use the algebra in which a natural number is represented as a positive integer. This algebra was used to specify the function *ntoi* in an earlier example. (Notice that the bindings given to the operator symbols $\$Zero$ and $\$Succ$ in this algebra are not the same as the bindings presumed in in the definition of p above. In general, they need not even have the same typings.) Thus, we get an algorithm expressed in ADL as:

```
pwr_2 = hom[nat] Nat{c := int; $Zero := 0, $Succ := \n 1+n} p
```

The equation satisfied by *pwr_2* is:

$$pwr\_2\, n = \textbf{if } n \bmod 2 \neq 0 \textbf{ then } 0$$
$$\textbf{else } 1 + pwr\_2\,(n \textbf{ div } 2)$$

To obtain an explicit representation of the factor that is a power of 2, the *Nat*-algebra can be modified to calculate that factor. This solution is

```
pwr_2' = hom[nat] Nat{c := int; $Zero := 1, $Succ := \n 2*n} p
```

Example 8. : Integer factorial. The factorial function was used in Example 4 to illustrate primitive recursion, but the type of the factorial defined there was *nat* → *int*, rather than the more usual type, *int* → *int*. The reason for the abnormal typing was to be able to define *fact* by a *nat*-catamorphism. Now that the combinator *hom* is available, that is no longer a requirement.

We can define a partition relation to recover the natural number structure of a non-negative integer and define the factorial function that is expected:

```
fact = snd o hom[nat] Nat{c := int * int;
                     $Zero := (0,1),
                     $Succ := \(m,n) (m+1, (m+1) * n)}
              (\n if n=0 then $Zero else $Succ(n))
```

Example 9. : Filtering a list

The function *filter p* : *list(a)* → *list(a)* reconstructs from a list given as its argument, a list of the subsequence of its elements that satisfy the predicate function $p : a$ → *bool*. This function could be directly constructed in terms of *list*-algebra catamorphisms. Instead, we propose an algebraic variety to represent the two cases that occur in filtering—an element of the list is either to be included or omitted.

```
signature Slist(a){type c;
               slist/c={$Nomore, $Include of a*c, $Omit of c}}
```

A definition of *filter p* can be given as a morphism of *slist*-algebras:

```
filter p = hom[slist] Slist(a){c := list(a);
                          $Nomore = Nil,
                          $Include = Cons,
                          $Omit = id}
               (\xs case xs of
                    Nil => $Nomore
                  | Cons(x,xs') => if p x then $Include(x,xs')
                                          else $Omit xs'
                end)
```

□

Example 10. : Quicksort

The Quicksort algorithm requires two functions, one that partitions a list,

$$part : int → list(int) → list(int) \times list(int)$$

and another that sorts a list,

$$sort : list(int) → list(int)$$

The function *part* can be defined as a *list*-catamorphism:

```
part a = red[list] List(int){c := list(int)*list(int);
                $Nil := (Nil,Nil),
                $Cons := \(b,(xs,ys)) if b<a then (Cons(b,xs),ys)
                                      else (xs,Cons(b,ys))}
```

The function *sort*, however, uses a divide-and-conquer algorithm with the structure of a binary tree. It can be expressed as a morphism of the following algebraic variety:

```
signature Btree(a){type c; btree/c = {$Emptytree, $Node of c*a*c}};

sort = hom[btree] Btree(int){c := list(int);
                $Emptytree := Nil,
                $Node := \(xs,x,ys) append xs (Cons(x,ys))}
            (\xs case xs of
                Nil => $Emptytree
              | Cons(x,xs') =>
                        let (ys,ys') = part x xs'
                        in $Node(ys,x,ys')
            end)
```

Notice that although the algorithm is controlled by a tree traversal, the sort function has type $list(int) \rightarrow list(int)$. There is no data structure corresponding to the data type $btree(list(int))$. This is a "treeless" tree traversal.

Exercise 9. Another form of bush

Given the following signature declaration,

signature *Bush'(a)*{type c; *bush'/c* = {*$Leaf'* of a, *$Branch'* of $nat*(nat \rightarrow c)$}}

construct a morphism of type $bush(a) \rightarrow bush'(a)$ that is invertible. (Construct its inverse, too.)

Exercise 10. Splitting a list more efficiently
The function *splitat* of Exercise 7, when defined by primitive recursion does more computation than is necessary. It recursively evaluates the function on the tail of a list that has already been successfully split. Redefine *splitat* in terms of *hom[list]*.

Exercise 11. Factors of a positive integer
Give a function, *factors*, that takes a positive integer N and a list of positive integers M to a list of the factors of N by M, and which satisfies the following equations:

$factors\ N\ Nil = Cons(N, Nil)$
$factors\ N\ (Cons(m, M')) =$
$\qquad\qquad Cons(m, factors\ (N/m)\ (Cons(m, M')))$ if m divides N
$factors\ N\ (Cons(m, M')) = factors\ N\ M'$ otherwise

Prove that your solution satisfies the equations.

6.1 Termination conditions for morphisms of non-free algebras

Two kinds of proof obligations are necessary to establish properties of ADL programs: (1) termination proofs establish the existence of total functions specified by combinator expressions and are associated with type correctness, and (2) verification of hypothetical propositions about type-correct (and therefore terminating) programs. We shall first address the proposition of termination of functions defined with the combinator *hom*, then take up the structure of proof rules to verify other propositions.

Recall that for a construction $hom[t]T(a)\{b; k\}p$ to be a t-algebra morphism, the partition relation p must be a left inverse of the structure function of a t-algebra, (τ, h). Since we do not know h in general, we require a condition that can be applied directly to p itself. Note that if p is a left inverse, it is also a right inverse to h on some subset of the elements of type a. Thus a well-typed partition relation is *formally* correct in the sense that it constructs results by well-typed application of operators of the signature T. However, its application to an arbitrary element $x : \tau$ might fail to be defined; x may not be in the codomain of h. The additional requirement can be stated in terms of a total ordering on a that must be furnished to discharge the proof obligation.

The following definition characterizes termination in terms of a predicate that can be associated with a partition relation. The idea is that elements of a domain satisfy the predicate only if they are elements of a well-founded ordering that is compatible with the partition relation. Then if the domain of the partition relation, p, is restricted to the set characterized by the predicate, termination of an expression $hom[s]\,A\,p$ will be assured by further establishing that $red[s]\,A$ is a catamorphism.

Definition 12. Let Σ be a parameterized signature, $\Sigma(a) = (S, \{\Sigma_s \mid s \in S\})$, where for each $s \in S$, $\Sigma_s = (c_s, [1..n_s], \{\ldots \kappa_i \text{ of } \sigma_{i1} \times \cdots \times \sigma_{im_i} \ldots\})$. Let $\{\tau_s \mid s \in S\}$ be a set of types (sets) and let D be a disjoint union of this set. That is, each element of D is a pair, (s, x), where $s \in S$ and $x \in \tau_s$. Let P be a predicate over D.

Suppose that $(\prec) \subseteq D \times D$ is a well-founded ordering on the set $\{x : D \mid P(x)\}$. We say that a sort-respecting function $p : D \to \bigcup_{s \in S} t(\tau_s)$ calculates a Σ-*inductive partition* of the sets $\{x : \tau_s \mid P(s, x), s \in S\}$ if

$$\forall x : \tau_s.\, P(s, x) \Rightarrow$$
$$\forall \kappa_i \in T.\, p(s, x) = \kappa_i(y_1, \ldots, y_{m_i}) \Rightarrow$$
$$\forall j \in 1..m_i \begin{cases} (t, y_j) \prec (s, x) & \text{if } \sigma_{ij} = c_t \\ \forall z : \tau_t.\, z \, elt\_s'\, y_j \Rightarrow (t, z) \prec (s, x) & \text{if } \sigma_{ij} = s'(c_t) \end{cases}$$

where $t \in S$ and s' is an unsaturated sort, $s' \notin S$, and elt_s' is an infix notation for the two-place predicate defined by cases:

$$z = x \Rightarrow z \, elt\_s'\, \kappa_i'(y_1, \ldots, x, \ldots, y_{m_i})$$
$$z \, elt\_s'\, y \Rightarrow z \, elt\_s'\, \kappa_i'(y_1, \ldots, y, \ldots, y_{m_i})$$

for all operators κ_i' in $\Sigma_{s'}$.
□

In the definition above, the predicate P characterizes a domain on which the morphism is well-defined. Any properties of the morphism deduced with the proof rules of the t-algebra will be valid only for points of the domain that satisfy P. When the signature is single-sorted, it is unnecessary to introduce a disjoint union of domain types and to pair each domain element with a sort to distinguish the set from which it is drawn.

In Example 7, a suitable subset and its well-ordering is the positive integers with the natural order, $(<)$. The partition relation p induces a Nat-inductive partition on this subset. In Example 8 the same ordering is used but the set is the non-negative integers.

For Example 9, a suitable ordering on $list(int)$ is $xs \prec ys$ iff $length\ xs < length\ ys$. With this ordering, the predicate "universally true" induces an $Slist$-inductive partition on $list(a)$.

For Example 10, the same ordering of lists by their length is compatible with the partition function used in the definition of $sort$, and induces a $Tree$-inductive partition of $list(int)$. The verification condition for termination of the function $sort$ of this example becomes

$$(xs = Cons(x, xs')) \wedge (part\ x\ xs' = (ys, ys')) \Rightarrow (ys \prec xs) \wedge (ys' \prec xs)$$

6.2 Proof rules for morphisms of non-free algebras

In Section 4.3, inductive proof rules for catamorphisms of signature algebras were discussed. Although the structure of morphisms of non-free algebras, defined with the combinator hom, involves the added complexity of a partition relation, these morphisms also have inductive proof rules that can be calculated from signatures. We shall not present an algorithm for calculating the rules, as this is complicated and technical, but shall illustrate the principle with examples for several of the varieties used as examples in the preceding sections.

Generalized Nat-induction The conclusion of a generalized induction rule is expressed in terms of a two-place predicate that relates the argument and the result of a morphism of a Nat-structure algebra. The argument variable is universally quantified over a domain characterized by a termination predicate for the morphism. The termination predicate is an external condition for logical validity of the rule—it is not expressed in the rule itself. While this may be regarded as a flaw in the logic from a foundational point of view, it has an advantage from a pragmatic viewpoint. Separating the proof obligations to show termination from those required to prove other properties affords flexibility in constructing deductions, and allows deductions to be modular.

The hypotheses of a generalized induction account for analysis of the argument of a morphism by the partition relation, as well as for construction of the result by the operators of the specified signature algebra. From the signature Nat, we derive the rule:

$$z : \tau_2$$
$$\forall x : \tau_1. \, (p \, x = \$Zero) \Rightarrow P(x, z)$$

$$\dfrac{g : \tau_1 \to \tau_1 \qquad s : \tau_2 \to \tau_2 \\ \forall x : \tau_1. \forall y : \tau_2. \, (p \, x = \$Succ(g \, x)) \Rightarrow P(g \, x, y) \Rightarrow P(x, s \, y)}{\forall (x : \tau_1 \mid T(x)). \, P(x, hom[nat] \, Nat\{c := \tau_2; \ \$Zero := z, \ \$Succ := s\} \, p \, x)}$$

in which T is a predicate characterizing a domain on which the morphism is defined (i.e. its computation terminates).

It is instructive to apply this rule to a simple example. Let

$$\tau_1 = int \qquad \tau_2 = int$$
$$p \, x = \textbf{if } x = 0 \textbf{ then } \$Zero \textbf{ else } \$Succ(x - 1)$$
$$z = 0$$
$$s = \lambda n \, n + 1$$

and interpret P as equality on integers. The termination predicate for this example must restrict the domain to the non-negative integers. The hypotheses of the generalized induction become

$$\forall x : int. \, (x = 0) \Rightarrow P(x, 0)$$
$$\forall x : int \, \forall y : int. \, (x \neq 0) \Rightarrow P(x - 1, y) \Rightarrow P(x, y + 1)$$

These conditions are satisfied if P is interpreted as equality in the algebra of integer arithmetic.

Generalized *List*-induction A rule for generalized *list*-induction follows the form of that for the signature *Nat*, but with an additional analysis function. When a domain element is partioned to match the template of the domain of the operator *$Cons*, a value of the list element type is produced, as well as a value of the type of the original domain. The rule is:

$$n : \tau_2$$
$$\forall x : \tau_1. \, (p \, x = \$Nil) \Rightarrow P(x, n)$$

$$\dfrac{g_1 : \tau_1 \to a \qquad g_2 : \tau_1 \to \tau_1 \qquad f : \tau_2 \to \tau_2 \\ \forall x : \tau_1. \forall y : \tau_2. \, (p \, x = \$Cons(g_1 \, x, g_2 \, x)) \Rightarrow P(g_2 \, x, y) \Rightarrow P(x, f(g_1 \, x, y))}{\forall (x : \tau_1 \mid T(x)). \, P(x, hom[list] \, List\{c := \tau_2; \ \$Nil := n, \ \$Cons := f\} \, p \, x)}$$

Exercise 13. State the generalized induction rule for the signature *Btree* given in Example 10. Use this rule to derive conditions that must be satisfied by the function *part*, as defined in the example, to verify that a result calculated by the function *sort* is a sorted permutation of a list given as its argument.

7 The ADL type system

Logical properties of structure-algebra morphisms can be derived by inductive proof rules. Each such property can be formalized as a predicate over a set. ADL types can be interpreted as sets, although as we have seen in Section 6.2, proof obligations arise in verifying that a syntactically legal term is semantically well-founded.

Since types are sets, the restriction of a type by a predicate defines a set that may be considered to be a subtype of a structurally defined type. We call such subtypes *domain types*. An ADL domain type is expressed with set comprehension notation, as for instance, $\{x : \tau \mid P(x)\}$, where τ is a structural type expression and P stands for a predicate. In the type system of ADL, domain types occur only on the left of the arrow type constructor. Domain types express restrictions in the types of functions.

Syntax of type expressions

typ	::= identifier	primitive types
	| typ $*$ typ	products
	| domtyp $\rightarrow$ typ	function types
	| identifier(typ [, typ])	datatypes

domtyp ::= typ

          \| {identifier : typ | Identifier(expr)}   restricted domain types

---

The Hindley-Milner type system is based upon a structural notion of type and is not expressive enough to distinguish among domain types of ADL. Thus, its type-checking algorithm is not powerful enough to ensure that a syntactically well-formed ADL expression is meaningful, but requires additional evidence as proof. Nevertheless, we find it useful to employ the Hindley-Milner type system as an approximation to ADL's type system. The Hindley-Milner type-inference algorithm is an abstract interpretation of ADL that approximates its type assignments. Whenever Hindley-Milner type checking asserts that an expression is badly typed, it cannot be well-typed in the ADL type system. When Hindley-Milner type inference assigns a type to an expression, that typing will be structurally compatible with any ADL typing of the expression.

For example, given a pair of ADL functions with typings $f : \{x : \tau_1 \mid P(x)\} \rightarrow \tau_2$ and $g : \{x : \tau_2 \mid Q(x)\} \rightarrow \tau_3$, a structural (Hindley-Milner) typing approximates the ADL typings as $f : \tau_1 \rightarrow \tau_2$ and $g : \tau_2 \rightarrow \tau_3$. It will judge their composition to be well-typed, with typing $g \circ f : \tau_1 \rightarrow \tau_3$. An ADL typing of the composition has the form $g \circ f : \{x : \tau_1 \mid R(x)\} \rightarrow \tau_3$, and it carries a proof obligation to show that $R(x) \Rightarrow P(x) \wedge Q(f\,x)$. To discharge the proof obligation requires a logical deduction based upon algebraic properties of the function f.

To determine whether a function application is well-typed is too complex for Hindley-Milner typing alone. To know that $f\,a$ is well-typed, one must furnish evidence that $P(a)$ holds. Function types in ADL may involve restrictions expressed in domain types, and these restrictions might include arbitrary arithmetic formulas. For this reason, ADL does not have principal types, nor unicity of types. Domain restrictions are needed to express the termination conditions for combinators that express morphisms of non-initial structure algebras.

Domain restrictions must be expressible with first-order predicates. As a practical consequence, this implies that a domain restriction cannot assert a property of the result of applying a function-typed variable. For example, given a function $f : \{x : \tau_1 \mid P\,x\} \to \tau_2$, we can express the typing of a function that composes its argument on the left of f as

$$\lambda g.\, g \circ f \; : \; (\tau_2 \to \tau_3) \to \{x : \tau_1 \mid P\,x\} \to \tau_3$$

The type of the formal parameter, g, is only structural; it requires no domain predicate to be imposed.

If, however, we attempt to type the function $\lambda h.\, f \circ h$ that composes its argument on the right of f, we find that it is impossible to do so with only a first-order domain predicate. The predicate must express that every point in the codomain of h satisfies the domain predicate P, and to express this restriction requires quantification over all points in the domain of h. The only kind of typing restriction that can be expressed of a function-typed variable is a domain restriction. Nevertheless, this can be quite powerful.

Given a proof that a function-typed variable satisfies a domain restriction at every occurrence in an expression, the variable may be abstracted from the expression and given a domain-restricted function type. For instance, suppose that in an expression $\lambda x.\, e : \tau_1 \to \tau_3$, the free variable f occurs in an applicative position and satisfies a structural typing $f : \tau_1 \to \tau_2$. If in addition, at every occurrence of f in e (each of the form $f\,e'$) one can show that $P\,x \Rightarrow R\,e'$, then the abstraction can be given a typing $\lambda f.\, \lambda x.\, e \; : \; (\{y : \tau_1 \mid R\,y\} \to \tau_2) \to \{x : \tau_1 \mid P\,x\} \to \tau_3$.

An application of a function $h \; : \; (\{y : \tau_1 \mid R\,y\} \to \tau_2) \to \tau_3$ to an argument $e' \; : \; \{y : \tau_1 \mid Q\,y\} \to \tau_2$ is judged to be well-typed if there is a proof that $\forall y : \tau_1.\, R\,y \Rightarrow Q\,y$. This condition ensures that any expression to which h's formal parameter might be applied will satisfy the restriction imposed by the domain predicate in the typing of e'.

8 Monads

Monads are mathematical structures that have found considerable use in programming. Knowing that a program is to be interpreted in a particular monad allows us to "take for granted" the structure of the monad without explicit notation. Common examples are monads of exceptions (we take for granted that exceptions are propagated, and shall only express unexceptional terms) and monads of state transformers (we take for granted that state is threaded through computations in a deterministic order).

Monads have been found useful in computer science relatively recently [Mog91, Wad90]. Monads have been used to explain control constructs such as exceptions [Spi90] and advocated as a basis for formulating reusable modules [Wad92].

A variety of monads cannot be specified with the sorted signature declarations available in ADL. Instead, there is a predefined variety, whose signature is

signature $Monad(a)\{$ **type** $M(a);$
$monad/M(a) = \{\$Unit$ of $a,$ $\$Mult$ of $M(M(a))\}\}$

In a monad specification, $M(a)$ can be substituted by a type expression in which the parameter a has only positive occurrences (with respect to the arrow constructor). Positive occurrences are defined in terms of predicates Pos_a and Neg_a, defined as follows:

$$Pos_a(a) = true$$
$$Pos_a(b) = true \text{ if } b \neq a$$
$$Pos_a(X * Y) = Pos_a(X) \wedge Pos_a(Y)$$
$$Pos_a(X + Y) = Pos_a(X) \wedge Pos_a(Y)$$
$$Pos_a(X \rightarrow Y) = Neg_a(X) \wedge Pos_a(Y)$$

$$Neg_a(a) = false$$
$$Neg_a(b) = true \text{ if } b \neq a$$
$$Neg_a(X * Y) = Neg_a(X) \wedge Neg_a(Y)$$
$$Neg_a(X + Y) = Neg_a(X) \wedge Neg_a(Y)$$
$$Neg_a(X \rightarrow Y) = Pos_a(X) \wedge Neg_a(Y)$$

where a and b denote atomic type expressions. For example, the following propositions are satisfied, according to the definition:

$$Neg_a(a \rightarrow b)$$
$$Pos_b(a \rightarrow b)$$
$$Pos_a((a \rightarrow b) \rightarrow a)$$

Neither Pos_a nor Neg_a holds of the expression $a \rightarrow a$, which contains both positive and negative occurrences.

A monad is not a free algebra; there are three equations to be satisfied:

$$mult_a^M \circ unit_{M(a)}^M = id_{M(a)} \tag{4}$$

$$mult_a^M \circ (map\_M \ unit_a^M) = id_{M(a)} \tag{5}$$

$$mult_a^M \circ mult_{M(a)}^M = mult_a^M \circ (map\_M \ mult_a^M) \tag{6}$$

There is another function that can be defined in terms of the components of a monad and it is often more convenient to use this function than $mult^M$. This is the natural extension,

$$ext^M : (a \rightarrow M(b)) \rightarrow M(a) \rightarrow M(b)$$

$$ext^M \ f =_{def} mult^M \circ map\_M \ f$$

It is easy to prove a number of identities for *ext*;

$$ext^M\ mult_a^M = id_{M(a)} \tag{7}$$

$$ext^M\ f \circ unit^M = f \tag{8}$$

$$ext^M\ (ext^M\ f \circ g) = ext^M\ f \circ ext^M\ g \tag{9}$$

$$ext^M\ id_{M(a)} = mult_a^M \tag{10}$$

$$ext^M\ (unit^M \circ f) = map\_M\ f \tag{11}$$

A function of the form $unit^M \circ f : a \to M(b)$ or $ext^M\ (unit^M \circ f) : M(a) \to M(b)$ is said to be *proper* for the monad, whereas a function with codomain $M(b)$ that cannot be composed in this way is said to be non-proper.

To extend a function whose domain type is a product, i.e. $f : a \times b \to M(c)$, the monad M must be accompanied by a *product distribution* function, $dist^M : M(a) \times M(b) \to M(a \times b)$. This allows us to form an extension $(ext^M\ f) \circ dist^M : M(a) \times M(b) \to M(c)$ that can be composed with a pair of functions in the monad.

Generally, there is no unique way to form a product distribution function. We require only a single coherence property of such a function, namely that

$$dist^M \circ (unit_a^M \times unit_b^M) = unit_{a \times b}^M \tag{12}$$

8.1 Monad declarations in ADL

Monads can be declared in a declaration format resembling an algebra specification for the monad algebra,

```
monad { name [(type expr)] (type id) = type expr;
        $Unit := expression,
        $Mult := expression}
```

The square brackets are meta-syntax to indicate that the first instance of *type expr.* is optional, depending upon the particular monad. A monad declaration is valid iff the *type expr* to the right of the equals contains only positive occurrences of the *type id* and the monad equations are satisfied. An ADL translator can check the first of these conditions but will not always be able to verify the equations automatically.

8.2 Some useful monads

There are several structures that will be recognized as features of programming languages and which correspond to monads.

Exceptions

$$\textbf{monad } \{Ex_i(\alpha) = \textbf{free}\{\$Just \text{ of } \alpha, \$exc_i\};$$
$$\$Unit := \lambda x \; Just(x),$$
$$\$Mult := \lambda t \; \textbf{case } t \textbf{ is}$$
$$Just(x) => x$$
$$\mid i => \$exc_i$$
$$\textbf{end}\}$$

where i ranges over identifiers, excluding "*Just*".

The keyword **free** is not a proper sort, but designates the carrier of the free algebra of the bracketed signature it precedes. This declaration defines an indexed family of monads that corresponds to a family of exceptions, indexed by identifiers.

For example, the type expression $Ex_{Nothing}(term(int))$ expresses a type whose proper values are in the datatype $term(int)$ and whose improper value is the identifier *Nothing*, an exception name. Since the type constructor of this particular monad has structure similar to that of an inductive signature, values in the monad can be analyzed by a **case** expression.

A function $f : a \to b$ that has been defined without thought of exceptions is "lifted" into a monad Ex_i by its map function, $map\_Ex_i \; f$. The lifted function, which is proper for the monad, propagates the exception i but neither raises this exception nor handles it. In ADL we designate a proper function of a given monad by the use of heavy brackets, $\llbracket f \rrbracket$.

A distribution function for the monad of exceptions that evaluates a pair from left to right is:

$$dist^{Ex_i}(x, y) = \textbf{case } x \textbf{ of}$$
$$Just(x') => \textbf{case } y \textbf{ of}$$
$$Just(y') => Just(x', y')$$
$$\mid i => i$$
$$\textbf{end}$$
$$\mid i => i$$
$$\textbf{end}$$

Alternatively, one could define a distribution function that would evaluate pairs from right to left.

State transformers The monad of state transformers affords a generic, functional specification of the use of state in computing. State can be of any type and the operations on a state component are not specified in the monad.

$$\textbf{monad } \{St[\beta](\alpha) = \beta \to \alpha \times \beta;$$
$$\$Unit := \lambda a \; \lambda b \,(a, b),$$
$$\$Mult := \lambda t \; \lambda b \, \textbf{let } (s, b') = t \, b \textbf{ in } s \, b'\}$$

The product distribution function specifies how a state component is threaded through the computation of a pair. Here is a left-to-right product distribution function:

$$dist^{St} = \lambda(s_1, s_2)\,\lambda b\, \mathbf{let}\ (a_1, b') = s_1\, b\ \mathbf{in}$$
$$\mathbf{let}\ (a_2, b'') = s_2\, b'\ \mathbf{in}$$
$$((a_1, a_2), b'')$$

State readers An important special case of state transformers occurs when a computation does not change the state. For such a case, we can use a simpler monad, the monad of state readers.

$$\mathbf{monad}\ \{Sr[\beta](\alpha) = \beta \to \alpha;$$
$$\$Unit := \lambda a\, \lambda b\, a,$$
$$\$Mult := \lambda t\, \lambda b\, t\, b\}$$

The product distribution function for state readers is unbiased as to order of evaluation of the components of a pair.

$$dist^{Sr} := \lambda(s_1, s_2)\,\lambda b\, (s_1\, b, s_2\, b)$$

The continuation-passing monad The well-known CPS transformation used in compiler design is another instance of a familiar monad.

$$\mathbf{monad}\ \{CPS(\alpha) = (\alpha \to \beta) \to \beta;$$
$$\$Unit := \lambda a\, \lambda c\, c\, a,$$
$$\$Mult := \lambda t\, \lambda c\, t\, (\lambda s\, s\, c)\}$$

in which β is a free variable ranging over types.

The CPS monad can be given a left-to-right product distribution function:

$$dist^{CPS} := \lambda(t_1, t_2)\,\lambda c\, t_1\, (\lambda x\, t_2\, (\lambda y\, c\, (x, y)))$$

It could also be given a right-to-left product distribution, but this is not usually done. The choice is completely arbitrary.

8.3 Interpreting an algebra in a monad

When the carrier of an algebra has the structure of a monad, we say that the algebra is interpreted in the monad. This allows us to specify functions that carry the monad operations "for free". For instance, if a Nat-algebra is interpreted in a monad $M(a)$, and $s : a \to a$, we can make the binding $\$Succ := \| s \|$ to designate $map^M\, s\ :\ M(a) \to M(a)$. If $x : a$ we could write $\| x \|$ to designate $unit^M\, x$. Interpreting an algebra in a monad affords a notational shortcut to specifying functions that are proper for the monad.

Example 11. Labeling a tree

Given the signature *Btree* of binary trees with labeled nodes, which was specified in Example 10, give an algorithm to copy a tree, replacing the labels on its nodes by a depth-first enumeration with integers beginning with 1 at the root.

If our task was simply to copy a binary tree, the *Btree* algebra that induces the identity catamorphism would satisfy our requirements. This algebra is given by

$$Btree(a)\{c := btree(a); \ \$Emptytree := Emptytree, \ \$Node := Node\}$$

However, an algorithm to enumerate the nodes of a binary tree must carry a count of the number of nodes already enumerated, as it traverses the tree. This count can be provided as an integer-typed state component in a *Btree*-catamorphism. To incorporate a state component, we shall re-interpret the identity algebra in a state-transformer monad, and modify it so that the label on each node of a tree is replaced by an integer value calculated from the state. The carrier of the algebra becomes $St[int](btree(int))$. The operator $\$Emptytree$ will be bound to the injection of a data constructor, *Emptytree*, into the monad algebra by an application of *unit_St*. We designate this standard operation by enclosing the data constructor in fat brackets.

The reinterpretation of $\$Node$ requires slightly more thought. Of its three arguments, the first and third will be state transformers and hence must be applied to state components to produce state-value pairs. To achieve a left-to-right enumeration, the subtree arguments of $\$Node(l, x, r)$ should act on a state component n as

$$\textbf{let } (l', n_1) = l\,n \textbf{ in}$$
$$\textbf{let } (r', n_2) = r\,n_1 \textbf{ in}$$
$$((l', r'), n_2)$$

which is just the meaning of the expression $dist\_St\,(l, r)\,n$.

The label in $Node(l, x, r)$ is to be replaced by the current value of the enumeration count and the state passed on must be incremented by one. With this in mind, the desired binding for $\$Node$ is

$$F = \lambda(l, x, r)\,\lambda n \frac{\textbf{let } ((l', r'), n') = dist\_St\,(l, r)\,(n+1)}{\textbf{in } (Node(l', n, r'),\ n')}$$

and the enumeration function, specified in ADL, is

$$c := St[int](btree(int));$$
$$\lambda t\ fst\,(red[btree]\ Btree(int)\{\$Emptytree := \|Emptytree\|,$$
$$\$Node := F\}\,t\,1)$$

□

Exercise 14. Breaking lines of text

Given a list of character strings representing individual words, form a list of strings representing lines of text with a length bound L given as a parameter. Fit as many words onto a line as it will contain without overflow. Separate adjacent words on a line by blank spaces counting one character. If a word is encountered whose length exceeds the bound, return an exception named *long_word*.

Exercise 15. Justifying lines of text

Extend the solution of Exercise 11 to justify text on both right and left margins by inserting additional blanks between words on a line to secure spacing as nearly even as possible on each line. If only one word fits on a line, left justify it.

9 Algebras of lambda terms

As an example of the style of high-level programming with algebras, we shall specify an interpreter for a lambda calculus. The strategy will be to first interpret the abstract syntax of lambda terms in a related abstract syntax for deBruijn terms, then to define substitution on deBruijn terms and produce an interpretation in which the *app* operator realizes β-reduction.

To begin, we shall need to declare algebra classes for lambda terms and deBruijn terms.

```
signature Term(a,b){type c;
            term/c = {$Var of b, $Abs of a*c, $App of c*c}}

signature Term'(a){type d;
            term'/d = {$Var' of a, $Abs' of d, $App' of d*d}}
```

The first translation is a catamorphism of *term*-sorted terms. An environment is needed to keep track of the bindings of identifiers. The interpretation of a term is then a function from environment to deBruijn term. We observe that this is the type of a state reader monad, which allows us to refer to the interpretation of the data constructor *App'* as it is lifted into the monad as a proper morphism.

```
dB = red[term] Term(string){c := Sr[list(string)](term'(int));
                $Var := \x \e Var'(depth x e),
                $Abs := \(x,t) \e Abs'(t(Cons(x,e)))
                $App := [|App'|]}
```

where the function *depth* counts the number of elements in the environment that precede x. In ADL, a function such as *depth* is not specified with recursion, but as a morphism of an appropriate algebra. For search of a list, we prefer not to use induction on the *list*-algebra itself, for that would traverse the entire list even if a successful outcome of the search had already been found. Instead, we construct a *nat*-morphism with the *hom* combinator. This allows the specification of a partition function that terminates the search when a matching element is found.

```
depth x = hom[nat] Nat{c := int;
                $Zero := 0,
                $Succ := add 1}
            (\xs case xs is
                Nil => $Zero
                | Cons(x',y) => if x=x' then $Zero
                                        else $Succ y
                end)
```

Next, we define substitution in deBruijn terms. The function *subst* takes three arguments: the term to be substituted, the term into which the substitution is to be made, and the binding height (number of surrounding abstraction constructors) of the second term. We shall formulate *subst N* as a *term'*-algebra morphism into an algebra whose carrier is an *int* state reader monad. This allows us to refer to the interpretation of data constructors in the monad.

```
subst N = red[term'] Term'{d := Sr[int](term'(int));
                    $Var' := \n \ct if n < ct then Var'(n)
                                    else if n = ct
                                         then lift N ct 0
                                         else Var'(n-1),
                    $Abs' := [|Abs'|] oo add 1,
                    $App' := [|App'|] o dist_Sr}
```

```
dist_Sr = \(f,g) \s (f s, g s)
```

In the definition above, we have made use of a convenient notational extension that extends function composition to curried functions. The meaning of $\underbrace{\circ \cdots \circ}_{n}$

is $\circ^n$, where $n \geq 1$ and

$$f \circ^1 g = f \circ g$$
$$f \circ^{n+1} g = \lambda x\, f\, x \circ^n g$$

Thus $f \circ\circ g = \lambda x\, \lambda y\, f\, x\, (g\, y)$ and $f \circ\circ\circ g = \lambda x\, \lambda y\, \lambda z\, f\, x\, y\, (g\, z)$.

The subordinate function *lift* has the task of modifying the deBruijn indices within the substituted term to compensate for the binding height of the context into which each substitution is made. Indices within N that correspond to local bindings are unchanged. Indices that correspond to bindings in the term's environment must be incremented by the binding height of the context. Thus there are two integer state components given as arguments of *lift*. The first represents the binding height of the context into which a substitution is made, and the second represents the height of local bindings within a subterm of N.

```
lift = red[term'] Term'{d := Sr[int](Sr[int](term'(int)));
                    $Var' := \n \ct \m if n < m then Var'(n)
                                       else Var'(n+ct),
                    $Abs' := [|Abs'|] ooo add 1,
                    $App' := [|App'|] o dist_Sr_Sr}
```

Contraction of a deBruijn term is accomplished by the following function:

```
contract = red[term'] Term'{d := term'(int);
                    $Var' := Var'
                    $Abs' := Abs'
                    $App' := \(M,N) case M is
                                    Var'(_) => App'(M,N)
```

```
| Abs'(y) => subst N y 0
| App'(_,_) => App'(M,N)}
```

The function *contract* performs a single contraction step but does not generally produce a term in weak head normal form, because the substitution of an abstraction for a variable in a term may produce new redexes. To weak-head-normalize a deBruijn term, the contraction step must be iterated along the normal-order spine of a term [Pey87]. An iterative control construct could be programmed in the coalgebraic part of ADL, although that topic is outside the scope of this chapter. However, we note that to verify that an iteration was well defined in ADL, one would be required to furnish a proof of its termination. For the example at hand, no such proof is possible, for termination of the iteration would imply normalizability of terms of an untyped lambda calculus, which is impossible in general.

10 Further work

In this chapter we have tried to convince the reader that there are compelling advantages to using the algebraic structure of functional programs in an explicit way. The advantages include better understanding of a program's control structure and the availability of explicit, detailed induction rules for reasoning about each structure that is used. Monads integrate naturally with algebras, providing explicit structure to the carrier type.

We have told only half the story, however. In the other half, there is an interesting type system for algebraic programs. Algebras also provide units of modularity for composing programs at a larger granularity. And there are dual structures, the so-called coalgebras, that lead to equally interesting families of control structures, related more naturally to iteration than to recursion.

Another untold benefit of algebraic program construction is the opportunity it presents to use powerful program transformation techniques. When the underlying control structure is manifest, less costly program analysis is needed to determine when transformation strategies may apply. Many transformations are in fact, simply directed instances of theorems provable by parametricity [SF93]. There are many opportunities that have not yet been exploited.

Acknowledgements
We would like to thank our colleagues, Jeff Bell, Jim Hook, Tim Sheard and Lisa Walton who have served as guinea-pigs in programming experiments with ADL and have delivered valuable criticism and valued encouragement. We have also benefited from stimulating discussions with Erik Meijer and John Launchbury.

A Syntax of ADL

The syntax $foo^{\{,\}*}$ means *foo* may be repeated zero or more times, with a ,
in between each instance. The $+$ is similar to $*$, but the item may be repeated
one or more times, and $++$ indicates *two* or more times. The angle brackets $\langle\ \rangle$
indicate optional items.

A.1 Base syntax

The non-literal terminals are *id* (identifiers) and *const* (special constants such as
integers and strings).

$$
\begin{array}{lll}
decl & ::= & \textbf{signature}\ id\ \langle(id^{\{,\}+})\rangle\{\ tvars\ ;\ sortsig^+\ \} \\
& & \textbf{cosignature}\ id\ \langle(id^{\{,\}+})\rangle\{\ tvars\ ;\ cosortsig^+\ \} \\
& & \textbf{val}\ valbind \\
& & \textbf{prefix}\ int\ id^+ \\
& & \textbf{infix left}\ int\ id^+ \\
& & \textbf{infix right}\ int\ id^+ \\[4pt]
tvars & ::= & \textbf{type}\ id^{\{,\}+} \\[4pt]
sortsig & ::= & id_{sort}\ /id_{carrier} = \{\ opdecl^{\{,\}+}\ \} \\[4pt]
opdecl & ::= & id \\
& & id\ \textbf{of}\ type \\[4pt]
cosortsig & ::= & id_{sort}\ /id_{carrier} = \{\ coopdecl^{\{,\}+}\ \} \\[4pt]
coopdecl & ::= & id\ :\ type \\[4pt]
type & ::= & id\ \langle(type^{\{,\}+})\rangle \\
& & type^{\{*\}++} \\
& & type_1\ \text{->}\ type_2 \\
& & (\ type\ ) \\
valbind & ::= & pat = expr \\[4pt]
pat & ::= & apat \\
& & id\ \textbf{as}\ pat
\end{array}
$$

$$apat \quad ::= \quad \_$$
$$id$$
$$(\; pat^{\{,\}*} \;)$$

$$rulepat ::= \quad \_$$
$$id$$
$$const$$
$$id \; pat$$
$$id \; \textbf{as} \; pat$$
$$(\; pat^{\{,\}*} \;)$$

$$expr \quad ::= \quad aexpr$$
$$appl$$
$$\backslash apat \; expr$$
$$\textbf{let} \; valbind \; \textbf{in} \; expr$$

$$appl \quad ::= \quad expr \; expr$$
$$expr \; id \; expr$$

$$aexpr \quad ::= \quad id$$
$$\$id$$
$$const$$
$$\texttt{map}[id]$$
$$\texttt{red}[id] \; algebra$$
$$\texttt{hom}[id] \; algebra$$
$$\texttt{gen}[id] \; algebra$$
$$\texttt{cohom}[id] \; algebra$$
$$\textbf{case} \; expr \; \textbf{of} \; rule^{\{-\}+} \; \textbf{end}$$
$$(\; expr^{\{,\}*} \;)$$

$$rule \quad ::= \quad rulepat \; \texttt{=>} \; expr$$

$$algebra ::= \langle id \langle (id_{typaram}^{\{,\}+}) \rangle \rangle \{ \; tybind \; ; \; opbind^{\{,\}+} \; \}$$
$$\langle id \langle (id_{typaram}^{\{,\}+}) \rangle \rangle \{ \; tybind^{\{,\}+} \; ; \; subalg^+ \; \}$$

$$tybind \quad ::= \quad id \; \texttt{=} \; type$$

$$subalg \quad ::= \quad id \{ \; opbind^{\{,\}+} \; \}$$

$$opbind \quad ::= \quad id \; \texttt{:=} \; expr$$

Notes:

- In *type*, * binds more tightly than ->, and -> associates to the right.
- In *sortsig*, $id_{carrier}$ must be declared in *tvars*, and each $id_{carrier}$ may only appear in one *sortsig*.
- The ambiguity of application in patterns and expressions is resolved by a precedence parser. Each *id* has an associated fixity (prefix or infix), precedence and, for infix, associativity. Precedence is a positive integer, with higher value indicating higher precedence (binds more tightly). These are assigned by a **prefix** or **infix** declaration. The default is prefix with precedence 9.
- No *id* may appear twice in a *pat* and no *id* may be that of a free algebra operator. In a *rulepat*, no *id* may appear twice, unless it is a free algebra operator.
- In an *algebra*, the *ids* bound in *tybinds* must correspond to the *tvars* declared in the algebra signature.

A.2 Derived forms

$id\ apat_1 \ldots apat_n = expr \qquad \Rightarrow id = \backslash apat_1 \ldots \backslash apat_n\ expr$

$\text{let } valbind^{\{\text{and}\}++} \text{ in } expr \qquad \Rightarrow \text{let } valbind^{\{\text{in let}\}++} \text{ in } expr$

$\text{if } expr_1 \text{ then } expr_2 \text{ else } expr_3 \Rightarrow \text{case } expr_1 \text{ of true => } expr_2 \mid \text{false => } expr_3$

References

[B⁺94] Jeffrey Bell et al. Software design for reliability and reuse: A proof-of-concept demonstration. In *TRI-Ada '94 Proceedings*, pages 396–404. ACM, November 1994.

[Bir86] Richard S. Bird. An introduction to the theory of lists. In M. Broy, editor, *Logic of Programming and Calculi of Discrete Design*, volume 36 of *NATO Series F*. Springer-Verlag, 1986.

[Bir88] Richard S. Bird. Lectures on constructive functional programming. In M. Broy, editor, *Constructive Methods in Computing Science*, volume 52 of *NATO Series F*. Springer-Verlag, 1988.

[CS92] Robin Cockett and Dwight Spencer. Strong categorical datatypes. In R. A. G. Seely, editor, *International Meeting on Category Theory, 1991*. AMS, 1992.

[Fok92] Maarten M. Fokkinga. *Law and Order in Algorithmics*. PhD thesis, University of Twente, Twente, The Netherlands, February 1992.

[Gog80] Joseph A. Goguen. How to prove inductive hypotheses without induction. In W. Bibel and R. Kowalski, editors, *Proc. 5th Conference on Automated Deduction*, volume 87 of *Lecture Notes in Computer Science*, pages 356–373. Springer-Verlag, 1980.

[GT79] Joseph A. Goguen and Joseph Tardo. An introduction to)BJ: A language for writing and testing software specifications. In *Proc. of Conference on Specification of Reliable Software*, pages 170–189. IEEE Press, 1979.

[GTW78] Joseph A. Goguen, James Thatcher, and Eric Wagner. An initial algebra approach to the specification, classification, correctness and implementation of abstract data types. In Raymond Yeh, editor, *Current Trends in Programming Methodology IV*, pages 80–149. Prentice-Hall, 1978.

[GW88] Joseph A. Goguen and Timothy Winkler. Introducing OBJ3. Technical Report SRI-CSL-88-9, SRI International, August 1988.

[Hag87] T. Hagino. *A Categorical Programming Language*. PhD thesis, University of Edinburgh, 1987.

[KB⁺95] Richard B. Kieburtz, Francoise Bellegarde, Jef Bell James Hook, Jeffrey Lewis, Dina Oliva, Tim Sheard Lisa Walton, and Tong Zhou. Calculating software generators from solution specifications. In *TAPSOFT'95*, volume 915 of *Lecture Notes in Computer Science*, pages 546–560. Springer-Verlag, 1995.

[KL94] Richard B. Kieburtz and Jeffrey Lewis. Algebraic Design Language— Preliminary definition. Technical report, Pacific Software Research Center, Oregon Graduate Institute of Science & Technology, January 1994.

[Mac71] Saunders MacLane. *Categories for the Working Mathematician*. Springer-Verlag, 1971.

[Mal90] Grant Malcolm. *Algebraic Data Types and Program Transformation*. PhD thesis, University of Groningen, 1990.

[Mee86] Lambert Meertens. Algorithmics—towards programming as a mathematical activity. In *Proc. of the CWI Symbposium on Mathematics and Computer Science*, pages 289–334. North-Holland, 1986.

[MFP91] Erik Meijer, Maarten Fokkinga, and Ross Paterson. Functional programming with bananas, lenses, envelopes and barbed wire. In *Proc. of 5th ACM Conf. on Functional Programming Languages and Computer Architecture*, volume 523 of *Lecture Notes in Computer Science*, pages 124–144. Springer-Verlag, August 1991.

[Mog91] Eugenio Moggi. Notions of computations and monads. *Information and Computation*, 93(1):55–92, July 1991.

[Pey87] Simon Peyton Jones. *The Implementation of Functional Programming Languages*. Prentice-Hall, 1987.

[SF93] Tim Sheard and Leonidas Fegaras. A fold for all seasons. In *Proceedings of the conference on Functional Programming and Computer Architecture*, Copenhagen, June 1993.

[Spi90] Mike Spivey. A functional theory of exceptions. *Science of Computer Programming*, 14:25–42, 1990.

[Wad90] Philip Wadler. Comprehending monads. In *Proc. 1990 ACM Conference on Lisp and Functional Programming*, pages 61–78, 1990.

[Wad92] Philip Wadler. The essence of functional programming. In *Conference Record of the Nineteenth Annual ACM Symposium on Principles of Programming Languages*, pages 1–14. ACM Press, January 1992.

Graph Algorithms with a Functional Flavour

John Launchbury

Oregon Graduate Institute
jl@cse.ogi.edu

Abstract. Graph algorithms have long been a challenge to program in a pure functional language. Previous attempts have either tended to be unreadable, or have failed to achieve standard asymptotic complexity measures. We explore a number of graph search algorithms in which we achieve standard complexities, while significantly improving upon traditional imperative presentations. In particular, we construct the algorithms from reusable components, so providing a greater level of modularity than is typical elsewhere. Furthermore, we provide examples of correctness proofs which are quite different from traditional proofs, largely because they are not based upon reasoning about the dynamic *process* of graph traversal, but rather reason about a static *value*.

1 Introduction

Graph algorithms do not have a particularly auspicious history in purely functional languages. It has not been at all clear how to express such algorithms without using side effects to achieve efficiency, and lazy languages by their nature have had to prohibit side-effects. So, for example, many texts provide implementations of search algorithms which are quadratic in the size of the graph (see [Pau91], [Hol91], or [Har93]), compared with the standard linear implementations given for imperative languages (see [Man89], or [CLR90]). What is more, very little seems to have been gained by expressing such algorithms functionally—the presentation is sometimes *worse* than the traditional imperative presentation!

In these notes we will explore various aspects of expressing graph algorithms functionally with one overriding concern—we refuse to give ground on asymptotic complexity. The algorithms we present have identical asymptotic complexity to the standard presentation.

Our emphasis is on depth-first search algorithms. The importance of depth-first search for graph algorithms was established twenty years ago by Tarjan and Hopcroft [Tar72, HT73] in their seminal work. They demonstrated how depth-first search could be used to construct a variety of efficient graph algorithms. In practice, this is done by embedding code-fragments necessary for a particular algorithm into a depth-first search procedure skeleton in order to compute relevant information while the search proceeds. While this is quite elegant it has a number of drawbacks. Firstly, the depth-first search code becomes intertwined with the code for the particular algorithm, resulting in monolithic programs. The code is not built by re-use, and there is no separation between logically distinct phases. Secondly, in order to reason about such depth-first search algorithms we have to reason about a dynamic *process*—what happens and when—and such reasoning is complex.

Occasionally, the *depth-first forest* is introduced in order to provide a *static* value to aid reasoning. We build on this idea. If having an explicit depth-first forest is good for reasoning then, so long as the overheads are not unacceptable, it is good for programming. In this paper, we present a wide variety of depth-first search algorithms as combinations of standard components, passing explicit intermediate values from one to the other. The result is quite different from traditional presentations of these algorithms, and we obtain a greater degree of modularity than is usually seen.

Of course, the idea of splitting algorithms into many separate phases connected by intermediate data structures is not new. To some extent it occurs in all programming paradigms, and is especially common in functional languages. What is new, however, is applying the idea to graph algorithms. The challenge is to find a sufficiently flexible intermediate value which allows a wide variety of algorithms to be expressed in terms of it.

In our work there is one place where we do need to use destructive update in order to gain the same complexity (within a constant factor) as imperative graph algorithms. We make use of recent advances in lazy functional languages which use monads to provide updatable state, as implemented within the Glasgow Haskell compiler. The compiler provides extensions to the language Haskell providing updatable arrays, and allows these state-based actions to be encapsulated so that their external behaviour is purely functional (a summary of these extensions is given in the Appendix). Consequently we obtain linear algorithms and yet retain the ability to perform purely functional reasoning on all but one fixed and reusable component.

Most of the methods in this paper apply equally to strict and lazy languages. The exception is in the case when depth-first search is being used for a true *search* rather than for a complete *traversal* of the graph. In this case, the co-routining behaviour of lazy evaluation allows the search to abort early without needing to add additional mechanisms like exceptions.

2 Representing graphs

There are at least three rather distinct ways of representing (directed) graphs in a language like Haskell. For example:

1. as an element of an algebraic datatype containing cycles constructed using laziness;
2. as an (immutable) array of edges; or
3. as explicit mutable nodes in the heap (working within the state monad).

The first of these is the most "functional" in its flavour, but suffers from two serious defects. First, cyclic structures are isomorphic to their unrolled counterparts[1], but graphs are not isomorphic to their unrolling. Each node of the graph could be tagged explicitly, of course. But this still leaves us with the second defect: cyclic structures are hard to preserve and modify. Hughes proposed lazy memo functions as a means of preserving cycles [Hug85], but these have not been adopted into any of the major

---

[1] In languages like Scheme which have object identity this is not the case, but this is at the (semantic) cost of tagging each cons-cell with a unique identifier.

lazy languages. And without them, something as simple as mapping a function over the graph will cause it to unfurl. In addition within any cycle, the graph structure is monolithic: any change to a part of it will force the whole cycle to be rebuilt. An exception to this may occur if the compiler manages to deduce some sort of linearity property which allows update-in-place, but then the efficiency of the algorithm may become a very delicate matter.

The second representation method lies somewhere on the border between "functional" and "imperative". Using arrays to store edge lists is a common practice in the imperative world, but the only array facility used is constant-time read-access (if the graph is static), so purely functional arrays are appropriate. This is the method we will focus on.

The final method is highly imperative, and is most appropriate when it is vital to be able to change the graph in-place (i.e. when a local modification should be globally visible).

2.1 Adjacency Lists

We represent a graph as a standard Haskell immutable array, indexed by vertices, where each component of the array is a list of those vertices reachable along a single edge. This gives constant time access (but not update—these arrays may be shared arbitrarily). By using an indexed structure we are able to be explicit about the sharing that occurs in the graph. In addition, this structure is linear in the size of the graph, that is, the sum of the number of vertices and the number of edges.

We can use the same mechanism to represent *undirected* graphs as well, simply by ensuring that we have edges in both directions. An undirected graph is a symmetric directed graph. We could also represent *multi-edged* graphs by a simple extension, but will not consider them here.

Graphs, therefore, may be thought of as a table indexed by vertices.

```
type Table a = Array Vertex a
type Graph   = Table [Vertex]
```

The type Vertex may be any type belonging to the Haskell index class Ix, which includes Int, Char, tuples of indices, and more. For now we will assume:

```
type Vertex = Char
```

We will make the simplifying assumption that the vertices of a graph are contiguous in the type (e.g. numbers 0 to 59, or characters 'a' to 'z', etc.). If not then a hash function will need to be introduced to map the actual names into a contiguous block. Because we assume contiguity, we commonly represent the list of vertices by a pair of end-points:

```
type Bounds = (Vertex,Vertex)
```

Haskell arrays come with indexing (!) and the functions indices (returning a list of the indices) and bounds (returning a pair of the least and greatest indices).

To further manipulate tables (including graphs) we define a generic function mapT which applies its function argument to every table index/entry pair, and builds a new table.

```
mapT :: (Vertex -> a -> b) -> Table a -> Table b
mapT f t = array (bounds t) [(v, f v (t!v)) | v<-indices t]
```

The Haskell function `array` takes low and high bounds and a list of index/value pairs, and builds the corresponding array in linear time.

Finally, it is sometimes useful to translate an ordered list of vertices into a lookup table which shows the position of the vertex in the list. For this we could use the function `tabulate`:

```
tabulate :: Bounds -> [Vertex] -> Table Int
tabulate bnds vs = array bnds (zip vs [1..])
```

which zips the vertices together with the positive integers $1, 2, 3, \ldots$, and (in linear time) builds an array of these numbers, indexed by the vertices.

2.2 Edges

Sometimes it is convenient to extract a list of edges from the graph. An edge is a pair of vertices. But, because some graphs are sparse, we also need to know separately what the vertices are.

```
type VE = (Bounds,[(Vertex,Vertex)])

edges :: Graph -> VE
edges g = (bounds g, [(v,w) | v <- indices g, w <- g!v])
```

To build up a graph from a list of edges we define a function `buildG`.

```
buildG :: VE -> Graph
buildG (bnds,es) = accumArray snoc [] bnds es
  where snoc xs x = x:xs
```

Like `array` the Haskell function `accumArray` builds an array from a list of index/value pairs, with the difference that `accumArray` accepts possibly many values for each indexed location, which are combined using the function provided as `accumArray`'s first argument. Here we simply build lists of all the values associated with each index. Again, constructing the array takes linear time with respect to the length of the adjacency list. So in linear time, we can convert a graph defined in terms of edges to a graph represented by a vertex table.

2.3 Simple operations

Following edges

To find the immediate successors to a vertex v in a graph g we simply compute `g!v`, which returns a list of vertices.

Transposing a graph

Combining the functions edges and buildG gives us a way to reverse all the edges in a graph giving the *transpose* of the graph:

```
transposeG :: Graph -> Graph
transposeG g = buildG (vs, [(w,v) | (v,w) <- es])
  where (vs,es) = edges g
```

We extract the edges from the original graph, reverse their direction, and rebuild a graph with the new edges.

OutDegree and InDegree

Using mapT we could define,

```
outdegree :: Graph -> Table Int
outdegree g = mapT numEdges g
  where  numEdges v ws = length ws
```

which builds a table containing the number of edges leaving each vertex.

Now by using transposeG we can immediately define an indegree table for vertices:

```
indegree :: Graph -> Table Int
indegree g = outdegree (transposeG g)
```

This example gives an early feel for the approach we develop in these notes. Rather than defining indegree from scratch by, for example, building an array incrementally as we traverse the graph, we simply reuse previously defined functions, combining them in a fresh way. The result is shorter and clearer, though potentially more expensive (an intermediate array is constructed).

There are two things to say about this additional cost. Firstly, the additional cost only introduces a constant factor into the complexity measure, so the essence of the algorithm is preserved. Secondly, recent work in the automatic removal of intermediate structures promises to come a long way to removing this problem. We will come back to this in Section 7.

3 Depth-First Search

The traditional view of depth-first search is as a *process* which may loosely be described as follows. Initially, all the vertices of the graph are deemed "unvisited", so we choose one and explore an edge leading to a new vertex. Now we start at this vertex and explore an edge leading to another new vertex. We continue in this fashion until we reach a vertex which has no edges leading to unvisited vertices. At this point we backtrack, and continue from the latest vertex which does lead to new unvisited vertices.

Eventually we will reach a point where every vertex reachable from the initial vertex has been visited. If there are any unvisited vertices left, we choose one and begin the search again, until finally every vertex has been visited once, and every edge has been examined.

In this paper we concentrate on depth first search as a specification for a *value* rather than on a process. The specified value is the *spanning forest* defined by a depth-first traversal of a graph, that is, a particular sub-graph of the original which, while it contains all the vertices, typically omits many of the edges.

The edges of the graph that are included in the spanning forest are (quite naturally) called *tree edges*. The omitted edges may be classified further with respect to the forest. Thus an edge in the graph which goes in the opposite direction to the tree edges is called a *back edge*. Conversely, a *forward edge* jumps more than one level from a vertex to one of its descendents (in the spanning forest). Finally, a *cross edge* is an edge which connects vertices *across* the forest—but always from right to left, there are no left-right cross edges. This standard classification is useful for thinking about a number of algorithms, and later we give an algorithm for classifying edges in this way.

3.1 Specification of depth-first search

As the approach to depth-first search algorithms which we explore in these notes is to manipulate the depth-first forest *explicitly*, the first step, therefore, is to construct the depth-first forest from a graph. To do this we need an appropriate definition of trees and forests.

A forest is a list of trees, and a tree is a node containing some value, together with a forest of sub-trees. Both trees and forests are polymorphic in the type of data they may contain.

```
data Tree a   = Node a (Forest a)
type Forest a = [Tree a]
```

A depth-first search of a graph takes a graph and an initial ordering of vertices. All graph vertices in the initial ordering will be in the returned forest.

```
dfs :: Graph -> [Vertex] -> Forest Vertex
```

This function is the pivot of these notes. For now we restrict ourselves to considering its properties, and will leave its Haskell implementation until Section 5.

Sometimes the initial ordering of vertices is not important. When this is the case we use the related function

```
dff :: Graph -> Forest Vertex
dff g = dfs g (indices g)
```

which arbitrarily uses the underlying order of indices as an initial vertex ordering.

3.2 Properties

What are the properties of depth-first forests? They can be completely characterised by the following two conditions.

(i) The depth-first forest of a graph is a spanning subgraph, that is, it has the same vertex set, but the edge set is a subset of the graph edge set.

(ii) The graph contains no left-right cross edges with respect to the forest.

Later on in the paper, we find it convenient to talk in terms of *paths* rather than single edges: a path being made up of zero or more edges joined end to end. We will write $v \longrightarrow w$ to mean that there is an edge from v to w; and $v \longrightarrow\!\!\!\!\!\rightarrow w$ to mean that there is a path of zero or more edges from v to w. It should be clear from the context which graph is being discussed.

The lack of left-right cross edges translates into paths. At the top level, it implies that there is no path from any vertex in one tree to any vertex in a tree that occurs later in the forest. Thus[2],

Lemma 1. *If* (ts++us=dff g), *then*

$$\forall v \in \text{ts} . \ \forall w \in \text{us} . \ \neg(v \longrightarrow\!\!\!\!\!\rightarrow w)$$

Deeper within each tree of the forest, there *can* be paths which traverse a tree from left to right, but the absence of any graph edges which cross the tree structure from left to right implies that the path has to follow the tree structure. That is:

Lemma 2. *If the tree* (Node x (ts++us)) *is a subtree occurring anywhere within* dff g, *then*

$$\forall v \in \text{ts} . \ \forall w \in \text{us} . \ v \longrightarrow\!\!\!\!\!\rightarrow w \Rightarrow v \longrightarrow\!\!\!\!\!\rightarrow x$$

So the only way to get from v to w is via (an ancestor of) x, the point at which the forests that contain v and w are combined (otherwise there would be a left-right cross edge). Thus there is also a path from v to x.

The last property we pick out focusses on dfs, and provides a relationship between the initial order, and the structure of the forest[3].

Lemma 3. *Let a and b be any two vertices. Write $\longrightarrow\!\!\!\!\!\rightarrow$ for paths in the graph* g, *and $\leq$ for the ordering induced by the list of vertices* vs. *Then*

$$\exists t \in \text{dfs g vs} . \ a \in t \wedge b \in t$$
$$\Leftrightarrow \exists c . \ c \longrightarrow\!\!\!\!\!\rightarrow a \wedge c \longrightarrow\!\!\!\!\!\rightarrow b \wedge (\forall d . \ d \longrightarrow\!\!\!\!\!\rightarrow a \vee d \longrightarrow\!\!\!\!\!\rightarrow b \Rightarrow c \leq d)$$

This Property says that:

$\Rightarrow$ given two vertices which occur within a single depth-first tree (taken from the forest), then there is a predecessor of both (with respect to $\longrightarrow\!\!\!\!\!\rightarrow$) which occurs earlier in vs than any other predecessor of either. (If this were not the case, then a and b would end up in different trees).

$\Leftarrow$ if the earliest predecessor of either a or b is a predecessor of them both, then they will end up in the same tree (rooted by this predecessor).

While these three properties are true of depth-first search spanning forests, but they are not complete. There are other useful properties not derivable from these.

---

[2] We use the notation ts++us to indicate any division of the list of trees in the forest, such that the order of the trees is preserved. Note that either ts or us could be empty. Also, we use $\in$ to indicate list membership and not purely for set membership.

[3] We further overload the $\in$ notation, to mean that both a and b occur as vertices within the tree t.

4 Depth-first search algorithms

Having specified depth-first search (at least partly) we turn to consider how it may be used.

Algorithm 1. Depth-first numbering

The first algorithm is straightforward. We wish to assign to each vertex a number which indicates where that vertex came in the search. A number of other algorithms make use of this *depth-first search number*, including the biconnected components algorithm that appears later, for example.

We can express depth-first ordering of a graph g most simply by flattening the depth-first forest in *preorder*. Preorder on trees and forests places ancestors before descendants and left subtrees before right subtrees[4]:

```
preorder :: Tree a -> [a]
preorder (Node a ts) = [a] ++ preorderF ts

preorderF :: Forest a -> [a]
preorderF ts = concat (map preorder ts)
```

Now obtaining a list of vertices in depth-first order is easy:

```
preOrd :: Graph -> [Vertex]
preOrd g = preorderF (dff g)
```

For many situations this is eactly what we want. However, it is sometimes useful to translate the ordered list into actual numbers. To obtain such a table of depth-first search numbers we can simply use the tabulate function from earlier:

```
preNums :: Graph -> Table Int
preNums g = tabulate (bounds g) (preOrd g)
```

Algorithm 2. Topological sorting

The dual to preorder is postorder, and unsurprisingly this turns out to be useful in its own right. Postorder places descendants before ancestors and left subtrees before right subtrees:

```
postorder :: Tree a -> [a]
postorder (Node a ts) = postorderF ts ++ [a]

postorderF :: Forest a -> [a]
postorderF ts = concat (map postorder ts)
```

So, like with preorder, we define,

---

[4] The use of repeated appends (++) caused by concat introduces an extra logarithmic factor here, but this is easily removed using standard transformations.

```
postOrd :: Graph -> [Vertex]
postOrd g = postorderF (dff g)
```

Again, using `tabulate` we could construct (in linear time) a table containing the post-order numbers of each of the vertices.

```
postNums :: Graph -> Table Int
postNums g = tabulate (bounds g) (postOrd g)
```

The absence of left-right cross edges in depth-first search forests leads to a pleasant property when any depth-first search forest is flattened in postorder. If there is a path from some vertex v to a vertex w later in the ordering, then there is also an even later vertex u (beyond w) which, like w is also reachable by a path from v. In addition, however, there is also a path in the other direction, going from u to v. We can make this precise as follows.

Definition 4. A linear ordering $\leq$ on vertices is a *post-ordering* with respect to a graph g exactly when,

$$v \leq w \wedge v \longrightarrow\!\!\!\!\rightarrow w \Rightarrow \exists u \,.\, v \longleftrightarrow\!\!\!\!\!\!\rightarrow u \wedge w \leq u$$

where $v \longleftrightarrow\!\!\!\!\!\!\rightarrow u$ means $v \longrightarrow\!\!\!\!\rightarrow u$ and $u \longrightarrow\!\!\!\!\rightarrow v$.

This property is so-named because post order flattening of depth first forests have this property.

Theorem 5. *The order in which the vertices appear in* postOrd g *is a post-ordering with respect to* g.

Proof. If v comes before w in a post order flattening of a forest, then either w is an ancestor of v, or w is to the right of v in the forest. In the first case, take w as u. For the second, note that as $v \longrightarrow\!\!\!\!\rightarrow w$, by Property 1, v and w cannot be in different trees of the forest. Then by Property 2, the lowest common ancestor of v and w will do.

We can apply all this to topological sorting. A topological sort is an arrangement of the vertices of a directed acyclic graph into a linear sequence $v_1, \ldots, v_n$ such that there are no edges (and hence no paths) from later (greater numbered) to earlier (lesser numbered) vertices.

This problem arises quite frequently, where the graph represents a set of tasks need to be scheduled, with the edges representing inter-task dependencies (an edge $v \longrightarrow w$ is interpreted as "task v must be done before task w"). The topological sort produces a linear ordering of the tasks in which none of the tasks depend on earlier tasks.

We define,

```
topSort :: Graph -> [Vertex]
topSort g = reverse (postOrd g)
```

Theorem 6. *If* g *is an acyclic graph, then* topSort g *produces a topological sorting of* g.

Proof. We write $\geq$ for the order of vertices from `topSort g`. Then $\leq$ is the reverse ordering, that is, the ordering given by `postOrd g`. Now, suppose that $v \geq w \land v \longrightarrow\!\!\!\!\!\rightarrow w$. Then,

$$w \geq v \land v \longrightarrow\!\!\!\!\!\rightarrow w \Rightarrow v \leq w \land v \longrightarrow\!\!\!\!\!\rightarrow w$$
$$\Rightarrow \exists u \, . \, v \longleftarrow\!\!\!\!\!\!\!\!\!\rightarrow u \land w \leq u$$
$$\Rightarrow v = w$$

as **g** is acyclic.

Algorithm 3. Connected components

Two vertices in an undirected graph are *connected* if there is a path from the one to the other. In a directed graph, two vertices are connected if they would be connected in the graph made by viewing each edge as undirected. Finally, with an undirected graph, each tree in the depth-first spanning forest will contain exactly those vertices which constitute a single component.

We can translate this directly into a program. The function `components` takes a graph and produces a forest, where each tree represents a connected component.

```
components :: Graph -> Forest Vertex
components g = dff (undirected g)
```

where a graph is made undirected by:

```
undirected :: Graph -> Graph
undirected g = buildG (vs, concat [[(v,w),(w,v)] | (v,w)<-es])
    where (vs,es) = edges g
```

The undirected graph we actually search may have duplicate edges, but this has no effect on the structure of the components. Furthermore, as the number of edges is at most doubled, neither is there any effect on the asymptotic complexity.

Algorithm 4. Strongly connected components

Two vertices in a directed graph are said to be *strongly connected* if each is reachable from the other. A strongly connected component is a maximal subgraph, where all the vertices are strongly connected with each other. The problem of determining strongly-connected components is well known to compiler writers as the dependency analysis problem—separating procedures/functions into mutually recursive groups. We implement the double depth-first search algorithm of Kosaraju (unpublished), and [Sha81].

```
scc :: Graph -> Forest Vertex
scc g = dfs (transposeG g) (reverse (postOrd g))
```

The vertices of a graph are ordered using `postOrd` (which, recall, includes a call to `dfs`). The reverse of this ordering is used as the initial vertex order for a depth-first traversal on the transpose of the graph. The result is a forest, where each tree constitutes a single strongly connected component.

The algorithm is simply stated, but its correctness is not at all obvious. However, it may be proved as follows.

Theorem 7. *Let a and b be any two vertices of $\mathbf{g}$. Then*

$$(\exists t \in \text{scc } \mathbf{g} . a \in t \wedge b \in t) \Leftrightarrow a \twoheadleftrightarrow b$$

Proof. The proof proceeds by calculation. We write $\mathbf{g}^T$ for the transpose of $\mathbf{g}$. Paths $v \twoheadrightarrow w$ in $\mathbf{g}$ will be paths $v \twoheadleftarrow w$ in $\mathbf{g}^T$. Further, let $\leq$ be the post-ordering defined by $\text{postOrd } \mathbf{g}$. Then its reversal induces the ordering $\geq$. Now,

$$\exists t \in \text{scc } \mathbf{g} . a \in t \wedge b \in t$$

$\Leftrightarrow$ {Definition of scc}

$$\exists t \in \text{dfs } \mathbf{g}^T \ (\text{reverse } (\text{postOrd } \mathbf{g})) . a, b \in t$$

$\Leftrightarrow$ {By Property 3}

$$\exists c . c \twoheadleftarrow a \wedge c \twoheadleftarrow b \wedge (\forall d . d \twoheadleftarrow a \vee d \twoheadleftarrow b \Rightarrow c \geq d)$$

$\Leftrightarrow \exists c . a \twoheadrightarrow c \wedge b \twoheadrightarrow c \wedge (\forall d . a \twoheadrightarrow d \vee b \twoheadrightarrow d \Rightarrow d \leq c)$

From here on we construct a loop of implications.

$$\exists c . a \twoheadrightarrow c \wedge b \twoheadrightarrow c \wedge (\forall d . a \twoheadrightarrow d \vee b \twoheadrightarrow d \Rightarrow d \leq c)$$

$\Rightarrow$ {Consider $d = a$ and $d = b$}

$$\exists c . a \twoheadrightarrow c \wedge a \leq c \wedge b \twoheadrightarrow c \wedge b \leq c \wedge (\forall d . a \twoheadrightarrow d \vee b \twoheadrightarrow d \Rightarrow d \leq c)$$

$\Rightarrow$ {$\leq$ is a post-ordering}

$$\exists c . (\exists e . a \twoheadleftrightarrow e \wedge c \leq e) \wedge$$
$$(\exists f . b \twoheadleftrightarrow f \wedge c \leq f) \wedge (\forall d . a \twoheadrightarrow d \vee b \twoheadrightarrow d \Rightarrow d \leq c)$$

$\Rightarrow$ {$e = c$ and $f = c$ using $(\forall d \ldots)$}

$$\exists c . a \twoheadleftrightarrow c \wedge b \twoheadleftrightarrow c$$

$\Rightarrow$ {Transitivity}

$$a \twoheadleftrightarrow b$$

which gives us one direction. But to complete the loop:

$$a \twoheadleftrightarrow b$$

$\Rightarrow$ {There is a latest vertex reachable from a or b}

$$a \twoheadleftrightarrow b \wedge \exists c . (a \twoheadrightarrow c \vee b \twoheadrightarrow c) \wedge (\forall d . a \twoheadrightarrow d \vee b \twoheadrightarrow d \Rightarrow d \leq c)$$

$\Rightarrow$ {Transitivity of $\twoheadrightarrow$}

$$\exists c . a \twoheadrightarrow c \wedge b \twoheadrightarrow c \wedge (\forall d . a \twoheadrightarrow d \vee b \twoheadrightarrow d \Rightarrow d \leq c)$$

as required, and so the theorem is proved.

To the best of our knowledge, this is the first calculational proof of this algorithm. Traditional proofs (see [CLR90], for example) typically take many pages of wordy argument. In contrast, because we are reusing an earlier algorithm, we are able to reuse its properties also, and so obtain a compact proof. Similarly, we believe that it is because we are using the depth-first search forest as the basis of our program that our proofs are simplified as they are proofs about *values* rather than about *processes*.

A minor variation on this algorithm is to reverse the roles of the original and transposed graphs:

```
scc' :: Graph -> Forest Vertex
scc' g = dfs g (reverse (postOrd (transposeG g)))
```

The advantage now is that not only does the result express the strongly connected components, but it is also a valid depth-first forest for the original graph (rather than for the transposed graph). This alternative works as the strongly connected components in a graph are the same as the strongly connected components in the transpose of the graph.

Algorithm 5. Classifying edges

We have already discussed the classification of graph edges with respect to a given depth-first search. Here we codify the idea by building subgraphs of the original containing all the same vertices, but only a particular kind of edge.

Tree edges are easiest, these are just the edges that appear explicitly in the spanning forest. The other edges may be distinguished by comparing preorder and/or postorder numbers of the vertices of an edge.

Only back edges go from lower postorder numbers to higher, whereas only cross edges go from higher to lower in *both* orderings. Forward edges, which are the composition of tree edges, cannot be distinguished from tree edges by this means—both tree edges and forward edges go from lower preorder numbers to higher (and conversely in postorder)—but as we can already determine which are tree edges there is no problem in extracting the remaining forward edges. The implementation of these principles is now immediate[5].

```
tree :: Bounds -> Forest Vertex -> Graph
tree bnds ts = buildG (bnds, concat (map flat ts))
  where  flat (Node v ts) = [(v,w) | Node w us <- ts]
                            ++ concat (map flat ts)

back :: Graph -> Table Int -> Graph
back g post = mapT select g
  where  select v ws = [ w | w <- ws, post!v<post!w ]

cross :: Graph -> Table Int -> Table Int -> Graph
cross g pre post = mapT select g
  where
    select v ws = [ w | w <- ws, post!v>post!w, pre!v>pre!w]

forward :: Graph -> Graph -> Table Int -> Graph
forward g tree pre = mapT select g
  where  select v ws = [ w | w <- ws, pre!v<pre!w] \\ tree!v
```

To classify an edge we generate the depth-first spanning forest, and use this to produce tables of preorder and postorder numbers. We then have all the information required to construct the appropriate subgraphs corresponding to the various sorts of edges.

---

[5] The use of (quadratic) list difference in forward is a minor infelicity—the second list is an ordered subsequence of the first so can be removed by a linear traversal of the first.

Algorithm 6. Finding reachable vertices

Finding all the vertices that are reachable from a single vertex v demonstrates that the dfs doesn't have to take all the vertices as its second argument. Commencing a search at v will construct a tree containing all of v's reachable vertices. We then flatten this with preorder to produce the desired list.

```
reachable :: Graph -> Vertex -> [Vertex]
reachable g v = preorderF (dfs g [v])
```

We could have used either flattening (pre- or post-order) but using preordering does not require any buffering of vertices—the vertices are placed in the list as soon as dfs places them in the spanning forest.

One application of this algorithm is to test for the existence of a path between two vertices:

```
path :: Graph -> Vertex -> Vertex -> Bool
path g v w = w 'elem' (reachable g v)
```

The elem test is lazy: it returns True as soon as a match is found. Thus the result of reachable is demanded lazily, and so only produced lazily. As soon as the required vertex is found the generation of the depth-first search forest ceases. Thus dfs implements a true *search* and not merely a complete *traversal*. To achieve this in a strict language like ML, for example, would require modifications to dfs to enable it to raise an exception at an appropriate time.

5 Implementing depth-first search

In order to translate a graph into a depth-first spanning tree we make use of a technique common in lazy functional programming: generate then prune. Given a graph and a list of vertices (a root set), we first generate a (potentially infinite) forest consisting of all the vertices and edges in the graph, and then prune this forest in order to remove repeats. The choice of pruning pattern determines whether the forest ends up being depth-first (traverse in a left-most, top-most fashion) or breadth-first (top-most, left-most), or perhaps some combination of the two.

5.1 Generating

We define a function generate which, given a graph g and a vertex v builds a tree rooted at v containing all the vertices in g reachable from v.

```
generate :: Graph -> Vertex -> Tree Vertex
generate g v = Node v (map (generate g) (g!v))
```

Unless g happens to be a tree anyway, the generated tree will contain repeated subtrees. Further, if g is cyclic, the generated tree will be infinite (though rational). Of course, as the tree is generated on demand, only a finite portion will be generated. The parts that prune discards will never be constructed.

5.2 Pruning

The goal of pruning the (infinite) forest is to discard subtrees whose roots have occurred previously. Thus we need to maintain a finite set of vertices (traditionally called "marks") of those vertices to be discarded. The set-operations we require are initialisation (the empty set), a membership test, and addition of an extra element. While we are prepared to spend linear time in generating the empty set (as it is only done once), it is essential that the other operations can be performed in constant time (otherwise we lose linearity of dfs).

The easiest way to achieve this is to make use of *state transformers*, and mimic the imperative technique of maintaining an array of booleans, indexed by the set elements. This is what we do. We provide an explanation of state-transformers in the Appendix, but as they have already been described in a number of papers [Mog89, Wad90, LPJ94], and already been implemented in more than one Haskell variant, we avoid cluttering the main text.

The implementation of vertex sets is easy:

```
type Set s = MutArr s Vertex Bool

mkEmpty :: Bounds -> ST s (Set s)
mkEmpty bnds = newArr bnds False

contains :: Set s -> Vertex -> ST s Bool
contains m v = readArr m v

include :: Set s -> Vertex -> ST s ()
include m v = writeArr m v True
```

A set is represented as a mutable array, indexed by vertices, containing booleans. To generate an empty finite set we allocate an appropriately sized array with every element initialised to False. Set membership, and augmenting the set with a new member are just done using array reading and writing.

Using these, we define prune as follows.

```
prune :: Bounds -> Forest Vertex -> Forest Vertex
prune bnds ts = runST (mkEmpty bnds 'thenST' \m ->
                       chop m ts)
```

The prune function begins by introducing a fresh state thread, then generates an empty set within that thread and calls the "procedure" chop. The final result of prune is the value generated by chop, the final state being discarded.

```
chop :: Set s -> Forest Vertex -> ST s (Forest Vertex)
chop m [] = returnST []
chop m (Node v ts : us)
  = contains m v 'thenST' \visited ->
    if visited then
      chop m us
    else
```

```
include m v          'thenST' \_  ->
chop m ts            'thenST' \as ->
chop m us            'thenST' \bs ->
returnST ((Node v as) : bs)
```

When chopping a list of trees, the root of the first is examined. If it has occurred before, the whole tree is discarded. If not, the vertex is added to the set represented by m, and two further calls to chop are made in sequence.

The first, namely, chop m ts, prunes the forest of descendants of v, adding all these in turn to the set of marked vertices. Once this is complete, the pruned sub-forest is named as, and the remainder of the original forest is chopped. The result of this is named bs, and a forest is constructed from the two.

All this is done lazily, on demand. The state combinators force the computation to follow a predetermined linear sequence, but exactly where in that sequence the computation is, is determined by external demand. Thus if only the top-most left-most vertex were demanded, then that is all that would be produced. On the other hand, if only the final tree of the forest is demanded, then because the set of marks is single-threaded, all the previous trees will be produced. However, this is demanded by the very nature of depth-first search anyway, so it is not as restrictive as it may at first seem.

At this point one may wonder whether any benefit has been gained by using a functional language. After all, the code looks fairly imperative. To some extent such a comment would be justified, but it is important to note that this is the *only* place in the development that destructive operations have to be used to gain efficiency. In addition, the complete encapsulation provided by runST guarantees that dfs has a purely functional exterior—the state cannot escape, not even to repeat calls of dfs. As far as the rest of the program is concerned, dfs *is purely functional*. Thus we have the flexibility to gain the best of both worlds: where destructive update is vital we use it, where it is not vital we can encapsulate it and use the full power of the lazy functional languages.

5.3 Depth-first Search

The components of generate and prune are combined to provide the definition of depth-first search.

```
dfs g vs = prune (bounds g) (map (generate g) vs)
```

The argument vs is a list of vertices, so the generate function is mapped across this (having been given the graph g). The resulting forest is pruned in a left-most top-most fashion by prune.

5.4 Is State Essential?

If paying an extra logarithmic factor is acceptable, then it is possible to dispense completely with the imperative features used in prune, and to use an implementation of sets based upon balanced trees, for example. Then set membership and adding elements to sets become logarithmic operations, hence the extra factor.

Even in this case, however, the set of marks has to be passed around *in a state-like manner*: when pruning a tree it is vital to know which vertices occurred in the earlier trees. Thus the code for dfs may remain entirely unchanged, and simply the definitions of the plumbing combinators and the set operations would be changed to reflect the alternative implementation.

Interestingly there is an alternative to using state *without losing asymptotic complexity*, and that is to use lazy arrays (as were implemented in LML for example, and discussed in the context of state transformers in Launchbury and Peyton Jones [LPJ]). In this case the dfs code would have to be altered, as the set membership test is combined in a single operation with adding a new element. That is, the test means "add a new element, and tell me if it was already in the set or not". Details of this technique have been exlpored by Johnsson [Joh].

6 Complexity Analysis

Models for complexity analysis of imperative languages have been established for many years, and verified with respect to reality across many implementations. Using these models it is possible to show that traditional implementations of the various depth-first search algorithms are linear in the size of the graph (that is, run in $O(V + E)$ time).

Corresponding models for lazy functional languages have not been developed to the same level, and where they have been developed there has not yet been the same extensive verification. Using such models (based on counting function calls) we believe our implementation of the depth-first search algorithms to be linear, but because these models have not been fully tested, we also ran empirical tests.

We took measurements on the strongly connected components algorithm, which uses two depth-first searches. Timings were taken on randomly generated graphs with up to 5000 vertices and edges, and we plotted the results. They are quite clear: the plotted points all lie on a plane, indicating the linearity of the algorithm.

As for constant factors, we currently estimate that we lose a factor of about 6 compared with coding in C by (a) using Haskell, and (b) using multi-pass algorithms. However, such figures are notoriously slippery, especially as the quality of the underlying implementation continues to improve.

7 Fusing the Phases

There has been a lot of recent work on program fusion (also known as deforestation) in the past few years. Most of this work finds its roots in Burstall and Darlington's fold/unfold transformations [DB76]. As the various depth-first search algorithms presented earlier are built component-wise in a multi-pass fashion, it makes sense to ask whether we can fuse the various phases. If we can, how similar are the results to traditional depth-first search algorithms?

7.1 Fusing the components of depth-first search

Even dfs itself was defined in two separate phases: generate an infinite (potentially) forest, and then prune it in a depth-first manner. The relevant code is as follows.

```
dfs g vs = prune (bounds g) (map (generate g) vs)

prune bnds ts = runST (mkEmpty bnds 'thenST' \m ->
                         chop m ts)

chop m [] = returnST []
chop m (Node v ts : us)
  = contains m v 'thenST' \visited ->
    if visited then
      chop m us
    else
      include m v         'thenST' \_  ->
      chop m ts           'thenST' \as ->
      chop m us           'thenST' \bs ->
      returnST ((Node v as) : bs)


generate g v = Node v (map (generate g) (g!v))
```

To fuse this into a single phase we first unfold the definition of prune.

```
dfs g vs = runST (mkEmpty (bounds g) 'thenST' \m ->
                    chop m (map (generate g) vs))
```

Secondly, we invent a new function snip which satisfies

```
snip m g vs = chop m (map (generate g) vs)
```

Now using fold/unfold steps we can transform this as follows (starting with a case analysis on the list argument):

```
snip m g [] = chop m (map (generate g) [])
            = chop m []
            = returnST []
```

and

```
snip m g (v:vs)
  = chop m (map (generate g) (v:vs))

  = chop m (Node v (map (generate g) (g!v))
                        : map (generate g) vs)

  = contains m v 'thenST' \visited ->
    if visited then
      chop m (map (generate g) vs)
    else
      include m v                          'thenST' \_  ->
      chop m (map (generate g) (g!v))      'thenST' \as ->
      chop m (map (generate g) vs)         'thenST' \bs ->
      returnST ((Node v as) : bs)
```

```
      = contains m v  'thenST' \visited ->
        if visited then
          snip m g vs
        else
          include m v        'thenST' \_  ->
          snip m g (g!v)     'thenST' \as ->
          snip m g vs        'thenST' \bs ->
          returnST ((Node v as) : bs)
```

Collecting all the pieces together we have the new definitions:

```
dfs g vs = runST (mkEmpty (bounds g) 'thenST' \m ->
                    snip m g vs)

snip m g [] = returnST []
snip m g (v:vs)
  = contains m v  'thenST' \visited ->
    if visited then
      snip m g vs
    else
      include m v        'thenST' \_  ->
      snip m g (g!v)     'thenST' \as ->
      snip m g vs        'thenST' \bs ->
      returnST ((Node v as) : bs)
```

This is much more like the traditional coding. Which of the versions is better? It depends what is wanted. Factorising the definition into components promises to make proofs about depth-first search itself easier, but having the two components fused is likely to be (marginally) more efficient, and does not rely of laziness. This latter point is important if these techniques are to be used in a strict language.

7.2 Moving Operations Across State Boundaries

In the previous section, we successfully moved a purely functional operation (map (generate g vs)) into the scope of a state thread simply by unfolding definitions. It was so easy because it was an *input* to the state operation that was being affected.

When we want to manipulate the *output* of a state thread we have to call on a little theory. To take a program of the form f (runST m) and move the f inside the state-thread, we use the following rule (from parametricity):

```
f (runST m) = runST (st f m)
```

where st is the function-part of the ST functor. That is

```
st f m = \s -> let (a,s')=m s in (f a,s')
```

Perhaps more convenient, however is to give an axiomatization with respect to thenST and returnST, which goes as follows.

```
st f (m 'thenST' (\v -> n)) = m 'thenST' (\v -> st f n)
st f (returnST a) = returnST (f a)
```

7.3 Topological sort

We take topological sort as an example. It was defined as a depth-first search followed by a flattening of the tree and a reversal of the list. Taking the definition and expanding out the definition of postOrd and dff gives:

```
topSort g = reverse (postorderF (dfs g (indices g)))

dfs g vs = runST (mkEmpty (bounds g) 'thenST' \m ->
                    snip m g vs)

snip m g [] = returnST []
snip m g (v:vs)
  = contains m v  'thenST' \visited ->
    if visited then
      snip m g vs
    else
      include m v       'thenST' \_  ->
      snip m g (g!v)    'thenST' \as ->
      snip m g vs       'thenST' \bs ->
      returnST ((Node v as) : bs)
```

We will write revPost for the composition of reverse and postOrderF. Pushing revPost into the state thread gives

```
topSort g = runST (mkEmpty (bounds g) 'thenST' \m ->
                    st revPost (snip m g (indices g)))
```

Again, we invent a new function definition. Let

```
revPostSnip m g vs = st revPost (snip m g vs)
```

Then, performing a case analysis on the list argument:

```
revPostSnip m g []
  = st revPost (snip m g [])
  = st revPost (returnST [])
  = returnST (revPost [])
  = returnST []
```

and

```
revPostSnip m g (v:vs)
    = st revPost (snip m g (v:vs))

    = st revPost
        (contains m v  'thenST' \visited ->
         if visited then
           snip m g vs
         else
           include m v       'thenST' \_  ->
```

```
      snip m g (g!v)    'thenST' \as ->
      snip m g vs       'thenST' \bs ->
      returnST ((Node v as) : bs))
```

Push the revPost all the way to the leaves of the state thread:

```
  = contains m v  'thenST' \visited ->
    if visited then
      st revPost (snip m g vs)
    else
      include m v       'thenST' \_  ->
      snip m g (g!v)    'thenST' \as ->
      snip m g vs       'thenST' \bs ->
      returnST (revPost ((Node v as) : bs))
```

Use the definition of postorderF, and the fact that reverse (xs++ys) = reverse ys ++ reverse xs (so long as xs is finite):

```
  = contains m v  'thenST' \visited ->
    if visited then
      revPostSnip m g vs
    else
      include m v       'thenST' \_  ->
      snip m g (g!v)    'thenST' \as ->
      snip m g vs       'thenST' \bs ->
      returnST (revPost bs ++ [v] ++ revPost as)
```

Now we introduce auxilliary names (ps and qs) for the result of applying revPost to as and bs, and express these renamings using returnST:

```
  = contains m v  'thenST' \visited ->
    if visited then
      revPostSnip m g vs
    else
      include m v                        'thenST' \_  ->
      (snip m g (g!v) 'thenST' \as ->
       returnST (revPost as))            'thenST' \ps ->
      (snip m g vs      'thenST' \bs ->
       returnST (revPost bs))            'thenST' \qs ->
      returnST (qs ++ [v] ++ ps)
```

Finally, pull the revPost operation across the calls to snip)

```
  = contains m v  'thenST' \visited ->
    if visited then
      revPostSnip m g vs
    else
      include m v                        'thenST' \_  ->
      st revPost
        (snip m g (g!v) 'thenST' \as ->
```

```
              returnST as))                    'thenST' \ps ->
          st revPost
            (snip m g vs     'thenST' \bs ->
             returnST bs))                     'thenST' \qs ->
          returnST (qs ++ [v] ++ ps)

      = contains m v  'thenST' \visited ->
        if visited then
          revPostSnip m g vs
        else
          include m v                         'thenST' \_  ->
          st revPost
            (snip m g (g!v))                  'thenST' \ps ->
          st revPost
            (snip m g vs)                     'thenST' \qs ->
          returnST (qs ++ [v] ++ ps)

      = contains m v  'thenST' \visited ->
        if visited then
          revPostSnip m g vs
        else
          include m v                         'thenST' \_  ->
          revPostSnip m g (g!v)               'thenST' \ps ->
          revPostSnip m g vs                  'thenST' \qs ->
          returnST (qs ++ [v] ++ ps)
```

Putting all this together gives the following definition for topological sort:

```
    topSort g = runST (mkEmpty (bounds g) 'thenST' \m ->
                    revPostSnip m g (indices g))


    revPostSnip m g [] = returnST []
    revPostSnip m g (v:vs)
      = contains m v  'thenST' \visited ->
        if visited then
          revPostSnip m g vs
        else
          include m v                         'thenST' \_  ->
          revPostSnip m g (g!v)               'thenST' \ps ->
          revPostSnip m g vs                  'thenST' \qs ->
          returnST (qs ++ [v] ++ ps)
```

We have successfully eliminated the intermediate spanning forest, but the result is still rather unlike a traditional implementation. The lists of vertices built up in the recursive calls are decidedly non-standard. A typical imperative solution would introduce a stack and push the vertices on to the stack as it went along. For example, it may be something like the following (assuming suitable definitions for mkStack, stackToList and push):

```
topSort g
  = runST (mkEmpty (bounds g)            'thenST' \m ->
           mkStack []                    'thenST' \s ->
           revPostSnip m s g (indices g) 'thenST' \_ ->
           stackToList s)

revPostSnip m s g [] = returnST ()
revPostSnip m s g (v:vs)
  = contains m v   'thenST' \visited ->
    if visited then
      revPostSnip m s g vs
    else
      include m v                        'thenST' \_  ->
      revPostSnip m s g (g!v)            'thenST' \_  ->
      push s v                           'thenST' \_  ->
      revPostSnip m s g vs               'thenST' \_  ->
      returnST ()
```

Again, which of these is "better"? The positioning of the push is rather subtle, and the choice of stack rather than queue even more so. If we had wanted the vertices in the other order (i.e. not reversed) then we would have had to make a different choice.

Can the second version be obtained from the first by techniques similar to those used earlier? If so, can the earlier techniques be automated? The answers to these questions are still far from clear.

8   Acknowledgements

This paper bears heavily on work by King and Launchbury [KL95] and much has been lifted verbatim. The additional material has benefitted from discussions with Alex Bunkenburg, and Tim Sheard.

Appendix

Imperative features were initially introduced into the Glasgow Haskell compiler to perform input and output. The approach is based on monads, and can easily be extended to achieve *in-situ* array updates and to allow the imperative actions to be delayed until their results are required. This is the model we use. The notation comes from [LPJ94]

We use the monad of state-transformers with type constructor ST which is defined:

```
type ST s a = a -> (a,s)
```

So elements of type ST s Int, say, are functions which, when applied to the state, return a pair of an integer together with a new state. As usual we have the unit returnST and the sequencing combinator thenST:

```
returnST :: a -> ST s a
returnST a s = (a,s)

thenST :: ST s a -> (a -> ST s b) -> ST s b
(m 'thenST' k) s = k a t  where  (a,t) = m s
```

The ST monad comes equipped with three basic array operations:

```
newArr  ::Ix i=> (i,i) -> a ->ST s (MutArr s i a)
readArr ::Ix i=> MutArr s i a -> i -> ST s a
writeArr::Ix i=> MutArr s i a -> i -> a ->ST s ()
```

The first, newArr, takes a pair of index bounds (the type a must lie in the index class Ix) together with an initial value, and returns a reference to an initialised array. The time this operation takes is linear with respect to the number of elements in the array. The other two provide for reading and writing to an element of the array, and both take constant time.

Finally, the ST monad comes equipped with a function runST.

```
runST :: (\/s . ST s a) -> a
```

This takes a state-transformer function, applies it to an initial state, extracts the final value and discards the final state. The type of runST is not Hindley-Milner because of the nested quantifier, so it must be built-in to Haskell. The universal quantifier ensures that in a state thread variables from other state threads are not referenced. For details of this see [LPJ94].

So, for example,

```
runST (newArr (1,8) 0     'thenST' (\nums ->
        writeArr nums 5 42 'thenST' (\_ ->
        readArr nums 5     'thenST' (\v ->
        returnST v))))
```

will return 42. This can be read as follows: run a new state thread extracting the final value when finished; create a new array indexed from 1 to 8 with components all 0; then bind this array to nums; write to array nums at index 5 the value 42; then read the component in nums at index 5 and bind this value to v; finally return value v. Note that the final expression returnST v is unnecessary as readArr returns a value. The parentheses immediately after 'thenST' are also unnecessary, as Haskell's grammar binds lambda expressions tighter than infix functions.

References

[CLR90] T.H.Corman, C.E.Leiserson, and R.L.Rivest, *Introduction to Algorithms*. MIT Press, MA, 1990.

[DB76]   J.Darlington and R.Burstall, *A System which Automatically Improves Programs*. Acta Informatica, 6(1), pp 41-60, 1976.

[Har93] R.Harrison, *Abstract Data Types in Standard ML*. John Wiley and Sons, 1993.

[Hol91] I.Holyer, *Functional Programming with Miranda*. Pitman, London, 1991.

[HT73]   J.E.Hopcroft and R.E.Tarjan, *Algorithm 447: Efficient Algorithms for Graph Manipulation*. Communications of the ACM, 16(6), pp 372-378.

[Hug85]   R.J.M.Hughes, *Lazy Memo Functions*. Proc. FPCA 85, Nancy, LNCS 201, Springer-Verlag, 1985.

[Joh]   T.Johnsson, *Efficient Graph Algorithms Using Lazy Monolithic Arrays*. unpublished.

[KL95]   D.King and J.Launchbury, *Structuring Depth-First Search Algorithms in Haskell*. Proc. POPL, San Francisco, CA, 1995.

[LPJ94]   J.Launchbury and S.Peyton Jones, *Lazy Functional State Threads*. Proc. PLDI, Orlando, FL, 1994.

[LPJ]   J.Launchbury and S.Peyton Jones, *State in Haskell*. LASC Special issue on State in Programming Languages, to appear.

[Man89]   U.Manber *Introduction to Algorithms—A Creative Approach*. Addison-Wesley, MA, 1989.

[Mog89]   E.Moggi, *Computational Lambda-Calculus and Monads*. Proc LICS, Asilomar, CA, 1989.

[Pau91]   L.C.Paulson, *ML for the working programmer*. Cambridge University Press, 1991.

[Sha81]   M.Sharir, *A Strong-Connectivity Algorithm and its Application in Data Flow Analysis*. Computers and Mathematics with Applications, 7(1), pp 67-72.

[Tar72]   R.E.Tarjan, *Depth-first Search and Linear Graph Algorithms*. SIAM J. of Computing, 1(2), pp 146-160.

[Wad90]   P.Wadler, *Comprehending Monads*, Proc. L&FP, Nice, France, 1990.

Springer-Verlag
and the Environment

We at Springer-Verlag firmly believe that an international science publisher has a special obligation to the environment, and our corporate policies consistently reflect this conviction.

We also expect our business partners – paper mills, printers, packaging manufacturers, etc. – to commit themselves to using environmentally friendly materials and production processes.

The paper in this book is made from low- or no-chlorine pulp and is acid free, in conformance with international standards for paper permanency.

Lecture Notes in Computer Science

For information about Vols. 1–848
please contact your bookseller or Springer-Verlag

Vol. 884: J. Nievergelt, T. Roos, H.-J. Schek, P. Widmayer (Eds.), IGIS '94: Geographic Information Systems. Proceedings, 1994. VIII, 292 pages. 19944.

Vol. 885: R. C. Veltkamp, Closed Objects Boundaries from Scattered Points. VIII, 144 pages. 1994.

Vol. 886: M. M. Veloso, Planning and Learning by Analogical Reasoning. XIII, 181 pages. 1994. (Subseries LNAI).

Vol. 887: M. Toussaint (Ed.), Ada in Europe. Proceedings, 1994. XII, 521 pages. 1994.

Vol. 888: S. A. Andersson (Ed.), Analysis of Dynamical and Cognitive Systems. Proceedings, 1993. VII, 260 pages. 1995.

Vol. 889: H. P. Lubich, Towards a CSCW Framework for Scientific Cooperation in Europe. X, 268 pages. 1995.

Vol. 890: M. J. Wooldridge, N. R. Jennings (Eds.), Intelligent Agents. Proceedings, 1994. VIII, 407 pages. 1995. (Subseries LNAI).

Vol. 891: C. Lewerentz, T. Lindner (Eds.), Formal Development of Reactive Systems. XI, 394 pages. 1995.

Vol. 892: K. Pingali, U. Banerjee, D. Gelernter, A. Nicolau, D. Padua (Eds.), Languages and Compilers for Parallel Computing. Proceedings, 1994. XI, 496 pages. 1995.

Vol. 893: G. Gottlob, M. Y. Vardi (Eds.), Database Theory – ICDT '95. Proceedings, 1995. XI, 454 pages. 1995.

Vol. 894: R. Tamassia, I. G. Tollis (Eds.), Graph Drawing. Proceedings, 1994. X, 471 pages. 1995.

Vol. 895: R. L. Ibrahim (Ed.), Software Engineering Education. Proceedings, 1995. XII, 449 pages. 1995.

Vol. 896: R. N. Taylor, J. Coutaz (Eds.), Software Engineering and Human-Computer Interaction. Proceedings, 1994. X, 281 pages. 1995.

Vol. 897: M. Fisher, R. Owens (Eds.), Executable Modal and Temporal Logics. Proceedings, 1993. VII, 180 pages. 1995. (Subseries LNAI).

Vol. 898: P. Steffens (Ed.), Machine Translation and the Lexicon. Proceedings, 1993. X, 251 pages. 1995. (Subseries LNAI).

Vol. 899: W. Banzhaf, F. H. Eeckman (Eds.), Evolution and Biocomputation. VII, 277 pages. 1995.

Vol. 900: E. W. Mayr, C. Puech (Eds.), STACS 95. Proceedings, 1995. XIII, 654 pages. 1995.

Vol. 901: R. Kumar, T. Kropf (Eds.), Theorem Provers in Circuit Design. Proceedings, 1994. VIII, 303 pages. 1995.

Vol. 902: M. Dezani-Ciancaglini, G. Plotkin (Eds.), Typed Lambda Calculi and Applications. Proceedings, 1995. VIII, 443 pages. 1995.

Vol. 903: E. W. Mayr, G. Schmidt, G. Tinhofer (Eds.), Graph-Theoretic Concepts in Computer Science. Proceedings, 1994. IX, 414 pages. 1995.

Vol. 904: P. Vitányi (Ed.), Computational Learning Theory. EuroCOLT'95. Proceedings, 1995. XVII, 415 pages. 1995. (Subseries LNAI).

Vol. 905: N. Ayache (Ed.), Computer Vision, Virtual Reality and Robotics in Medicine. Proceedings, 1995. XIV, 567 pages. 1995.

Vol. 906: E. Astesiano, G. Reggio, A. Tarlecki (Eds.), Recent Trends in Data Type Specification. Proceedings, 1995. VIII, 523 pages. 1995.

Vol. 907: T. Ito, A. Yonezawa (Eds.), Theory and Practice of Parallel Programming. Proceedings, 1995. VIII, 485 pages. 1995.

Vol. 908: J. R. Rao Extensions of the UNITY Methodology: Compositionality, Fairness and Probability in Parallelism. XI, 178 pages. 1995.

Vol. 909: H. Comon, J.-P. Jouannaud (Eds.), Term Rewriting. Proceedings, 1993. VIII, 221 pages. 1995.

Vol. 910: A. Podelski (Ed.), Constraint Programming: Basics and Trends. Proceedings, 1995. XI, 315 pages. 1995.

Vol. 911: R. Baeza-Yates, E. Goles, P. V. Poblete (Eds.), LATIN '95: Theoretical Informatics. Proceedings, 1995. IX, 525 pages. 1995.

Vol. 912: N. Lavrac˘, S. Wrobel (Eds.), Machine Learning: ECML – 95. Proceedings, 1995. XI, 370 pages. 1995. (Subseries LNAI).

Vol. 913: W. Schäfer (Ed.), Software Process Technology. Proceedings, 1995. IX, 261 pages. 1995.

Vol. 914: J. Hsiang (Ed.), Rewriting Techniques and Applications. Proceedings, 1995. XII, 473 pages. 1995.

Vol. 915: P. D. Mosses, M. Nielsen, M. I. Schwartzbach (Eds.), TAPSOFT '95: Theory and Practice of Software Development. Proceedings, 1995. XV, 810 pages. 1995.

Vol. 916: N. R. Adam, B. K. Bhargava, Y. Yesha (Eds.), Digital Libraries. Proceedings, 1994. XIII, 321 pages. 1995.

Vol. 917: J. Pieprzyk, R. Safavi-Naini (Eds.), Advances in Cryptology - ASIACRYPT '94. Proceedings, 1994. XII, 431 pages. 1995.

Vol. 918: P. Baumgartner, R. Hähnle, J. Posegga (Eds.), Theorem Proving with Analytic Tableaux and Related Methods. Proceedings, 1995. X, 352 pages. 1995. (Subseries LNAI).

Vol. 919: B. Hertzberger, G. Serazzi (Eds.), High-Performance Computing and Networking. Proceedings, 1995. XXIV, 957 pages. 1995.

Vol. 920: E. Balas, J. Clausen (Eds.), Integer Programming and Combinatorial Optimization. Proceedings, 1995. IX, 436 pages. 1995.

Vol. 921: L. C. Guillou, J.-J. Quisquater (Eds.), Advances in Cryptology – EUROCRYPT '95. Proceedings, 1995. XIV, 417 pages. 1995.

Vol. 923: M. Meyer (Ed.), Constraint Processing. IV, 289 pages. 1995.

Vol. 924: P. Ciancarini, O. Nierstrasz, A. Yonezawa (Eds.), Object-Based Models and Languages for Concurrent Systems. Proceedings, 1994. VII, 193 pages. 1995.

Vol. 925: J. Jeuring, E. Meijer (Eds.), Advanced Functional Programming. Proceedings, 1995. VII, 331 pages. 1995.

Vol. 926: P. Nesi (Ed.), Objective Software Quality. Proceedings, 1995. VIII, 249 pages. 1995.

Vol. 927: J. Dix, L. Moniz Pereira, T. C. Przymusinski (Eds.), Non-Monotonic Extensions of Logic Programming. Proceedings, 1994. IX, 229 pages. 1995. (Subseries LNAI).